QUICK GUIDE TO THE TEXT

This text is organized around the Interstate School Leaders Licensure Consortium Standards and provides a bridge from the theory of school administration to the practical problem solving in which school principals and other leaders engage.

Hallmark Features

- A solid research base relates directly to practice in the field, giving the text a real-world authenticity.

- Contains chapter-ending activities, selected readings, and thirty case studies as supplemental learning tools.

- The book's four sections are organized around the Interstate School Leaders Licensure Consortium (ISLLC) Standards and focus on the key issues that form the heart and soul of effective leadership. Located in page margins throughout the text, references to ISLLC Standards assist students in linking their knowledge base with basic standards.

- Constant attention is given to issues of learning and teaching and the creation of powerful learning environments. Each standard is supported by a list of elements that provide greater specificity to each standard. A complete list of all seven standards along with their associated elements is located in Appendix B.

- Thirty case studies with scoring rubrics throughout the text, similar to the School Leaders Licensure Exam (SLLA) exam items and referenced to the standards, provide great practice opportunity and preparation for the actual exam.

- An integrated focus on learning organizations and learning communities highlights the changing role of the principal as a transformational leader working with teachers, parents, and children to create a successful school.

For information about what is new to this edition, please see the back cover.

The Principal

Creative Leadership for Excellence in Schools

SEVENTH EDITION

The Principal

Creative Leadership for Excellence in Schools

Gerald C. Ubben

University of Tennessee, Knoxville

Larry W. Hughes

University of Houston, Professor Emeritus

Cynthia J. Norris

Lincoln Memorial University

Boston   Columbus   Indianapolis   New York   San Francisco   Upper Saddle River
Amsterdam   Cape Town   Dubai   London   Madrid   Milan   Munich   Paris   Montreal   Toronto
Delhi   Mexico City   São Paulo   Sydney   Hong Kong   Seoul   Singapore   Taipei   Tokyo

Vice President and Editor in Chief: Jeffery W. J
Executive Editor and Publisher: Stephen D. Dra
Editorial Assistant: Jamie Bushell
Vice President, Director of Marketing: Quinn P
Senior Marketing Manager: Christopher Barry
Senior Managing Editor: Pamela D. Bennett
Production Editor: Mary Harlan
Project Manager: Clara Bartunek
Senior Art Director: Jayne Conte
Cover Designer: Suzanne Behnke
Cover Art: Getty Images. Inc.
Full-Service Project Management: Niraj Bhatt/A
Composition: Aptara®, Inc.
Printer/Binder: Courier Westford
Cover Printer: Lehigh/Phoenix Color
Text Font: Times

Credits and acknowledgments borrowed from other sources and reproduced, with permission, in this textbook appear on appropriate page within text.

Every effort has been made to provide accurate and current Internet information in this book. However, the Internet and information posted on it are constantly changing, so it is inevitable that some of the Internet addresses listed in this textbook will change.

Library of Congress Cataloging-in-Publication Data

Ubben, Gerald C.
   The principal: creative leadership for excellence in schools / Gerald C. Ubben, Larry W. Hughes,
Cynthia J. Norris. —7th ed.
     p. cm.
   ISBN-13: 978-0-13-715837-9
   ISBN-10: 0-13-715837-8
   1. School principals—United States.   2. School management and organization—United States.   3. School supervision—United States. I. Hughes, Larry W. II. Norris, Cynthia J. III. Title.
   LB2805.U2 2010
   371.2′012—dc22

                                                                                            2010006098

10 9 8 7 6 5 4 3 2 1

www.pearsonhighered.com

ISBN-13: 978-0-13-715837-9
ISBN-10:   0-13-715837-8

BRIEF CONTENTS

CONTENTS

PREFACE

This seventh edition of *The Principal* continues to reflect the evolution in the roles of educational leaders and the mounting demands to rewrite their job descriptions every year. Increased tasks in areas such as instructional leadership, data analysis, technology utilization, and community relations are requiring principals to expand their toolbox of skills.

New to This Edition

To keep pace with the changing times, we have enhanced this edition in the following ways:

- Organized the text around the new *Educational Leadership Policy Standards: ISLLC 2008* as adopted by the National Policy Board for Educational Administration
- Focused emotional intelligence tied to situational leadership as well as added a broadened discussion of professional learning communities by considering spontaneously formed *communities of practice*
- Introduced a new section in the chapter on decision making that discusses at length the part that *stakeholders* play in arriving at just, defensible, and implementable decisions
- Added a totally new chapter on administrator uses of electronic technology, including communication strategies using Twitter, social networks such as Facebook and LinkedIn, blogs and podcasts on school websites, school information systems, and telephone message delivery systems.
- Expanded the section on school mission statements and suggested ways of gathering, analyzing, and applying school-based data
- Added to the staffing chapters by including material on reduction in force (RIF) as well as new designs for the deployment of elementary and middle school staffs.
- Introduced a new section in the school and community chapter that deals extensively with *helicopter parents*. Guidelines are presented.
- Updated the chapter on legal rights and responsibilities to include relevant new cases and discussions about dress codes, religious practices and zero-tolerance edicts. Ways to stay out of trouble while maintaining a civilized and legal school environment are proposed. Also covered are single-gender classrooms, employment issues, and prayer and religion in the classroom.
- Added four new cases and revised several others to update concerns that confront the principal. Topics in the new cases and revisions include possible sexual harassment, recruitment, dress codes, and community pressure groups.
- Updated selected readings in all chapters to reflect current scholarly work.

New Standards

Clear and consistent standards can help guide the way for administrator preparation programs and for administrators who are growing in their careers. Standards give leaders the tools they need to meet new demands. The Council of Chief State School Officials (CCSSO), through the Interstate School Leaders Licensure Consortium (ISLLC), has recently published the new *Educational Leadership Policy Standards: ISLLC 2008* as adopted by the National Policy Board for Educational Administration (NPBEA). The new standards continue to shift the focus as follows:

- From technical skills to interpersonal skills
- From director to consensus builder and motivator
- From resource allocation to accountability for learning processes and results
- From campus administrator to integrator of school and community services
- From policy recipient to policy participant

The knowledge, skills, and concepts expected through these standards should be viewed holistically. That is, they are generic and integrated for all school leaders through a variety of positions. The standards reflect an emphasis on student outcomes with emphasis on student-completed artifacts.

This edition of the Principal includes margin notes referencing the more critical ISLLC 2008 standards for each chapter subsection to help readers relate the concepts of the book to the standards. Adopters of the textbook can access a password-protected website to use the Test Bank and PowerPoint presentations developed by the authors to assist instructors teaching the course. (Contact your local publisher's representative.)

The Principal continues to be based on the research about linkages between school leadership and productive schools, especially in terms of outcomes for children and youth. It supports the understandings that formal leadership in schools is a complex, multifaceted task that requires continual learning and that effective school leaders must be strong educators anchoring their work on the central issues of learning, teaching, and school improvement. School leaders must also be moral agents and social advocates for the students and communities they serve. Additionally, they must make solid connections with stakeholders, empowering them to create learning communities that value and care for others as individuals and as members of the educational community.

The efforts of NPBEA have moved standards to the next level to form a framework that provides an excellent base for the organization of school leader preparation programs. The six ISLLC 2008 standards focus only on the key issues that form the heart and soul of effective leadership. Constant attention is given to issues of learning and teaching and the creation of powerful learning environments. Each standard is supported by a framework of functions that provide greater specificity to each standard. (A complete list of all six standards along with their associated functions is located in Appendix B.)

Content Organization

This book is organized into four parts centered on the ISLLC 2008 standards developed specifically for school leaders. Each of the four major parts of the book is framed with one or two of the standards as its major theme.

Part One: Creating a Vision of Leadership and Learning

Standard 1: An education leader promotes the success of every student by facilitating the development, articulation, implementation, and stewardship of a vision of learning that is shared and supported by all stakeholders.

Standard 5: An education leader promotes the success of every student by acting with integrity, fairness, and in an ethical manner.

Part Two: Developing a Positive School Culture

Standard 2: An education leader promotes the success of every student by advocating, nurturing, and sustaining a school culture and instructional program conducive to student learning and staff professional growth.

Part Three: Managing the Organization

Standard 3: An education leader promotes the success of every student by ensuring management of the organization, operation, and resources for a safe, efficient, and effective learning environment.

Part Four: Interacting with the External School Environment

Standard 4: An education leader promotes the success of every student by collaborating with faculty and community members, responding to diverse community interests and needs, and mobilizing community resources.

Standard 6: An education leader promotes the success of every student by understanding, responding to, and influencing the political, social, economic, legal, and cultural context.

We continue to try to put a proper balance between two covers of the book so that aspiring and practicing administrators may find intellectual challenge as well as cause to reflect on what, with effort and analysis, "might be." It is our hope that we have provided good balance between the theoretical and the practical and the bridge that connects them.

Thank you to the following reviewers: Frank D. Adams, Wayne State College; Robert Kladifko, California State University, Northridge; Marilynn Marks Quick, Ball State University; and Annie Ritter, Webster University.

As before, we continue to hope that the readers will find this book to be useful now and on the job. Let us know.

The Principal

Creative Leadership for Excellence in Schools

PART ONE

Creating a Vision of Leadership and Learning

The school leaders of the twenty-first century must have knowledge and understanding of the purpose of education and the role of leadership in modern society as well as various ethical frameworks and perspectives on ethics, the values of the diverse school community, professional codes of ethics, and the philosophy and history of education. They should also believe in, value, and be committed to the ideal of the common good, the principles in the Bill of Rights, the right of every student to a free quality education, bringing ethical principles to the decision-making process, subordination of one's own interest to the good of the school community, accepting the consequences for upholding one's principles and actions, using the influence of one's office constructively and productively in the service of all students and their families, and development of a caring school community. The Educational Leadership Policy Standards: ISLLC 2008 Standard 5 supports these characteristics.*

> **Standard 5: An education leader promotes the success of every student with integrity, fairness, and in an ethical manner.**

Likewise, the educational leader must have knowledge and understanding of the goals of learning in a pluralistic society; the principles of developing and implementing strategic plans; systems theory; information sources, data collection and data analysis strategies; effective communication; and effective consensus-building and negotiation skills. They must also believe in, value, and be committed to the educability of all; a school vision of high standards of learning; continuous school improvement; the inclusion of all members of the school community; ensuring that all students have the knowledge, skills, and values needed to become successful adults; a willingness to continuously examine one's own assumptions, beliefs, and practices; and doing the work required for high levels of personal and organization performance. The Educational Leadership Policy Standards: ISLLC 2008 Standard 1 supports these requirements.

*ISLLC-Interstate School Leaders Licensure Consortium.

1

Standard 1: An education leader promotes the success of every student by facilitating the development, articulation, implementation, and stewardship of a vision of learning that is shared and supported by all stakeholders.

Part One addresses Standards 1 and 5 and the functions that accompany them.

1

The Principal

A Creative Blend of Substance and Style

Leadership, in the final analysis, is the ability of humans to relate deeply to each other in the search for a more perfect union. Leadership is a consensual task, a sharing of ideas and a sharing of responsibilities, where a "leader" is a leader for the moment only, where the leadership exerted must be validated by the consent of followers, and where leadership lies in the struggles of a community to find meaning for itself.

—WILLIAM FOSTER[1]

The role of the school principal has evolved considerably since the days of the little red schoolhouse. Currently, it is cast under the umbrella of *school improvement* and carries with it enormous moral and ethical challenges to build community among diverse and ever-changing populations.

School improvement, fueled by the No Child Left Behind legislation, presents a dual role for the school principal. First, principals must be accountable for the academic progress of all students entrusted to their care. Second, they must facilitate the social and emotional development of all students regardless of age, race, creed, or intellectual capacity. These combined roles constitute a moral obligation, which Fullen[2] suggests means "making a difference in the life chances of all students—more of a difference for the disadvantaged because they have further to go."

The principal must foster a climate of collegial support and community through which this complex task might be accomplished. Community encompasses the notion of task commitment as well as a deep and abiding relationship that sustains that task. Leading from this perspective requires nurturing rather than coercing, sustaining, and challenging rather than directing.

The principal, then, is the pivotal point—the catalyst—for what happens in the school. Principals must face their conceptual, human, and technical[3] obligations with courage and dedication. It is a challenging, yet rewarding, task for those willing and prepared to accept the position.

In this chapter we introduce the principal as an instructional leader and address the roles and responsibilities of the principal's position. The chapter discusses the context in which the role is enacted, the individual within the role, and the nature of the role within the context.

We begin by viewing these dimensions through a social systems theory.[4] This theory presents organizations as total systems with all parts working together in a complete and integrated manner. Everything that occurs within the organization, or school, is really a blending of two important dimensions: the institutional and the individual. The institutional dimension refers to the organization, whereas the individual dimension considers the personal, which includes the leader and all members of the organization. These components must work together to accomplish the school's goals.

Social Systems Theory

We begin our discussion of the roles and responsibilities of the school principal by considering the individual and institutional forces that help shape that role. The social systems theory of Getzels and Guba[5] reflects the interplay of these forces. Essentially, the theory posits two dimensions to the organization: the nomothetic (institutional) dimension and the idiographic (personal) dimension (see Figure 1.1).

Institution refers to the organization and its necessary functions that must be carried out according to certain expectations. *Roles* are the official positions and offices that have been established to carry out the organization's purpose and functions. The behaviors that are to comprise a role are called *role expectations.* Every role has certain normative responsibilities, and these will

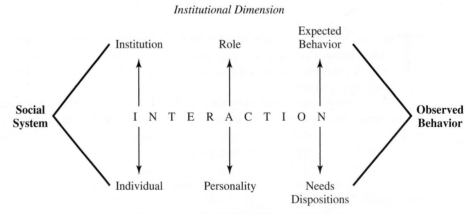

FIGURE 1.1   Depiction of a Social Systems Theory

Source: Larry W. Hughes and Gerald C. Ubben, *The Elementary Principal's Handbook: A Guide to Effective Action,* 4th ed. Boston: Allyn & Bacon, 1994, p. 22. Used with permission.

differ by role. It is the interaction of the institutional and idiographic dimensions within that role that results in the observed behavior of individuals in the organization.

It is essential that principals know the role expectations of the principalship position and that they understand their own personality dimensions and needs dispositions. They must, then, consider how these factors might shape their particular role expectations and influence their behavior within the principalship role. They must also be aware of other roles within the organization and how personal as well as institutional expectations affect those roles.

Personality in the context of the social systems model may be defined as the "dynamic organization within an individual of those 'needs-dispositions' that govern his [or her] unique reactions to the environment."[6] In other words, each individual is a complex of previous experiences that have provided him or her with differing orientations to life, to organizations, and to other people. These experiences affect a person's sense of what is pleasurable, important, and real. They determine the expectations that they bring to the role.

The challenge to the principal is to try to address both individual and organizational needs to achieve as much congruence as possible. The greater the congruence, the more productive the organization is. This congruence creates interdependence between the individuals and the organization. The result is enhanced growth for the individual and greater productivity for the organization. At the same time, it is important that the principal understands when it might be appropriate, and indeed desirable, to try to influence organizational expectations toward more positive directions. Such is the essence of leadership!

Viewed systemically, organizational expectations represent the collective expectations of individual members. These expectations can also be viewed from an individual or subgroup perspective, thereby raising various questions such as these:

- What does the group expect the organization to accomplish, and what expectations does the group have for the principal within the leadership role?
- What do individual members and subgroups expect from the organization and its leader and from each other?

The School Improvement Plan Applied to Systems Theory

The School Improvement Plan, which will be discussed more fully in Chapter 4 of this text, is designed as a framework for all that happens within a school setting. If viewed from a systems approach and properly facilitated by the school principal, this plan can serve as a central focus for leadership. The written plan reflects the important *institutional dimension* since it specifies the task or purpose that the school desires to accomplish. This plan is shaped by various stakeholders who, through consensus, specify the school's purpose and direction. Individual *roles* and responsibilities are identified for plan implementation. Each specified role has organizational *expectations* for task accomplishment. All institutional dimensions combine to represent a holistic plan. Note, however, that the plan is merely the written *intent* for task accomplishment. Much more is required of the leader.

Intent, alone, is not enough for task accomplishment; there must be purposeful action taken on the plan. This requires that the *individual dimensions* of social systems theory work in concert with the institutional dimensions. Individual expectations must blend with institutional expectations. Individuals must contribute to the plan's design and must become committed to its realization for actual school improvement to occur. A community must evolve—it must be committed to a shared purpose.

The orchestrator of this complex process of school improvement must be the school principal. Just as the orchestra conductor directs a symphony, so, too, must the principal feel the pulse of the school, move with the rhythm of expectations and human needs, and create from diverse perspectives a harmonious community dedicated to the task. How successful the principal is in this endeavor will be greatly dependent on the nature of the organizational context in which the school operates, as we shall see in the following section.

The School: The Context for Leadership

The responsibilities of school leadership are best understood when viewed within the organizational context in which leadership takes place. Indeed, Fullen[7] states that "the leader's job is to help change context—to introduce new elements into the situation that are bound to influence behavior for the better." Within context, leaders are identified to guide groups of people who have come together to fulfill a purpose. Leaders are in service to organizations, to the individuals who comprise those organizations, and to the clients that the organization serves. As Hodgkinson[8] suggests, "The context of schooling is a complex fabric woven from the threads of individual lives—teachers, students, parents, and citizens—the threads of group culture and the social threads of politics and economics."

One way of viewing various organizational contexts is to consider them from the viewpoint of metaphors. Morgan[9] has presented several metaphors of organizational context that we will consider here: machines, organisms, and brains. As we view these contexts, note that leaders influence the nature of organizational context, and, in turn, leaders are influenced by the contexts in which they operate.

Schools as Machines

Schools, viewed as machines, exhibit many qualities reflective of the Scientific Management Era, where efficiency and highly structured tasks characterized much of the organization's daily operation. Schools designed in this fashion are closed systems, unaware of, or unresponsive to, the changing needs of their internal and external environments. This is a major disadvantage when considering the evolving needs of a complex society. Often, in such settings, the needs of the disadvantaged and minorities are not adequately met, and failure is the result. Nieto[10] suggested, "Failure to learn does not develop out of thin air; it is scrupulously created through policies, practices, attitudes and beliefs."[11] Characterized by a bureaucratic hierarchy, machine-driven schools are tightly coupled, policy-driven settings that tend to stifle the initiative and creativity of organizational members. Leaders of such schools attempt to control both power and knowledge and "manage" the organization and its people so that order, predictability, and tradition are maintained.

On the surface all may seem balanced and smooth running, but there is a tendency in such stagnant environments for decay to occur. These organizations face a real danger of becoming outdated and obsolete. When organizations are designed as machines, there is a tendency to manage rather than lead, for there is comfort in stability. Even schools that normally would exhibit more open environments can become machine driven. Under threat, these schools and their leaders sometimes revert to a machine-type model as they attempt to tighten up their standards and be "accountable" in the face of criticism. We see this tendency today in many schools that view the mandate for school improvement merely from a test-score perspective. These schools become test driven rather than student centered. The moral purpose of leadership is much more than the manipulation of test scores. As stated by Fullen,[12] "Moral purpose of the highest order is having a system where all students learn, the gap between high and low performers becomes greatly reduced, and what people learn enables them to be successful citizens and workers in a morally based knowledge society."

Schools as Organisms

Schools, characterized as organisms, or natural systems, exhibit growth and adaptive qualities. Centered on interdependence and collaboration, these schools emphasize individuality, uniqueness, and self-renewal. Such educational settings are responsive, open organizations that meet the changing needs of their internal and external environments. In such schools, principals serve as facilitators of a shared mission that unites organizational members through purposeful commitment. Standardization of method is far less important than the results achieved or the impact realized. Human needs are acknowledged and met while growth is facilitated. In this context, uniqueness is appreciated as individuals are encouraged to maximize individual potential. Diversity is viewed as a strength that provides greater synergy to the organization.

Schools as Brains

Learning organizations, characterized as thinking/learning models, reflect the brain metaphor. Schools of this type emphasize reflective, problem-finding approaches for the improvement of current conditions and practices. This will be discussed in more detail in Chapter 2 when we consider schools as learning communities. It is important to note, however, that schools must be designed appropriately to facilitate learning communities. The image is one of holistic thoughts, where both the rational and intuitive dimensions of problem solving come into play. Knowledge and power are widely dispersed throughout the organization. This exchange of ideas enables adaptation to occur and new designs and approaches to be generated. Schools organized as brains are characterized by community; knowledge is not only shared and stored but it is generated. Principals are facilitators who enable the free flow of communication and exchange of ideas and who set forth conditions that foster the empowerment of others.

Reflection

In viewing these metaphorical contexts from the perspective of schools, we can apply questions that help paint a vivid picture of each setting. As you reflect on these environmental contexts, consider these significant questions concerning each one of the previously described organizational contexts:

- What would be the purpose of education?
- What would be the role of the principal? (director, facilitator, developer?)
- What would be the role of the teacher? (laborer, craftsperson, professional, artist?)
- What would be the role of the learner?
- What would learning look like?

There is embedded in organizational context both implicit and explicit expectations of what the organization should accomplish and what the leader should provide to the process of goal fulfillment. Sarason[13] has noted:

> Existing structure of a setting or culture defines the permissible ways in which goals and problems will be approached. Not so obvious, particularly to those who comprise the structure, is that existing structure is but one of many alternative structures possible in that setting and the existing one is a barrier to recognition and experimentation with alternative ones.

As you answered each of the previous questions, you did, in fact, explore organizational beliefs and platforms from which leadership is cast. A formal platform is comprised of a series of statements reflecting beliefs, values, and visions for education.[14] Platforms help people clarify personal and organizational expectations. But what are the influences that shape these expectations and that determine those platforms?

School Expectations

Organizational expectations are influenced by various sources: the school community, school district mandates and policy, state and federal policies and directives, court decisions, the general public, the educational profession itself, and various interest and professional groups. Individuals and subgroups within organizations also have their own set of expectations that grow out of their unique experiences, their personalities and individual needs, and, in many cases, their political agendas. All play a part in shaping organizational expectations, as well as the expectations the organization holds for its leaders.

Expectations for schools tend to become generalized and perpetuated over time by one's past experiences in school settings. For instance, overexposure to a certain organizational context might result in a feeling of comfort that "this is the way things are done around here." Although a status-quo perspective does enable the preservation of many important traditions and structures, it can also have negative results. In many cases, these past experiences create expectations, which may cause schools to become outdated and obsolete in their purpose. This is especially true as school environments change and new and crucial needs arise. Sarason[15] addressed this issue when he suggested that schools are very difficult to change because most everybody at some point has *been there.* Recognizing this danger and being cognizant of the need to restructure schools to better meet the needs of changing society, many groups have endeavored to change outdated expectations and to redesign the environmental context, or the structure, that surrounds the school.

In this area, the school principal can exert a tremendous influence in elevating the expectations of the school community. In addition, some professional organizations have given a more concentrated effort toward raising and standardizing school expectations and the expectations for its leaders. School expectations have been challenged by the research in effective schools as well as by national reports, such as *A Nation at Risk*[16] and *The Carnegie Report.*[17] The expectations for school principals as leaders of restructured schools have also been challenged. Two major leaders in this arena, the National Policy Board[18] and the Interstate School Leaders Licensure Consortium (ISLLC),[19] have developed national standards that attempt to bring greater clarity and direction to the role of school principal.

Tightly Coupled and Loosely Coupled Organizations

Often, there is great difference of opinion as to what constitutes "good schooling" and good leadership within schools. As a result, schools often find themselves trying to muddle through their tasks with little true sense of direction or clear understanding of expectations. The very nature of schools and schooling makes it difficult to come to agreement on expectations, even within a particular school setting. Weick[20] has referred to this in terms of the "tightly coupled" versus "loosely coupled" phenomenon. Organizations that are tightly coupled are characterized by four important qualities: (1) there are clear rules and expectations, (2) rules and expectations are disseminated and understood by all organizational members, (3) monitoring of performance is consistent and frequent, and (4) corrective feedback results from assessment results. There is balance and order within the structure that is set; it is a rational system. This tightly drawn system is reflective of the machine metaphor, which carries with it expectations for structure, standardization, and control.

Schools, in contrast to such organizations, are not rational entities; instead, schools are much more loosely coupled and unpredictable. Although there are general expectations for all schools, each school must redefine those expectations based on the things that are not always "clear-cut" and predictable. This opens the door for real leadership to occur. Principals in such settings have greater opportunity to personalize their organizations and voice their own expectations and the expectations of others within their organizations than do principals in more rationally ordered settings. Although broad, general expectations exist for all schools, there is great variety among schools in interpreting those expectations based on their own unique needs. Here is where a school principal, by orchestrating a carefully developed School Improvement Plan, can help chart the pathway for *real* school improvement. This plan must first give careful attention to an important question: *What should be?* Each school must redefine its own expectations based on the influences it encounters within its own unique setting and on the changing needs of those individuals within the setting.

Leadership Perspectives

It is easy to govern schools based on a set of "standardized expectations"; it is a far greater challenge to examine those expectations according to the needs of the individuals within the setting. Leaders become either reactive or proactive in their response. The reactive mode requires only management of a prescribed order; the proactive mode requires leadership. The managerial style, often referred to as *transactional leadership,* is reminiscent of the machine metaphor and places all power and responsibility in the hands of the principal. Adherence to the purpose is based on a reactive response supported by positional and coercive power. It is an exchange of "a day's work for a day's pay" with little thought to purposeful commitment.

Certainly, the administrator should be a custodian and preserver of the basic traditions, values, goals, and history of the organization as well as a guardian of all that is good and productive. In that sense, the leader operates as a manager. At the same time, if the organization is to maintain its vitality and meet the needs of its people and of the larger context it serves, the leader must also be a proactive questioner of current practices and a transformer of policies, procedures, and practices that are counterproductive for the organization and its members. The leader must facilitate schools that are not only productive disseminators of knowledge, but that also guard and preserve the democratic rights of all individuals within that context. To do so is to practice social justice. The leader must help elevate and orchestrate higher purposes for the good of all. In other words, a careful consideration of "what should be" will result in a vision where all members are afforded the highest possible opportunities for maximum development regardless of race, age, gender, or intellectual capabilities. In that sense, the leader is transformational. The organistic model and the brain model come into play.[21] The *transformational leader* shares power, inspires others to leadership, and encourages participation and involvement of all members in executing the school's purpose.

Contrasting the Transactional and Transformational Leader

In his classic work, *Leadership,*[22] Burns coined the terms *transactional* and *transformational* leadership. These two leadership approaches are, from his perspective, completely different styles that have little to do with each other. He sees these styles as being opposite ends of a continuum, with the leader having certain dispositions that govern their style. The transactional leader operates from a power base of rewards and punishments and endeavors to gain the cooperation of followers on an "exchange" basis. Little personal commitment results from this exchange, because it depends on merely understanding the duties and making sure they are accomplished as directed. Leadership in this sense is viewed as a function of organizational position. It is concerned with reacting to presented problems by orchestrating people and tasks to accomplish stated goals. Viewed from this perspective, the school principal focuses on tightly coupled objectives, curriculum, teaching strategies, and evaluation. The teacher is viewed as a "laborer" with administration determining not only the "what" but the "how." The machine metaphor is very much in place.

Transformational leadership, on the other hand, inspires others toward collaboration and interdependence as they work toward a purpose to which they are deeply committed. It is a leadership style based on influence and is accomplished when leaders "delegate and surrender power *over* people and events in order to achieve power over accomplishments and goal achievement."[23] Sergiovanni has referred to transformational leadership as a "value-added" approach, since the focus is on a tightly coupled purpose that determines the "why" rather than the "what" and "how." The teacher is seen as a "craftsman, professional, or artist" rather than laborer,[24] with the organizational context being organistic or brain metaphor oriented. Foster[25] agrees with Burns that these two styles are cut from a different cloth; yet there are others who view the skills as being closely related and building on each other.

Representative of those who see this connection are Bass and Avolio,[26] who presented a first- and second-order change theory. They contend that leaders must manage before they can lead. During first-order change, the leader is concerned with understanding subordinates' needs, providing them appropriate rewards for their contributions, and helping them clarify the connection between their goals and those of the organization. It is only after this is accomplished, Bass and Avolio suggest, that the leader really inspires others to greater values awareness, encourages their commitment to the goals of the organization, or fosters their personal or professional growth. During this later stage, the leader becomes transformational.

The questions now become: Where does transformational leadership take place? Are all persons in leadership positions transformational leaders? Is only the "designated leader," or the school principal, a transformational leader? Is transformational leadership equated with school effectiveness as determined by stated goals and objectives? Is it possible to be a transformational leader and not manage?

These questions are fertile ground for debate. Both Sergiovanni[27] and Foster[28] have provided a perspective. In Sergiovanni's model of the effective instructional leader (discussed in Chapter 2 of this text), a continuum of leadership skills is presented. The lower three skills—technical, human, and educational—are viewed as basic skills for determining competence as a leader. In other words, these are the necessary skills for good management of the organizational setting and establishment of the basic foundation for effective educational productivity. A school principal would need to attend to all of these skills in adequate fashion to be considered competent; to do less would denote incompetence. The highest two skills—symbolic and cultural—need to be in place before a principal is considered effective (or, in our terminology, "transformational"). This hierarchy is reflective of the theory expressed by Bass[29] and suggests that if an individual is to be transformational *within the principalship role,* he or she must, in fact, have in place a foundation of good management practice to do so. To be an effective symbolic and cultural principal-leader assumes that the foundation of competent management is already in place. However, as Burns suggested, "Leadership is *not merely* a managerial tool."[30]

Foster takes transformational leadership beyond the role of the principal by suggesting that transformational leadership results from "mutual negotiations and shared leadership roles."[31] He continued, "Leadership cannot occur without followership and many times the two are exchangeable. . . . Leaders normally have to negotiate visions and ideas with potential followers, who may in turn become leaders themselves, renegotiating the particular agenda."[32] Certainly, Sergiovanni's[33] notion of the four substitutes for leadership discussed in Chapter 2 supports this idea.

Ethical Responsibilities of Transformational Leadership

Foster[34] suggests that transformational leaders operate from four important characteristics. First, they are *educative.* They help the organization learn. They assist organizational members in important discoveries:

- What has taken place in the school's history?
- What guiding values have helped to shape its culture?
- What is the school's purpose?
- What is power distributed throughout the organization?

Second, they are *critical.* They help organizational members examine current conditions and question their appropriateness for all individuals. They encourage individuals to make a difference in the situations that seem unjust or inappropriate by taking action in positive ways.

Third, transformational leaders are *ethical.* They encourage self-reflection, democratic values, and moral relationships. They strive to influence people to reach higher levels of values consciousness.

Fourth, they are *transformative.* Their leadership is aimed toward social change through elevation of human consciousness. They seek to build a community of individuals who believe they can make a difference.

Single-Loop and Double-Loop Learning

A learning model by Argyris[35] helps in better understanding these different leaderships perspectives. Argyris defined two kinds of learning: a single-loop and a double-loop process. "*Single-loop learning* rests in an ability to detect and correct error in relation to a given set of operating norms." It consists of three steps:

1. A norm, or a standard, for operation is established. (What should be?)
2. Monitoring occurs to determine if any discrepancies exist between current conditions and the established norm. (What is?)
3. Corrective action is taken to ensure that conditions are congruent with the previously established norm. (Needs and a plan for correction are identified.)

The single-loop process promotes stability and predictability based on an established norm. It is assumed that what the organization is trying to accomplish is what it *should be* doing. Little consideration is given to the evolving nature of the internal and external school environment. The organization operates as a closed system.

"*Double-loop learning* depends on being able to take a 'double look' at the situation by questioning the relevance of operating norms."[35] It is a four-step process:

1. A norm, or a standard, for operation is established. (What should be?)
2. Monitoring occurs to determine compliance with the established norm. (What is?)
3. If a discrepancy exists, leaders ask "Why?" (Why is it as it is?)
4. Corrective action takes place, which may
   a. bring conditions back in line with the norm (What should be?) or
   b. establish a new norm. (A *new* look at "what should be")

Double-loop learning encourages growth and development, for it responds to the inevitable changes that occur within the school's internal and external environment. Rather than accepting a goal or norm as being "correct," time is spent in questioning that norm in light of changing needs.

Single-loop learning is a *problem-solving process*. Double-loop learning is both *problem solving* and *problem finding*. In school improvement, it is important to question the current norms and practices to see if they meet the needs of *all* groups.

Management and Leadership

Good management creates a necessary state of orderliness and certitude to aspects of the school organization, but not to the exclusion of a necessary state of turmoil as new goals and processes are established and as the school family addresses new challenges and struggles to create an even more productive future.

This begins to describe the difference between leadership and management. Management is status quo oriented and assumes a highly stable environment. As Argyris[36] explained in the single-loop process discussed earlier, the job of the manager is to keep things moving correctly according to the norm that has already been set. There is an assumption made that the standards or norms that have been previously established are appropriate ones, and the task is to see that conditions are aligned with the established goals. If things are not operating effectively, it is the job of the manager to see that corrective action is taken to bring things back into balance. Management operates from a problem-solving perspective with little attention given to questioning the appropriateness of established norms.

The notion of leadership is much different. Leaders build on the status quo, to be sure, but they go well beyond it. As in a double-loop process, they continually reexamine the norm to determine if what the organization *is doing* is what it *should be doing.* As Foster stated, "Leaders always have one face turned toward change."[37] There is a constant reexamination of current conditions and a formulation of new possibilities. Leadership is a problem-finding as well as problem-solving approach. It is a dynamic process that challenges the organization to higher levels of consciousness and growth.

Certainly, good principal leaders also manage, but they manage with a leadership perspective! A different mental set characterizes the leader-manager. These principals use their perceptions of changes that are needed to work both inside and outside the organization to map new directions, to secure new resources and refocus existing resources, and to respond to the realities of a very unstable present and, at times, an unforeseeable future. To such leaders, change is inevitable—the challenge is to make the most of it in increasingly more productive ways.

The Principalship: The Role in Context

Leadership as Philosophy in Action

ISLLC 1

When school principals enter their schools, they bring with them their values, beliefs, and philosophies. Principals lead from their values! The impact of the principal's leadership is felt, and is dependent on, what the principal values, and the clarity and commitment the principal displays toward those values.

Earlier, we discussed the individual and organizational (nomothetic) expectations for the various roles within an organization. Regardless of the organization's expectations for the role of "principal," or the expectations held by various individuals or subgroups within the organization, the individual within the role must weigh his or her own expectations against those demands and determine how the role will be shaped. What the principal personally values gives form and substance to the role of principal.

Values shape the direction of leadership, provide the distinctive character of that leadership, and determine the passion that influences others to follow. Leadership, then, results from a relationship forged on the anvil of respect and personal regard. Leadership is nurtured by the values that ultimately unite individuals, from however dissonant their perspectives.

The principal's values impact the school in two very important ways. First, the principal's values determine *preservation and guardianship.*[38] The principal's values determine what remains stable or unchanged. Second, the principal's values determine the *nature of transformation and change.* Values determine what the principal recognizes as being unjust or inappropriate for the human beings served, the nature of the problems identified and solved, the quality of critique (or questioning of current practice), and the direction that change take.[39] Norris stated that "values shape personal dreams and visions"[40] and Kouzes and Posner suggested that these values are "the guiding principles in our lives with respect to personal and social ends we desire and with respect to moral conduct and personal competence such as honesty and imagination."[41]

Espoused Values and Values in Use

Values are both espoused, or voiced, and demonstrated in actions. What principals believe is their *espoused theory.* What they demonstrate that they believe through their actions is their *theory in use.* It is important that there be congruence between what principals *say* is important, or valued, and what they actually *do* or demonstrate is important by their actions. A congruence between these two is the basis of leader *credibility.*[42] A discrepancy between what leaders say and do leads to mistrust and an inability to influence the behavior of others.

Leadership is dependent on credibility! Credibility, then, has everything to do with values, but to fully appreciate this fact, it is important to have a clear understanding of the nature of values. The following section presents a model for interpreting the level of one's value consciousness.

Leadership from a Values Perspective

The values that an individual leader possesses form a continuum that ranges from a transactional style (or managerial mindset) to a transformational (leadership) one. In understanding how values shape these perspectives, let us consider values development as classified through the work of Hall.[43] In Hall's view, values acquisition is a developmental process that proceeds through cycles of growth resulting in four *phases of consciousness* (discussed in the next section). Hall has suggested that movement from one phase to the next requires that an individual become conscious (aware) of that stage by (1) understanding the world from that perspective, (2) perceiving himself or herself as functioning within that world, or (3) having human needs he or she wishes to satisfy within that phase. A stage of values consciousness is governed not only by the goals or needs the individual seeks to satisfy within that phase but also by the means, or skills, necessary to actualize those goals. Hall has theorized that leaders must possess the skills needed to operate at a particular consciousness level before that level can be appreciated or valued. A leader leads at the level of values consciousness attained.

Hall's Phases of Consciousness

Here, we explore each phase of consciousness and discuss its implications for leadership.[44]

Phase One.   The major emphasis at this phase of consciousness is *survival.* The individual is highly motivated to remain safe and to preserve things in a stable, secure manner. There is a great need during this phase to ensure that life is predictable and that it conforms to known patterns. During periods of increased stress or uncertainty, the individual experiences enhanced need for self-preservation and less tolerance for ambiguity. Since structure, predictability, and control give the illusion of "safety," principals who operate from this phase of values consciousness often seek comfort in the tried and true and find the machine metaphor compatible with their needs. Individuals at this phase of consciousness are consumed with their own self-interests and have less empathy for others; their stages of leadership is transactional.

Phase Two. The need for *social interaction* becomes prevalent at this stage of consciousness. The individual reaches beyond his or her need for self-preservation to appreciate the needs of others. There is an increasing desire to belong at this stage—not only within family and social groups but also to organizations. Organizational affiliation is viewed as adherence to rules, policies, and procedures; therefore, an administrator at this phase strives to operate "by the book," yet at the same time project a caring, considerate attitude toward subordinates. Since schools are viewed as "families," there is emphasis on collegiality and a desire to foster a sense of belonging among the staff. Leadership remains transactional.

Phase Three. *Individuality* emerges during phase three as a creative response to life takes the place of institutional conformity. During this phase, the individual begins to become his or her own person. There is increased motivation for self-actualization and a more genuine recognition of the dignity and worth of others. Empathy and a deeper respect for human life are present. Leaders at this phase of values consciousness find the organistic metaphor a compatible view of organizational context. They emphasize the uniqueness of individuals and their need for continued development. They have model toward a more transformational style of leadership.

Phase Four. Individuals at this phase begin to think from a more *global, systemic perspective.* They experience an increased desire for harmony, community, and the integration of values, beliefs, and ideas. Principals begin to view the world beyond the borders of the school with a deepening appreciation for the larger community and for societal issues. Principals take on a proactive stance, becoming more involved in the critical questioning of current practice. There is a transformational aspect to leadership that seeks to make a difference in education and in the lives of others. A strong desire to build community in its truest sense emerges.

Implications for Leadership Development

Through personal reflection, leaders encounter their beliefs, strengthen their convictions, and challenge their thinking toward higher levels of moral commitment. The values that principals embrace form the basis of what they perceive to be important in their schools. Values form the building blocks for a personal vision of what should be. Senge[45] discusses the importance of vision development and refers to it as "personal mastery." It is the task of leaders to discover and clarify their values as a foundation for guiding their schools.

Leadership and Vision

Vision has been defined as "the capacity to create and communicate a view of the desired state of affairs that induces commitment among those working in the organization."[46] *Create, communicate,* and *commitment* are the key words. Organizational study after study, whether that organization is in the public sector or the private sector, a school or a business, reveals that leaders have vision. Bennis[47] found that the key ingredient among executives of highly successful organizations was "compelling vision." Others, both before and after the Bennis inquiry, have found much the same thing. Norris,[48] for example, called it "creative leadership" and wrote,

> Leadership is creative to the extent that the leader:
>
> - has a wide knowledge of educational theory and principles;
> - possesses the ability to analyze current situations in light of what should be;
> - can identify problems;
> - can conceptualize new avenues for change.

She continued, "Creative leadership requires that the leader make full use of the analytical as well as the intuitive mind."[49] Visionary leaders ask such questions as these: Who are the human beings that inhabit the school setting? What are the needs of these individuals? What unique problems face them as they seek to bring meaning to their lives? Vision, then, is asking questions about what might be, standing for something, making certain others know what that "thing" is, and determining appropriate courses of action for getting to expressed goals.

Shared Vision and Authority

Increasingly important is the notion of *shared vision* and the part that the principal plays in fostering the empowerment of others. Commitment to any endeavor is strengthened greatly when others have the freedom to express their own visions of what should be and are encouraged to contribute their unique talents and ideas to the resolution of important issues that concern them. The principal encourages responsibility by allowing the autonomy and authority to match the task.

Leadership Style and Emotional Intelligence

Goleman[50] posits a direct link between emotional intelligence and effective leadership. He points out that emotional intelligence (EI) is as important as cognitive ability in determining one's effectiveness as a leader. He suggests that EI is comprised of four main capabilities:

- Self-awareness—a sense of self-worth based on understanding one's emotions, strengths, and limitations and the impact they have on others
- Self-management—the ability to manage one's emotions, responsibilities, and opportunities as well as, being trustworthy and oriented toward excellence
- Social awareness—empathy toward others, a sense of organizational needs, and recognition of and action toward meeting the needs of others
- Social skill—visionary leadership and influence as well as the ability to communicate, foster change, manage conflict, and inspire others toward collaboration and cooperation

It is important that leaders work to develop all areas of emotional intelligence in order to effectively lead their organizations.

Different EI capability areas tend to promote different leadership styles; each style affects organizational members in a different way Table 1.1 demonstrates this connection.

TABLE 1.1   Leadership Style, Emotional Intelligence Capabilities, and Impact on Others

LEADERSHIP STYLE	EMOTIONAL INTELLIGENCE CAPABILITIES	IMPACT ON OTHERS
Coercive	Initiative, achievement	Compliance
Authoritative	Self-confidence, empathy, vision	Commitment
Affiliative	Empathy, communication, relationship	Contentment
Democratic	Collaboration, team building	Collaboration
Pacesetting	Initiative, responsibility, achievement	Challenge
Coaching	Self-awareness, empathy, development	Growth

Adapted from: D. Goleman, "Leadership That Gets Results." *Harvard Business Review* (March–April 2000): 78–90.

The most effective leaders are those who employ all six of the leadership styles and apply each one appropriately. Four styles—the authoritative, democratic, affiliative, and coaching— appear to produce the best organizational climate and performance.

Goleman's research indicates that the most effective single style in producing a results-oriented climate is the authoritative style. Authoritative leaders are visionaries who inspire people and gain their commitment by showing them how their work fits into a larger purpose for the organization. "An authoritative leader states the end but generally gives people plenty of leeway to devise their own means. Authoritative leaders give people plenty of freedom to innovate, experiment, and take calculated risks."[51]

The results of Goleman's study suggest that school principals are most effective when they can sense organizational needs and orchestrate their style repertoire to meet the evolving needs of the organization. Goleman's study supports earlier contingency management studies suggesting that there is no single approach to effective leadership given the diverse and constantly changing needs of today's schools.

Roles and Functions

The role of the principal will vary from place to place as a result of organizational and community expectations. Nevertheless, the *functions* that must be managed by the principal are similar, regardless of where the position is located or how many students there are.

Five functional aspects compose the principalship. Four of these take place inside the school; the other occurs in interaction with the outside world. The "inside" functions include curriculum development, instructional improvement, student services, and financial and facility management. The "outside" function is community relations.

The dimensions of leadership and management cut across these five functions. Leadership is the way principals *use themselves* to create a school climate characterized by student productivity, staff productivity, and creative thought. Think of good management as the systematic application of an array of skills to provide for an orderly and efficient school environment. Figure 1.2 depicts the relationship of the five functions and the two dimensions.

FIGURE 1.2   The Five Functions and Two Dimensions of the Principalship

Source: Larry W. Hughes and Gerald C. Ubben, *The Elementary Principal's Handbook: A Guide to Effective Action,* 4th ed. Boston: Allyn & Bacon, 1994, p. 5. Used with permission.

Research and development efforts of such professional organizations as the National Association of Secondary School Principals (NASSP)[52] and the National Association of Elementary School Principals (NAESP)[53] have uncovered discreet skills, the presence of which determines effectiveness. Research done by NASSP[54] notes abilities that are important to a successful school administrator. More recently, the National Policy Board (NPB) has incorporated many of these skills as part of its national standards for school principals.[55] The six NASSP abilities include the following:

- Ability to plan and organize work
- Ability to work with and lead others
- Ability to analyze problems and make decisions
- Ability to communicate orally and in writing

Each of the five functions is vitally important for school success, and each requires the principal to exercise good managerial skills as well as leadership. The remainder of this text will focus on these specific functions and will discuss the dispositions, knowledge, and skills necessary for effective principal leadership.

A Leadership Challenge

ISLLC 3

Today's school principals have been charged with the task of shaping their schools to become outstanding examples of productive learning. Principals are challenged to clarify their own values, beliefs, and positions and to engage proactively with others in the redesign and improvement of their schools. They are expected to establish conditions that foster personal empowerment and enhanced development of organizational members and to orchestrate shared power and decision making among an array of individuals both internal and external to the school setting. At the same time, principals are encouraged to build a community of leaders and learners who will effectively shape the school environment to champion increased productivity among students. Truly, it is an exciting time to be a school principal!

Summary

School leadership is best understood in relation to the context in which that leadership takes place. In this chapter we have explored organizational context based on the metaphors of machines, organisms, and brains. Through that exploration, we have examined individual and group expectations and the part they play in determining the nature of the principalship as well as the principal's role within that context.

The concepts of transactional and transformational leadership have also been explored as a way of understanding the importance of principals' values and ethical responsibilities within their role. We have stressed the importance of principals becoming reflective leaders concerned with their own development and leadership artistry.

ACTIVITIES

1. Review Case Studies 12, 19, and 24 at the end of this book. Apply the concepts expressed in this chapter. What implications do the various views of transformational leadership have for managing and leading? What relevance has social systems theory? Which, if any, of Morgan's metaphors might describe the organization in each case?

2. Turn to the ISLLC standards in Appendix B. Review the functions listed with Standards 1 and 5. Reflect on which of the standard items relate directly to the material presented in this chapter. Do these standards better reflect the concepts of transformational or transactional leadership? Identify one function from each standard to link directly to a concept or idea discussed in Chapter 1.

ENDNOTES

1. William Foster, "Toward a Critical Theory of Educational Administration," in *Leadership and Organizational Culture,* ed. T. J. Sergiovanni and J. E. Corbally (Urbana: University of Illinois Press, 1984).
2. Michael Fullen, *Change Forces: The Sequel* (Philadelphia: Falmer Press, 1999), p. 1.
3. R. Katz, "Skills of an Effective Administrator," *Harvard Business Review 52,* no. 5 (1974): 90–102.
4. Jacob W. Getzels and Egon G. Guba, "Social Behavior and the Administrative Process," *School Review 65* (Winter 1957): 423–441.
5. Ibid.
6. Ibid.
7. Michael Fullen, *The Moral Imperative of School Leadership* (Thousand Oaks, CA: Corwin Press, 2003), p. 1.
8. Christopher Hodgkinson, *The Philosophy of Leadership* (Oxford, England: Basil Blackwell Publisher Limited, 1983).
9. Garath Morgan, *Images of Organizations* (Cambridge, MA: Sage, 1986).
10. Sonia Nieto, *The Light in Their Eyes: Creating Multicultural Learning Communities* (New York: Teachers College Press, 1999).
11. Ibid.
12. Fullen, *The Moral Imperative,* p. 1.
13. Seymour Sarason, *Revisiting the Culture of the School and the Problem of Change* (New York: Teachers College Press, 1996), p. 27.
14. T. Sergiovanni, "Leadership as Cultural Expression," in *Leadership and Organizational Culture,* ed. T. J. Sergiovanni and J. E. Corbally (Urbana: University of Illinois Press, 1984).
15. Sarason, *Revisiting the Culture of the School and the Problem of Change.*
16. In its 1983 report, *A Nation at Risk,* the National Commission on Excellence in Education challenged the schools to overcome what they saw as a "rising tide of mediocrity."
17. The Carnegie Foundation for the Advancement of Teaching, *An Imperiled Generation: Saving Urban Schools* (Princeton, NJ: Princeton University Press, 1988). This report discusses the negative environmental factors within school settings that hinder learning in the urban areas.
18. The National Policy Board (NPBEA) is sponsored and supported by the Association of Colleges for Teacher Education, Association of School Business Officials, Council of Chief State School Officers, National Association of Secondary School Principals, National Association of Elementary

School Principals, American Association of School Administrators, Association for Supervision and Curriculum Development, National Boards Association, National Council of Professors of Educational Administration, and University Council for Educational Administration.

19. The Interstate School Leaders Licensure Consortium is a program of the Council of Chief State School Officers. Representatives from 24 state education agencies and various professional associations drafted the standards that have been developed by this committee. They were written to be compatible with the new National Council for the Accreditation of Teacher Education (NCATE) *Curriculum Guidelines for School Administration.*

20. Karl Weick, "The Significance of Culture," in *Organizational Culture,* ed. P. Frost, L. Moore, M. Lewis, C. Lundenberg, and J. Martin (Beverly Hills, CA: Sage, 1985).

21. Nieto, *The Light in Their Eyes.*

22. James Burns, *Leadership* (New York: Harper, 1978).

23. Ibid.

24. Thomas Sergiovanni, "Leadership and Excellence in Schooling," *Educational Leadership 41* (February 1984): 4–13.

25. Foster, "Toward a Critical Theory of Educational Administration."

26. Bernard Bass and Bruce Avolio, eds. *Improving Organizational-Effectiveness through Transformational Leadership* (Thousand Oaks, CA: Sage, 1993).

27. Thomas J. Sergiovanni, *Moral Leadership: Getting to the Heart of School Improvement* (San Francisco: Jossey-Bass, 1992).

28. Foster, "Toward a Critical Theory of Educational Administration."

29. Bass, *Leadership and Performance Beyond Expectations.*

30. Burns, *Leadership.*

31. Foster, "Toward a Critical Theory of Educational Administration."

32. Ibid., p. 42.

33. Sergiovanni, *Moral Leadership.*

34. Foster, "Toward a Critical Theory of Educational Administration."

35. Chris Argyris, *Reasoning, Learning and Action: Individual and Organizational* (San Francisco: Jossey-Bass, 1982).

36. Ibid.

37. Foster, "Toward a Critical Theory of Educational Administration."

38. Hodgkinson, *The Philosophy of Leadership.*

39. Ibid.

40. Cynthia Norris, "Developing Visionary Leaders for Tomorrow's Schools," *NASSP Bulletin 74* (May 1990): 6–10.

41. James Kouzes and Barry Posner, *The Leadership Challenge* (San Francisco: Jossey-Bass, 1987).

42. Ibid.

43. Brian Hall, *The Development of Consciousness: A Confluent Theory of Values* (New York: Paulist Press, 1986).

44. Ibid.

45. Peter Senge, *The Fifth Discipline: The Art and Practice of the Learning Organization* (New York: Doubleday, 1990).

46. Warren Bennis, "Transformation Power and Leadership," in *Leadership and Organizational Culture,* ed. T. J. Sergiovanni and J. E. Corbally (Urbana: University of Illinois Press, 1984).

47. Ibid.

48. Cynthia Norris, "Cultivating Creative Cultures," in *The Principal as Leader* (2nd ed.), ed. Larry W. Hughes (New York: MacMillan, 1999).

49. Ibid.

50. Daniel Goleman, "Leadership That Sets Results," *Harvard Business Review* (March-April 2000): 78–90.

51. Ibid., p. 84.

52. NASSP has available a variety of descriptive materials and research reports, including validation studies. Write to NASSP, 1904 Association Drive, Reston, VA 22091. The NASSP process is designed for the K–12 spectrum; the skills identified are generic and applicable for elementary as well as secondary school principals.

53. NAESP has developed a similar set of skills for elementary school principals.

54. In the NASSP there are actually 12 discrete skills and attributes: problem analysis, judgment, organizational ability, decisiveness, leadership, sensitivity, stress tolerance, oral and written communication, personal motivation, educational values, and range of interests. What is described here are the more general categories of skills.

55. The National Policy Board distinguished between the academic knowledge base and the professional knowledge base by organizing subject content into work-relevant patterns that make expert knowledge functional.

SELECTED READINGS

Bass, Bernard, *Transformational Leadership Development* (Palo Alto, CA: Consulting Psychologist Press, 1990).

Beckner, Weldon, *Ethics for Educational Leaders* (Boston: Pearson Press, 2004).

Burns, James McGregor. "Prologue," in *Leadership* (New York: Harper, 1978).

DePree, Max. *Leadership Is an Art* (New York: Dell Publishing, 1990).

Fullen, Michael. *The Moral Imperative of School Leadership* (Thousand Oaks, CA: Corwin Press, 2004).

Gardner, Howard. *On Leadership* (New York: Free Press, 1990).

Gardner, Howard. *Leading Minds: An Anatomy of Leadership* (New York: Basic Books, 1995).

Gilligan, Carol. *In a Different Voice* (Cambridge, MA: Harvard University Press, 1993).

Greenleaf, R. K. *Servant Leadership: A Journey into the Nature of Legitimate Power and Greatness* (New York: Paulist Press, 2002).

Katz, Michael, Noddings, Nell, and Strike, Kenneth. *Justice and Caring: The Search for Common Ground in Education* (New York: Teachers College Press, 1999).

Moore, B. "Improving the Evaluation and Feedback Process for Principals," *Principal 88*, no. 6 (2009): 38–41.

Noddings, Nell. *Educating Moral People* (New York: Teachers College Press, 2002).

Portin, B. "The Roles That Principals Play." Retrieved June 4, 2009, from *Educational Leadership 61*, no. 7(2006): 14.

Rooney, J. "What New (Young) Principals Need to Know." *Educational Leadership 66* (2008): 84–85.

Tschannen-Moran, M. "Fostering Teacher Professionalism in Schools: The Role of Leadership Orientation and Trust." *Educational Administration Quarterly 45*, no. 2 (2009) 217–247.

2 The Learning Community

Community celebrates the dignity and worth of self and others, fosters the empowerment of both and encourages and supports the maximum development of human potential for the benefit of the common good.

—Cynthia Norris et al.[1]

Principals are challenged to be developers, or catalysts, for human and organizational development. This is an awesome task requiring awareness, commitment, and a genuine concern for the welfare of others. Development cannot be considered without first addressing the concept of *empowerment*, which means "to enable." We believe it is the responsibility of the school principal to ensure that conditions are present that enable individuals and organizations to develop their highest potential. Although personal empowerment must come from within the individual person, the principal can foster a climate conducive to risk taking, personal contribution, and challenge.

ISLLC 2

The orientation toward development is consistent with the concept of servant leadership discussed in Chapter 1. Viewed from a servant leadership perspective, a developer is in "service" to others, fostering the greatest opportunities for their growth. As the leader takes time to consider others' needs, there is a renewed emphasis on an "ethic of care."

This chapter takes the position that the context most conducive for inspiring individual and organizational development is the *learning community*. In the following discussion, we build the concept of a learning community, talk about the conditions that facilitate its enactment, and discuss the role that the leader plays in fostering its development. In understanding learning communities, it is first necessary to consider the nature of groups.

Sociological and Psychological Nature of Groups

Groups have both a sociological (group) and a psychological (individual) dimension. The sociological dimension is concerned with how the group itself develops and how it, in turn, interfaces with other groups. The school would be considered a group that contains within it many subgroups. Examples of these subgroups are departments, teams, schools within schools, study groups, and cooperative learning groups. Other forms of subgroups include those based on gender or ethnicity. Each subgroup interacts with the larger school, with other subgroups within the school, and with groups in the larger environment. In turn, the larger group, or the school, must interface with all the individual subgroups and with other schools, as well as with the umbrella group, or school district.

In schools that are not sensitive to the issues of social justice, there is sometimes a failure to give equal attention to all groups and their needs. This failure greatly impedes the development of the school as a true learning community. Even beyond the parameters of the official school district, other groups react with the school and its subgroups. Parent groups, support agencies, and state departments of education are but a few examples. Ways of working with many of these groups are discussed in later chapters concerning public relations, special education, and legal issues.

The psychological nature of groups involves the individual *within* the group. Of particular interest is the nature of the individual's development and how it is affected by the dynamics of the group. What factors create or impede individual development? Of interest, as well, is the impact that the individual, in turn, has on the group. How does the individual influence group development? How might the individual lessen the effectiveness of the total group? How might the group impede the development of the individual? All of these concerns are dealt with as we consider learning communities.

Reciprocity

A major concept relevant to understanding group and individual development is the notion of *reciprocity.* Based on the word *reciprocate,* which means to "give back," reciprocity enables individuals and groups to respond in productive ways to the influence of each other. As one entity grows and is strengthened, it provides influence and opportunity to the other, thereby encouraging mutual development. This exciting notion lies at the heart of what a learning community is. Researchers have explored the idea of reciprocity by examining groups, called *cohorts.*[2] Cohorts are becoming typical service-delivery models in educational administration programs throughout major universities. Next, we discuss some major findings from this cohort research and provide a model that has implications for learning communities in schools.

Cohort Model

The model shown in Figure 2.1 is the result of researchers'[3] work with cohorts across four university settings over a six-year period. The researchers suggest that cohorts that operate as true groups are characterized by four important qualities: interaction, purpose, interdependence, and individual growth. The first three qualities, demonstrated by the outer points of the triangle, determine the strength or cohesiveness of the group, or cohort. The outer points of the triangle demonstrate this interconnection. The inner portion of the triangle represents the individual development that tends to happen when groups become cohesive, interdependent entities.

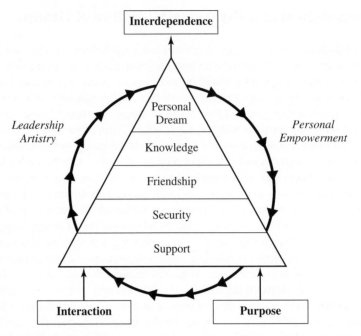

FIGURE 2.1   The Cohort Model

Source: Adapted from C. Norris and B. Barnett, Cultivating a New Leadership Paradigm: From Cohorts to Communities. Paper presented at the University Council for Educational Administration Annual Meeting, Philadelphia, 1994. Used with permission

Individual development includes the following characteristics believed to occur in developmental fashion: support, security, friendship, knowledge, and realization of the personal dream.

Let us discuss each of these components of a community in detail and apply the related concepts to schools.

Interaction.   Interaction, which serves as the foundation of a community, is enhanced through frequent opportunities for individuals to come together. Initially, group members are more closed in their willingness to connect with each other. Often, barriers are built that impede a free exchange of ideas, and group members may be somewhat hesitant to reveal themselves to each other. The size of the group also plays a part in increasing interaction. In groups over 20, it is more difficult to ensure that opportunities are provided for all to contribute. It is important that the principal foster a climate of openness and trust and that many opportunities are made available for individuals to share thoughts and ideas.

Interaction builds connections and encourages trust among members. It moves the group from a mere discussion of ideas to a deeper level of exchange, which Senge[4] terms "dialogue." As Norris[5] states:

> Positive involvement and accountability for group goals and purposes are intensified when members interact and consider the issues surrounding their aims and purposes. They learn from each other as ideas are shared and they question and confirm their direction and purpose. It is interaction that ultimately paves the way for a deeper understanding of, and commitment toward, group purpose—the second ingredient in a true learning community.

Purpose.   Purpose unites the group in a meaningful way and creates a community from a mere gathering of individuals. Purpose must evolve from among group members if it is to be meaningful. Each person must see in that purpose something of value if he or she is to become committed toward its achievement. When individuals, through collective dialogue, determine their own purpose, they work more diligently to achieve their objectives.

Interdependence.   Interdependence results from group commitment toward a shared purpose. As individuals work together to achieve something they all value, they begin to appreciate the talents and contributions each brings to the task. They understand more fully that their efforts are intensified as others join with them in the same cause. This is certainly true in teacher professional learning communities; it is equally true among students in collaborative learning groups and similar settings. Again, however, note that the previously mentioned qualities of a learning community must be present before interdependence results. Nieto[6] makes this point when she talks about establishing cooperative learning groups as a way of meeting the needs of students in multicultural settings. "Cooperative learning, for example, can take place in the most uncooperative and oppressive of settings, while extraordinary and high level learning can happen in traditional-looking classrooms with nailed-down seats in rigid rows."

Individual Growth.   In true communities, individuals become the benefactors. Individuals grow in a climate of support and security. The exchange of ideas fosters a dialogue that challenges this growth and provides a sustaining force for the individual's development. Within a sustaining community, individuals progress in their development. They move from feelings of support to a sense of security. This increase in trust brings about deepening friendships and high levels of enhanced learning. Their knowledge of content increases as does their knowledge of self. Through affirmation and feedback, individuals become more aware of their own values and develop a deepening understanding of their own purposes.

Learning Communities

Learning communities are concerned with growth and continuous self-renewal of both individuals and organizations. The leader is, therefore, responsible for *building organizations* where people are continually expanding their capabilities to shape their future—leaders are responsible for learning.

ISLLC 2   Linda Lambert,[7] in *Building Leadership Capacity in Schools,* states that leadership for learning is a collective responsibility. She defines leadership this way: "The key notion in this definition [of leadership] is that leadership is about learning together, and constructing meaning and knowledge collectively and collaboratively."[8] Learning organizations never "fully arrive," for their tendency is to search continually for new possibilities and opportunities for growth. An organizational context, such as the brain metaphor discussed in Chapter 1, enables the organization to assimilate and store past knowledge, but also to construct new knowledge through the shared experiences, ideas, and perceptions of all group members. Each individual group member becomes a resource of knowledge for all others, and the organization becomes a catalyst for thinking and learning.

   Note, however, that *learning communities* do not evolve until a strong base of *community* is present. This is illustrated in Figure 2.1. As shown, support, security, and friendship form the foundation for knowledge acquisition. A major mistake made in many schools today is attempting to institute learning teams without paying careful attention to the underlying foundation for collaboration.

Systems Thinking

Many contemporary writers have presented their views of just what constitutes a learning community. Perhaps one of the most succinct definitions is that given by Senge,[9] who suggests that learning organizations are distinguished by five important characteristics:

1. *Systems Thinking.* In learning organizations/communities there is a connection between all aspects of the organization. What happens in one part affects all other parts. The uniting thread becomes the shared vision or purpose. Within true learning communities, there is also *reciprocity* of individual and group development and responsibility of each party to the other. Rather than independence or dependence, there is *interdependence* within the learning setting.
2. *Personal Mastery.* Knowledge is seen as an avenue for greater *self-awareness and understanding* that, in turn, fosters appreciation of others. Within true learning communities, there is recognition and appreciation of individual potential, and the opportunity to develop that potential is present.
3. *Team Learning.* In learning communities there is a *deliberate effort to* build settings in which true *dialogue* rather than mere discussion is the order of the day. School leaders (principals or teachers) eliminate the top-down *sage on the stage* perspective. The learning environment fosters meaningful connections within learning settings for faculty as well as students.
4. *Challenging Mental Models.* A climate of continual questioning, problem finding, and *exploration of possibilities* becomes the natural mode of operation within learning communities. This double-loop learning process becomes the basis for the transformation of current realities.
5. *Shared Vision.* In learning communities, all community members are encouraged to explore their beliefs and values, to test those values in the context of real learning experiences, to question "conditioned" assumptions, and to search for the common bonds of understanding that unite all members.

Mezirow[10] speaks of the learning that takes place in such settings as "transformational learning," for it is learning that changes the individual's perspective. As an example, a group might examine current school structure related to philosophy, policy, and procedures. Through dialogue, the groups members may then question the appropriateness of the structure for all groups and decide to take action to move the school toward a different direction.

Transformational Learning

Transformational learning produces a change in personal perspective and causes individuals to behave in different way. It differs from informational learning, which merely presents knowledge about a content area. Transformational learning is defined by Mezirow as learning that "uses a prior interpretation to construe a new or revised interpretation of the meaning of one's experience in order to guide future action."[11]

As transformational learning takes place, individuals proceed through a series of important steps. Through these steps:

- They examine past experiences in relation to the present situation (centrality of experience).
- They become aware of contradictions in their thinking (critical reflection).
- They change their assumptions based on dialogue with others (rational discourse).

This progression in thinking is brought about through collective inquiry in a nurturing environment, Mezirow[12] speaks of true learning communities as "holding environments." They provide group members with both support and challenge.

Nieto,[13] too, discusses the important role that collective inquiry plays in the learning process. She contends that children from minority backgrounds are not often exposed to a wide variety of viewpoints; therefore, they need opportunities to explore, the views of others. This can be accomplished through collective sharing of experiences—known as *critical pedagogy*. In this process, "students use their experiences to extend their learning," and student voice is honored and used in the classroom teaching. Neito views empowerment as both "the *purpose* and *outcome* of critical pedagogy." She sees student empowerment resulting from a "redefinition of relationships between and among teachers and students, parents, and administrators."[14]

Within these nurturing or holding environments, individuals develop a deep sense of belonging and personal empowerment. But what exactly is empowerment, and what are the principles on which it is built?

Empowerment

Empowerment is "the act of increasing either one's own or other's influence over life's circumstances and decisions. . . . It conveys a psychological sense of personal control or influence and a concern with social influence."[15] Not only does empowerment concern personal influence but it also radiates from the individual a sense of self-actualized behavior that Maslow terms the *creative ego*.[16] Such behavior includes these characteristics:

1. *Openness to Experience.* The individual exhibits a lack of rigidity of beliefs, perceptions, and ideas. There is also a greater tolerance for ambiguity and a more receptive attitude toward possibilities.
2. *Internal Locus of Evaluation.* The individual exhibits an internal ability to self-evaluate and to rely on individual judgment in determining personal worth.
3. *Ability to Toy with Elements and Concepts.* The individual exhibits a spontaneous exploration of thoughts and ideas as well as a creative response to situations.
4. *Lack of Fear.* The individual exhibits self-acceptance and confidence and a greater willingness to venture forth and try new ideas.

What, then, can a principal do to enhance conditions that will facilitate such individual empowerment and, in turn, influence greater productivity within the organization? Rath and colleagues[17] have suggested three theories that might guide principals' actions. Those theories are the theories of needs, values, and thinking.

Needs Theory.   As pointed out by such theorists as Maslow and Alderfer,[18] emotional security is a basic need that provides a foundation for other higher-level needs. Emotional security depends on the climate and conditions under which one works. Effective schools research is but one example of the literature supporting the need for a positive climate that allows for freedom of expression, risk taking, and exploration. Goleman[19] has discussed the important relationship between *interpersonal intelligence* and *academic achievement,* or professional success. According to Goleman, without the full development of emotional intelligence, academic growth will not be maximized.

Research on learning communities suggests that emotional security also develops most effectively when individuals feel that they have a support group. Learning communities seem to promote this sense of emotional security so necessary for empowerment to occur.

Values Theory.   A second theory that supports empowerment is the values theory. We have already discussed the importance of principals becoming aware of their own values and visions for education. Without a clear purpose and clarification of one's values, it is difficult to lead with *credibility* and to have the vision required for leadership. It is important that teachers and students also have opportunities to clarify their values and to share in development of the vision and purpose for the school. Opportunities for discussion groups, thinking meetings,[20] and values clarification activities can enhance the students' emotional intelligence and provide a closer bond between the students and the school. In a later chapter on curriculum, we discuss this concept as part of humanistic curriculum theory. The concept is revisited in the chapter on school discipline, when we consider the formation of advisory groups and other counseling services. Teachers, too, should be provided opportunities to explore their values through such avenues as platform development[21] study groups, and work on school improvement plans.

Thinking Theory.   We have previously discussed the importance of dialogue and critical inquiry to a sense of personal empowerment. Individuals, through this collaborative exchange, gain the support and challenge necessary for transformational learning to occur. Teachers gain the skills and confidence to assume leadership in school affairs when they are sustained in such holding environments.

Teacher Empowerment

Some leaders grant teachers "professional authority" based on "seasoned craft knowledge and personal expertise" rather than relying on traditional authority based on a traditional power base. Sergiovanni has referred to this practice as providing "substitutes for leadership."[22]

Sergiovanni considered the use of substitutes for leadership to be a moral leadership process whereby individuals are given the authority and responsibility to apply their own professional knowledge to the decisions that relate to their own educational responsibilities. It is a concept that treats teachers as professionals who operate from an intrinsic, or individual, view of their career. This value-added approach depends on four basic "substitutes" for leadership being in place:

1. *School Norms.* A shared covenant unites individual members in a committed effort to realize common values and beliefs.
2. *The Professional Ideal.* Organizational members accept their individual responsibility for student learning and for their own professional development.

3. *Collegiality.* Individuals collaborate in mutual support yet assume individual responsibility for their own growth and leadership.
4. *Rewarding Work.* Work is meaningful and individuals feel accountable for their own success and the success of their students.

Instructional Leadership

The original models of instructional leadership were driven by an effective schools concept that placed the school principal at the apex of learning. There is still relevance in considering the dimensions of that leadership as guides for establishing a shared leadership effort in which the principal serves as *a facilitator of the process.* As pointed out by Sergiovanni, what truly guides the direction of this process is centered in the "professional ideal" rather than in directives that come from a top-down perspective. All elements of the learning community must come together in a meaningful way before this can take place. Sergiovanni listed the following five leadership skills or forces, available to principals as they facilitate a professional learning community.[23]

1. *Technical Forces.* Technical forces include being a good manager and applying good planning, organizing, coordinating, and controlling techniques to ensure optimum effectiveness of the organization—for example, efficient office management practices, good scheduling techniques, and appropriate use of goals and objectives. Technical behaviors are basically the activities that would ensure good, efficient management.
2. *Human Forces.* These behaviors emphasize human relations skills, good motivational techniques, and good morale building within the organization. The appropriate use of participatory management is an integral part of these behaviors, which become major contributors to the climate of the school.
3. *Educational Forces.* External forces focus on the conceptual knowledge of education. Skills include the ability to diagnose educational problems, carry out the functions of clinical supervision, evaluate educational programs, help develop curriculum, implement staff-development activities, and develop good individual educational programs for students.
4. *Symbolic Forces.* These behaviors demonstrate to others those things that the leader believes important and of value to the organization. They involve *purposing*—"that continuous stream of actions by an organization's formal leadership which has the effect of inducing clarity, consensus, and commitment regarding the organization's basic purposes."[24]
5. *Cultural Forces.* These behaviors focus on strengthening the values and beliefs that make the school unique. The leader attempts to build traditions of the school around those things most highly valued. This is done by sharing with others what the school most values; by orienting new members of the group—students, staff, and parents—to the values and beliefs of the organization; by telling stories of past glories to reinforce these traditions; or simply by explaining the standard operating procedure that is expected to be used.

The cultural forces of leadership bond students, parents, and teachers together as true believers in the school. A special sense of personal worth and importance grows out of membership in the organization. Likewise, learning communities produce more effective high-performance schools. We turn our attention now to some of the characteristics of high-performing organizations.

High-Performance Organizations

ISLLC 1

The phrase *high-performance organization* has now come into common usage. We first discovered it in an unfortunately obscure work by Marshall.[25] He described five conditions in schools that could be labeled high performing. Such schools have the following characteristics:

1. An outcome-based learning environment in which high standards of education, social development, and health are achieved by all learners
2. An outcome-based environment in which the system of instructional decision making and delivery responds to each learner's needs, interests, abilities, talents, styles of learning, and styles of living
3. An outcome-based environment in which curriculum assessment and human resources development are mutually reinforcing
4. An outcome-based environment in which the resources for learning are planned, focused, and managed by teams of educators with input from parents and other citizens
5. An outcome-based environment in which communication and community involvement are an integral part of the human resource and economic development of the community

Sergiovanni observed that in a high-performance school, the principal deemphasizes "top down hierarchies and detailed scripts that tell people what to do." Rather, the principal connects "people to outcomes rather than rules. . . . The key to effective leadership is to connect workers tightly to ends, but only loosely to means."[26]

Senge has offered a perspective and a structure for the improvement of the instructional processes that is consistent with this concept. His thesis is fundamental to principals who wish to lead their schools to new heights of performance. Senge described the skills needed to build what he labels "learning organizations." In such an organization, the leader's responsibility is to provide opportunities for the staff to engage in "generative" learning. As organizational members learn, their capabilities and perceptions expand.[27] In a similar vein, Cordeiro pointed out, "An organization that generates learning is able to grow and develop in an infinite number of ways. Most organizations are adaptive but not also generative. Schools have become proficient at adapting [others'] models."[28]

Others' models or another school's problem solution may not in any way appropriately address problems and challenges confronting one's own school. Adaptation may simply result in frustration and in a local problem not being solved. In the learning organization, people ask *why* a condition is the way it is and devise ways to address the "whys." The focus is on the problem, not on the symptoms.

Goal Setting

High-performing organizations are characterized by committed, energetic people who sit down together, examine problems confronting their organization, and figure out ways to overcome these problems. Tanner called this "breaking the bonds of isolation" and creating a "climate of professional inquiry."[29] The principal's job is to facilitate this exchange by asking these questions:

- Why are we doing what we are doing? (a goals question)
- What are we doing? How are we going about achieving our goals? (a process question)
- Can it be done a better way? (an evaluation question)

Principals engage staff, students, and community in goal setting and problem solving because all are stakeholders and each, to one degree or another, has a contribution to make and responsibilities to assume for why things are as they are. Four assumptions guide the principal:

1. People at the working level tend to know the problems best.
2. The face-to-face work group is the best unit for diagnosis and change.
3. People will work hard to achieve objectives and goals they have helped develop.
4. Initiative and creativity are widely distributed in the population.

These assumptions undergird the high-performance organization.

It is axiomatic that any effective organization must have a clear sense of direction. Once developed, the goals need to be explicated by specific objectives, and the accomplishment of these objectives must be manifest in instructional activities in the classroom.

Well-understood, well-advertised goals for schools and classrooms are absolutely essential. School climate, consistency in decision making, and accountability for what happens in the instructional delivery system—three very different aspects of schools that aspire to high performance—result from the nature of the goals that are established and *the nature of the goal-setting process.* Stated simply, "The glue that holds together the myriad actions and decisions of highly effective principals . . . [are] the goals that they and their staff have developed for the school and a sense of what their schools need to look like and to do in order to accomplish those goals."[30]

Those who work collectively to construct and implement the goals for an organization may be part of what Wenger[31] refers to as a community of practice. Communities of practice are formed through shared interest and mutual engagement. They arise when people have a passion for something that they do together. Through mutual engagement, they continue to learn. This shared learning is transformational in nature, for it not only enhances the learning of the individual, but it adds to the collective knowledge of the organization as well.

A Model for Instructional Leadership

Effective instructional leadership requires a complex set of relationships between principals and their beliefs and the surrounding environment of the school. The principal's values and previous experiences, as well as the expectations of the community and the institution in which the principal finds the school, all must be taken into account.

Values and Beliefs of the Principal. What a principal values and believes should be passed on to all children are the things that become the principal's contribution to the school. When principals are asked what they think is most important for children to learn, they will usually have a particular area of interest high on the priority list about which they are most willing to talk. Most principals will emphasize basic skills as being important. But beyond the basic skills emphasis, the priority list can become very diverse.

A principal's beliefs about the ability of all children to learn is extremely important. In most of the research about high-performing schools, principals have a strong belief in and commitment to the ability of all children to learn regardless of race, social conditions, or gender. These beliefs are extremely important because staff members will become attuned to what they believe the principal considers important. This contributes strongly to the establishment of a school culture characterized by high expectations for all.

Community Influences and Expectations.   The local community also exerts great pressure on a principal's behavior. Principals of inner-city schools find a high percentage of their time being spent on student behavioral problems that are a direct outgrowth of community and domestic problems at home. High unemployment and high crime rates, poverty, and hunger directly affect the school and expectations for the school. The principal of the highly affluent suburban school is heavily influenced by community demands and expectations of high achievement. National Merit scholarships, high SAT scores, entrance into the Ivy League colleges, and the athletic stature of the school all become pressures on the principal.

ISLLC 4

The demands and expectations for a school can change, however. Academic demands for a school can be expressed by a call for high test scores. Some communities will even demand academic excellence that goes beyond mere competence to call for the development in children of attributes such as arts appreciation, curiosity, creativity, interpersonal competence, problem-solving skills, critical thinking skills, strong work ethics, and communication skills.

Communities also influence a principal's behavior by their willingness to contribute resources directly to the school in the form of funds and services. If large amounts of money must be raised outside of regular revenue channels by such means as school-based fund-raising activities by children or volunteers, the funds often will be directed to particular interest areas. Parents and community volunteers contributing their time directly to various projects in the school program can be another major influence.

Good instructional leaders are able to harness the interests of the community, taking advantages of its strengths while at the same time focusing on its needs. Over time, an effective instructional leader will even mold the community's expectations for the school, changing satisfaction with mediocrity or special interests to expectations for excellence in the entire program.

Institutional Influences.   Every school is influenced by the organization of which it is a unit. A local school is one part of an intricate network of units nested together into districts, regions, and states. The autonomy of the local school varies greatly from school district to school district and, interestingly, even within districts. All schools have mandates relative to federal, state, and local programs, but some principals are much more effective than others in tailoring these programs to meet the needs of their local schools. For example, in one school district the principal complained about the effort of the central office to impose a districtwide curriculum on his school; he cited how the district was presently highly decentralized, allowing the judgment of the local staff to prevail in curriculum matters. He went on to complain how imposing a districtwide curriculum would reduce his role to simply that of a curriculum manager instead of a leader. Another principal in the district, however, saw the same set of circumstances as an opportunity to bring together additional resources to meet the problems of her school. She got most of her teachers onto the curriculum committees and volunteered her school as a pilot for the project. She also commented that her school's enthusiastic participation in some projects gave her increased power to say no to other influences when necessary.

Institutional influences on the local school also can be seen in the availability of both materials and human resources. School principals often find their time consumed with raising money for this or that project, which detracts from their major role as instructional leaders. Efforts to obtain grants that relate directly to the good of the school can legitimate, but funding activities through candy sales and bazaars are generally misdirected efforts and consume valuable time.

The quality of the faculty and staff of a school represents another major institutional constraint or influence. Most often, upon assuming a principalship, principals inherit a staff from their predecessors. Efforts to influence the staff may initially be limited to organizational and staff-development activities. Yet, positively influencing the quality of the staff through the selection process may be the most important long-term action of the principal. In fact, some research suggests that principals are effective because they have a staff that allows them to behave as they do. The level of authority given to a principal in employing staff becomes a major factor over time in the principal's ability to influence the development of the staff.

Summary

The focus of this chapter has been on the principal as builder of a learning community that contributes to a high-performance school. The principal has been cast as a facilitator of the learning process. We have stressed, however, that leadership in instructional and curricular endeavors is not the sole province of the principal. Indeed, high performance can occur only as leadership is encouraged to emerge from stakeholders—staff, students, and the community. Setting high standards and exemplifying these is an essential leadership act of the principal, nonetheless. It is the principal who is in the position to facilitate staff development, orchestrate time, and schedule factors so that teachers have opportunities to work together to solve instructional and curricular problems.

ACTIVITIES

1. Review the elements of a learning community. Apply each of the five characteristics to your own school and indicate by example the degree to which your school exemplifies these qualities. What strategies would you, as principal, engage in to overcome any weaknesses?
2. Review Case Studies 9, 10, and 17 at the end of this book. For any or all, analyze the problem presented and, applying the concepts developed in this chapter, set forth a strategy for overcoming the problem. You do not have to solve the problem, but you must accept it as *your* problem. Based on reasonable (and stated) assumptions, provide a framework wherein you expect the problem would be mitigated, if not solved.
3. Turn to the ISLLC Standards found in Appendix B. Review the functions listed with Standards 1 and 5. Reflect on which of the standard items relate directly to the material presented in this chapter. How is the concept of empowerment reflected in ISLLC Standard 1? Identify one function to link directly to a concept or idea discussed in Chapter 2.

ENDNOTES

1. Cynthia Norris, Bruce Barnett, Margaret Bassom, and Diane Yerkes, *Developing Educational Leaders, A Working Model: The Learning Community in Action* (New York: Teachers College Press, 2002), p. 5.
2. Cynthia Norris and Bruce Barnett, *Cultivating a New Leadership Paradigm: From Cohorts to Communities.* Paper presented at the University Council for Educational Administration Annual Meeting, Philadelphia, 1994.
3. Cynthia Norris, Bruce Barnett, Margaret Bassom, and Diane Yerkes, "The Cohort: A Model for Developing Transformational Leadership," *Theory Into Practice 27,* no. 3/4 (Fall/Winter 1996): 146–164.
4. Peter Senge, *The Fifth Discipline* (New York: Doubleday, 1990), p. 9.
5. Cynthia Norris, "Comparative Learning Within a Learning Community," in *My Place, Your Place, Our Place: Education*

for the Neighborhood and the World, ed. Glenda Ross, Dianna Popova, Gerald Ubben (Knoxville: University of Tennessee, 2005), pp. 130–138.

6. Sonia Nieto, *The Light in Their Eyes: Creating Multicultural Learning Communities* (New York: Teachers College Press, 1999), p. 108.

7. Linda Lambert, *Building Leadership Capacity in Schools* (Arlington, VA: Association for Supervision and Curriculum Development, 1998).

8. Ibid., p. 7.

9. Senge, *The Fifth Discipline.*

10. J. Mezirow, "Learning to Think Like an Adult: Core Concepts of Transformational Theory," *Adult Education Quarterly 44,* no. 4 (2000): 158–172.

11. Ibid.

12. Ibid.

13. Nieto, *The Light in Their Eyes: Creating Multicultural Learning Communities.*

14. Ibid.

15. Louis Rath, Merrill Harmin, and Sidney B. Simon, *Values and Teaching* (2nd ed.) (Columbus, OH: Merrill, 1978), pp. 27–28.

16. Abraham Maslow, "Toward a Psychology of Being," in *The Creativity Question,* ed. A. Rothernburg and C. Housman (Durham, NC: Duke University Press, 1976), pp. 296–305.

17. Rath, Harmin, and Simon, *Values and Teaching.*

18. C. P. Alderfer, *Existence, Relatedness, and Growth: Human Needs in Organizational Settings* (New York: Free Press, 1972).

19. Daniel Goleman, *Emotional Intelligence* (New York: Bantam Books, 1995).

20. William Glasser, *School Without Failure* (New York: Harper and Row, 1969) and *Control Theory in the Classroom* (New York: Harper and Row, 1986). Both of these books share considerable insight into ways that values clarification can be facilitated

21. Thomas Sergiovanni and Robert Starratt, *Supervision: A Redefinition* (6th ed.) (New York: McGraw-Hill, 1998).

22. Thomas Sergiovanni, *Moral Leadership: Getting to the Heart of School Improvement* (San Francisco: Jossey-Bass, 1992).

23. Thomas J. Sergiovanni, "Leadership and Excellence in Schools," *Educational Leadership 41* (1984): 4–13.

24. Ibid.

25. R. Marshall, *Restructuring the American Work Place: Implications for the Public Sector* (Eugene, OR: Labor Education Research Center, University of Oregon, 1992). LERC Monograph Series.

26. Thomas Sergiovanni, "The Roots of School Leadership," *Principal 74,* no. 2 (November 1994): 6–9.

27. Senge, *The Fifth Discipline.*

28. P. Cordeiro, "The Principal's Role in Curricular Leadership and Program Development," in *The Principal as Leader* (2nd ed.), ed. Larry W. Hughes (New York: Macmillan, 1999), p. 133.

29. Laurel N. Tanner, "The Practical Affairs of Improving Teaching," in *The Principal as Leader,* ed. Larry W. Hughes (New York: Macmillan, 1999), pp. 190, 194.

30. Kenneth Leithwood, "The Principal's Role in Teacher Development," in *Changing School Culture through Staff Development: 1990 Yearbook of the Association for Supervision and Curriculum Development.* ed. Bruce Joyce (Alexandria, VA: ASCD, 1990), pp. 71–90.

31. Etienne Wenger, *Communities of Practice: Learning, Meaning and Identity.* (Boston; Cambridge University Press, 1998).

SELECTED READINGS

Blasé, Joseph, and Peggy C. Kirby. *Bringing Out the Best in Teachers: What Effective Principals Do* (Newbury Park, CA: Corwin Press, 1991).

Christman, J. B., and J. A. Sopovitz. "Small Learning Communities that Actually Learn: Lessons for School Leaders." *Phi Delta Kappa 86* (2005): 649–651.

David, J. L. "Small Learning Communities." *Educational Leadership 65,* no. 8 (2008): 84–85.

DuFour, R. "What Is a Professional Learning Community?" *Educational Leadership 61,* no. 8 (2004): 6–11.

DeFour, Richard, and Robert Eaker. *Professional Learning Communities at Work: Best Practices for Enhancing Student Achievement* (Bloomington, IL: National Educational Service, 1998).

Griffin, Gary A. "Leadership for Curriculum Improvement: The School Administrator's Role," in *Critical Issues in Curriculum. The 87th Year-book of the National Society for the Study of Education,* ed. Laurel Tanner (Part 1, pp. 244–266) (Chicago: University of Chicago Press, 1988).

Hammond, Linda Darling. *The Right to Learn* (San Francisco: Jossey-Bass, 1997).

Hord, S. "Professional Learning Communities: Educators Work Together toward a Shared Purpose." *Journal of Staff Development 30,* no. 1 (2008): 40–43.

Hord, S., and S. Hirsh. "The Principal's Role in Supporting Learning Communities." *Educational Leadership 66,* no. 5 (2009): 22–23.

Huffman, J. "The Role of Shared Values and Vision in Creating Professional Learning Communities." *NASSP Bulletin 87* (2003): 21–32.

Huffman, J. B., and A. L. Jacobson. "Perceptions of Professional Learning Communities." *International Journal of Leadership in Education 6* (2003): 239–250.

Javius, E. L. "Skills for courageous leaders." *Leadership 38,* no. 3 (2009): 30–32.

Johnson, R. "Using Collective Wisdom." *Principal Leadership (Middle School Ed. 6,* no. 4 (2005): 37–38.

Kelehear, Z. "Mentoring the Organization: Helping Principals Bring Schools to Higher Levels of Effectiveness." *NASSP Bulletin 87,* no. 637 (2003): 35–47.

Lambert, Linda. *Building Leadership Capacity in Schools* (Arlington, VA: Association for Supervision and Curriculum Development, 1998).

Lambert, Linda. "A Framework for Shared Leadership." *Educational Leadership 59* (2002): 37–40.

Lampress, B. "Ten Strategies for Staff Empowerment." *Principal Leadership (High School Ed.) 4* (2004): 32–37.

Leithwood, Kenneth A. "The Principal's Role in Teacher Development," in *Changing School Culture through Staff Development: 1990 Year-book of the Association for Supervision and Curriculum Development,* ed. Bruce Joyce (pp. 71–90) (Alexandria, VA: Association for Supervision and Curriculum Development, 1990).

Little, J. "Inside Teacher Community: Representation of Classroom Practice." *Teacher College Record 105* (2003): 913–946.

Meier, Deborah. *In Schools We Trust: Creating Communities of Learners in an Era of Testing and Standardization.* (Boston: Beacon Press, 2002).

Norris, Cynthia. "Cultivating Creative Cultures," in *The Principal as Leader,* ed. Larry W. Hughes (2nd ed.) (New York: Macmillan, 1999).

Norris, Cynthia, Bruce Barnett, Peggy Basam, and Diane Yerkes. *Developing Educational Leaders, a Working Model: The Learning Community in Action* (New York: Teacher's College Press, 2002).

Protheroe, N. "Professional Learning Communities." *Principal 83,* no. 5 (2004): 39–42.

Schaps, E. "Creating a School Community." *Educational Leadership 60* (2003): 31–33.

Schomburg, G. "The Principal as a Systems Thinker." *Principal* (March/April 2008): 20–26.

Senge, Peter. *The Fifth Discipline* (New York: Doubleday, 1990).

Senge, Peter, et al. *Schools That Learn:* A *Fifth Discipline Field Book* (New York: Doubleday, 2000).

Sergiovanni, T. J. "Collaborative Cultures and Communities of Practice." *Principal Leadership 5* (2004): 48–52.

Zepeda, S. J. "Leadership to Build Learning Communities." *The Educational Forum 68,* no. 2 (2004): 144–151.

3

Decision Processing and Decision Making at the School Site

It's vain to do with more what can be done with less.

—OCCAM'S RAZOR, WILLIAM OF OCCAM[1]

Before we begin our discussion of the prime activity of the principalship—facilitating decision making—we need to establish the parameters. No treatment of the subject can be complete without discussing the environment within which decisions occur. To do that, we need to consider those who are affected by the decisions, that is, the stakeholders.

Stakeholders

There is much in the literature these days about involving stakeholders in decision making. What and who are the stakeholders? The word *stakeholder* can be defined as a person or a group with a direct interest, involvement, or investment in something. In a school, for example, that would be the staff members—professional and nonprofessional—the students, parents or caregivers, associated organizations such as parent–teacher groups and booster clubs, local businesses, and, in fact, all of the taxpayers. Isn't that everybody? Yes it is, and that is why the simple blandishment that school leaders must "involve the stakeholders in decision-making practices" sometimes rings falsely. How does one "involve everyone" in decision making? Silly question, but the blandishment is also silly.

The important issue is *who* specifically to involve? And *when?* And *to what degree?* A decision involving a single student narrows the search for stakeholders to the student, the caregiver, any teacher who is involved, and the principal or principal's delegate. A decision to seek additional tax monies to build a new building involves many more people or representative of these people. Board members, key businesses, parents, staff members, community leaders, and students all may have important roles to play in that activity. In the process, a myriad of decision-making situations occur that require, to some degree, an assessment of who the key stakeholders are and what the nature of their involvement should be.

The main concern is to correctly identify who the appropriate stakeholders are in any given problem and the most useful way to engage these persons. Will the best form of engagement be a focus group, a task force, an action committee, an informative newsletter, or some other device? What will be the nature of the involvement? Advice, consent, and information exchange are all involvement activities; none is uniformly appropriate.

In this chapter, all of the foregoing possibilities will be examined. Also, two classic models of decision processing will be presented as will conceptualizations to guide decision processing and decision making. The chapter concludes with discussions of how to effectively use problem-solving work groups and dead horse beating to solve persistent problems.

For perspective, we began this chapter on decision making with a citation to an ancient philosopher and scientist William of Occam. Decision making and decision processing can be, by nature, complex procedures. These acts are also the essential acts of leadership, whether that leadership is manifest in active groups of teachers, a council including parents, or just the principal. Occam, however, gives us a perspective. He prescribed that given sufficient information, the simplest solution is most often the best solution. Note the words *given sufficient information*. Getting sufficient information often presents a most difficult problem. It is in the information-gathering process, however, that great opportunities exist for maximum involvement of others in the decision-making process.

Let us begin by illustrating decision processing with a case that demonstrates the several elements of the process and the mistakes that can be made.

Decision Making: A Perspective

We think of decision making as the result of a problem-solving process rather than simply a final, visible act. To achieve good decisions, it is necessary to engage in problem analysis and select the best decision process. Even seemingly simple problems require some thought and anticipation of consequences. This need not take a long time, but delaying action even for a few moments to mull an issue can save a lot of heartburn. Consider the following case.

CASE STUDY

Mickey Felder, a veteran bus driver, came into my office (L.W.H) one morning about 10:00 A.M. I had begun my first superintendency of this 2,300-student district just over two months earlier. It was now the end of September.

"Chief," he said, "we've got a problem on the Bus 5 route I drive." I told him to sit down and asked him what *our* problem was. [Mistake number 1; I was not the one who makes up the bus routes.]

He continued, "As you know [I didn't know], when Bus 5 begins its route, it soon gets to the grade-level crossing at North Thomas Street. Every morning at the time I'm starting out to pick up the children, there is a scheduled freight train that blocks the crossing. I wait and wait. What happens is that this makes me late to Southeast Elementary School, which is where I finish my route. The principal and teachers are complaining because the kids are reaching school after the final bell.

"What I want to do is start my route by going in the other direction—the direction that I would normally be coming in on at the end of my route. Then I could avoid the freight train delay because the tracks would be clear then and the kids would arrive at school on time. Can do?"

My response was, "Makes sense to me Mickey, go ahead. Just tell your riders so they know what is happening." A simple problem was solved and I went on to the other work of the day.

It was *not* a simple problem, and things were not as they seemed. In fact, the immediate result was a lot of unnecessary pain, confusion, and embarrassment. The pain involved me, the transportation supervisor, some parents, and ultimately Mickey Felder. (But it was I who inflicted the pain on Felder.) The embarrassment was mine only. Why? The facts came out:

- There was no regular morning freight train on the North Thomas Street crossing.
- Small as it was, the school system did have a transportation supervisor.
- Mickey changed the direction of the route only in the morning. So, those children who were picked up first were left off last in the afternoon.
- There was an arterial highway on the route. The route had been structured originally to provide pickup on the home side of these children. Now they had to cross the road.
- Mickey Felder was having a feud with three of the parents of the children served by his bus. These children were early boarders and lived on the arterial highway.

These first four facts were easily obtainable, but that's not the important point. The important issue was that the decision was not mine to make! The first step in any rational decision process is to decide to whom the decision "belongs." Was this my problem to begin with? Nope. It belonged to the transportation supervisor who would have sorted it out in a minute.

As it developed, my hasty decision—made without any information search—caused a rift with another stakeholder: the transportation supervisor. We didn't know each other well; we hadn't worked together long enough to have developed a trusting relationship. He was rumored to have wondered aloud what I thought were the kind of decisions he should be making—how to reorganize the curriculum, perhaps. (It took a lot of time and reassurance to repair that relationship.) In addition, there were a lot of angry parents, children were placed in a hazardous position, and much time had to be spent with an insubordinate bus driver. That's a high price to pay for quick action and a stupid decision.

Decision Settings

Problems occur in a variety of forms; they differ in content, in the process by which the problem is addressed, and in the kind of impact made on the organization and the people in the organization. When should one make a straightforward unilateral decision? When should one involve others in the agonizing process of consensus?

The answer is not difficult to see in the extreme. If the situation is a fire in the basement, an order is issued to clear the building; one does not call a committee together to achieve consensus on which fire exits to use. (However, it would not be inappropriate to involve affected groups or individuals in advance in the development of policies and procedures for how to cope with such emergencies.) It is more useful to think about decision settings than about specific decisions.

Problems may fall into two general decision settings: structured settings (routine, recurring issues) and multialternative, unstructured, or innovative settings.

Structured Decision Settings

Many things that happen in the school organization are recurring in nature. The basis for an orderly, goal-oriented school is an array of proven, reliable, productive activities that are instituted, monitored, and terminated by an appropriate set of habituated decisions.

The range of responses to any given issue may be clearly limited by law, policy, and/or custom as well as by time constraints and the maturity of the group affected by the decisions. The principal can expect certain kinds of problems to recur frequently and regularly, given a particular environment or set of circumstances. Routine response mechanisms to these are expected by members of the staff so that they can go about their work with a minimum of disruption. To the maximum degree possible, the decisions and decision processes that respond to recurring activities should be routinized.

Need for Written Policies.   Arranging conditions in the school so that recurring problems are resolved with a minimum of disruption and false starts can be readily achieved. A school building policy and rules and regulations manual developed with the assistance of staff and students is essential.

Such a manual should contain statements of basic responsibilities of teachers, counselors, administrators, and classified personnel in each of five functional aspects of the school: pupil personnel services, staffing and staff relations, building management and financial operations, public relations, and curriculum and instructional development. The roles and responsibilities of various personnel with respect to matters pertaining to the functional aspects are carefully delineated, lines of communication are spelled out, and common procedural questions are answered. Importantly, too, the document should spell out student responsibilities—the rules and regulations by which every student is expected to live.

In such a manual, the delegation of specific management tasks to designated people will ensure a necessary degree of stability. This document clarifies the "who is to do what" question and it permits the principal to manage by exception rather than by direct participation in all decisions.

Importance of Routine Decision Processes.   In a well-managed school, routine day-to-day activities are carried on without the constant involvement of the principal. The primary responsibility of the principal is not the routine operation of the building but rather the creation of organizational conditions whereby school operations may be readily modified to meet changing demands and opportunities.

Thus, structured or routine decision making, while encompassing problem situations running from the highly important to the mundane, is best formalized. The result will be relatively little stress on individuals or the organization as decisions are promulgated and implemented. Such is often not the case in settings wherein a variety of responses are available *(multialternative)* or in settings where no acceptable alternatives are apparent *(unstructured or innovative)*.

Multialternative, Unstructured, and Innovative Settings

Even though many of the decisions that need to be made in and about the school are structured and only a limited number of options are available, frequently there are issues for which a wide array of alternative actions is available, and the principal may be confronted with a seemingly endless

ISLLC 3

number of possibilities. Many of these alternatives may appear nearly equal in value, *or* there may be an inadequate information base from which to determine the efficacy of the alternatives.

Unanticipated problems, unique situations, and fast-changing conditions are characteristics of organizational life. Decisions in such situations often require "leaps into the unknown"—creative problem resolution that by its very nature produces both individual and organizational stress. In these decision settings, one needs to move from rational decision making to creative decision making.

It is not a once-and-for-all change, however. Generating creative responses to unstructured problems requires some structuring and a return to rational processes when the alternatives are ultimately weighed and an action plan is developed. The generation of alternatives and creative responses requires the combination of some rational processes, frequent abrupt changes to creative processes, and then a return to the rational process. Problem definition, for example, is a rational process, and goal setting or mission statements require rational processes. On the other hand, the development of alternative solutions is an intensely creative process.

Groups or individuals do not have to be *either* creative or rational. Problem-solving groups, or individuals, make use of both orientations and must do so to be effective. Creative processes in the work organization need a structure or framework to be useful. Totally nongoal-oriented think tanks are a luxury most organizations cannot afford on an ongoing basis. Organizational creativity is goal oriented.

Techniques for Unstructured, Innovative Decision Making.   Several techniques can be used to address problems of an unstructured nature. Five of these—brainstorming, structured absent group, nominal group, focus groups, and consensus decision making—are generally descriptive of the possibilities.

Brainstorming.   Brainstorming has as its only purpose the generation of ideas, no matter how impractical the ideas may seem at first consideration. Whereas the usual kinds of meetings or conferences tend to be noncreative, a brainstorming group devotes itself *solely to creative thinking.* To function properly, the group remains, during the period of the brainstorm, completely divorced from the mundane world. The role of the group leader is one of facilitator rather than gatekeeper.

ISLLC 3

The best recording method is to write ideas on a flip chart. Using flip charts keeps the ideas visible and thus stimulates other ideas. Moreover, when the session ends, the paper can be duplicated and circulated to group members.

At some point following the brainstorming session, the group reconvenes for the purpose of judging and modifying the ideas. This session is one of analysis. The purpose is to select those ideas that singly or in combination with other ideas seem to provide a creative solution to the problem.

From the analysis session, the group decides on the four or five solutions that offer a basis for the systematic resolution of the problem. At this point, the group may engage in any number of systematic planning approaches and work the solutions into an implementation phase.

A criticism of the brainstorming technique is that the results may be affected by peer pressure (or hierarchical pressure if it is a vertically organized group). Also, unless the leader is especially well skilled, a few outspoken members may dominate, thereby reducing the number of contributions from other members. To avoid this, many leaders turn to either the structured absent group or to the nominal group technique.

Structured Absent Group.   This technique does not require a group to convene. Individuals are asked to participate in a simulation activity in which each is presented a case study describing an organizational issue. Included are a modest amount of descriptive data. The organization may be fictitious, but the issue is real. Individuals are asked to respond to three items:

1. Given the issue, what do you think is the problem? What might be some subproblems?
2. What might be two or three actions of a short-term nature that could be expected to reduce the intensity of the problem?
3. Suggest at least two actions or processes that might ultimately resolve the problem.

The responding individuals submit their suggestions to the person charged with ultimately working on the problem. A variation on this is to have the individuals actually meet as a problem-solving group to share their solutions and arrive at an action plan. This latter variation is similar to the nominal group technique described next.

Nominal Group.   As in brainstorming, a small group convenes to focus on an organizational problem. However, the use of this technique requires that although members of the group work on an identified problem in the presence of each other, they do so without immediate interaction.

Once the problem is explained by the convenor, group members are given a few minutes, individually, to write as many alternative solutions to the problem as possible. After the time has elapsed, a presentation of alternatives occurs. Participants give one alternative solution at a time, which is posted on flip chart paper. This continues in round-robin fashion until all alternatives are posted. No discussion of alternatives takes place until all of the alternatives have been recorded.

The value of the process is that divergence is encouraged because alternatives are developed privately. A disadvantage, of course, is that unlike brainstorming, there is no way for one individual's idea to spark another individual. Nevertheless, a "creative tension" occurs because participants are aware that others are working on the same problem and they also know that everyone's product will be displayed.

Focus Groups.   Focus groups have been used under a variety of names in organizations for a long time. Focus groups are collections of persons who are called together to consider a single issue. In the school organization, it could be a problem such as where to locate a particular school, and community members might be involved. Or, it could be a curriculum reorganization issue or an issue of how best to organize to have students perform better on state-mandated examinations.

Important data about the issue are shared with the group (for example, in the instance of the school location problem, data might include traffic patterns, growth rates, district policies, etc.). A discussion leader and a recorder are provided and the group examines the issue. The recorder notes important points that are raised, the nature of agreement and disagreement, and the intensity of emotion about aspects of the issue. These data are collected and later reported to a school leader or a group of leaders who consider the points raised and use the elements of discussion to formulate a path of action.

ISLLC 3   *Consensus Decision Making.*   One of the most difficult and perhaps the lengthiest options open to school leaders is to engage appropriate staff in consensus decision making. The process is difficult because all judgments about final actions must be withheld until the sessions are complete; it can be lengthy because included staff members are asked to consider the problem and offer suggestions about the best solution. No decision is made until all agree that they can support an agreed-upon course of action.

In a session, the problem is presented to the affected or representative group. Any relevant information is gathered and presented. A discussion about the issue ensues and is conducted by the leader or the one who has convened the group. Alternative possibilities are suggested by any group member and a discussion about alternatives ensues. At this point, a rational decision model is followed. Ultimately—sooner or later—the leader polls the group. Polling is permitted but simple vote counting and majority rule is not. The group is striving for the best decision, not majority rule, and the best decision is the workable answer that all will support regardless of whether it is the answer any one individual wants.

The leader needs to encourage diverse opinions; the group is not seeking unanimity but rather collaboration and ultimate support for the decision. Fullan[2] points out the differences between "like-minded consensus" and collaboration. From Fullan's perspective, effective collaborative environments encourage more diversity in opinions. The good leader, therefore, does not accept too readily what appears to be unanimity when engaging in a consensus decision process.

Consensus decision making takes time and often requires more than one group meeting. It is not a process one chooses for routine decision making or for mundane issues. But if the issue is an important one, and if general support for implementation in the organization is required, it is the best way to go.

Decision Processing: Classic Models

An array of problem-solving processes is at the disposal of the school administrator: from a unilateral "this is what must be done" telling process to engaging work groups in consensus decision making. The effective principal uses a range of techniques and processes to arrive at the maximum feasible decision.

Probably no models give specific insights into the complexities and dynamics of decision making more than those developed by Maier, Vroom and Yetton, and Vroom and Jago. Some of you might feel that although the Vroom–Jago model is interesting, it would be impractical and certainly contrary to Occam's razor to sit down and move through the various options when engaging in an emergency confronting the school organization. To those of you, we simply ask: What are the options? It does not take long to collect a little information and consider alternatives. And, that is what the models suggest. Vroom–Jago, as is the Maier model, is a thought process, not a puzzle. It will tell the leader what the best decision *process* ought to be but not what the decision should be.

An enterprising principal or assistant principal will recognize immediately that no one is going to ponderously go through the Vroom–Jago decision tree for every decision that needs to be made. After all, time is a valued commodity. A single walk down the hall to get to the gymnasium because there is a fight will result in several encounters with staff members, students, and maybe even parents, each of whom has a question about something and perhaps wants some sort of decision. No one does not enter the decision tree for these sorts of things even though one does consider the elements quickly. If it is a complex question and involves other people, however, the principal must delay a decision until more information is available.

A judgment is made on these occasions. And, here is where one might intuitively go not to Vroom–Jago but to the Maier model. Into which quadrant does the problem fit? Is it a technical problem? Is it a problem of no technical significance but one the group cares about? Answers to these questions tell a person when the issue is complex enough to consider the decision tree. They tell a person when the relatively small time required for thinking out the problem would result in a decision process that is worth the effort.

Principals and assistant principals are not going to try to stop an emergency while they cogitate about an intellectual model of decision processing. The models are to help leaders understand the complexities of major decision making and the impact and possible success of any particular decision process. The models are to be used to help, not to impede, movement toward a goal.

Both the Vroom–Jago and Maier models are consistent with the necessary approach for greater involvement of staff and others in decision making.

The Maier Model

Maier and Verser[3] have discussed the need for decision makers to consider two discrete elements: the requirements that a decision be one that is of high quality and that the decision be one that carries with it the likelihood that subordinates will accept it.

Decision quality refers to decisions in the problem-solving process that have to do with achieving organizational goals and maintaining control, aside from any consideration of subordinate motivation. Is the decision technically sound? Is it based on the best information available?

Decision acceptance refers to the degree of commitment required of stakeholders to implement the decision. Acceptance is crucial when the administrator depends on subordinates to implement a decision. Although it is not possible to know unerringly when to involve others in a decision-making process, who those others should be, or what the nature of their involvement should be, there is always a need to consider the feelings, attitudes, and skills of those who will be charged with implementing the decision. Any decision that will require behavioral change will probably require stakeholder commitment. The nature of involvement will depend in great part on the complexity of the problem to be solved, the degree to which those affected by the decision will be required to behave differently for the decision to be properly implemented, and the degree to which stakeholders will accept a unilateral decision.

Quadrant Interaction.   Using the two factors of technical expertise needed (quality of decision required) and need for group acceptance (hearty compliance and/or behavior change required) as prime determinants, a quadrant model can be developed to help answer the involvement question.

The quadrant in which both the quality of the decision and the need for stakeholder acceptance are high presents the greatest challenge to the leader. Into this quadrant fall those decisions that require much in the way of technical expertise and knowledge in order for a good decision to be reached. In addition, no matter how technically superior the solution may be, in order for that solution to be put into effect much work-group acceptance will be necessary. That is, the decision must fall within the stakeholders' "zone of hearty compliance." Without consideration of the needs and opinions of the group, compliance may not occur; this may be so for several reasons: because an apparent solution is contrary to present practice or present attitudes; because it requires work-group members to perform in ways that are initially more difficult or for which they have not been trained; because of the simple lack of agreement about the efficacy of the decision; or for any number of other reasons, including threat, fear, distrust of administrators, or anger. If any of the previous conditions can be assumed, then something beyond a simple, unilateral decision process probably will be required. What kinds of issues might fall within this quadrant? Any curricular change certainly would, as would budget development. Changes in school policies affecting large numbers of students and school constitutional questions would also seem to fit here. Operating in this quadrant will require good human relations skills as well as technical competence in the subject under review.

The quadrant requiring a high level of acceptance depicts situations where group feelings may be intense, but great technical expertise is not required because the subject is not a complex one. Any number of resolution schemes are available; the appropriate one must be fair and sensitive to the needs and desires of the work group. Assignment of unpaid extracurricular duties, balanced work schedules for routine duties, and school calendar development, among myriad other decision situations, might fall into this category. Among appropriate ways to handle problems in this quadrant would be the formation of advisory committees, delegation of decision making to standing or ad hoc bodies, or informal consultation with leaders of the groups affected.

The high-quality–low-acceptance quadrant contains the kinds of decisions that affect the quality of the organization in a technical sense but do not have a great impact on the human side of the enterprise. Equipment selection, design of conflict-free schedules, and the design of a management information system, among other examples, might fall into this quadrant.

In the remaining quadrant (low-acceptance–low-quality), neither great technical competence nor sensitive human relations is a critical consideration. What is needed is a concrete act to resolve a simple problem. Time is the only critical element. A decision has to be made in a timely fashion so that people in the organization can go about their work in an orderly, efficient, and knowledgeable manner.

The Maier model is a good analytical tool. It emphasizes that selection of the best decision process will result from an analysis of the nature of the problem and the nature of the work group.

Vroom and Yetton[4] and Vroom and Jago[5] have extended these concepts and provided a basis for choosing the decision process most likely to result in the maximum feasible decision. Effective leadership, as manifested in good decision making, depends on understanding the conditions of a problem situation, assessing correctly how much participation or "power sharing" is required to be successful, and establishing the form that the participation should take.[6]

The Vroom–Jago Decision Process Model

In an early research effort, Vroom and Yetton developed a decision tree to assist the executive in arriving at the best decision process. It was on this work that Vroom and Jago based their later research. Vroom and Yetton established five possible actions by the executive when it came to attempting to reach a decision, which were labeled AI, AII, CI, CII, and GII.

With an AI decision, the executive simply reviews the information that is available and makes a decision. AII decisions involve the use of another person or persons in the collection of information, either with or without knowing why the information is being collected. AI and AII are strictly unilateral decision processes.

In the CI decision process, the executive shares the nature of the problem with an individual subordinate, or with some subordinates *separate* from each other, seeks advice, and then makes the decision, which may or may not follow the advice. CII is where the executive convenes a group of subordinates and collectively these people examine the problem. Again, however, the executive makes the final decision, which may or may not follow the advice provided. The advantage here, if all present have important information, is that ideas and information are shared and synergy is possible.

In a GII decision process, all of the elements for consensus decision making are present. The executive shares the problem with the related group and the group, as a whole, generates and evaluates ideas and possible solutions. The executive serves as convenor and may even serve as chair of the convened group but makes no attempt, beyond that of any other group member, to influence the direction of final decision. The executive is willing to implement any solution that has the support of the group.

Both AI and GII may appear to be the riskiest of the procedures, but neither is any more or less risky than the other three processes. What one is looking for is the process that will most likely result in the best route to a maximum feasible decision.

How does a leader choose the procedure most likely to result in a good decision—one that is technically sound and that the work group will work hard to implement, to use Maier and Verser's quality and acceptance dimensions? The choice is determined by several aspects of the situation within which the problem exists. It depends, as well, on leader judgments about the nature of these aspects. One can never avoid the responsibility for making good judgments about the nature of the situation; no model will exclude the leader from this. Five aspects seem to require a judgment:

1. A clear definition of the problem (What is it that is *not* what is desired?)
2. The amount of information that the leader and subordinates have, or, if more information is needed, whether it is known where this information is. This determines the degree to which the problem is "structured." In an "unstructured" problem, there is no information currently available, or it is not known where to get the necessary information, or there is an array of possible responses. A highly structured problem is one for which there is policy or legal guidance.
3. Whether it is likely that subordinates will accept a unilateral decision from the leader
4. Whether it is likely that subordinates will cooperate with the leader or with each other to try to collectively reach a good decision
5. The amount and intensity of disagreement the leader perceives among subordinates about preferred alternatives

Vroom and Jago thus continued the Vroom and Yetton research and added refinements and enhancements. The conceptual framework and the basic assumptions remain unchanged, however.

Time-Driven Considerations.   The available time to resolve an issue may impinge greatly on the degree to which members of a work group can be involved in problem solving and the form that this involvement takes. CII and GII decision procedures require an investment of time considerably greater than the other procedures. Is the problem important enough—that is, is group commitment necessary and is a high-quality decision required—to justify the expenditure of the labor hours that will be required?

Even if the quality of the decision is not crucial (i.e., there are a number of alternatives, any one of which would adequately resolve the issue), but acceptance is critical and not likely to result from a unilateral decision, then an investment of time will be necessary. Judicious use of time, however, is an important consideration, however. CII and GII decision processes do use up both the time and the energy of subordinates and peers. A 4-hour group meeting between the principal and an advisory group of eight others consumes 36 labor-hours of work time. What other important activities had to be delayed or not done because of the meeting?

Development-Driven Considerations.   Much may be gained from broad participation in decision making by a school staff and school community. Such involvement encourages idea sharing, trust, high performance standards, and work-group effectiveness. It also capitalizes on the abilities of the informal leaders on the staff.

However, skills in decision making need to be nurtured, and work groups need to be helped to improve these skills. Consider a school or a department with many new personnel or a school functioning under a mandate for site-based management and similarly a mandated teacher and/or community advisory council. If group members have heretofore been relatively uninvolved and unfamiliar with decision making in an organizational context, there is work to be done by the principal. The principal might employ a CII or a GII process on less intense problems with a new group as a way to provide a basis for group members to learn to work together. Later in this chapter we discuss how to set an appropriate framework for group decision making.

The Decision Tree.   Help in selecting the most likely process to lead to the maximum feasible decision is available in the form of a decision tree. Eight questions, to be answered yes or no, form the branches of the tree. These questions are addressed *only* after the problem to be solved has been satisfactorily defined.

1. How important is the technical quality of this decision?
2. How important is subordinate commitment to the decision?
3. Does the leader have sufficient information to make a high-quality decision?
4. Is the problem well structured?[7]
5. If the leader were to make the decision alone, is it reasonably certain that subordinates would be committed to the decision?
6. Do subordinates share the organizational goals to be attained in solving this problem?
7. Is conflict among subordinates over preferred solutions likely?
8. Do subordinates have sufficient information to make a high-quality decision?

Implications of Decision-Processing Models

Use of tools such as the Maier model or the Vroom–Jago decision tree for problem analysis does not remove the need for sensitive judgment. Indeed, the effective use of these models requires the highest order of sensitivity. The leader is seeking the maximum feasible decision—the decision that offers promise of long-term problem resolution or problem mitigation *and* the one that those most affected will work to carry out. The processes described here are designed to take the leader to this sort of decision.

What one has, with the rational decision processes just presented, is a basis for reducing the risks and analyzing the strengths and weaknesses of relative positions. The decision tree, the Maier model, and any of a number of other rational processes are tools for the manager to use to arrive at a maximum feasible decision. The models are not a substitute for thinking; rather, their purpose is to stimulate thinking to provide the basis for sound judgments.

Problem Solving

The organization, or the work group, or the principal is faced with either an unwelcomed event or by a need to choose a course of action to achieve certain predetermined goals. There is, in fact, a problem to be solved.

Viewing decision making as problem solving has the advantage of delaying an act or judgment until there is a reasonable basis for acting in a certain way. Moreover, not all problems are worthy of responses. Some issues, on just a little reflection, will be "solved" only at the price of creating a larger problem of a different nature. Other issues are just not all that important and may be simply ignored. Still other issues are someone else's responsibility and should be referred to that person or group. The first decision, then, that needs to be made is defining the nature and severity of the problem. The second decision is to determine to whom the problem belongs.

Figure 3.1 depicts a rational problem-solving/decision-making model. Whether the problem is complex, such as how to respond to an issue raised by a pressure group, or simple, such as what to do with a sick student, the process is the same. How to deal with a sick student may not take much time, but assuming the student really is ill and that it is the principal or assistant principal's problem, clearly the rest of the problem fits into Figure 3.1.

In an analysis of the problem, the legal ramifications and school district policy are considered. This provides a framework for decision making. Alternative solutions might include sending the student back to the classroom but with instructions to the teacher that the student should not participate in class activities, or sending the student to a health room until school is over for the day, or sending the student home or to a hospital. Each of the alternatives must be evaluated in light of the severity of the problem, the feasibility of the solution, the age of the student, the time of the day, and the anticipated consequences of the particular action. For example, is there a responsible person in the home who can take care of the sick student?

How long should such a process take? In the instance of the sick student, probably no more than five minutes or less for the administrator who knows the policies and the student. In the instance of an upset pressure group of citizens, the process will require more time but the steps are the same to reach a sound judgment in a timely manner.

Once a judgment is made and is implemented, the results must be evaluated. Did it work? Why or why not? Was the school, or the student, or the group better off or worse off?

The Work Group as a Problem-Solving Unit

The school executive is looking for the best solutions to problems—routine and nonroutine. Such solutions will not occur in an organization of interacting humans unless processes are employed that make appropriate use of the collective intelligence of these humans. Thus, effective principals deliberately and frequently engage their staff in problem-solving activities.

ISLLC 3

ISLLC 3

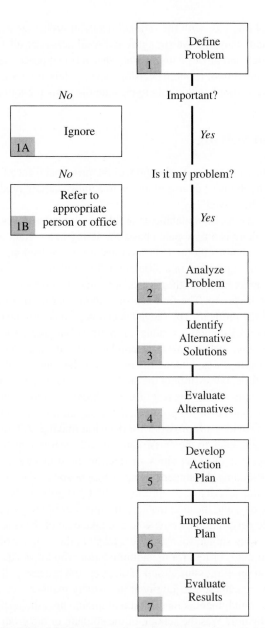

FIGURE 3.1   Rational Decision Making: Steps in Systematic Problem Solving

Productive relationships develop as a result of engaging in important activities together. It is then possible for the strengths and weaknesses of members to be known, revealing who can be counted on for what kinds of expertise. Knowing where certain kinds of expertise exist permits the principal to create effective teams to focus on troubling schoolwide issues, existent or anticipated. Thus, effort spent to help a work group develop problem-solving skills will pay rich dividends.

Setting Realistic Decision-Making Limits

Regardless of the maturity of the staff, few problem-solving groups can be permitted to operate completely unfettered. Real-world constraints are always factors. Any group charged with helping to resolve an issue needs to know the rules of the game if the expectation is a decision that can be implemented. The following considerations provide a solid basis for maximum effective use of problem-solving groups:

1. Decide if the task force is to be advisory in nature. That is, is it a CII or is it a GII? Are decisions to be suggestions only, or is the group to be charged with coming up with final decisions?
2. Cooperatively set a realistic time line. This would include further data collection periods, preparation of final reports, generation of new program alternatives, and the anticipated implementation date, among other milestones.
3. Establish a tentative budget for the project phases. Possible line items include released time costs, materials costs, transportation, and meals.
4. Review any districtwide policies or state laws that might impinge on the nature of any resolution scheme. For example, is there a systemwide or statewide adopted basal reading series that must be lived with no matter what? Does the state provide for experimental programs?
5. Establish the "essential conditions" that any decision must fit in order to be acceptable. Budget is a frequent essential condition; the solution *must not* exceed a specified amount.
6. Set up regular interaction sessions about progress and findings.

Working at the Operational Level

Most problems are better addressed and solved at the operational level without interference from a superordinate structure. In such instances, the superordinate structure serves as a support unit, providing resources as might be needed and performing in an oversight role only.

The argument in favor of such a practice is that autonomy is placed appropriately, permitting maximum latitude in decision making at the lowest possible operating level. The problem-solving work group (PSWG) is an action group. It resolves problems rather than simply identifying them.

A PSWG is a small group of workers with similar responsibilities who voluntarily meet for an hour or more each week to discuss school-related problems, investigate causes, recommend solutions, and take corrective action. It is organized horizontally rather than vertically. No structural changes are required in the organization; it fits into any existing structure. Several features distinguish the PSWG:

- The PSWG consists primarily of a regular work group (e.g., department, grade-level, or cross-level group of teachers, counselors, etc.; such a group is not limited to the professional staff).
- Membership is voluntary.
- The group meets regularly once a week.

- The group solves problems rather than identifying problems for the principal or others to solve.
- The PSWG is imbued with appropriate authority and a modest budget.

The PSWG requires administrative support, which may take the form of providing a meeting place and time off from instructional duties to meet. The principal may or may not be a member of the PSWG, but someone who is a part of the school's administrative team is a member. The role of the participating administrator is that of convenor and facilitator. Having an administrator in the group ensures upward communication.

Problem Solving and Dead Horse Beating

The essence of problem solving is determining *what* is the problem? Problem definition is necessary for problem solution. Consider this example of the British drill team:

> A British drill team of five entered the stage. Four of the uniformed group began to march in cadence. They did a close order drill. They presented arms. A 20-minute show ensued. The fifth uniformed person simply stood at attention. This was puzzling to spectators. What does number 5 do? Why does he just stand there at attention? No one knew until an old soldier informed him. "You see," he said, "in the mid-nineteenth century this was a mounted group. They would ride in on five horses and dismount. Number 5 would hold the reins of the horses and the others would do the drill. They have never got rid of number 5 even though his purpose is no longer needed."

Many organizations are like this. They have some number 5s—person who no longer serve in a purpose that is functional or necessary, or offices that really do not serve to do anything vital, or programs that are not producing the desirable results.

Healthy organizations continually subject themselves to examination to discover if there are number 5s functioning. Are all the paraprofessionals properly assigned to areas of greatest need? When was this last examined? How are the male students doing compared to female students? Would grouping by gender be a justifiable experiment and practice? How long have the reading instructors used the current series? Is it serving as well as other possible approaches? How do you know?

When things are not going well—students are dropping out, teacher turnover is high, the learning curve is down, attendance is poor—what is it that should be done? What should be done when the school is not adapting to changing conditions or when a school system's practices are not working or are not working well? Many strategies have been tried, and some strategies that do not work have been labeled "beating a dead horse." How many of such strategies have you observed? Examine Figure 3.2 for a reporting of poor but common approaches to problem solving. Better ways are available, and they have been expressed in this chapter.

Michael Fullan[8] suggests that reform and change will never occur in schools until the nature of the school context is changed to allow greater decision making and empowerment for staff members and other stakeholders. The models presented in this chapter provide the basis for encouraging that empowerment, which will make for better problem solving and stronger schools.

FIGURE 3.2   Beating a Dead Horse: Programs That are not Working

* Arrange a visit to other sites to see how they ride dead horses. [See how others are failing.]

* Appoint a group to revive the dead horse. [Keep pushing the old idea.]

* Create a training session to improve riding skills on a dead horse. [Train others about implementing the old idea.]

* Change requirements so that the horse no longer meets the standard of dead. [Lower the standards.]

* Increase funding or bonuses to improve the horse's performance. [Offer incentive pay for running an ineffective program.]

* Declare that no horse is too dead to beat. [Keep doing it again and again.]

* Do a study to see if outsourcing will reduce the cost of riding a dead horse. [Let some other group also fail; spreads the blame.]

* Buy a computer program to enhance dead horse performance. [Impose technology.]

* Declare a dead horse is less costly than a live one. [The program is cheaper, so keep it even if it isn't working.]

* Hire a consultant to show how a dead horse can be ridden. [Employ some "experts" in the old idea.]

* Promote the dead horse to a supervisory position. [Get the horse out of the way! Pass on the damage.]

Summary

The essential executive act is decision making. Decision making is problem solving—or it ought to be. But decisions are not made very well in a vacuum. Moreover, few decisions are made in the organization that do not affect the lives of others and require others to behave differently tomorrow than they did today.

Thus, the final act—the decision—must be subject to an intellectual process. The first step is to discover what the problem is. Subsequent steps (the decision-making process) may require creative approaches and the wisdom of others in the work group.

Much research about decision processing has been conducted over the years. One of the most useful applications of this research has been the Vroom–Jago model. In this approach, various conditions existing in a problem situation are subjected to analysis, and the decision maker is led to a decision process that is most likely to result in a maximum feasible decision.

It is important for decisions to be made and problems solved at the appropriate level. In schools, staff at the building levels—operating under the concept of enlightened suzerainty—can be expected to develop good solutions to troubling issues. Successful teams select a process for making decisions at the start of their work, one that is fair to everyone on the team. Planning for effective decision making is essential.[9]

ACTIVITIES

1. Reflect on the Maier model. Identify problems or issues that in your own experience would have fallen into each of the quadrants. What actually occurred in each of these incidents? How might the incident have been handled?
2. Review Case Studies 3, 10, and 29 at the end of this book. Apply the Vroom–Jago decision tree. Use both the development-driven and the time-driven tree. Pay particular attention to your statement of the problem. Discuss your approach with a small group of colleagues. Try to achieve consensus on both the nature of the problem and the maximum feasible decision process.
3. Turn to the ISLLC standards found in Appendix B. Review the functions listed with Standard 1. Describe which decision processes you would use to implement "the vision is developed with and among stakeholders." How would you carry it out?

ENDNOTES

1. *Occam's razor* is a rule in science and philosophy stating that entities should not be multiplied needlessly. In other words, there is little need to overanalyze and generate too many possibilities. This rule is interpreted to mean that the simplest of two or more competing theories is preferable and that an explanation for unknown phenomena should first be attempted in terms of what is already known. This is also called *law of parsimony*. William of Occam (sometimes Ockham), 1285?–1349?, was an English scholastic philosopher who rejected the reality of universal concepts. This got him in trouble with the Roman Catholic Church.

   The importance of this role is that given two or more choices, when data are available, the simplest solution is frequently the best solution. This is a commonsense warning against unnecessarily complicated solutions, especially to practical problems. That does not mean, however, that the simplest answer to a question is always or even often the best answer.
2. Michael Fullan, *Change Forces: The Sequel* (London: Falmer Press, 1999), p. 36.
3. Norman R. F. Maier and Gertrude C. Verser, *Psychology in Industrial Organizations* (5th ed.) (Boston: Houghton Mifflin, 1982), p. 173.
4. Victor H. Vroom and Philip W. Yetton, *Leadership and Decision-Making* (Pittsburgh: University of Pittsburgh Press, 1973).
5. Victor H. Vroom and Arthur G. Jago, *The New Leadership: Managing Participation in Organizations* (Englewood Cliffs, NJ: Prentice-Hall, 1988).
6. Maier's work and the works of Vroom and Yetton, as well as Vroom and Jago, are based on earlier concepts advanced by Simon. Simon's "Zone of Acceptance" model was based on two questions: Is the issue relevant to others in this organization? Do others in this organization have the expertise to deal with the issue? If the answer to both of these questions is "no," then whatever decision is made is likely to fall within the subordinate's zone of acceptance. If the answer is "yes," then, according to Simon, there is a need to engage others in an examination of alternatives or, at least, in the collection of additional information. Herbert A. Simon, *Administrative Behavior* (New York: Macmillan, 1947).
7. A "structured" problem is one in which the decision maker knows three components of the problem: the current state (what "is"), the desired state (the desired outcome or what ought to be), and the mechanisms needed to get from one to the other (the processes). The problem, in effect, is programmable; creative solutions are not needed. The more structured a problem, the less likely great participation of others in the solution is necessary.
8. Michael Fullan, *The New Meaning of Educational Change* (4th ed.) (New York: Teachers College Press, 2007).
9. Harvard Business Essentials, *Creating Teams with an Edge* (Boston: Harvard Business School Press, 2004). This is a useful book for those interested in developing an effective management team or school advisory council.

SELECTED READINGS

Breiter, A., and D. Light. "Data for School Improvement: Factors for Designing Effective Information Systems to Support Decision Making in Schools" [Electronic Version]. *Educational Technology & Society, 9,* no. 3 (2006): 206–217.

Fullan, Michael. *The New Meaning of Educational Change* (4th ed.) (New York: Teachers College Press, 2007).

Greenfield, William G. "Leading the Teacher Work Group," in *Current Issues in School Leadership,* ed. Larry W. Hughes (Mahwah, NJ: Lawrence Erlbaum, 2005), Chapter 14.

Harvard Business Essentials. *Creating Teams with an Edge* (Boston: Harvard Business School Press, 2004).

Holcomb, Edie L. *Students Are Stakeholders, Too* (Thousand Oaks, CA: Corwin Press, 2007).

Leech, D., and C. Fulton. "Faculty Perceptions of Shared Decision Making and the Principal's Leadership Behaviors in Secondary Schools in a Large Urban District." *Education (Chula Vista, Ca) 128,* no. 4 (2008): 630–644.

Lovely, S., and S. Smith. "Selective Abandonment: How and When to Say No." *Principal Leadership (High School Ed.) 5,* no. 3 (2004): 35–38.

Rooney, J. "Sharing the Decisions." *Educational Leadership 62* (2004): 84–85.

Vroom, Victor H., and Arthur G. Jago. *The New Leadership: Managing Participation in Organizations* (Englewood Cliffs, NJ: Prentice-Hall, 1988).

4 School Improvement through Systematic Planning

*If you don't know where you are going, It doesn't
much matter what you do.*

—ALICE IN WONDERLAND[1]

his chapter describes a process of organizing for school improvement through a systematic plan of action. It also describes some of the tools that may be used to aid in systematic planning.

The principal's role in instructional leadership discussed in Chapter 2 pointed out the importance of beliefs and values in establishing a vision for the school. Out of the vision and the underlying values the principal holds about education, he or she should develop expectations for the school.

Expectations may begin from a person's individual values or may start from ideas suggested or mandated by others, but eventually they must grow to the collective expectation of a larger set of stakeholders of the school. Plans for improvement should grow out of these expectations.

Efforts to bring about change or initiate something new for one's school should usually begin with a plan. Good local school planning involves the translation of concepts, ideas, beliefs, and values into a vision of what a good school should be, as well as a clarification of the general mission for the school.

The idea of school improvement suggests a change of some type within the organization. Often, we may think of a document as being the end product of the planning, but the real focus should be on the process. As Hall and Hord noted, "Change is a process not an event."[2] The learning community essential to high-performance organizations discussed in Chapter 2 is an appropriate vehicle through which to develop strategic or school improvement plans.[3] However, keep in mind that involving a wide array of participants who are stakeholders in the school is critical to the success of the process. Furthermore, the process must entail more than the participation in the decision-making process—it must involve the "teacher as learner" in the fashion described by Fullan and colleagues.[4] If school improvement is to be successful in implementation as well as in planning, school leaders must ultimately transform schools into places for teachers to learn continuously about their content areas and ways to promote student achievement.

Most often the plan is for improvement of an existing, ongoing school. Therefore, planning begins with gathering and analyzing information about the existing school program and the community and students it serves. The planning continues with the review or development of the stated school mission and beliefs held about education. The third task is to determine goals and expectations for student learning and how to measure them. Analysis then turns inward to a comparison of current instructional and organizational practices to research-based indicators of high-performing systems. Analysis of data generated from these steps provides the basis for the development of an action plan for school improvement. The final step is the implementation of the plan and the recording of the results.

The Principal's Role

Schools really can make a difference in the achievement levels of students, but a school is usually only as good or bad, as creative or sterile, as the person who serves as the head of that school. Research on effective schools highlights the role of the principal in establishing goals and objectives for the school. What do effective principals do?

> Principals of effective schools are strong instructional leaders who know how to manage time and money effectively . . . they concentrate on priority goals . . . they set as their main goal the acquisition of basic skills . . . effective principals have high expectations for all students and they will enlist the support of others in meeting common goals.[5]

The principal is the one person in a school who can oversee the entire program because of his or her interest in the success of the entire school and all of its parts. Therefore, the principal is in the best position to provide the necessary sense of direction to the various aspects of a school. The most effective principals have a clear sense of purpose and priorities and are able to enlist the support of others toward these ends.

Many of the problems of direction within a school organization are subtle, will be difficult to solve, and require great conceptual and technical knowledge of curriculum, instruction, and learning. The principal must have the necessary understanding to find proper and just solutions to these problems and many others like them.

Above all, it is absolutely necessary for the principal to involve others. The success of any school improvement rests with the active involvement of all stakeholders in the school. From the collective gathering of baseline data, through the hammering out of the collective beliefs and goals, to the review of expectations for student learning, to the ultimate decisions of how to improve the school, a wide variety of people must be involved for their ideas and for their ultimate ownership.

Gathering Baseline Data

Data-driven decision making is a major theme of the previous chapter and is clearly illustrated by the flowchart in Figure 3.1. What kinds of data are available about one's school? How might these data be organized to help make wiser decisions? What data should be gathered to help better profile the school?

The National Study of School Evaluation (NSSE)[6] has proposed a framework for data-driven decision making with four major steps:

1. *Mining the Data.* Collect and organize pertinent data and information from four major categories: (a) student performance data, (b) student and community characteristics, (c) school and staff characteristics, and (d) stakeholder perspectives.
2. *Analyzing the Data.* Analyze and synthesize the data to create knowledge. Analysis should lead to an understanding of the school's strengths, limitations, and emerging issues of importance. Data should be disaggregated by appropriate subgroups so that comparisons can be made. Emphasis should be on both problem finding and problem solving. Where possible, data should be translated into concrete terms (i.e., 92% average daily attendance means almost three weeks of instruction missed per child on average during the course of a year).
3. *Communicating the Data.* Develop a shared understanding of the meaning of the data. Construct narrative summaries with clear, concise major points of analysis. Include graphic overviews with tables and charts. Seek feedback from the users to help refine the process of data collecting and analysis. Organize into learning communities to promote shared learning through ongoing conversations about the meaning and application of data.
4. *Using the Data.* Place an emphasis on improvement planning purposes rather than data for reporting purposes. Improvement efforts should be based on the use of objective data rather than fads, traditions, or anecdotal evidence. Use the analysis of data to guide the selection of goals and objectives for improvement and establish baseline measures to help monitor progress over time. Examine data as a function of organizational learning and a tool for instructional improvement.

A school generates a massive amount of data each year for each child. Data are often not used effectively because of the difficulty in linking related pieces of information together. For example, imagine a database of all the information gathered on one child across his or her school career—all the tests, major assessments, teachers, attendance, discipline records, grades, and so on. Now multiply that by the number of children currently in your school and add those who have matriculated or transferred out during the past three years. This is the data set needed along with the ability to cross-reference many of the components to carry out the analysis suggested. The task of gathering and maintaining current as well as historic records is sometimes referred to as *data warehousing* and the process of retrieving and reporting data-based management systems.[7]

Demographic Data

Basically, principals are looking for descriptive or demographic information about their students, staff, and parent and community involvement with their schools. A list[8] of what data principals might gather is as follows:

Student Data

- Enrollment history (length of time in current school and previous school)
- Attendance, tardiness (percent)

- Living in one-parent or two-parent household
- Ethnicity, gender
- Parental education level
- Free/reduced price lunch (percent and number)
- Academic assistance program enrollments (percent and number) (special education, bilingual, ESL, gifted, etc.)
- Program or course enrollments (percent and number) (regular academic, vocational, advanced placement, etc.)
- Number of retentions
- Office discipline records
- In-school and out-of-school suspensions (with reasons)
- Expulsions (with reasons)
- Dropouts (percent and number)
- Postgraduation activities (college, military, employment)

Community Data

- Description of community residents by age, level of education, race, marital status, income, education, and so on
- Economic and social conditions of the community
- Measures of the extent of involvement of the community in the school
- Residents with school-age children (percent and number)
- Other youth-serving organizations in the community and services available

Staff Data

- Size and deployment of staff
- Summary of staff qualifications (degrees and institution, certifications, years of experience)
- Staff absenteeism (number of days, sequence of days, days of week, reason, etc.)
- Outside interests (hobbies, travel, businesses, etc.)

Student Outcome Data

Each year, assessment or achievement information is gathered from students to determine each child's individual academic progress. Many of these same data can be used in a collective way to assess the performance of the school and its various programs. The data are usually of most value for analysis when they are recorded in such a way as to allow trend analysis across three or more years, as shown in Figure 4.1. These data are particularly useful when they can be disaggregated by logical demographic categories such as those listed in the student and staff data sections just shown. This means that each item of data carries the identifying number of the student who generated it. In this manner, trend information can be calculated across years. Some of the data are easily quantifiable, allowing for statistical analysis, whereas others are more qualitative in nature, allowing only for classification by demographic category. Assessment data[9] commonly gathered by schools include these:

- Standardized norm-referenced achievement tests
- Writing assessments
- Competency tests (criterion referenced—measured against predetermined curriculum standards)

Subject Area	2008	2009	2010	2011	2012
Reading	54	55	56	57	56
Language	53	52	53	54	53
Math	51	53	54	55	54
Science	56	54	53	54	52
Social Studies	53	53	54	53	52

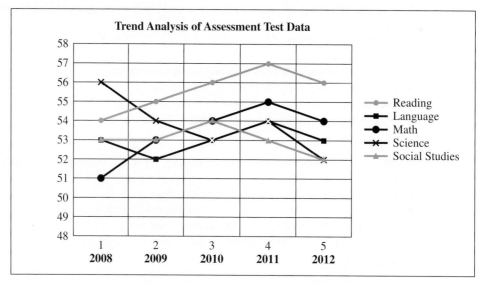

FIGURE 4.1   Ubben Elementary School Trend Analysis of Assessment Test Data

- End-of-course assessments
- Gateway tests (required for passage to higher grade or graduation)
- SAT/ACT
- Early childhood assessments (readiness tests)
- Authentic assessment artifacts (portfolios, performances, projects, products, etc.)

School Processes

Before school leaders can seriously think about how they want to change or what they wish to become, they must consider and describe who they currently are. Baseline data are necessary as the platform from which to help identify current strengths and weaknesses and ultimately as the platform from which to launch new strategies. Here is a list of categories to include in this description of the school. Remember, the point is to describe current actions—on a day-to-day basis—with an eye on evaluation of each process to suggest possible changes.

- *Curriculum and its articulation across grades and subjects.* Have we done curriculum mapping? Are we aligned with state standards?
- *Instruction and current instructional strategies employed.* How are we identifying and dealing with students' individual differences? How does this inform our instruction?

- *All the ways students are grouped for instruction and with what student/teacher ratios.* Are students heterogeneously grouped? Homogeneously grouped? Both? Do class or group sizes vary significantly and if so why?
- *Learning and teaching spaces and how we use them.* Do we organize spaces to facilitate learning communities?
- *How we schedule time and its allocation across the curriculum.* Is time strictly controlled from the office, or do teachers or learning communities have flexibility in the use of time?
- *How we identify and track student learning.* What are our measures of student progress? How frequently do we measure? How do we track individual student progress across multiple years?
- *What we do when a student is not learning at an expected rate.* How do we identify problems and how quickly does the system respond? Do we have a response to intervention (RTI) system in place?
- *How we handle individual differences in learning styles and abilities of students.* Does our practice suggest we really believe in individual differences and/or multiple intelligences?
- *Our philosophy and practice of classroom management (discipline).* Do we have good classroom management procedures in place and are they working?
- *Personal relationships among teachers, and among teachers and students.* Does our school have a good organizational climate that is conducive to learning?

This list is by no means an all-inclusive list. Many other categories and questions can be included.

Perceptual Data

Another very important data source to help profile a school can be found in the opinions and attitudes of the school's stakeholders. Recall that stakeholders are individuals who have some reason to believe they are part of the school community. For example, stakeholders could be students, parents, community members and local business employees, school faculty and all other staff members, administrators in the building as well as those in a district office, and others. Valuable information can be gathered from stakeholders through informal contacts, but carefully prepared surveys sent to representative samples of the stakeholder groups often allow for easier data analysis and reporting.

Many tools are available to measure the perceptions of stakeholders on school dimensions such as culture,[10] climate,[11] organizational health,[12] teacher efficacy,[13] teacher empowerment,[14] and school leadership.[15] All of them relate at least indirectly to student performance and all can provide insight to inform a school improvement plan. The faculty members of the school are a significant stakeholder group because of their in-depth knowledge and history of the school as well as their great influence on the school's future direction.

Organizational Climate and Health Data. There are a number of good instruments that draw on teachers' perceptions of their school to assist in an evaluation of the climate or health of the organization. School climate is a system of shared values, norms, and tacit assumptions that hold a school together and give it a distinctive identity.

The Organizational Climate Description Questionnaire (OCDQ)[16] is available in revised form with versions for elementary, middle, and secondary schools. It measures these dimensions:

supportive principal behavior, directive principal behavior, restrictive principal behavior, Intimate Teacher behavior, and disengaged teacher behavior. The 42-item instrument produces a score for the school based on an open to closed continuum and offers norms that allow comparisons with other schools.

The Organizational Health Inventory (OHI)[17] goes a step beyond simply measuring climate to a broader vision of a healthy organization. A healthy school is one in which the institutional, administrative, and teacher levels are in harmony, and the school meets functional needs as it successfully copes with disruptive external forces and directs its energies toward its mission. The five dimensions, or subtests, of the OHI are institutional integrity, collegial leadership, resource influence, teacher affiliation, and academic emphasis. The OHI is available in an elementary, middle, and secondary form.

Survey Materials   Survey forms for stakeholders are available from various educational organizations; one example is the NSSE Opinion Inventories.[18] The NSSE inventories include separate survey forms for each stakeholder group and include questions about quality, strengths, and limitations of the school as well as quality changes over time. The results for each school are compared with a national sample.

In many cases, it is better for the principal to develop his or her own survey materials when specific program areas or problems are to be targeted. A needs assessment instrument can be created by using belief statements as a base. A series of items that can be rated on a five-point Likert-type rating scale, ranging from strongly disagree to strongly agree, are developed for each belief statement. An illustration of a needs assessment statement follows:

SA	**A**	**N**	**DA**	**SD**	
1	2	3	4	5	Programs and varied instructional techniques are provided to respond to each student's individual needs and differences.

Statements can be grouped into logical categories, weighted, and scored. For example, if belief statements are organized around concepts from the effective schools research—including time, climate, basic commitment, staff, curriculum, leadership, and evaluation—several assessment items could be written for each of the categories. Responses can be divided by the number of items in the category in order to be viewed equally. This will allow comparison between categories for later priority determination. Figure 4.2 gives a complete illustration of a needs assessment instrument, including a weighted scoring sheet that is organized around effective schools concepts.

Survey Administration

Whenever a survey is to be administered, these questions always arise: Whom should we survey? How should we do it? It is not always necessary to survey everyone, it is important to follow the general rules of survey research to ensure that the results are truly representative of the population. Surveys distributed and collected on site with a captive audience produce the highest rate of return. Surveys handed out to whichever adult happens to walk in the building often are not truly representative of the community. Surveys sent home with students often don't get returned. Think through and develop a plan for survey administration that fits your stakeholder group to ensure maximum return.

FIGURE 4.2   Needs Assessment

School Excellence Inventory

Directions: Rate the following Items on a scale of 1 to 5 to reflect your opinion of your school.
(1 = Low . . . 5 = High)

	(Low)			*(High)*
1. Students have favorable attitudes toward school and learning.	1	2	3	4	5
2. Students' learning is frequently evaluated using curriculum-referenced materials.	1	2	3	4	5
3. The staff has high expectations for the students and adults with whom they work.	1	2	3	4	5
4. Students' time-on-task behavior is maintained at a high level because:					
a. A climate of order and discipline has been established.	1	2	3	4	5
b. Limited time is used in maintaining order.	1	2	3	4	5
c. Classroom management tasks have been "routinized" to maximize available instructional time.	1	2	3	4	5
d. The school staff has made a commitment to maximize learning time by reducing impediments to learning and interruptions of the school day.	1	2	3	4	5
5. Each student and parents receive regular feedback regarding the student's progress.	1	2	3	4	5
6. Student attendance rates are high.	1	2	3	4	5
7. There is a clear understanding of what the school believes in and stands for, which includes:					
a. An academic focus.	1	2	3	4	5
b. A belief that all students have the ability to learn.	1	2	3	4	5
c. An expectation that each student will learn.	1	2	3	4	5
d. High expectations for each student.	1	2	3	4	5
8. Teachers regularly utilize techniques to assure that all students are learning.	1	2	3	4	5
9. Staff members are evaluated regularly.	1	2	3	4	5
10. Programs and varied instructional techniques are provided in order to respond to each child's individual needs and differences.	1	2	3	4	5
11. Students feel valued and successful.	1	2	3	4	5
12. Individual help is provided to students when needed.	1	2	3	4	5
13. School staff members exhibit a high degree of concern and commitment for the achievement and well-being of each student.	1	2	3	4	5
14. The principal is effective because:					
a. He or she understands the process of instruction and accepts the responsibility for being an instructional leader.	1	2	3	4	5
b. He or she is an able manager.	1	2	3	4	5
c. He or she has high attainable expectations for the students and adults with whom he or she works.	1	2	3	4	5
d. He or she has goal clarity (a clear sense of purpose and priorities) and is able to enlist the support of others in understanding, accepting, and accomplishing those ends.	1	2	3	4	5

(continued)

FIGURE 4.2   Needs Assessment (*continued*)

	(low)				(High)
e. He or she recognizes the importance of (and actively involves) the people who work in and who are served by the school.	1	2	3	4	5
f. He or she assists the school staff in implementing sound instructional practices.	1	2	3	4	5
15. Students receive prompt feedback on their work.	1	2	3	4	5
16. A high level of staff and student morale exists.	1	2	3	4	5
17. Members of the school staff are cooperative and supportive of each other.	1	2	3	4	5
18. The curriculum:					
a. Emphasizes mastery of basic skills.	1	2	3	4	5
b. Is well defined.	1	2	3	4	5
c. Is appropriately sequenced and articulated from grade to grade and from subject to subject.	1	2	3	4	5
d. Includes clearly defined learner goals.	1	2	3	4	5
e. Is regularly evaluated.	1	2	3	4	5
19. Techniques are used to pinpoint individual student's strengths and weaknesses.	1	2	3	4	5
20. The staff is competent and continues to grow and learn.	1	2	3	4	5
21. The school is open to and encourages participation and involvement by parents and other citizens.	1	2	3	4	5
22. Parents, students, and staff place a high priority on learning.	1	2	3	4	5
23. Students are instructed at the appropriate level of difficulty.	1	2	3	4	5

Summary Sheet
School Excellence Inventory

Time	Climate	Basic Commitment	Staff	Curriculum	Leadership	Evaluation
#4a = ___	#1 = ___	#7a = ___	#3 = ___	#10 = ___	#14a = ___	#2 = ___
#4b = ___	#6 = ___	#7b = ___	#9 = ___	#18a = ___	#14b = ___	#5 = ___
#4c = ___	#11 = ___	#7c = ___	#13 = ___	#18b = ___	#14c = ___	#8 = ___
#4d = ___	#16 = ___	#7d = ___	#17 = ___	#18c = ___	#14d = ___	#12 = ___
Total = ___	#21 = ___	#22 = ___	#20 = ___	#18d = ___	#14e = ___	#15 = ___
÷ 4 = ___	Total = ___	Total = ___	Total = ___	#18e = ___	#14f = ___	#19 = ___
	÷ 5 = ___	÷ 5 = ___	÷ 5 = ___	Total = ___	Total = ___	#23 = ___
				÷ 6 = ___	÷ 6 = ___	Total = ___
						÷ 7 = ___

Electronic surveys using the Internet or telephone texting are becoming popular ways to administer surveys in some communities. Of course, only people with Internet access or texting capabilities on their cell phones are going to be reached. See Chapter 14 for more details on electronic surveys.

Determining Vision and Mission

Every school must strive for quality. When improvement is seen in a school's quality, it is usually because the school has a vision of what quality represents and a sense of direction toward creating a quality program. The sense of direction can be developed through the creation of a statement of beliefs (vision), a set of goals (mission), and specific objectives to be achieved (outcomes). Each of these three levels—beliefs, goals, and objectives—has a specific purpose in the planning process and each contributes in determining direction and showing interrelationships (see Figure 4.3).

A *statement of beliefs* can be thought of as a foundation or a philosophy for the school and should represent the collective thinking of the staff and community representatives. For example, the statement "Every child can learn and achieve mastery" is a statement of belief. It is part of one's philosophy of education.

A *goal statement* indicates of intended direction (mission) relative to a belief statement (vision). For example, a school goal could be "Successful learning experiences will be provided for every child each day." This is a specific statement of intent. A goal, however, often can be something that a school strives toward but may never totally achieve.

Just as goals should be an outgrowth of a philosophy or belief, *objectives* should be extensions of goals. Objectives are more specific than goals and should be obtainable, often within a stated period of time. Here is an illustration of a program objective: "Instructional objectives will be developed by the staff for the reading and math curricula this year."

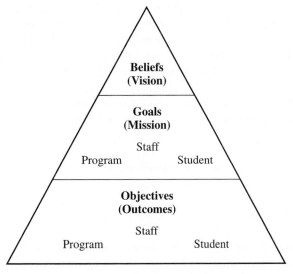

FIGURE 4.3 Determining Direction and Purpose for the School

Total quality management (TQM) speaks of performance goals and process goals. These suggest that some goals or objectives will be stated in such a manner that they are measurable in some meaningful way. An example might be "Unit test scores, when charted over time, will show overall class improvement." However, Deming, in laying out the principles of TQM, cautions against setting work standards that prescribe numerical quotas.[19]

Framework for Establishing Beliefs or Vision Statements

The vision, beliefs, and philosophy for a school should relate to societal expectations, wants and needs of the community, and the individual differences of children. A list can best be organized with an outline or framework of concepts and ideas to be included. There are many different ways such a framework can be organized. Three different frameworks, or structures, are described next.

Evaluative Criteria Framework.   *Evaluative criteria* guidelines of the national accrediting associations suggest considerations should be given to the following:

- Relevance of the statement of philosophy to the larger purpose of the American democratic commitment
- Attention to intellectual, democratic, moral, and social values, basic to satisfying the needs of the individual and his or her culture
- Recognition of individual differences
- The special characteristics and unique needs of elementary school children
- Concern for the nature of knowledge and for the nature of the learning process as they apply to learners and their total development
- Consistency of philosophy with actual practice
- Identification of the roles and relationships expected of the community, the student, the teacher, and the administration in the educational process of the school
- The role of the elementary school program of the school district and the importance of the articulation with other elements of the overall educational program
- The responsibility for making a determination as to a desirable balance among activities designed to develop cognitive, affective, and psychomotor demands
- The relationship of the school and all other educational learning centers
- The responsibility of the school toward social and economic change
- The accountability of the school to the community it serves[20]

Effective Schools Framework.   The research done over 30 years ago by Edmonds, Brookover, Lezotte, and many others highlighted seven main correlates of effective schools.[21] An *effective school* was defined as one that is achieving high and equitable levels of student learning. All children will learn essential knowledge, concepts, and skills needed to be successful at the next level of schooling. The seven correlates are as follows:

1. *Clear School Mission.* The mission needs to include the concept of learning for all.
2. *High Expectations for Success.* The climate should reflect what the staff truly believes and demonstrate that all students can obtain mastery of essential content areas.

3. *Instructional Leadership.* The principal acts as the instructional leader and communicates the school mission to the staff and community.
4. *Frequent Monitoring of Student Progress.* Academic progress is measured frequently. The results of assessments are used to improve instruction.
5. *Opportunity to Learn and Time on Task.* Directed instructional time is maximized greatly reducing noninstructional activities.
6. *Safe and Orderly Environment.* Orderly, purposeful atmosphere must be free from the threat of physical harm. The school climate is conducive to learning.
7. *Home/School Relations.* Partnerships are established with parents who assist in their child's education.

What is unique about these correlates is that they represent some of the first research-based characteristics of schools that were producing better student learning. Studies found that public schools can make a difference even with children of poverty. Replication research in recent years reaffirms the original findings.

Essential Schools Framework   The Coalition of Essential Schools has developed a set of common principles around which their member schools organize their schools. These principles also can be a framework for establishing belief and vision statements.[22]:

1. Learning to use one's mind well
2. Less is more, depth over coverage
3. Goals applicable to all students
4. Personalization
5. Students-as-workers, teacher-as-coach
6. Demonstration of mastery
7. A tone of decency and trust
8. Commitment to the entire school
9. Resources dedicated to teaching and learning
10. Democracy and equity

These three frameworks for identifying beliefs statements obviously have some degree of overlap. But each also has a certain rationale for its own structure. The school might elect to use one of the three frameworks or create its own structure from a combination of them. One or more belief statements can be written for each of the areas on the outline.

Vision and Mission Development Process

The process of establishing a sense of direction in a school must be a dynamic one involving teachers, community members, and, in some cases, students. In reality, the interaction and debate of the processes in determining what the document is to include is more important than the product itself, because the vision and mission are important only if they are alive. Beliefs must be kept alive in the minds of staff and community, and those people must feel that the goals and objectives relative to those beliefs are appropriate.

Staff/Community Consensus.   The initial formulation as well as the regular reviews and updates of the belief statements should be done using a staff/community/student consensus model. The participants are separated into writing teams consisting of three to five members, including all members of the faculty. Each writing team should be structured to create maximum internal variability. This means that each team should have teachers from different grade levels, subject areas, and experience background. If community members and students (secondary) are participating, one or more should be assigned to each writing team.

Each writing team should be given a complete list of belief topic areas. The team's task will be to write one or more statements regarding what it believes for each of the topics. For example, if one of the topic areas asks the team to list its beliefs regarding curriculum, the members might ultimately write a statement such as this: "We believe that the school staff should collectively review the basic objectives and strategies for teaching and learning and periodically reexamine and reconstruct objectives in view of current curricular priorities."

Each writing team should develop statements for each aspect of the belief framework. This may require 6 to 12 or more statements from each writing team. Upon completion of the initial writing task, each writing team is asked to select one representative member from the group to meet with a similar member from each of the other teams to form a consensus team to discuss the statements written by each team on the first topic. A second representative should be identified for the second topic as well as a third and fourth until all writing team members are representing their team to a consensus team consisting of one member from each of the other writing groups. Figure 4.4 illustrates the writing team–consensus team structure.

These newly formulated consensus teams review the written statements on the assigned topic from each of the writing teams and select, combine, and rewrite the submitted statements until they have developed a series of statements on the assigned topic that their group accepts. Each team representative then takes the newly combined set of statements on the team's topic back to his or her original writing team for discussion, additional modification, or ratification.

If the original writing team feels that the rewrite of the consensus team does not reflect the original team's beliefs, team members should modify the consensus team's work. The consensus

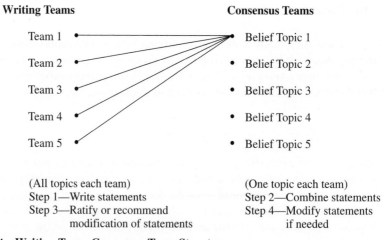

FIGURE 4.4   Writing Team–Consensus Team Structure

team would then be reconvened to consider the recommended modifications. If necessary, the statements may go back and forth several times. The other consensus teams are carrying out the same procedures for their topics. The final set of belief statements developed by a school using this process is shown in Figures 4.5 and 4.6

FIGURE 4.5   Sample High School Vision and Mission Statement

Vision

We believe that Manor High School is a unique educational environment. Its uniqueness is exemplified in certain aspects of its design. It is designed to meet the individual needs of a larger percentage of students than is possible in the traditional system; to avoid a mass-produced, molding effect; to provide a distinctly pleasant atmosphere for learning; to foster respectful relationships; and to serve the community.

We believe that all students have needs that must be fulfilled. We believe that all students are unique as individuals—that they develop at different rates and in different manners. We believe that students have a natural desire to learn independence, responsibility, self-assertion, democratic ideas, and the skills necessary to solve present and future problems.

We believe the role of the student is to involve himself or herself responsibly in the learning experience.

We believe that learning is evidenced by a behavioral change. It is a continuous process that takes place in the home, community, and school.

We believe that the role of the teacher is (1) to design learning opportunities and (2) to provide each student for whom he or she is responsible the freedom to learn what the student needs to take a productive and rewarding part in society. The teacher is an advisor and sharer.

We believe that teaching and learning can best be accomplished through interaction and involvement of students, staff, administration, and community.

We believe that the administration is responsible for supplying and maintaining all the physical accouterments of the school. The principal is to be an instructional leader but shares with students, teachers, and community the task of facilitating and coordinating learning. His or her leadership should be participatory and not authoritarian.

Mission

The mission of Manor High School is to establish a student and community learning center with high expectations for student performance designed to facilitate stimulating learning experiences and harmonious social interactions in which each individual has the opportunity to realize his or her full potential.

It is our endeavor to develop the following qualities to a high degree through conscientious and dedicated guidance and instruction. These qualities are:

1. The self-evaluative ability of the individual

2. The positive attitude of the individual toward himself or herself and others

3. The independence and responsibility in the individual

4. The creativity in the individual

5. The ability to be self-assertive

6. The acquiring of knowledge relative to both the mental and physical needs and abilities of the individual

7. The critical thinking and decision-making ability of the individual

8. The ability of the individual to contribute to and to make his or her way in our society

FIGURE 4.6   Sample Elementary and Middle School Belief and Mission Statements

Pi Beta Phi K–8 Belief Statements

*We believe the instruction of each child is the shared responsibility of the student, school, family, caregiver, and community.

*We believe school should be safe, nurturing, and accepting of all students to allow the opportunity for maximum growth.

*We believe that the school should be sensitive to the needs of all stakeholders in creating the learning environment and policies that support it.

*We believe that students should learn to understand and respect the rights and responsibilities of being an American citizen.

*We believe that appropriate assessments are necessary to meet the physical, emotional, academic, and social needs of every student.

*We believe that effective decision-making skills are essential for the lifelong well-being of all students.

*We believe each student is responsible for learning, attendance, and attitude and that this personal responsibility is the foundation for assuming the stewardship of our community and environment.

Inskip Elementary School Belief Statements

- Student learning is the chief priority of the school.

- All students can learn.

- Each student is a valued individual with unique physical, social, emotional, and intellectual needs and should be provided with a variety of instructional approaches.

- A student's self-esteem is enhanced by positive relationships and mutual respect among and between students and staff.

- A safe and physically comfortable environment promotes student learning.

- A variety of methods should be used to allow students to demonstrate their understanding of essential skills.

- Teachers, administrators, parents, and the community share the responsibility for advancing the school's mission.

Lonsdale Elementary School Mission Statement

We endeavor to give all students the opportunity for a quality education that develops content knowledge, skills, and attitudes that will enable them to meet their maximum potential in a structured, safe environment. We prepare our students to become independent, lifelong learners and productive, responsible citizens.

Glen Lake Elementary School Mission Statement

The mission of the Glen Lake School community is to inspire in all learners the motivation and confidence to reach their highest potential by providing challenging and meaningful learning experiences in a safe, caring, and respectful environment.

West Valley Middle School Mission Statement

The mission of the West Valley Middle School community is to Inspire students to be Resourceful, Respectful, and Responsible citizens by providing a challenging and safe learning environment.

Clarifying Expectations for Student Learning

What should be the expected outcomes for students? What does the principal want his or her students to know and be able to do? What values does the principal wish his or her students to hold? The goal of this phase of the school improvement is to gain clarification through the development of a shared set of expectations for student learning and achievement. Most important is the need for all those who have a stake in the success of the school to agree on the broad areas of knowledge, skill, and abilities that students should be able to demonstrate when they exit from the highest grade in the school. This shared consensus of student-desired outcomes can provide the stakeholders of the school—students, parents, staff, and community—with a clear sense of direction and purpose for the education of children in the school. Student performance is the real purpose for efforts at improvement and the reason behind any school improvement planning process.

Shared Vision Process

Once again, the process of developing a shared vision of student expectations is critical to the success of any plan developed. A committee process with all stakeholder groups participating is extremely important. A shared vision is the desired outcome.

The process of developing a shared vision should begin with a review of the documents previously developed as part of the improvement planning. These include the beliefs (vision) and goals (mission) statement and a review of the data gathered for the school profile. Analysis of these documents will help to identify stakeholder expectations, and the assessment and evaluation results will help identify current learning levels. The statements of expectations for student learning to be developed should reflect, when finished, the beliefs and goals identified in the vision and mission statement.

The next step by the student outcomes committee should consist of two reviews of current practice and thought. The first should be a review of current research and theory of instruction methods and learning. Chapter 7 provides a basis for this type review. The second review should be of current school, district, state, and national goals for student learning. Several different frameworks or approaches to curriculum design are discussed in Chapter 6. Most of the national curriculum organizations (e.g., National Council of Teachers of Mathematics, National Council for Social Studies, National Council of Teachers of English) have published goals and standards in their respective program areas. The NSSE has several support documents to help local schools with developing goals for student learning.[23]

Based on the reviews of vision and mission, the previously developed school profile, and current practices in learning and standards for curriculum, the next step is to develop statements of desired results for student learning. The statements should include the desired knowledge, skills, and abilities that a well-educated child should be able to demonstrate. They should be stated clearly to show what the student should know or be able to do.

If these tasks of identifying desired results of student learning are done thoroughly for all curriculum areas, the project becomes a monumental. In fact, it becomes a major component of the curriculum audit process. The entire process must be seen as a multiyear, multicycle process and part of a larger five-year strategic plan for the school, with only small parts of the entire process becoming the focus each year. For this reason, only a manageable number of schoolwide goals should be identified for immediate attention.

A review of student learning needs should become the basis for the identification of goals to be initially targeted for action. Once again, a review of the data gathered in the school profile, along with the desired outcomes for the students, should be the basis for the needs assessment. Be careful to base the assessment on a broad review of student achievement. Do not get caught in the trap of looking at standardized achievement data because those data are easiest to use or because others are emphasizing those data. Rather, make an effort to look at a broad base of student performance data. For example, portfolios of student work, essays or writing projects, oral presentations, group projects, open-ended problem-solving situations, self-assessment, peer assessment, term projects or research projects, and performance activities often are more valid measures of student performance.

A tentative list of 5 to 10 goals should be identified for initial consideration with 2 or 3 goals becoming the major focus. Others can be added later when success is observed with the first set. If too many goals are initiated, focus is lost and positive results are harder to achieve. Be sure to continue to review all goals, recommendations, and decisions with the stakeholder committee for its consideration and acceptance.

Analysis of Instructional and Organizational Effectiveness

The purpose of this analysis is to examine the quality of the work of the school on behalf of student learning. If schools look only at the desired results of student learning and pay no attention to the processes whereby the learning can take place, little will be accomplished.

A dual focus on the quality of the work of students and on the quality of the work of the school is required for school improvement to take place. The school's strengths and weaknesses should be identified. This can be done through a review of the literature on school organization as well as by observing quality practices in other schools throughout the nation.

Think of the school structural framework as an integrated system with each of the several organizational components closely related to one another. Systems theory requires that specific thought be given to each of several organizational components of the program: (1) curricular organization, (2) instructional processes, (3) student grouping practices, (4) staff organization, (5) the scheduling of learning time, and (6) facility utilization and design. Although the six components can be separated for discussion purposes, the program that results for any particular school must give detailed attention both to the contribution that each component makes to the achievement of the goals and objectives of the school and the development of each component in such a way that it is compatible with the other five components. For example, a belief statement may speak to the importance of meeting the individual needs of each child. From this belief statement a goal of individualizing instruction might be selected. This instructional format must then be supported with a student grouping plan, staffing plan, and schedule. In turn, if the staffing selection proposes team teaching, the facility utilization design should provide appropriate work spaces for teaching teams.

The organizational components are not equally important and should not be considered as equals, nor are they independent entities. Decisions regarding the organization of the curriculum and instructional program should be made first. These must logically be based on the beliefs and goals for the school. The other four components serve the first two.

The first step should be the review of *best practices* for effective schools as described in current educational research. Chapters 6, 7, 11, and 12 provide reviews of current literature and ideas on each of these instructional organization components designed to bring about maximum student achievement and learning. Review in conjunction with the vision, beliefs, mission, and goal process started earlier in the improvement process.[24]

Several other areas should be considered in the review of organizational effectiveness. These are less directly connected to the instructional systems but are nevertheless critical to the overall effectiveness of the school:

- *Practices of Leadership in the School.* Do the leaders support teaching and learning, develop schoolwide plans for improvement, make decisions that are research based, make decisions using collaborative techniques, monitor instruction, and manage the organization for safe operation and an efficient learning environment?
- *Learning Community Building.* Is there evidence of a good working climate in the school, with the staff functioning as a energized supporting learning organization? Is there a good working relationship in the school that engages parents and families as partners in the learning process? Is there a collaborative network with community members and groups, youth-serving agencies, clergy and government leaders, and leaders in higher education and business?
- *Use of Technology.* Is there evidence that newer technologies of modern communication and computing are being integrated into the management of the school and the instructional programs of the school, providing students with a variety of skills and opportunities for expanded learning?

Documenting current practice in the school is the second step in the process of investigating the instructional and organizational effectiveness. This should be done using several approaches:

- *Document Review.* Instructional organization in schools is supposed to be well documented. Curriculum frameworks, lesson plans, teacher assignments, student schedules, minutes from faculty meetings and team meetings, and daily bulletins all provide insight into the reality of how instruction is currently organized and managed. These documents should provide a basis for analysis. On the other hand, if these documents do not exist or are very sketchy in the information they provide, the message may be there a lack of instructional organization.
- *Faculty Survey.* Survey the faculty regarding instructional practices currently being used. The School Excellence Inventory shown in Figure 4.2 focuses on instructional practices. The NSSE Survey of Instructional and Organizational Effectiveness[25] covers many of the identified topics, but the principal may wish to develop his or her own instrument tailored to specific questions and needs.
- *Observation and Interview.* An interview and observation schedule may be developed to gather information about instructional and organizational practices in the school. Although these data are often more difficult to summarize and illustrate in graphic form, they offer an opportunity for greater depth of analysis with reasons why certain things are as they are.

Summarize the findings of the investigation into instructional and organizational practices in the school and compare them to what was found in the literature regarding "best practices." From this analysis, identify school priorities for building and strengthening the instructional and organizational program of the school. Be sure to remember the "systems" nature of many of these organizational structures and that they need to be considered collectively when contemplating change.

Finally, return to the stakeholders, particularly the school faculty, for consensus. Select, with faculty involvement, from the priority list those instructional and organizational components that best support desired learning goals from the earlier analysis that clarified expectations for student learning and set priorities and targets for improvement.

By this time, the School Improvement Committee and school stakeholders have completed a school profile with a heavy emphasis on data; constructed a vision, mission, beliefs, objectives document with the involvement of each stakeholder group; identified appropriate learner outcomes for the school with targeted areas for improvement; and completed an analysis of the instructional and organizational structures of the school with priorities identified that complement those selected in the learner outcome section. The next task will be to build a plan of action.

Action Planning/Project Management

Action planning is what professional planners label *programming an objective,* and that label is descriptive. The action plan contains the following elements:

- A description of the several activities necessary to achieve an objective
- The relationship of these activities to each other
- The assignment of specific responsibilities to individuals who will see to the implementation of the activities
- A time frame and chronology of activities and events
- An evaluation process

There are no guarantees that the plan will succeed in solving the existing problem; that is why the last element of the plan provides for an evaluation. The activities in the plan may be best thought of as "hypotheses"—more than a hunch, perhaps; certainly more than a hope; nevertheless, not certainties. Therefore, it is necessary to evaluate the efficacy carefully, not only of the total project but also of the specific activities composing the project.

Once the action plan is developed, project management is in great part a monitoring process. The project manager may be the principal but not necessarily so. Any person on the staff with good administrative skills and an interest in the project may be a likely candidate to become the manager.

This gives the principal an excellent way to develop and capitalize on the leadership skills of staff members, including assistant principals, faculty, and resource or support personnel. Adequate resources must be provided to the person to put in charge of managing a project; these may include released time and secretarial service as well as a budget.

Analyzing the Problem

Always take care that the presumed problem is adequately analyzed before moving into an elaborate action plan. It is at the problem analysis point that a force field analysis proves helpful.

Force Field Analysis.   Kurt Lewin,[26] applying certain physical laws to the organizational setting, concluded that things stay the way they are in organizations because a field of opposing forces is in balance. One way to think about a problem situation is to regard the situation as being as it is because of positive ("driving") and negative ("restraining") forces that are equal in strength. The driving forces are current conditions and actions present in the organizational environment (or in the community, or even in society as a whole) which are such that change is encouraged. Restraining forces are conditions or actions, which are such that change is discouraged or inhibited. These can be thought of as negative, or "minus," forces in the developing equation.

The force field concept issues from the physical law that a body at rest (in equilibrium) will remain at rest when the sum of all the forces operating on it is equal to zero. The body will move only when the sum is not zero, *and it will move only in the direction of the unbalancing force.*

It is not difficult to observe this phenomenon in organizations. The productivity of a school staff, the state of the school/community relations program, the success level of the intramural program, among any number of other observable situations are all subject to explanation (and change) by force field analysis. A thing is where it is because the sum of the *power* of the counterbalancing plus and minus forces is equal to zero—and the situation is "frozen."

Power is a key word here because equilibrium is not achieved by a simple equal *number* of forces. It is the strength of the force that is important. One overwhelming positive force (e.g., the infusion of huge amounts of federal or state dollars) may be quite sufficient to change dramatically the nature of a science program that had suffered from lack of equipment, inadequately prepared teachers, and lack of community concern. Similarly, a large, vocal, and interested religious group might impact mightily on the nature of a science curriculum in any particular community, despite research evidence about inquiry methods, adequate budget, well-trained teachers, or bright students, among any number of other forces that would otherwise be generative of good programming.

Movement (i.e., change) will take place only when an imbalance is created. An imbalance will occur by eliminating forces, by developing new forces, or by affecting the power of existing forces. The imbalance "unfreezes" the current situation, the situation will change, and a new state of equilibrium will be achieved. To recapitulate, an imbalance may be created in several ways:

- Addition of a new force(s)
- Deletion of a force(s)
- Change in the magnitude or strength of any of the forces

Any plan that is developed after force field analysis is conducted will probably make use of all three ways of creating an imbalance.

There is evidence, however, that attempting to increase only positive forces creates much tension in the system, and often the intensity of the restraining forces correspondingly increases. This leaves the organization no better off, and sometimes worse off, because of new tensions. The best results occur when the first effort is directed to reducing the intensity of the restraining forces. Also, there may be little or nothing that can be done about some of the forces—a few may be imponderables, others simply may be outside the control of organization members.

Engaging in force field analysis focuses thinking and may result in a restatement of the problem. Often, what appeared to be the problem is really a symptom; one of the identified "restraining forces" is actually the problem that requires attention. Thus, a principal, project manager, and staff must have open minds at the early stages so that energies are ultimately focused on the right issues and not dissipated on things that are only symptomatic.

CASE STUDY

You are the principal of a middle school with an enrollment of 800 students. The composition of the student body is racially and ethnically heterogeneous, with perhaps few more children from families at the lower end of the community's economic continuum.

During the gathering of data for your School Improvement Plan, you become aware that all might not be well with the reading program in your school. The students in grades 7 and 8 do not seem to be reading as well as might be expected. There are a number troubling indicators.

As you review scores on standardized tests, the Iowa Test of Basic Skills among these, you observe that your students, in the main, are well below norms for the system as a whole and for the nation. Several of your teachers have also expressed concern about the reading skills of their students. The librarian has commented about a low circulation rate even among the usually more popular children's books. Senior high school principal colleagues have remarked to you that the incoming students from your school seem to have less well-developed reading skills.

As you examine the situation, you reach the conclusion that something is functionally wrong with the reading program, and the anticipated outcome—adequately skilled readers—is not being realized. You decide your reading program should become one of the targeted areas for your School Improvement Plan.

An example of a partial force field analysis of this problem appears in Figure 4.7. In any given real situation, many forces beyond those suggested in the example could exist. When conducting such an analysis, it is important to focus only on *what is,* not on *what might be* or on what one wishes were so. The purpose of the force field analysis is to get the problem under an analytical lens, so that a feasible solution (action plan) can be developed either to solve or ameliorate the problem.

FIGURE 4.7   Example of a Force Field Analysis

Problem: The pupils in Hughes Middle School are not developing good reading skills.

FACILITATING FORCES (+)	RESTRAINING FORCES (−)
Instructional Materials Center	Student transiency (over district average)
Full-time librarian	Bilingual population
Budgeted for 3 aides	Bimodal distribution of teachers (many
Funded ESL program	first year)
New reading series	New reading series program; no in-service
Assistant principal is a reading specialist	Parental involvement in school activities slight
State mandated and funded tutorial program	Little study room in homes—high number of apartment
Most children walk to school (no bus students)	and project dwellers
Expressed teacher concerns	Teacher turnover above district average
Flexible schedule	Single-parent and two-wage earner homes (people not
	readily available)
	No role models
	Staff overload

Generating Action Plans

Once the force field analysis has been completed, it is time to generate ideas for activities that, if accomplished, could be assumed to help solve the problem. Creative thought is what is sought. To do this, a principal could lead the staff in any of the three techniques for "unstructured" problem solving described in Chapter 3. Brainstorming or the nominal group techniques most easily lend themselves to this. There is one caveat: If the solutions generated do not relate in any way to the pluses and minuses in the force field analysis, they probably should be discarded. Unless the activity is such that it would seem to reduce a negative or strengthen a positive, that activity cannot be expected to help solve the problem.

The Indiana Principal's Leadership Academy has developed a good model for goal action plans. The plan begins with the identification of the vision and goal and then leads the user through a planning and documentation process. The Indiana Goal Action Plan (GAP) is shown in Figure 4.8

FIGURE 4.8   Goal Action Plan

Goal Action Plan

Participant's Name _____ Group # _____

GAP # and Name of GAP _____

1. **VISION:** For the particular problem being addressed create a vision of the best that you can imagine having happened as this problem is corrected. Write the vision statement as if the improvement already exists.

2. **GOAL(S):** There may be a number of worthy goals that apply to your vision. For this plan select only one goal and write it as an outcome statement that is measurable. Other goals for your vision will require other action plans.

3. **PLAN:** Mentally, walk through and outline the methods, strategies, people, and resources, which can be used to guarantee the attainment of the goal.

4. **TIMELINE:** List specific tasks to be done, determine how to get needed resources, and set appropriate dates by which each step will be completed.

5. **ANTICIPATED PROBLEMS:** List things that are potential obstacles, such as . . . resistant people, personal shortcomings, etc.

6. **PREVENTIONS:** Develop strategies to either prevent or remove barriers. Begin to list resources for assistance.

7. **BASELINE:** This is to be an observable indication of how you or your school performs now in the goal area of your Goal Action Plan.

8. **EXPECTATIONS:** MINIMUM—The smallest measure of improvement you will accept.

   SATISFACTORY—An average acceptable measure of improvement.
   EXCELLENCE—Evidence of great achievement or level of improvement.

9. **PROOF:** The demonstration or documentation that will prove to others that you successfully met your challenge and achieved your goal(s).

10. **CELEBRATION:** Celebrate success! Choose the most pleasurable and appropriate way to enjoy your achievement.

Source: Goal Action Plan, Indiana Principal's Leadership Academy, Indiana Department of Education, www.doe.in.gov/TitleI/pdf/leadership-teams/team_planning_sheet.doc

FIGURE 4.9   Action Planning: The Problem Resolution Document

Project: Improving the reading skills of seventh- and eighth-grade students at Hughes Middle School

Project Manager:	Kay Weise, Assistant Principal
Completion Date:	June 1*
Start Date:	August 15

ACTIONS	START/COMPLETE	RELATION TO FORCE FIELD (WHAT +/−)	COORDINATOR
Volunteers Program	10/1-cont.	#5(−)	Holland
After-school study program	11/1-cont.	#6(−)	Norris
"Why I Read" speakers	11/1–6/1	#9(−)	Carspecken
New teacher in-service program: Reading in subject areas	8/15–2/15	#6(+) #9(+) #3(−)	Craig
Reader of the Month Award	9/15–6/1	#1(+) #2(+)	Tanner
"Here's an Author"	2/1–3/1	#9(−)	Strahan
Story-Telling Time	10/5–5/15	#2(+) #3(+) #10(+)	Miller

*The first two actions continue beyond June.

along with instructions for completing each category. This goal action plan works extremely well for small but important tasks or as a subset of the planning documents needed for larger more complex projects, such as those covered later in this chapter. It also makes good use of force field analysis data, such as the data shown in Figure 4.7.

Using the Project Planning Document

ISLLC 3

Complex problems require the use of a planning document. The resolution of simple problems may not require an involved procedure; nevertheless, the logic and steps in the project planning document are applicable and should at least be a mental process. The document is the project manager's guide and serves also as a monitoring device.

Figure 4.9 illustrates a comprehensive problem resolution document. Using the previous case as an example, the project goal is stated, activities are delineated, target dates are established, and specific persons are identified who have assigned responsibilities for the implementation of the activities.

In many instances, a specific activity may be especially complex and composed of several components to be carried out before the activity is accomplished. The responsible person would develop a similar document for use with his or her team, and the project would be desegregated to another level. The point is, with such a document, tasks are clearly spelled out, and all are made aware of precisely what it is that is being attempted, how, who is responsible, when, and for what.

Putting the Plan into Operation

The project has now been separated into a series of activities. Complex activities have been subdivided into elements or events, the completion of which will conclude the activity; responsibilities have been assigned and accepted. Before proceeding, there is need to establish realistic target dates, develop the project calendar, and put into place a monitoring and evaluation process. Project planning computer software is of great assistance in organizing and managing large projects.[27] Each of the activities and documents listed in this section can be efficiently developed with a good software planning package.

Establishing Target Dates

Establishing precise starting and completion times for the project as a whole, as well as for each of the separate project activities, is critical.[28] In order to establish realistic completion dates, those involved in the project must understand (1) the nuances of the problem; (2) certain organizational realities, including, for example, requisitioning and purchasing procedures and time lines; and (3) the capabilities of the staff. If these conditions are met, then it is possible to set realistic target dates. To do this, the project team raises two questions: If unanticipated problems arose—strikes, floods, a championship basketball team—what would be the most pessimistic date by which this project could be completed? Then this question is asked: If all went well—no one became ill, adequate resources were available, the purchasing department finally got its act together—what would be the most optimistic date by which this project could be completed? The realistic target date is a point midway between the pessimistic and optimistic dates.

The Project Calendar: Gantt Charting

Once the activities and tasks have been delineated, the specific elements of the more complex activities detailed, and responsibilities assigned, the master schedule needs to be developed and posted. This is developed in the form of a *Gantt chart*. Figure 4.10 depicts a Gantt chart for the case study presented earlier. In the Gantt chart, each project activity is listed, along with the elements or tasks composing each activity and an indication of the targeted starting and completion dates of every entry.

Preparing the Master Project Document

The preparation of a master project document is an important responsibility of the project manager. The document may simply be a loose-leaf binder within which is placed the comprehensive problem resolution document, key personnel checklist, Gantt chart, minutes of team meetings, and any diary entries or other notes that might help future project managers. Such a document is of great assistance in the monitoring and evaluation process.

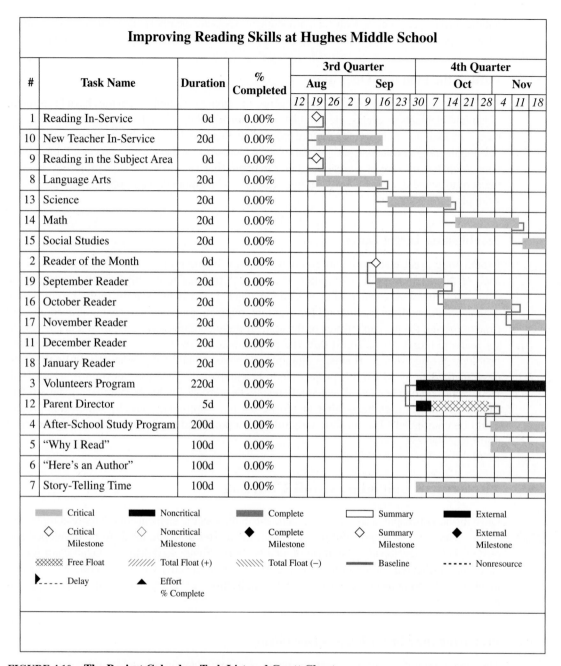

#	Task Name	Duration	% Completed	3rd Quarter							4th Quarter			
				Aug			**Sep**				**Oct**		**Nov**	
				12	19	26	2	9	16	23	30	7	14	21	28	4	11	18
1	Reading In-Service	0d	0.00%												
10	New Teacher In-Service	20d	0.00%												
9	Reading in the Subject Area	0d	0.00%												
8	Language Arts	20d	0.00%												
13	Science	20d	0.00%												
14	Math	20d	0.00%												
15	Social Studies	20d	0.00%												
2	Reader of the Month	0d	0.00%												
19	September Reader	20d	0.00%												
16	October Reader	20d	0.00%												
17	November Reader	20d	0.00%												
11	December Reader	20d	0.00%												
18	January Reader	20d	0.00%												
3	Volunteers Program	220d	0.00%												
12	Parent Director	5d	0.00%												
4	After-School Study Program	200d	0.00%												
5	"Why I Read"	100d	0.00%												
6	"Here's an Author"	100d	0.00%												
7	Story-Telling Time	100d	0.00%												

Improving Reading Skills at Hughes Middle School

Legend:
- Critical
- Noncritical
- Complete
- Summary
- External
- ◇ Critical Milestone
- ◇ Noncritical Milestone
- ◆ Complete Milestone
- ◇ Summary Milestone
- ◆ External Milestone
- Free Float
- Total Float (+)
- Total Float (−)
- Baseline
- Nonresource
- Delay
- ▲ Effort % Complete

FIGURE 4.10   The Project Calendar: Task List and Gantt Chart

Monitoring and Evaluating the Project

The project manager's responsibility is to help the project team stay on schedule. This does not mean daily, or even weekly, supervision; it does mean frequent conversations with individual activity coordinators and regular team meetings for the purpose of information sharing and midpoint corrections.

Other monitoring devices are available to the principal or project manager to help keep the project on target or to adapt to changes in the environment. Prominent posting of the Gantt chart will serve as both advertisement and stimulator.

Conducting Summative Evaluation

If regular monitoring has been occurring, then formative evaluation has been taking place. What remains to be developed is the summative evaluation. That is, how will the principal know if the project resulted in the desired outcome? Are things better? What worked? What did not work? What should be continued? What should not be continued?

To lend specificity, clarity, and form to the evaluation process, think of the several activities as "hypotheses." In the case study, it was believed that if certain activities were carried out, students would evidence better reading skills. These hypotheses must be tested, for it is pointless to engage in a series of activities if there are no provisions to determine whether the results were sufficient to justify continued expenditure of resources.

At the beginning of any project, it is important to state the indicators of achievement that the project staff is willing to accept as evidence of movement in the direction of the desired outcome. These indicators best come from restatements of the symptoms of the problem as originally stated. In the case study, some of the symptoms were these:

- Standardized test scores were below system norms.
- Circulation rates of library books were low.
- Caustic comments were received from senior high school principals.
- Teachers in the building expressed concerns.
- Teacher turnover is high.

Changes in these conditions provide a basis for evaluating the effectiveness of the project. A review of test data, surveys of teachers and administrators, circulation rates, and formal and informal feedback from students and parents are all available tools for determining whether the project was successful. Moreover, it may be that certain of the activities were more productive than others. This, too, needs to be investigated and any changes made so that energies and other resources are focused for maximum benefit.

Summary

The subject of this chapter has been goal setting and systematic problem identification and resolution using the *school improvement process* as the vehicle for change. Schools exist in an environment of change. The productivity of any particular school organization will depend in great part on the ability of leaders to analyze current conditions and future challenges, develop goals, and implement strategies for attaining the goals.

Instituting a process for identifying needs and developing a plan to resolve these needs in a manner consistent with system needs, are critical to effective building-level leadership. Action planning and project management are fundamental skills that must be employed to meet this challenge satisfactorily.

ACTIVITIES

1. Review Case Studies 6, 25, 26, and 29 at the end of this book. Apply the goal-setting and strategic planning concepts expressed in this chapter. How might you proceed in addressing the problems cited in these cases? Set forth a strategy to overcome the problem.
2. Review the activities at the end of Chapters 9 and 14 for further planning activities.
3. Turn to the ISLLC standards found in Appendix B. Review the functions listed with Standard 1. Review the vision, mission, and belief statement for your school. Do the actions of your school staff reflect these

statements? Are they posted or distributed to your stakeholders?
4. Does your school have a written school improvement plan? If so, review the plan. How is it being implemented? How long has it been in place? What results can be seen? How is the community involved?
5. Go to the Allyn Bacon website at http://www.pearson-highered.com/educator/product/Principal-The-Creative-Leadership-for-Excellence-in-Schools/9780205481378.page#top for more information on school improvement plans.

ENDNOTES

1. Comments of the Cheshire cat to Alice *(Alice in Wonderland)* upon her request for directions after admitting she didn't know where she wanted to go.
2. G. Hall and S. Hord, *Change in Schools: Facilitating the Process* (Albany: State University of New York Press, 1987), preface.
3. Most school improvement plans follow a strategic planning model.
4. M. Fullan, B. Bennett, and C. Rolheiser-Bennett, "Linking Classroom and School Improvement," *Educational Leadership 47,* no. 8 (1990): 13–19.
5. *Good Schools: What Makes Them Work* (Washington, DC: National School Public Relations Association, 1980).
6. From the National Study of School Evaluation (NSSE) *School Improvement: Focusing on Student Performance,* http://www.advanc-ed.org/accreditation/school_accreditation/resourcess_and_tools/? This website has a planning guide that provides a data-driven and research-based framework for improving student learning and strengthening the instructional and organizational effectiveness of schools. The guide includes planning resources, rubrics, templates, and sample reports to help schools develop and tailor improvement plans to meet the specific learning needs of their students.
7. Chapter 14, Technology Applications for School Management, provides more detail regarding software for these data management tasks.

8. It is best if these data can be maintained in a database by child, along with achievement data and grades. The data can then be tallied for demographic descriptions but can also be used to divide students into demographic groups for achievement comparisons. For example: How do the grades of children who come from one-parent homes compare with those from two- parent homes?
9. Chapter 7 provides more detailed information on how assessment data might be used.
10. S. Gruenert and J. Valentine, *School Culture Survey* (Columbus, MO: Middle Level Leadership Center, 2008).
11. There are several popular climate instruments available. The OCDQ was developed originally by Halpin and Croft in 1963. Both the revised version of the OCDQ and the OHI are available at http://www.waynekhoy.com under research instruments.
12. W. K. Hoy and D. J. Sabo, *Quality Middle Schools: Open and healthy* (Thousand Oaks, CA: Corwin Press, 1998).
13. M. Tschannen-Moran and A. Wollfolk Hoy, "Teacher Efficacy: Capturing an Elusive Construct," *Teaching and Teacher Education 17,* (2001): 783–805.
14. P. M. Short, and J. S. Rinehart, "School Participant Empowerment Scale: Assessment of level of empowerment within the School Environment." *Educational and Psychological Measurement 52* (1992): 951–960.
15. V. A. Anfaraq, Jr., K. Roney, C. Smarkola, J. DuCette, and S. Gross, *The Developmentally Responsive Middle*

Level Principal: A Leadership Model and Measurement Instrument. (Westerville, OH: National Middle School Association, 2006).

16. Copies of the various versions of the OCDQ as well as scoring instructions are available at http://www.waynekhoy.com/ocdq-re.html.

17. The OHI is also available at http://www.waynekhoy.com/ohi-e.html.

18. The NSSE Opinion Inventories are designed for teachers, students, parents, and community members to address a series of issues of concern to most schools. The survey forms are available from the National Study of School Evaluation, 1699 East Woodfield Road, Suite 406, Schaumburg IL 60173.

19. Mary Walton, *The Deming Management Method* (New York: Perigee Books, 1986), p. 33.

20. *Elementary School Evaluative Criteria* (Arlington, VA: National Study of School Evaluation, A Guide for School Improvement, 1973), pp. 39–40.

21. Correlates of Effective Schools, Association for Effective Schools, Inc., Michigan.

22. The website for the Coalition of Essential Schools is www.essentialschools.org.

23. NSSE Indicators of Schools of Quality published in collaboration with the Alliance for Curriculum Reform provides a broad review of both schoolwide goals for student learning as well as specific instructional area goals.

24. Although the improvement planning process discussed in this chapter appears to be a step-by-step linear process, it is best done as an interactive process with each section influencing and being influenced by the other components. In other words, an idea discovered while developing this section of the analysis of instructional and organizational structure may cause a committee to modify a belief or change the wording in a vision statement or somewhere else in the plan.

25. The NSSE Survey of Instructional and Organizational Effectiveness is available from the National Study of School Evaluation, 1699 East Woodfield Road, Suite 406, Schaumburg IL 60173.

26. Kurt Lewin, *Resolving Social Conflict* (New York: Harper & Row, 1948), pp. 125–141.

27. The Gantt chart illustration (Figure 4.10) uses Project Scheduler 6 for Windows by Scitor Corporation. There are many other good planning programs on the market, such as Microsoft Office Project.

28. In not all cases will the completion of one activity, or one component, depend on another, but sometimes this will be so. Even when this is not so, it is vital that activities be completed on time. When a project is complex and has many interrelated parts, it may be necessary to institute the Program Evaluation Review Technique (PERT). PERT will depict the order in which each of the activities and any subactivities must occur, as well as the relationship of one activity, event, or element to another.

SELECTED READINGS

Anfara, V. A., Jr., K. Roney, C. Smarkola, J. DuCette, and S. Gross. *The Developmentally Responsive Middle Level Principal: A Leadership Model and Measurement Instrument.* (Westerville, OH: National Middle School Association, 2006).

Bernhardt, V. L. "Data Tools for School Improvement." *Educational Leadership 62* (2005): 66–69.

Borman, G. D., G. M. Hewes, L. T. Overman, and S. Brown. "Comprehensive School Reform and Achievement: A Meta-analysis." *Review of Educational Research 73* (2003): 125–230

Earl, L., and S. Katz. "Painting a Data-Rich Picture." *Principal Leadership 5* (2005): 16–20.

Fullan, Michael G. *Change Forces: Probing the Depth of Educational Reform* (London: Falmer Press, 1993).

Fullan, Michael G. "Turning Systemic Thinking on Its Head." *Phi Delta Kappan 77,* no. 6 (1996): 420–423.

Gardner, Howard. *Multiple Intelligences: The Theory in Practice* (New York: Basic Books, 1993).

Hardin, D. "Leadership Capacity for Lasting School Improvement." *NASSP Bulletin 87* (2003): 79–82.

Hewson, K., and L. Adrian. "Action Planning: Rowing in the Same Direction." *Principal 88,* no. 1 (2008): 48–51.

Kidron, Y., and M. Darwin. "A Systematic Review of Whole School Improvement Models." *Journal of Education for Students Placed at Risk, 12,* no. 1 (2007): 9–35.

Kelly, L. K., and L. W. Lezotte. "Developing Leadership through the School Improvement Process." *Journal of School Improvement, 4,* no. 1 (2003).

Picciano, A. G. *Data Driven Decision Making for Effective School Leadership* (Upper Saddle River, NJ: Pearson Education, 2006).

Popham, J. *The Truth about Testing an Educator's Call to Action* (Alexandria, VA: Association for Supervision and Curriculum Development, 2001).

Reeves, D. "Making Strategic Planning Work." *Educational Leadership 65* (2008): 86–87.

Sanders, W. L., and S. R Horn. "Research Findings from the Tennessee Value-Added Assessment System (TVAAS) Database: Implications for Educational Evaluation and Research." *Journal of Personnel Evaluation in Education,12* (1998): 247–256.

Developing a Positive School Culture

The school leaders of the twenty-first century must have knowledge and understanding of student growth and development; applied learning theories; applied motivational theories; curriculum design, implementation, evaluation, and refinement; principles of effective instruction; measurement, evaluation, and assessment strategies; diversity and its meaning for educational programs; adult learning and professional development models; the change process for systems, organizations, and individuals; the role of technology in promoting student learning and professional growth; and school cultures. They should also believe in, value, and be committed to student learning as a fundamental purpose of schooling; the proposition that all students can learn; the variety of ways in which students can learn; lifelong learning for self and others; professional development as an integral part of school improvement; the benefits that diversity brings to the school community; a safe and supportive learning environment; and preparing students to be contributing members of society. The Educational Leadership Policy Standards: ISLLC 2008 Standard 2 supports these characteristics.

Standard 2: An education leader promotes the success of every student by advocating, nurturing, and sustaining a school culture and instructional program conducive to student learning and staff professional growth.

Part Two addresses this standard and the functions that accompany it.

5 Creating a Positive Learning Climate

> *We have to assure these children that while they are with us*
> *they are safe and will be treated well. For some that may be*
> *all we can do but we must do that. We may not be able to*
> *control what goes on in any child's life before or after school.*
> *But here they will be not abused and they will be treated*
> *fairly. And they will be protected and they will be respected.*
> *And we're going to help them learn how life can be.*
>
> —KARON RILLING[1]

It Happens in Many Schools

Two boys begin to fight. A crowd gathers. Threats are yelled, one boy to the other. An assistant principal and two teachers soon appear and quell the fight. "That's the third time this week," says your assistant. The onlookers fade away and return to their other activities. The scuffling boys are asked what the difficulty is. "He's a racist," yells one. "Am not. You bullied me," says the other. The story unfolds and, as in most such instances, the stories vary from individual to individual. What are the facts? Who knows?

Such things happen even in well-ordered schools. But, as in all cases, it is important to gather some facts and determine if the incident is just one of those childhood disagreements or if it represents a symptom of a greater problem. What are some questions to be asked in the quiet of an office? Try these:

- How old were the combatants? Has this happened with these two before? (Middle school boys "square off" a lot; it seems related to age and maturity.) How is your counseling program?

- Does this happen often in your school? Is it nearly always gender related?
- Among the students, is there racial tension? Or economic tension?
- Have there been reports from faculty about student disagreements and threatened fights?

What the school leaders are looking for, even in a cursory way, is whether the school is dealing with the normal interactive behavior of young people in a certain stressful situation or whether there are indications that a poor learning climate generally exists. Children and young people fight sometimes, although in orderly schools, not often. There are other ways to handle disagreements, and young persons need to know what these are and use them.

When this story was told to a practicing high school principal in a suburban school, he smiled and said: "Fighting? I wish I had only that to deal with. Talk to me about drugs in the restroom or about teachers being threatened. Talk to some of my counselors about pregnant 12-year-olds. Help me manage a social skills laboratory to get some of these kids ready for a job."

So, the problem is complex. So are the solutions.

This chapter focuses on the elements of the humane school—a school of which children and youth and staff want to be a part, a school that is orderly and caring.

How can such a school be developed, nurtured, and maintained? Our hope is that the material that follows will provide insights and guidance to processes that sustain the humane and productive school. We will discuss such topics as the school as a culture, positive student control, guidance and counseling programs, and issues such as classroom practices and dealing with violence and gangs.

Positive Student Control

Good schools are characterized by high standards, high expectations, and a caring environment. Good schools are also invariably orderly places. Misbehavior is dealt with quickly, fairly, openly, and without recrimination. Importantly, in good schools, the entire school community knows what the expectations are, supports these expectations, and understands and supports the rules that are designed to ensure a positive learning climate. Faculty and students seem to care about each other.

Analyses of leadership styles reveal that principals in good schools are assertive and academically oriented. The discipline code is clear. Good principals are mobile and highly visible in the halls, classrooms, and cafeteria. They spend much time monitoring behavior, troubleshooting, and conferring with teachers and students.

For more years than we care to think about, we have been actively engaged in working with principals and school faculties throughout the United States and other nations. Few things are universally true in this world, but we have *never* been in a school that had a productive learning environment that was not also orderly. The schools were not always quiet, but they were always orderly. Students and teachers were going about the business of learning in an efficient, effective, and caring way.

Staff, students, and parents knew what the rules were and worked hard to see that they were followed. Transgressions were dealt with quickly, fairly, and without lingering resentments. In these schools it was the uniform practice to follow the principles of substantive and procedural due process in spirit and in practice.

ISLLC 2

Study after study and myriad reports from practicing principals reveal four essential ingredients of the maximally productive environment for learning and positive student control:

1. Clear, firm, and high teacher and administrator expectations
2. Consistent rules and consequences that directly relate to breaking these rules
3. A decided and well-implemented emphasis on the self-esteem of all students
4. Public and private acknowledgment and rewarding of positive behavior by students

The School as a Culture

Schools have a complex student society, and many things go on in a school that seemingly have little relationship to the curriculum. All of these "things," including the curriculum, have a mighty impact on the learning climate of the school. Creating a positive learning climate requires a great understanding of the needs of learners, which are varied and only partly addressed by a formalized set of classroom and cocurricular activities.

ISLLC 2

The real or perceived normative behavior of a student body will determine reward or punishment practices, teacher and administrator attitudes and behaviors, and even teacher and administrator attrition rates. Some schools in a community may be classified as "tough" schools; others as "good places to work"; most often, these references reflect normative student behavior patterns. But normative behaviors and mass actions to the contrary, a student body is composed of many bodies. Although certain groups may determine in great part the "accepted" behavior, the student who walks through the door of the principal's office is an individual complex of forces that may or may not epitomize the student body.

> The most significant change in school culture happens when school leaders, teachers, and students model the values of and beliefs important to the institution. The actions of school leaders are noticed and interpreted by others as "what's important." A school leader who acts with care and concern for others will develop a school culture with similar values. The leader who ignores the value and input of others places a stamp of approval on selfish behaviors and attitudes.[2]

What is the school like? How do people—staff, students, and parents—feel about each other and the place where many spend most of the school year? There are any number of school climate and school culture instruments available.[3] A simple examination of any list of educational instruments will reveal these. But we like one that was developed several years ago by a practicing principal of a middle school in a downtown area of a medium-sized city. It's never been standardized; it's not even copyrighted; and there is no scoring key. But the answers will tell you much about how persons feel about the place in which they are working.

Essentially, the instrument asks questions that reveal attitudes and dispositions about the school and about those who are in the school. Figure 5.1 depicts the device that many principals use. Add to it and modify it to suit your own needs. It is important to keep the tone positive. The principal is trying to discover not only what might be getting in the way but also what is helping. Some principals call the instrument "This School Is a Good School But. . . ." Its name makes no difference; what the school leaders (and the staff, students, and parents) are looking for are insights about how things might be improved at the relationship levels.

FIGURE 5.1   About My School

This school is a good school. It could be better if . . .

1. In this school a lot of the students . . .

2. Poor kids here . . .

3. Those who go out for sports and make the team . . .

4. The teachers frequently . . .

5. When trouble happens, I . . .

6. Counselors around here . . .

7. The best thing this school has going for it is . . .

8. One of the things I don't like in this school is . . .

9. My teachers . . . [or My students . . .]

10. Students who are different [of a different race] from [me] [each other] often . . .

11. ADD and/or MODIFY. (Now prepare the same instrument for the staff—certificated and noncertificated—and each complete the form. Do you see any differences within the groups and between groups? What does that mean?)

Development of a Positive Program

The principal of a school has a particular responsibility to lead the staff in developing school policies to control student behavior. This is not to suggest that the principal personally should write the policy, but it is the principal who must develop the procedures by which the staff can establish a philosophy of behavior, disciplinary procedures to be followed, and techniques for corrective action.

ISLLC 2

Fundamental to an orderly learning climate are well-understood, appropriate, and consistently applied rules and procedures. Once the rules are in place, there are two equally important conditions that must be met: The rules must be promulgated in a manner that ensures understanding by all affected, and there must be regular and systematic evaluation of the need for and efficacy of existing rules. Times change, needs change, and appropriate response patterns change. Rules should be examined routinely in view of whether they continue to serve the intended purpose in an effective and efficient manner.

Five Premises about the School Environment and Students

Our discussion about schooling and student behavior is based on five premises:

1. Schooling occurs in a group context. Therefore, the behavior of any individual student will instantaneously have an impact on the behavior of other students.
2. Learning occurs best in an orderly environment.
3. An orderly environment can be best achieved by policies and strategies that promote self-regulation of behavior (internal control) rather than policies and strategies that try to force compliance with elaborate control mechanisms and overuse punishment (external control).

4. The environment is enhanced when the staff behaves in an orderly and internally controlled way.
5. The rules to guide behavior should be simple, well-known, and continuously reinforced.

Good Teaching

Greek mythology tells the story of Procrustes. Procrustes was a robber. He sat by the wayside and captured travelers. On to an iron bed, he would tie the traveler. If the person was too long for the bed, he would chop off the parts of the body that exceeded the bed; if the person was too short, he would stretch the body until it fit. Too tall or too short until all the visitors were the same size—they would fit the bed and be equally dead.

Trying to teach all of the students in the same classroom or of the same age group the same way is simply invoking Procrustes, and making the students equally "dead." There are better, more effective ways to teach. And a positive school culture starts in the classroom.

Good Rules

ISLLC 2, 3

It is axiomatic that if staff and students are to be held accountable for certain standards, these expectations must be established and promulgated *ahead of their application* in a manner that makes them easily disseminated, learned, and understood. A principal has the responsibility to prescribe reasonable controls for the efficient day-to-day operation of the schools.

What is "reasonable"? A rule of thumb applied most frequently by the courts is: "Does the regulation enhance the education of the children, promote their interest and welfare, and is it for the common good of education?" It is implicit that regulations be within the legal authority of the school district. Regulations beyond the province of the school board are not enforceable. A long-standing decision has held that "boards are not at liberty to adopt according to their humor regulations which have no relevance to the schools' purposes."[4] This would be no less true in the matter of rules and regulations prescribed by the principal.

Moreover, although it is sound practice to develop procedures and guidelines that provide for consistency of school operation, conscious parsimony will serve best. Developing long lists of dos and don'ts in an attempt to cover every contingency can create a school climate in which the name of the game becomes beating the system—a climate in which staff and students often derive a perverse joy from testing the limits.

Neither the extreme of rules for every occasion nor its opposite, no rule at all, is sensible. Principals within the school and teachers within the classroom have the right *and the obligation* to determine reasonable policies governing the conduct of their charges, not only to maintain a proper educational climate but also for safety.

Learning Communities: Smallness Is Good

Much attention has been directed to so-called small-school plans as a way of organizing schools at the elementary, middle, and high school levels. It is a way to reduce the size of the school unit and provide for a more intimate learning environment. The research effort has been considerable.[5] Others have been conducting research about the effectiveness of smaller class units.[6]

Oxley[7] reported that "an interdisciplinary team of teachers shares a few hundred (or fewer) students in common and has responsibility for their educational progress, provides for a large part of their instructional day in a physical space devoted to this purpose, and exercises maximum flexibility to act on knowledge of student needs." The focus is on student-centered curriculum and instruction.

The school-within-a-school concept has been current in the literature for some time. It has been successful under various organizational frameworks. The significance seems to be a decided lack of anonymity for students and their teachers. According to Oxley, the concept has four elements: autonomous decision making (by teachers), a unique identity, joint understandings of expectations between teachers and students, and teachers made responsible for their own professional development.

Other Factors Influencing Behavior

ISLLC 2, 3

Other conditions well within the control of the school administrator and staff contribute to the learning climate. Disorder and lack of control in schools are frequently a result of the existence of large, impersonal masses of students. Students' feelings of alienation and teachers' feelings of helplessness must be recognized and can be addressed by the reorganization of schools into smaller learning communities. The school-within-a-school concept *is* relevant, as are small classes.[8]

Most of the severe disciplinary problems are caused by a very small percentage of the students. Special facilities and methods are needed to manage the more severely disruptive students if they cannot be handled effectively in the classroom. Crisis intervention centers, "adaptive behavior classes," and in-school suspensions, among a number of other common practices, respond to this problem.

The principal's own behavior and activities will help set the tone. A principal who helps teachers develop good disciplinary practices, a principal who maintains direct contact with students, and a principal who is visible and active in the hall, cafeteria, and library is critical to a good learning climate.

ISLLC 2

"Hoopla."   The efficacy of public rewards for achievement cannot be underestimated. Hoopla is not hokey; the most productive organizations, in private and public sectors, make much of measured progress toward goals and of individual accomplishment. Acknowledgment of achievement shouldn't be limited to only students; the entire school family—custodians, bus drivers, teachers, counselors, and all the rest—deserve public recognition for jobs well done.

Effective methods of acknowledgment abound: T-shirts, public ceremonies, special parking privileges, positive time-out, bulletin board exhibits, standing ovations at assemblies, stars and stickers, Number One clubs, prizes, badges, friendly taps on the shoulder, and the list could go on. The point is that praise, sincerely given, works.

Hoopla is also important to help individuals recognize their own achievements without benefit of others' approval. Self-approval is sustaining. Teachers can help students in this by asking them to share a personal accomplishment that they are proud of but that others may not know about. Principals can do the same with the staff.

Adult Visibility.   Community volunteer programs, which have increasing numbers of parents and other citizens, in the schools are a great help in reducing the incidence of violence and gang activity. We are not referring simply to "parent patrols" in the halls and the like, although this is one type of activity that has shown some success. Any of a variety of volunteer programs that increase the conspicuous visibility of adults—and particularly parents—in the schools will help. Children report feeling safer when adults are around. And, although they will largely be ignored by adolescents, an adult presence often provides a reassuring or at least a constraining influence.

We conclude this section with a climate-setting note by Achilles and Smith. They point out what is wrong with some schools and what can be right.

> If they had a free choice, most people would not willingly stay where they felt unwanted, unwelcomed, and unappreciated: they would not go to a daily job where they felt harassed and where they found it impossible to do well. . . . Children quickly learn the espoused and sometimes conflicting norms of the school workplace and whether or not people at the school seem to like them and want to teach them.[9]

Violence and Disorder

At one time, people did not think of schools as being dangerous places. But these times are days of unrest, and days of courage, too. Violence in schools, just as any instance of violence in the nation and internationally, is everyone's problem. In regard to school violence, the nation clearly insists that everyone accept responsibility for making schools a safe environment—students, teachers, administrators, parents, and the general citizenry.

Violence is a way that the uninformed or the unskilled or the criminally disposed or the frustrated try to level the playing field to make up for domestic abuse, for lack of child support, for foster parents, for public housing, for grungy rentals, for juvenile detention, or for a host of other perceived and real injustices. And acts of violence are often manifested in the schools of the nation, where children, youth, and adults interact in a social setting.

Keeping It a Fair Playing Field

Casella[10] states:

> If the discipline policy calls for punishing all individuals caught in confrontations, then poor youths will be punished most, because they are most likely to be involved in confrontations that middle-class youths [are not] due primarily to structural factors involving high rates of violence in neighborhoods and families, social isolation, and lack of opportunities leading to economic and social success. In addition, punitive discipline negatively affects poor students because it supports practices that can be, at the very least, biased and sometimes racist. (p. 26)

If Casella is correct, then what may appear to be a fair policy and one that, if uniformly applied, should result in an equitable environment, often fails to meet the judgment of good sense. Schools all over the country are discovering this to be the case. It looks so easy: Transgress and we don't even have to think about it—you are out! But there is *no* policy that, if *unthinkingly* albeit uniformly applied, will result in fair play.

Consider the following: A junior high school girl was suspended from school for accepting an aspirin from a classmate. (The classmate was also suspended.) The reason was that medications not under prescription and on file were banned in this school. A 13-year-old boy was suspended summarily for bringing a weapon to school. He was bringing a Civil War–minted knife to display to his history class. He had no prior permission to do this. The knife was in a scabbard and carried in a paper bag.*

These seem to be clear overreactions to keeping a school safe and healthy. Yet, the safety and well-being of students and staff do require vigilance and well-understood policies, rules, and regulations. Perhaps you can think of other examples of such excesses. How would you, as a principal, respond to the cases just mentioned? What sorts of policies and regulations would you develop with your faculty and the caregivers or parents who place the care of their children with you? Could your students be of help in the development of safe school policies? We would answer yes. And, yes, we would argue that parents and staff be included in the development of these policies.

Gangs

Policies and procedures that decrease gang activity may be best developed locally to meet local needs. Some general considerations can be found in the research and literature, however. Figure 5.2 identifies some steps a school staff can take if there is evidence of gang activity on the campus. Gangs are *not* loose social networks. Even though the attraction may be protection and friendship, *the goal of a gang is control and social intimidation.* Gangs operate outside of the civilized social fabric and in lawless ways.

FIGURE 5.2   There Is a Gang in the House

Steps to Be Taken If Gang Activity Is Suspected

School administrators should:

- Establish the school as neutral ground and adopt a no-tolerance policy for gang activity.
- Distinguish between youthful misbehavior and delinquent or criminal acts.
- Cooperate with other social agencies, including the police or sheriff's department, to train school personnel in how to identify and handle gang members.
- Create a mechanism for mediating student conflicts, including consideration of peer mediation.

Teachers should:

- Treat all students fairly and consistently.
- Incorporate gang issues into class lessons; address rights and responsibilities of citizens, decision making, and problem-solving skills.
- Establish good lines of communication with parents or caregivers.
- Be aware of community resources that are available.

---

*These incidents are not made up. They actually occurred in public schools that were imposing some sort of zero-tolerance policy and were reported in reliable newspapers.

FIGURE 5.3   There May Be Gangs

There may be gangs if . . .

Graffiti: Unusual or indecipherable signs, symbols, alphabets, and nicknames on walls, notebooks, papers, and clothing might be signals of gang presence.

Colors: Members of gangs often reveal a subtle or obvious choice of clothing or color of clothing, or wear specific brands or styles of clothing, hats, shoes, jewelry, or haircuts, or may wear their clothing in distinctive ways, such as one jean leg rolled up.

Handsigns, Handshakes, or Unusual Language: Members often have unusual ways of greeting or signaling each other.

Initiations: Otherwise unexplainable wounds, skin carvings, tattoos, bruises, or injuries may be the result of gang initiation ceremonies.

Behavior Changes: Sudden changes of moods or behavior, as well as unexplainable poor grades, can signal gang involvement.

Generally speaking, a gang is a group that meets the following criteria:

- The group has a name and an identifiable leader or leadership structure.
- The group maintains a geographic, economic, or criminal activity "turf."
- Members associate on a regular and continuous basis in school and out of school.
- The group has visual symbols—insignia, greeting patterns, distinguishing dress, and so on—that readily identify one as either a member or nonmember.
- The group engages in delinquent or criminal activity. Delinquent and/or criminal activity is what differentiates a gang from organizations that often are otherwise visually consistent with stereotypic images of a gang.

School personnel need to become familiar with the symbols, terms, phrases, and other identifiers of gang presence. Figure 5.3 describes telltale signs suggesting the presence of gangs in the school.

The School as a Safe Haven

Schools should be safe places regardless of the nature of the neighborhood from which the students come. This means a zero-tolerance policy for major transgressions. No weapons, no controlled substances, no graffiti—this must be the policy of the school, and all personnel and all students need to be advised of this and what to do when these are discovered. What should be done if this policy is violated? Report it, immediately. The principal's responsibility is to get the transgressor out of contact with the rest of the student body *immediately*. If it is a criminal act, then other agencies need to get involved as well.

The school is not the only agency that has a stake in an orderly and safe environment. Large and small communities are depending more and more on an interagency approach. On any principal's phone list ought to be the numbers of the police juvenile division, Child Protective Services

ISLLC 3

officers, juvenile court officials, Crime Stoppers organizations, and any departments of youth development, whatever they might be entitled. Additionally, the school records office needs to have
the number and name of the responsible adult in the youth's home. Some success has been achieved
in such cities as Chicago, Baltimore, and Knoxville, among others, where schools and mayors' offices have moved to develop formal councils and networks to provide for interagency cooperation.

The Counseling Program

Counseling programs are too often thought of as an array of activities extended to the classroom by a designated person called a guidance counselor. Our position is that this approach is
totally inadequate and at times counterproductive to the needs of students. A good counseling
program needs to include teachers in a direct and organized way and avoid overreliance on
guidance counselors.

ISLLC 2

Guidance counselors often experience the highly unrealistic expectations of their
colleagues. In these days of troubling anonymity in large school units, of drop-ins and spiritual
drop-outs, an approach different from that, which locates all counseling responsibilities in one
office, is required. The need is for a total school commitment to the counseling function.

A different way of organizing counseling services is needed *not* because trained *guidance*
counselors aren't important, but because in their skills are not being used maximally. The function
of counseling is so critical to the development of students that a better approach must be employed.

Student advisement and guidance in the elementary and middle schools especially should remain the function of the classroom teacher, and a continued effort should be made to include teachers as part of a counseling team in the secondary schools as well. The main problem the classroom
teacher faces in organizing an effective student advisement program is usually one of time. There
are ways, however, to gain time for student counseling. Organizing activities and dividing some of
the responsibilities with other appropriate personnel can assist teachers in this endeavor.

Nevertheless, the basic advisement and guidance functions to be performed for a particular
student need to be in the hands of a single professional—someone who has a picture of the
whole student. A person designated as school guidance counselor with the usually recommended
student-to-counselor rates of 300 to 1 cannot be expected to develop such relationships; only
perfunctory interpersonal encounters are probable. It is absurd to think otherwise.

Advisor–Advisee Systems

A teacher–student advisement system can result in better student counseling. In one such system,
each teacher assumes responsibility for the curricular decisions and learning goals for a particular group of students. The ratio of students to advisor is based on the total student-to-staff ratio in
the school. Many schools involve every professional staff member in the school, including the
principal, librarian, and specialists. Involving everyone reduces the ratio and also provides every
staff member with direct student contact on an individual basis. Advisors become mentors.

ISLLC 2

In this approach, a school is divided into clusters, with a counselor and a principal or
assistant principal acting as administrative head. The counselor serves as a "master-advisor" for
15 to 20 teachers advisors. The teacher/advisor has no more than 15 students for whom counseling
is performed.

The teacher/advisor's primary role is to work individually with students in much the same way that formerly was expected of the guidance counselor. The guidance counselor's role is that of expert-consultant to groups of teachers. The teacher/advisor is both friend and advocate and strives to know the student in ways well beyond what a teacher can with the usual classroom loads. He or she is a person to whom the student can talk freely about school problems and work through solutions.

Not all teachers are personally disposed or equally able in such a role. Care needs to be taken to adequately prepare the staff for the role. In-service skill sessions will need to be developed and a good monitoring system maintained if the approach is to work well.

Among the many positive outcomes of such a system, is the reduction of anonymity felt by many students in schools, both large and small. Shyness, transience, previous bad experiences with schooling, poverty, among other symptoms of at-risk students—and the simple human need of all of us for an anchoring friendship in times of need—can be dealt with effectively with a teacher/advisor system.

Organizing Counseling Activities

Three basic counseling activities need to be carried out: group counseling, individual student counseling, and parent conferences.

Group Counseling. Group guidance activities can be of a variety of types. The underlying concept is the advisor's responsibility to aid the students in developing good peer relationships, good personal problem-solving skills, and good attitudes about learning.

Individual Counseling. Individual counseling has two purposes. First, it provides the opportunity for each student to interact with his or her advisor as a friend and confidant. Second, it provides for frequent program planning and evaluation conferences. At the least, biweekly conferences are suggested, and these should function as the main stage for academic planning. The following comments of a teacher describing the preparation for and conduct of counseling sessions are illustrative:

> For each of my students, I have a file folder in a box next to my desk. Every paper completed by that student is placed in that folder after it has been appropriately graded or reviewed. It remains there until the night before our scheduled appointment. Each night I take home the folders of the three students I am to see the next day and regroup and review their papers according to subjects. I also review my notes from earlier conferences with each student and look at the goals we established in previous weeks. I then write down tentative goals that I have in mind for the student for the next two-week period. The next day when that student comes to my desk for his conference, I review with him his schedule of activities and the amount of time that he has spent in each subject area. We then go over his papers and I ask if he is having any particular problems. I will note for him problems I have identified from my review. Next, we look to see whether previously set goals have been achieved and begin our discussion of which goals and learning activities should come next. I prefer that each of my students set goals for themselves rather than for me to always have to suggest them. We each write down the goals agreed upon and identify some of the activities to be done toward each. As might be expected, most are continuations of previously laid plans, but if new interests or needs have developed, these are to be included. Finally, a cover letter is stapled to the entire collection of papers to be taken home to the parent.

FIGURE 5.4   Setting and Recording Student Goals

Advisement Conference Report

Student Name	Term
Advisor	Date

A. Goals set by student and teacher:

B. Adjustments/accomplishments toward previously set goals:

C. Additional teacher comments:

D. Additional student comments:

E. Next conference date: _____

Some teachers prefer to develop systems and forms with which to set and record goals. These can be shared with parents and be made a part of the student's yearly diagnostic file. An example of such a form is shown in Figure 5.4. Such record development and record keeping are greatly facilitated by only a modest use of readily available data-based software programs formatted for the kind of computers that the school owns.

Parent Conferences.   Regular conferences with parents or guardians contribute to the development of a positive learning climate. In addition to as-needed "crisis" conferences, direct relationships between teacher and home should occur in the form of schoolwide planned parent–teacher conferences two or three times a year. These conferences must be carefully organized and scheduled.

ISLLC 4

There are many factors to consider for these schoolwide programs to be successful. For example, two working parents in a home might preclude attendance at parent–teacher conferences scheduled during the normal school day. Similarly, single-parent homes present scheduling problems. Transportation may be a factor, especially if schools are organized on something other than a neighborhood basis. Magnet school programs, for example, present special problems. These and other constraints can be overcome if there is a sincere desire on the part of teachers and other school personnel to do so.

Organizing the conferences can be made a task of a group comprised of community members and teachers, perhaps the responsibility of a parent–teacher organization (PTO) task force. Again, one must be sure that the group that is assigned the task of organizing the effort is generally representative of the neighborhood or community that the local school serves. Also, the bilingual, multicultural norms of school and community members must be considered.

Establishing a Good Advisement Program

Maximum flexibility in advisor assignments can be achieved through the expanded team concept. This will help keep the advisor-to-student ratio reasonable. Advisors should schedule meetings regularly with advisees, both on a group basis and individual basis. The total weekly commitment

ISLLC 3

Figure 5.5   Student Advisement Schedule (week 1 in a two-week cycle; 15 minutes each conference)

	Monday	Tuesday	Wednesday	Thursday	Friday
8:00 Early bus arrivals	David Thomas	Betty Baitland	Bart Herrscher	Maria Hernandez	Makeup
	Classes begin				
11:45	*Lunch*				Makeup
12:15	Douglas Edward	Lori Albright	Rebecca Hughes	Kevin Arthur	
3:00	*Classes end*				
3:10 Late bus departing	Phyllis Selter	Kymberli Nyberg	Will Weber	Kelli Jones	Makeup

to advisor/guidance functions of an individual nature should be approximately four hours per week during the school day while students are available and two hours after school, or when parents are available. Group guidance activities can be built into the regular school schedule, setting aside approximately 30 minutes each day, for a total of 2½ hours each week.

A regular appointment calendar on a two-week rotation should be established, with each student aware of the designated time well in advance of the conference. Figure 5.5 is an example of such a schedule.

Providing adequate time for teacher–student or teacher–parent conferences is of top priority. The more flexible the school program, the easier it is to schedule conferences during the school day. An effective way to provide more conference time is to lengthen the school lunch period an additional 15 or 20 minutes. The provision of an expanded noon activities program, as well as opening the study and instructional media areas, can provide for students who are not having conferences.

Selecting the Advisor.   The advisor must be able to talk with each student on a friendly, personal basis. For this to be accomplished, a good personality match between advisor and student is essential. This is best achieved if several choices for advisor assignment are available. Alternatives for advisor assignment for each student exist when the guidance program is operating on a team or expanded team basis. After staff and students have become acquainted in the fall term, each staff member is assigned an appropriate number of advisees, keeping in mind the needs of each individual student and which team member might best meet those needs.

A school organizational structure that greatly enhances the effectiveness of the advisement program is multiage grouping. This approach places students with a particular team for two or three years; each student keeps the same advisor during that entire period.

Role of the Guidance Counselor

The guidance counselor has a particularly important function. In the system just described, the guidance counselor must assume six responsibilities:

ISLLC 3

1. Become attached to a team and assume an advisor responsibility in order to keep in close touch with the program and with the other specialists within the school
2. Function as a school referral agent for problems identified by the advisor and faculty

3. Conduct diagnostic work beyond that possible for teachers to do

4. Administer and supervise the advisement program. The level of advisement activities proposed in this chapter far exceeds that typically carried out in school. To operate well, a good advisement program requires constant attention, encouragement, and coordination.

5. Provide and direct staff-development activities in the techniques of advisement, including teacher training for both group guidance functions as well as individual student academic diagnostic work and techniques for personal counseling. A major portion of the guidance counselor's role should be spent directly in staff-development activities.

6. Assist the teachers in establishing and maintaining a good in-class student personnel record system. These are the records maintained by the teacher for day-by-day counseling and academic prescriptions.

Student Services

Student services include all of the special support functions outside of the curricular and cocurricular offerings at the building level that impinge on the development of the student. The array of services offered by a school district adds a necessary quality to the individual school operation. The student services professional provides technical services and additional professional insight in the diagnosis, prescription, and treatment of individual learner difficulties as well as balanced programs for all learners. The principal's role is crucial. It is the principal who must provide for the organization, coordination, and articulation of such services at the building level.

ISLLC 4 Most school systems have a number of specialists available to the student to meet needs beyond those that can be met by the regular school staff. Each school should have someone designated to coordinate the special services needs for the school. The guidance counselor is an appropriate referral agent to determine needs for services, as well as for identifying the proper source for those services.

It is good practice for principals to prepare and disseminate a list of available services, as well as a list of people to contact for those services, so that teachers, parents, and other community members will know to whom they can turn for help with particular problems. On such a list would be counselors, including guidance, special education, and attendance; school psychologists; special education resource teachers; pathologists; teachers for the homebound; reading specialists; diagnosticians; and other special personnel provided by the district.

Principal's Role in Coordination and Articulation

With respect to the delivery of student personnel services, the principal is truly the person in the middle—not as a gatekeeper but as a facilitator. Referrals, if not routed directly through the principal, should at least be made with an information copy to the principal. Why? *Everything that goes on in and around the school is the responsibility of the principal,* and that includes proper delivery of support services. The reason for centralizing many student personnel services is because of the systemwide impact of these services. In addition, individual school needs vary widely enough to make it more efficient to centrally house some services to provide maximum access in time of need. Such a model works well, provided the principal recognizes a responsibility to continually be aware of student and teacher needs in the building and to investigate whether their needs are being met in a timely and efficient manner by the student personnel services division.

Summary

For many children and teenagers the school may be the only stable thing in their lives. For some, it is the only place they can get a decent meal. For these and others, it may be the only place they are safe from an otherwise hazardous and unstable world. And for these and others, school may be the only place where they may be rewarded for behaving and succeeding in socially acceptable ways. School should be a place where every student can learn what a civilized world there can be. And so we return to the thoughts of administrator Karon Rilling: "And they will be protected and they will be respected. And we're going to help them learn how life can be."

There is a growing effort by school administrators and teachers to aggressively address issues of bullying, racial tension, and other elements of a poor school culture. Most are accepting the challenges set forth by Houston middle school principal Lisa Weir when she recently said in a newspaper article: "I don't know if we can sit here and say we are going to change the culture but I want to believe we can."[11]

ACTIVITIES

1. Review Case Studies 22, 24, and 25 at the back of this book. Assume data provided relate to a school for which you are principal. Respond to all of the situations. Given the information provided, any reasonable assumptions, and the concepts presented in this chapter, address the issues.
2. Review Case 19. Role-play a counseling session with Timmy.
3. Turn to the ISLLC standards found in Appendix B. Review the functions listed with Standard 2. Reflect on which of the standard items relate directly to the material presented in this chapter. Identify one function to link directly to a concept or idea discussed in Chapter 5.

ENDNOTES

1. Karon Rilling, Ed.D., central office administrator, Austin (Texas) Independent School District, speaking to a graduate class of aspiring principals at the University of Houston.
2. Angus J. MacNeil, "Culture, Climate, and School Outcomes," in *Current Issues in School Leadership,* ed. Larry W. Hughes (Mahwah, NJ: Lawrence Erlbaum Associates, 2005), p. 296.
3. See, for example, Wayne Hoy, J. C. Tarter, and B. Kottcamp, *Open Schools/Healthy Schools: Measuring Organizational Climate* (London: Sage, 1991).
4. *State v. Fond du lac Board of Education,* 63 Wisc. 234, 23 NW 102, 53 Am. Rep, 1985.
5. D. Oxley, *Small Learning Communities Implementing and Deepening Practice* (Portland, OR: Northwest Regional Educational Laboratory, 2004).
6. See the work of Charles Achilles, reported variously by him and others, but recently available in L. W. Hughes (ed.), *Current Issues in School Leadership* (Mahwah, NJ: Lawrence Erlbaum Associates, 2005), Chapter 7, Class Size and Learning.
7. Oxley, *Small Learning Communities Implementing and Deepening Practice,* p. 1.
8. Charles M. Achilles, *Let's Put Kids First, Finally* (Thousand Oaks, CA: Corwin, 1999).

9. C. M. Achilles and P. S. Smith, "Stimulating the Academic Performance of Children," in *The Principal as Leader* (2nd ed.) ed. L. W. Hughes (Upper Saddle River, NJ: Prentice-Hall, 1999), Chapter 9.

10. R. Casella, "Violence and Threats of Violence," in *Current Issues in School Leadership,* ed. L.W. Hughes (Mahwah, NJ: Lawrence Erlbaum Associates, 2005), Chapter 2.

11. Lisa Weir, principal, Memorial Middle School, Houston Independent School District.

SELECTED READINGS

Bencivenga, A. S., and M. J. Elias. "Leading Schools of Excellence in Academics, Character, and Social-Emotional Development." *NASSP Bulletin 87* (December 2003): 60–72.

Fields, L. "Handling Student Fights: Advice for Teachers and Administrators." *The Clearing House 77* (2004): 108–110.

Fishbaugh, Mary Susan, Gwen Schroth, and Terry Berkeley. *Ensuring Safe School Environments: Exploring Issues—Seeking Solutions* (Mahwah, NJ: Lawrence Erlbaum Associates, 2003).

Freiberg, H. Jerome. *School Climate Measuring: Improving and Sustaining Healthy Learning Environments* (Philadelphia: Falmer Press, 1999).

Guldin, M. "Please Respect Me!" *Principal Leadership (High School Ed) 9* no. 5 (2009): 24–27.

Habegger, S. "The Principal's Role in Successful Schools: Creating a Positive School Culture." *NAESP Principal 88* no. 1 (2008): 42–46.

Hirst, R. K. "Reducing Discipline Referrals in Middle School." *Principal 84* (2005): 51.

Hoy, Wayne K., and J. C. Tartar. *The Road to Open and Healthy Schools: A Handbook for Change* (London: Sage, 1991).

Hughes, Larry W. *Current Issues in School Leadership* (Mahwah, NJ: Lawrence Erlbaum Associates, 2005). See especially Chapters 2, 7, 10, and 16.

Johnson, S., and C. Johnson. "Results-Based Guidance: A Systems Approach to Student Support Programs." *Professional School Counseling 6* (2003): 180–184.

Kinney, P. "Safety Relies on Climate. "*Principal Leadership (Middle Sch Ed),* no. 5 (2009): 54.

Lambert, J. "Easing the Transition to High School." *Educational Leadership 7* (2005): 61–63.

Protheroe, N. "A Schoolwide Approach to Discipline." *Principal 84* (2005): 41–44.

Peterson, K., and T. Deal. *Shaping School Culture* (San Francisco: Jossey-Bass, 2003).

Roberts, Warren G. *Bullying from Both Sides* (Los Angeles: Corwin Press, 2005).

Syversten, A. K., C. A., Flanagan, and M. D. Stout, "Code of Silence: Students' Perceptions of School Climate and Willingness to Intervene in a Peer's Dangerous Plan" [Electronic Version]. *Journal of Educational Psychology 101,* no. 1 (2009): 219–232.

Wolk, S. "Joy in Schools." *Educational Leadership 66* (2008): 8–15.

6

The School Curriculum

The purpose of school is not merely to help students achieve academically in school, but to prepare them to lead fulfilling lives.

—ELLIOTT EISNER[1]

L
eadership involves both conservation and innovation. Nowhere is the proper balance between the two more crucial than in the development and management of the school curriculum. As facilitators of these tasks, principals need a thorough knowledge of curriculum theory and philosophy. This knowledge provides a foundation for understanding the purpose and goals of the presented curriculum and creates a greater awareness of how the curriculum might be enhanced to meet the needs of their particular school population. This chapter will explore leadership of the curriculum and the various tasks and dimensions of that responsibility. In addition, the chapter will provide an overview of various curriculum orientations and their implications for enriching the standard curriculum. We begin by considering the principal's role in the administration of the curriculum.

The Principal's Role in Curriculum Administration

The school principal must be an instructional leader. In Chapter 2, we discussed the important role that the principal plays in fostering the empowerment of teachers and in providing the structures that promote "substitutes for leadership,"[2] thereby enabling teacher leadership to emerge. The principal's role as facilitator of that development has everything to do with curriculum leadership. When teachers are allowed to take ownership for their own classrooms, the role of the principal moves far more solidly into the transformational leadership arena than in the transactional one. Providing oversight and leadership from an influential power base rather than from authoritative control allows curriculum-related tasks such as these to be accomplished through shared responsibility:

- Analyzing what subjects, topics, knowledge areas, skills, and abilities should be taught in the school
- Designing, developing, or modifying courses; selecting the knowledge, skills, and abilities to be included; organizing content outlines, objectives, lesson plans, activities, test items; and so on
- Delivering the curriculum; determining the array of available courses; sequencing courses or units; scheduling courses with concern for balance, flexibility, availability, and the like
- Evaluating the curriculum by determining the congruence among course objectives, content taught, and student evaluation, as well as reviewing the relevance of the curriculum for the students and community served.

Of course, the major participants in many of these tasks will be teachers and possibly subject area supervisors. On the other hand, as the field continues to grow in site-based management, coupled with magnet schools and schools of choice, the principal will need to take major oversight responsibility for the restructuring of the curriculum for the local school. Understanding curriculum orientations is a beginning point.

Understanding Curriculum Theory

Curriculum administration is a dynamic rather than static process. It is crucial that the principal and all others who lead in the design and adoption of the school curriculum have an understanding of the philosophical frameworks that help shape curriculum. This knowledge is important, in two

ways: for understanding more completely the nature of the presented curriculum (the conservator's role) and for being prepared to more effectively restructure that curriculum in response to the emerging needs of those being served (the innovator's role).[3] Viewing the organization from a systemic perspective, the leader provides direction as a conservator of curriculum content and delivery, as well as an innovator and advocate for necessary change.

McNeil[4] presented four basic threads of curriculum theory: humanistic, social reconstuctionist, technological, and academic. He provided a frame for understanding these four varied philosophical orientations by considering their respective purposes, how they view the roles of teacher and learner, and the advantages and disadvantages of each orientation. The first two, humanistic theory and social reconstructionism, are cast in the realm of contemporary philosophy stemming from the philosophies of progressivism and reconstructionism[5] and promote the following basic instructional objectives:

- To promote democratic social living
- To improve and reconstruct society; education for change and social reform[6]

The last two, technological and academic curriculum theory, are cast in the realm of traditional philosophy stemming from perennialism and essentialism.[7] These philosophies promote the following objectives:

- To educate the rational person; to cultivate the intellect
- To promote the intellectual growth of the individual; to educate the competent person[8]

Each of the four curriculum orientations will be discussed in detail in the following sections.

The Humanistic Perspective

Purpose.   The humanistic perspective centers on the individual. Emphasis is on maximizing the potential of the individual in all areas: cognitive, affective, and psychomotor. It is a holistic approach to learning. Educating the whole child takes precedence over mere academic achievement. Humanistic curriculum is aimed toward the concepts of individual meaning, freedom, integrity, and autonomy. Based on the theories of such humanists as Abraham Maslow[9] and Carl Rogers,[10] the notions of self-actualization and personal meaning are emphasized. A premium is placed on the "joy of learning" with attention being given to the development of "peak experiences" where cognitive and affective learning take place simultaneously.

Affective development is an integral part of the humanistic curriculum. The focus is on self-awareness and on forming moral and ethical principles for oneself, rather than on "teaching" values as is advocated in many character education programs currently in vogue. Values clarification[11] techniques are often part of the curriculum that stresses the development of intrapersonal and interpersonal intelligence, referred to by Goleman[12] as emotional intelligence. Goleman compared his work with the writings and research of several others, such as Salovey,[13] Gardner,[14] and Sternberg,[15] and concluded that the following domains of emotional intelligence listed by Salovey seem most important to frame his work:

- Knowing one's emotions
- Managing emotions
- Motivating oneself
- Recognizing emotions in others
- Developing relationships[16]

The Principal's Role.   The principal's influence is a necessary ingredient for successfully integrating the humanistic curriculum approach into the school setting. The principal serves as a role model for the important values and behaviors necessary for shaping this curriculum orientation. Human respect forms the cornerstone of humanistic education, and it is the principal who sets the tone and serves as a model for the human relationships necessary to accomplish curriculum goals.

The Teacher's Role.   Central to the humanistic curriculum is the emotional relationship established between the teacher and the student. Trust, acceptance, and mutual understanding form the cornerstones of this relationship. The teacher seeks to establish an atmosphere for learning that enables and calls forth the potential often not recognized by the student alone. A climate of acceptance allows for risk taking, experimentation, and growth as the teacher serves as facilitator of the learning experience. Rogers expressed these qualities in his book, *Freedom to Learn.*[17] The research on effective schools[18] also presents many humanistic characteristics as necessary conditions for the climate that should surround learning.

The Student's Role.   In this approach, the student takes personal responsibility for learning and behavior. Self-direction is encouraged both cognitively and affectively. Students learn to accept and deal with the responsibilities associated with their own behavior as well as learn to form their own opinions and to think creatively. Emphasis is placed on personal independence and autonomy that carries with it the responsibility for one's own actions. It is an intrinsic process designed to foster mature thinking and behavior.

Approaches to Humanistic Education.   The affective dimensions of learning have been emphasized for some time in schools, but generally in the field of counseling. Rogers is a major contributor in shaping the concepts and applications of this approach to the classroom. His book, *Freedom to Learn,* and his emphasis on counseling have been important contributions to this view of curriculum.[19] Glasser has had a similar impact with his work concerning *reality therapy*[20] and the group process approaches to learning that he classifies as *thinking meetings.*[21] Self-awareness and self-discipline are the primary goals in the work of both these researchers rather than the external controls often emphasized in formal discipline plans. The student is encouraged to think for himself or herself and to form opinions and make judgments based on rational consideration of self and others. The student is taught to take responsibility for his or her own learning and behavior through the application of natural consequences.

An emerging interest in humanistic education is also reflected in the concept known as *confluent education.* In this curriculum model, the emphasis is on integration of the affective domain with the cognitive domain in the development of lesson materials. It is often referred to as an "add-on" approach, since emotional domains, attitudes, and values are included with the traditional subject matter. This is done so that the student may experience personal significance in what he or she is learning. The following would be present in a confluent lesson:

- Participation of all in a democratic learning experience
- Integration of thinking, feeling, and responding
- Relevant subject matter that touches the needs and lives of students
- Focus on self as the center of the learning experience
- Aim . . . [is] toward development of the total person within a human society[22]

In all aspects of the humanistic curriculum, there is an emphasis on the holistic nature of learning, or the Gestalt, which is the greatest advantage of this curriculum model. Its integrative nature encourages students to make connections, develop critical awareness, and respond in meaningful, personal ways to their learning experiences.

A Critique.   Major critics point to the difficulty in providing a sequential presentation of concepts and skills with this approach and to its overemphasis on the individual rather than the group. Others see the development of the individual as a necessary precursor to development of the group[23] and view the humanistic curriculum as an approach that encourages civic responsibility and service to others.

Social Reconstructionism

Purpose.   Those who advocate this approach view the curriculum as the agent of social change. Curriculum is considered the vehicle for bringing about needed changes in the social order and is designed to help individuals and groups elevate their oppressed conditions, thereby improving their opportunities to participate fully in a democratic society.

Social responsibility involves finding ways to become an integral part of the group and to come to consensus on important social matters. In this curriculum approach, major emphasis is on developing a strong values base from which to respond and take action relative to the many problems facing society.

Social reconstructionists view an effective curriculum as having three major cornerstones: "It must be *real,* it must require *action,* and it must teach *values.*"[24] Major emphasis is on learning that is relevant to the learner and that is central to the issues students face in their daily lives. No real learning occurs until action is taken on that learning; learning is activity dependent. Social responsibility is central to the purpose of knowledge acquisition.

Social reconstructionists, For example, Michael Apple,[25] Henry Giroux,[26] and Jeannie Oakes,[27] consider current public education to be "reproducing" a social order that is not always consistent with democratic principles and one that continues to maintain a stratified social order. They advocate critical examination of current situations within schools and the use of curriculum as a means of liberating all students to an equal access to a meaningful education. It is their belief that such practices as ability grouping and pullout programs tend to perpetuate a stratified social order.

Closely aligned with the ideas of the reconstructionists are the curriculum futurologists who advocate studying emerging trends and taking action to prevent "bad" futures. Leading proponents of this approach[28] advocate building curriculum by planning the future. These writers do not suggest that students be assisted in *adapting* to a future imposed on them, but that they *take action to prevent* those things that loom as destructive tendencies. Critical theory, or consciousness, separates social reconstruction from social adaptation. Social adaptation is based on an analysis of society but is aimed at helping students adapt to an impending future rather than to question it and take responsible action to prevent it.

The Principal's Role.   The principal's role is leadership oriented. It calls for a continual examination of current practices and the effects of current curriculum on the lives of students.
Principals must serve as values consciousness raisers,[29] problem finders, and visionary leaders who can enable all constituents to be actively engaged in the learning process. In Chapter 1, we discussed the moral and ethical responsibilities that are central to principal leadership in this curriculum orientation. Principals must take special note of situations in which the "hidden curriculum"[30] is creating oppressive situations for certain groups of students and take action to prevent unfair or undemocratic practices from taking place.

The Teacher's Role.   The teacher serves as a facilitator of the learning process. It is the teacher's task to assist students in identifying their interests and connecting those interests to a national and world perspective.[31] In many cases, the teacher serves as a bridge between the community and the student in regard to the special interests that the student might have. Gaining the cooperation and collaboration of outside agencies in establishing service projects and other community-related partnerships is also a part of the teacher's role.

Within the classroom setting, the teacher must be skilled in establishing and working with groups and in promoting opportunities for collaboration among students. Social reconstructionism is a natural curriculum orientation for reinforcing the notions of learning communities (dealt with in Chapter 2).

Approaches to Social Reconstructionism.   Current examples of this curriculum have become prevalent in today's schools: problem-based learning,[32] action learning, and multicultural education. Each of these has implications for student learning as well as teacher learning. In Chapter 13, we discuss five models of staff development for teachers. Two of the models (inquiry and school improvement process) relate to this concept. The social reconstruction orientation to curriculum is also closely related to the current notions of inclusion, cooperative learning groups, teaming, and cohorts, all of which are discussed in other chapters. Now we will discuss a current application of this curriculum orientation: action learning. We will also consider some implications of multicultural education.

Action Learning.   Some 400 seniors in a midwestern high school performed tasks in the community as part of their twelfth-grade social studies class. More than 90 percent of the senior class chose to do community service instead of writing a research paper. The students worked in a variety of endeavors, including political campaigns, voter registration drives, elementary and junior high schools, daycare centers, nursing homes, county recreation departments, and other places where they were needed. The only criterion for selecting placements was that the students work with people, not in clerical jobs. Finding placements for such a large number of students was facilitated by holding a community fair each fall. Community agencies that desired student assistance set up tables or booths and the students shopped around for a volunteer opportunity that interested them and met their time and transportation limits. Students did their volunteer work during unscheduled time during the school day or after school.

Action learning is based on the concept of young people learning by doing and tying this concept into the idea of learning by serving. Learning takes place through a combination of direct experiences and associated instruction or reflection. The purposes that action learning can serve and the student experiences it can offer vary greatly from school to school. The focus can be on "service learning," which connotes activities centered on self-development. All the varied approaches, however, put the emphasis on the personal involvement of young people in the wider community and recognition that learning does and should take place outside the classroom. Actual learning situations can include volunteer services, internships, community surveys and studies, social and political action, shadowing a person to explore a career role, living in another culture, and work experience. Of course, many of these activities are common to some vocational programs, but in fields such as math, English, health, history, and government, the practice to go along with the theory is less common.

Schools that offer action learning identify a variety of objectives for their program:

1. Contribution to a young person's social development and his or her sense of responsibility for the welfare of others
2. Intellectual development—academic subjects take on added significance when students can apply their classroom knowledge to real problems
3. Career education—being able to see firsthand and participate in a variety of possible job roles
4. Benefits to the school—breaking down the barriers between the school and the wider community
5. Benefits to the community—the ability to provide many community services that would not have been possible without student volunteer help

Organizing for Action Learning.   Many different action learning programs have been implemented, each with its own unique characteristics. Analyses of these different programs show five basic types of action learning situations, ranging from minimum integration with the school program to almost total involvement. From least involvement to most, the action learning programs are described here.

A Volunteer Bureau. The school or the student identifies volunteer activities. The work is done during unscheduled time, study hall time, or before or after school. In some cases, arrangements are made for half-day release of all students participating in the volunteer program on a particular day of the week. The staff coordinator of volunteer programs is valuable in providing coordination to the program by identifying and placing students, following up, and reviewing students' work. Each student usually has the prime responsibility for initiating his or her community experience, with the school providing a coordinating function.

Community Service for Credit. The same basic plan arranged as a volunteer bureau can be carried out but adding to it some form of academic credit for student participation. The school may actively promote the program or the student may possibly still be the initiating agent.

Laboratory for Existing Course. Projects organized in conjunction with regular courses are used often in lieu of research papers or other assignments. Students may engage in community activity during school hours or after school, depending on their schedules. Often, as the students become more involved in community projects, course content begins to be altered toward the more practical, useful information, emphasizing teaching systematic observation, data gathering, and community involvement.

Community Involvement Course. A formalized course in community involvement draws on the major features of the laboratory idea (from the previous model) along with the service for course credit concept. The course, though, has its entire structure organized around community involvement and draws all of its data for the course directly from the community. A course title such as Student Community Involvement might be appropriate.

The Action Learning Center. The center leads the students and teachers into the community, where they gain their total experience. This type of course is often interdisciplinary in nature and may be staffed by specialists who repeat the experience several times each year for different groups. Projects such as mountain camp-outs, canoe trips, rebuilding deteriorated homes, and other forms of community action are illustrative of this idea.

Action Learning Guidelines. Guidelines for directing action learning programs have been proposed by the National Association of Secondary School Principals:

1. The program must fill genuine needs of adolescents and of society in involving youth in tasks that are recognized as important by both young people and adults.
2. It must provide a real challenge to students, offering them an opportunity to extend their skills and their knowledge.
3. An opportunity for guided reflection on the service experience is necessary and this opportunity should be continued during the period of service.
4. Successful programs provide participants with the sense of community—that special feeling that comes from sharing a goal and working toward it with others.
5. A learning-by-serving experience should contribute to the knowledge that adolescents need regarding career options open to them in the adult world and offer some opportunities to work cooperatively with competent adults who are models for these options.

6. In format, the program must be both structured and flexible. Many projects have failed because they were too rigid to respond to changing conditions, and others have been unsatisfactory because they were too loosely structured to bring out a clear and continued sense of direction.

7. The program must promote a genuine maturity by allowing young people to exercise adult responsibility and be held accountable for their actions. This means, among other things, that students should actively participate in decision making and governance of the project in which they are learning by serving.

8. The stimulus for a worthwhile project or program can come from innumerable sources, so keep your eyes and minds open for leads as to needs, people, and places. Be particularly alert to hints that young people themselves may drop. They often are closer to the subtle but serious needs of the community than are school teachers and administrators.

9. Try to determine the optimal life span for a given learning-by-serving project and make this an element in planning and administration of the program. Probably more than most other aspects of secondary school curriculum, learning-by-serving programs have a constant need for new blood.

Multicultural Education.   Multicultural education is a field of study that is seen as five dimensional: the integration of content, the construction of knowledge, the reduction of prejudice, the promotion of equity, and the promotion of an empowering school culture and social structure.[33] Certainly, it is about social change through the educational process.

In *The Light in Their Eyes: Creating Multicultural Learning Communities,* Sonia Nieto[34] discusses some basic guidelines in the field. She begins by considering this question: What is learning? She posits that it is comprehensive and takes place in context rather than being restricted merely to academic achievement. Learning, she suggests, develops from social relationships and the actions of individuals. Children need to learn to think and problem solve through collaboration, Socratic questioning, and reflection. These tools assist them in the construction of their own learning. Learning can be enhanced or hindered by the attitudes and beliefs of teachers and administrators within school settings. Nieto presents five principles of learning that she considers essential to a good multicultural curriculum:

ISLLC 2

- *Learning is actively constructed.* Meaning is developed out of experience and through the active construction of knowledge. It is enhanced through dialogue and the development of "habits of mind."
- *Learning emerges from and builds on experience.* Although the experiences of multicultural children differ from those of the mainstream population, they do have important experiences, attitudes, and behaviors that should be utilized in the learning setting. Teacher's attitudes toward these experiences make a difference in the learning of these students.
- *Learning is influenced by cultural differences.* Teachers sometimes fail to consider the impact of culture on the learning process and therefore do not always acknowledge the individual differences of students.
- *Learning is influenced by the context in which it occurs.* In a caring environment, children feel supported and respond in positive ways. On the other hand, regimented, demoralizing climates foster poor self-concept and restrict learning.

■ *Learning is socially mediated and develops within a culture and community.* All children are capable of learning; however, the opportunities for that learning must be made available. Teacher attitude and behavior, along with school structure, can influence the degree of access the student has to learning.

Critique.   One of the major criticisms of the social reconstruction curriculum is that few agree on what is best for the future or present society. As McNeil suggested, "We can expect accelerated curriculum development along reconstructionist lines whenever there is a need to resolve a conflict in values. Such a need often exists in multi-cultural neighborhoods."[35] Within these communities there are certainly differing values, customs, and languages, which can create disagreements about just what the nature of the curriculum should be. As parents become more involved with the schools and schools with the community, there will likely be more opportunities for conflict between the groups as to *what should be taught* and *how it should be taught.*

Technological Curriculum

Purpose.   Often referred to as the *measured curriculum,* this conception of curriculum contains such elements as "behavioral objectives, time on task, sequential learning, positive reinforcement, direct instruction, achievement testing, mastery in skills and content, and teacher accountability."[36] This curriculum orientation is based on general systems philosophy that emphasizes specification of instructional objectives, precisely controlled learning activities designed to achieve those objectives, and criteria for determining mastery of the objectives stated. The curriculum is highly skill based and operates heavily at the lower levels of knowledge acquisition (i.e., knowledge, comprehension, and application). Its purpose is to systematize learning and make it more predictable, reliable, and measurable.

The Principal's Role.   Certainly, the principal functions as a manager in this orientation, although challenging organizational members toward goal accomplishment is a leadership activity. It is the job of the principal to see that things are being taught as they have been designed, to monitor and keep track of progress, to challenge through high expectations, and to ensure that teachers produce high gains in student productivity. In this orientation there is a high degree of authority and oversight to see that what is expected to be accomplished is being accomplished. The principal operates very much in the context of the machine metaphor in the technological orientation with more of an emphasis on a transactional approach than a transformational one.[37]

The Teacher's Role.   The teacher's task is to manage the curriculum that has already been established and to teach according to the "how to" that has been determined. In that sense, the teacher functions almost like a laborer or craftsperson rather than a professional or artist.[38] The teacher must closely monitor students' progress and take responsibility for their success or lack of it.

Approaches to Technological Curriculum.   The technological curriculum is very much present in the form of basic skills acquisition, mastery learning, time on task, curricular alignment, directive teaching models, and other models of sequential curriculum delivery. (Many of these are discussed in Chapter 10.) In a later section of this chapter, we will discuss curricular alignment and planning. For these reasons, little attention is given to the application of this curriculum orientation at this time.

Critique.   One of the major criticisms of the technological orientation is its limitation for con-cept teaching and learning. With its primary focus on basic mastery and lower levels of thinking, it does little to inspire higher-order thinking processes such as analysis, synthesis, and evaluation of concepts. Although more straightforward tasks might be taught more readily by a sequential approach, some believe that the technological approach "is a limited tool for nonprocedural tasks and may even hinder proficiency."[39] Related to this limitation is its almost exclusive focus on subject matter, or cognitive development, to the exclusion of the person, or affective dimension. In defense of this measured curriculum, however, there are some benefits that structure, sequence, and accountability have brought about. As Klein suggested,

> It is compatible with some of the major educational outcomes valued by society—a store of knowledge about the world, command of the basic processes of communication, and exposure to new content arenas. But this conception and design of curriculum cannot accomplish everything students are expected to learn.[40]

Academic Curriculum

Purpose.   The purposes of the academic curriculum are to train minds and to teach students to do research.[41] This orientation to curriculum is based on the idea of a "storehouse of knowledge" that has been handed down from the past and that contains a "body of truths" that is fixed and absolute. In this approach, there is a core of knowledge that every student should possess, and learning is acquiring knowledge through the disciplines. The emphasis is on cognitive development with particular stress on critical thinking based on a rational consider-ation of "truths." Truths are contained in the "three Rs, as well as liberal studies or essential academic subjects."[42]

Much emphasis in this orientation is placed on excellence and maximizing one's potential in the academic realm. Subject matter is important for its own sake, and greater degrees of importance are placed on some subjects than others. The forms and structure of knowledge are as important as the content itself. More recently, however, applications of this curriculum approach have emphasized integrated studies rather than the isolated content previously emphasized.

Efforts to create better integration of concepts have resulted in the redesign of curriculum delivery and often the redesign of schools. One such example is the incorporation of small learning communities within large high schools. These communities are often designed as academies that focus on a concentration of specific disciplines. Through in-depth study in a concentrated area, students gain a deeper understanding of the content presented.

The Principal's Role.   Certainly, the principal must model and encourage excellence! A model of high motivation to achieve must be exemplified. Lifelong learning should be celebrated throughout the school, and the principal should assume a major responsibility to ensure the com-petence of teachers through high standards and supervision.

The Teacher's Role.   The teacher is a disseminator of knowledge or a "sage on the stage." Since teachers serve as authorities relative to their subject areas, they plan and direct the learning activities with less input from students. The mode is typically direct instruction, with little attention devoted to group involvement or creative thinking activities.

ISLLC 2

Approaches to Academic Curriculum. Some of the more current applications of the academic curriculum include a renewed interest in a core curriculum in both the university and public school arenas. The back-to-basics movement and the idea of a national curriculum advocated by writers such as Hirst[43] and others tend to reinforce this idea. A particularly popular application of the academic model is the *Paideia Proposal,* which emphasizes a uniform educational system based on a course of study including such offerings as philosophy, literature, history, mathematics, natural science, and fine arts. It focuses on critical thinking and moral judgment and eliminates such "frills" as vocational education.

A second approach to the academic curriculum can be found in the concept of integrated studies. This movement is particularly popular in the middle school movement and is facilitated through the use of teams. Chapter 7 of this text addresses ways in which schools can be structured for maximum utilization of this approach.

Critique. This academic approach has been criticized by some for being too "adult focused" and uninspiring to students. There appears to be too much emphasis on content and not enough on process. In addition, there is little emphasis on the application of knowledge, which makes relevance even more difficult to establish.

Each of the orientations presented is important to consider as a "piece" of the total curriculum available to students. Certainly no single model has all that is needed to produce a balanced curriculum. The most effective curriculum is one in which there is a blend of several approaches. We now turn our attention away from *why we teach what we do* to *what we teach and how it should be taught.*

Curriculum Analysis

The introduction to this chapter discusses the pressures schools face in determining the curriculum. The school staff must have an orderly, logical way of going about the task of making curriculum decisions. The first step is often one of determining if the curriculum decision is theirs to make. Many states have curriculum requirements imposed by their legislatures or state departments of education. In other cases, local boards of education determine what subjects are to be taught. In reality, few, if any, decisions on course offerings or the number of hours of instruction in a certain subject are left to the local school.

The local school's role in curriculum analysis generally has two domains. One is to select a few elective offerings for the curriculum; for most schools, this is a relatively minor part of the overall curriculum. The more significant task is the responsibility to determine the content to be taught in almost every course in the school. Policymakers may determine course offerings by title, but rarely do they dictate the detail of the knowledge, skills, and abilities (KSAs) to be included within the courses. States often provide curriculum guides and some local school districts will provide prescribed content outlines, but usually the detail of what is to be taught is left up to the local school.

The responsibility for determining the detail of curriculum content for the school needs to be assumed by the professional staff of the school under the leadership of the principal. If the staff does not act collectively, the task will go by default to the individual teacher or the author of the selected textbook.

ISLLC 2

The determination of the content (KSAs) of virtually every course and subject offered by the school should be the result of a joint effort by two or more faculty members. Curriculum requests, such as the ones mentioned at the beginning of this chapter, should be submitted to the appropriate faculty curriculum team for consideration.

Curriculum committees can be organized around either a grade level or subject matter. Grade-level committees develop the content for the entire curriculum for a particular grade. This is a common elementary school approach, but it is becoming popular as a way to review middle school and high school curriculum as well. This approach emphasizes the *horizontal* dimension of the curriculum, which usually includes all the subjects available to a student at a given time. When a student is said to participate daily or weekly in social studies, English, science, mathematics, health, art, music, and physical education, one is describing the horizontal dimension of the curriculum. The horizontal structure of most U.S. schools is relatively uniform, and curricular areas are almost standard among schools and among grade levels. The horizontal balance remains about the same from year to year, providing students with equal amounts of time in each subject area.

Schools that are departmentalized, such as some upper elementary and junior high schools, have an additional problem with horizontal organization. The departmentalization creates *compartmentalization,* and the several disciplines taught are often not well coordinated or integrated for the students but taught as separate and unrelated bodies of knowledge.

An interdisciplinary curriculum using combinations of subjects offers ways to reestablish the integration of school subjects. In the lower elementary grades, this is best represented with so-called whole-language programs. This is a pedagogical movement away from discrete skills sequencing in the teaching of reading, for example. The approach integrates listening, speaking, reading, writing, and critical thinking. The whole-language approach is based on literature and subject matter and is heavily based on student experience rather than issuing from teacher-prepared worksheets and other didactic materials.

Subject matter curriculum committees develop the content for a particular subject area such as social studies. The committees review and plan social studies content for all courses within one discipline for combinations of grades, such as K–5, 6–8, or 9–12. This subject matter approach is effective in providing good vertical articulation for the curriculum.

The sequence of the skills or topics taught within a particular course of study over time—week by week, semester to semester, or year to year—represents the *vertical* dimension of the curriculum. Many resources are available to provide suggestions to the school or system's staff in the development of curriculum guides, including objectives and test items for vertical organization.

Curriculum Design and School Improvement

Each school serves a unique community. Therefore, each school must ultimately take responsibility for the design and development of its own curriculum. The principal provides the leadership for these tasks working through the faculty. The faculty curriculum committees organized for curriculum analysis can build on their earlier curriculum analysis efforts and continue with the design and development tasks.

ISLLC 2

Effective schools research identified the importance of a well-designed curriculum structure to the development of effective schools. The recommended structure included for each subject or

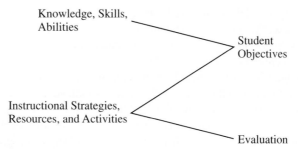

FIGURE 6.1   Curriculum Structure

course is a list of knowledge, skills, and abilities; specific student outcomes to be accomplished; well-designed lesson plans with instructional strategies, activities, and resources identified and matched to expected outcomes; and evaluation items created for each objective with a recommended mastery level for the evaluation. Each of these components is coordinated to achieve congruence throughout the curriculum, as shown in Figure 6.1.

Objectives and test items developed for the various course structures should be analyzed for the depth of learning they require. A classification system such as Bloom's Taxonomy[44] provides a method to determine the level of learning being expected of students. Bloom's Taxonomy of Cognitive Objectives, which includes the domains of knowledge, comprehension, application, analysis, synthesis, and evaluation, is valuable in ensuring that high-order skills are developed within the various disciplines.

The course outlines, objectives, and tests should be used by all teachers in the school who might be teaching that particular subject at that grade level. These curriculum structures, in some cases, may be based on a state-approved curriculum, may be organized around a particular text series developed by a districtwide curriculum committee, or may be constructed by the teacher or teachers in an individual building. The prescribed curriculum should be at least the work of two or more professionals and determined in concert by their joint effort.

Any discussion of curriculum must heed the effects of maturation on changes in student interests and needs. Several notions in particular are significant when considering the organization of a school. The first is that all children do not mature at the same rate; thus, all are not ready for the same curriculum at the same time. The difference in maturation of boys and girls is obvious, both physically and mentally. The same variation in size, mental capacity, interests, and needs also exists within children of the same gender at a given age, only to be in a different balance or relationship after several more years of maturation. These differences should have a bearing on both instructional techniques and curriculum offerings, as well as on ways of grouping students.

Curriculum Delivery

Although curriculum delivery may seem to be largely the responsibility of the teaching staff, many major delivery tasks encompass the entire school, thereby requiring the leadership of the principal. These include determining which courses are to be offered, sequencing courses and/or units, and scheduling courses with concern for curriculum balance, continuity, flexibility, and availability. In addition, materials and equipment must be made available for quality instruction in today's world of changing technology.

An important aspect of curricular organization from the effective schools research is the concept of *curricular alignment*.[45] Once a structured curriculum has been adopted and supposedly implemented for each subject area, the questions become: Are the teachers following it? Is the content presented to the students the same as indicated by the stated curriculum? The teacher who takes the student only two-thirds of the way through the prescribed topics for the year is out of alignment with the planned curriculum. The classroom teacher who spends an inordinately large amount of time on his or her favorite topic and slights or ignores the prescribed topics is out of alignment with the agreed-upon curriculum.

The concept of curricular alignment is particularly significant when accountability for learning is important. If the school's evaluation system of either standardized achievement tests or criterion-referenced tests is matched to the anticipated curriculum, a serious curricular alignment problem could lower test scores significantly for students who were never given the opportunity to master the content measured by the tests. Curricular alignment includes, therefore, the alignment or coordination of what is taught with what is to be measured.

Curricular alignment, however, is more global than just the match between what is taught and what is measured. It also encompasses the articulation and coordination of the school's philosophy to goals, goals to objectives, objectives to instruction, and instruction to evaluation. For example, if the school's philosophy includes the statement "We believe critical thinking and decision-making skills are important for every student to develop," then a goal should exist such as "to provide courses that help students develop critical thinking skills." Objectives also need to exist that speak to developing critical thinking skills—to illustrate, "a student will be able to demonstrate critical thinking skills by (1) defining a problem, (2) identifying and judging information relative to the problem, and (3) solving the problem and drawing conclusions." Instructional activities at a variety of levels of sophistication need to be incorporated into the several different courses, and, finally, test items need to be utilized that are designed to measure critical thinking skills. The lack of any of these items may result in curricular misalignment.

If good teaching is an art, should classroom teachers have the freedom to change, adapt, and take advantage of unique opportunities for learning as they evolve? Freedom in the classroom certainly is desirable, but it can be thought of primarily as a concern of teaching technique or strategy and should not necessarily be a problem of content or curriculum unless a teacher drifts too far from a prescribed curriculum. If that occurs, then maybe it is time to evaluate the approved curriculum or otherwise indicate to teachers that they are expected to follow the agreed-upon plans.

Curriculum Flexibility

It is important for schools to give adequate attention to individual differences and varying maturity rates and levels and to recognize that student interests and needs are broadly based. The organization of a school program must account for these needs, interests, and capabilities in all their diversity and provide learning experiences that will motivate all students.

ISLLC 2

If individual differences are to be recognized, both the vertical and horizontal dimensions of the curriculum require flexibility. Figure 6.2 illustrates the three different rates of learning. Since most children vary from the norm, the curriculum needs to be organized to allow each child to progress individually, as shown by lines A, B, and C.

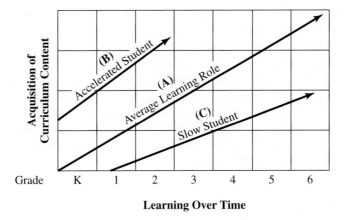

FIGURE 6.2   Impact of Individual Differences and Rates of Learning on Curriculum Needs

The organization must allow both child B and child C access to appropriate information as it is sequenced according to the difficulty of concepts and materials. The achievement of the student over time will depend, then, on the capability of the student to learn and the time committed to that subject.

In subjects such as reading and mathematics, the traditional assumption has been that all basic skills are taught in the elementary school. However, because of their slow maturation rates, many children in fact have not learned these basic skills at a satisfactory level in each grade. Therefore, these subjects must be continued through the middle school years and on into high school.

Curriculum Continuity

How much freedom should a student have to pursue needs and interests when curriculum selection is determined? Should a student have unlimited choice, or should he or she be guided according to some plan? Should the student have few curricular choices and be expected to take all required subjects? How can the school arrange curricular opportunities for the student who can move rapidly up a vertical skill sequence ladder, for the student who progresses at a slower rate, for the student who wants or needs an extremely broad range of content areas, and for the student who must concentrate on basic skills? In the past, educators have not differentiated for individual students but have provided a very basic curriculum for everyone, allowing for little variation. This traditional curriculum included the same basic subjects in each year of a child's education.

Curriculum Balance

The school is under frequent pressure to expand its curricular offerings. However, the time available for instruction has remained relatively constant although there is increasing interest in extending the length of the school year. Even so, only a limited number of hours each day are available for instruction. Difficult and sensitive decisions must be made to determine what alterations in the curriculum offer the best promise of an enhanced learning environment. Frequently, too, many aspects of the curriculum and the time allotted are mandated by state rules and regulations.

ISLLC 1

Nevertheless, there are many aspects of the curriculum that are at the discretion of local boards of education and schools.

Each school should have guidelines to use in making good decisions about these discretionary aspects and to provide a balanced curriculum free from momentary fads or the wishes of special-interest groups. John Goodlad, in his book *A Place Called School,*[46] suggests that adequate attention be paid to each of the "five fingers" of the curriculum each year. His five fingers, which come from the Harvard report published in *General Education in a Free Society,* are mathematics and science, literature and language, society and social studies, the arts, and vocational programs. Goodlad indicates that he feels elementary programs are too heavily directed toward language arts and mathematics.

Summary

The school principal plays a leadership role in curriculum design and administration. Various curriculum orientations form the foundation for determining not only *what* is being taught but what *should be* taught and *why.* Curriculum design is an important joint responsibility between principal and teachers. In this chapter, and we have presented a foundation for analyzing the curriculum and adapting it to fit the unique needs of the school.

ACTIVITIES

1. Reflect on the curriculum structure and offerings in your own school. Identify one or more areas where restructuring should take place. Why do you believe so? Apply the concepts of this chapter to your school. How would you proceed to restructure your school's curriculum?
2. Review Cases Studies 7, 13, 16, and 29 at the end of this book. Analyze the problems presented and apply the curriculum concepts developed in this chapter. What approach would you use in addressing the problems? Set forth a strategy to overcome the difficulties faced by the school as well as ways to deal with individuals in the cases.
3. Turn to the ISLLC standards found in Appendix B. Review the functions listed with Standard 2. Reflect on which of the standard items relate directly to the concepts of curriculum presented in this chapter. How do the concepts of curriculum development and organization match Standard 2? Identify one function to link directly to a concept or idea discussed in Chapter 6.

ENDNOTES

1. Elliot Eisner, "What Is the Purpose of School?" *ASCD Update 32,* no. 19 (December 1990): 4.
2. Thomas Sergiovanni, *Moral Leadership: Getting to the Heart of School Improvement* (San Francisco: Jossey-Bass, 1992).
3. Christopher Hodgkinson, *The Philosophy of Leadership* (Oxford, England: Basil Blackwell Publisher, 1983).
4. John McNeil, *Curriculum: A Comprehensive Introduction* (3rd ed.). (Boston: Little, Brown, 1985).
5. Allan Ornstein, "Philosophy as a Basis for Curriculum Decisions," in *Contemporary Issues in Curriculum,* ed. Allan C. Ornstein and Linda Behar-Horestein (Boston: Allyn & Bacon, 1995).
6. Ibid., p. 16.
7. Ibid.
8. Ibid.
9. Abraham Maslow, "A Theory of Motivation," *Psychological Review* (July 1943): 388–389.
10. Carl Rogers, *Freedom to Learn for the 1980s* (2nd ed.). (Columbus, OH: Merrill, 1988).
11. Values clarification is a technique quite common in gifted education. It is based on the idea that the learners should be able to explore their own feelings and values and make their own choices.

12. Daniel Goleman, *Emotional Intelligence* (New York: Bantam Books, 1995).

13. Goleman credits Salovey as being the first one to coin the term *emotional intelligence* in an article with John Mayer entitled "Emotional Intelligence," in *Imagination, Cognition, and Personality 9* (1990): 185–211.

14. Howard Gardner, *Multiple Intelligences: The Theory in Practice* (New York: Basic Books, 1993).

15. Robert Sternberg, *Beyond I.Q.* (New York: Cambridge University Press, 1985).

16. Goleman, *Emotional Intelligence,* p. 43.

17. Rogers, *Freedom to Learn.*

18. Effective schools research is usually divided into correlates. One of those correlates, the school climate, addresses many of the principles of humanistic curriculum in terms of setting the tone of the setting and the relationship between teacher and student.

19. Carl Rogers, *Client-Centered Therapy* (Boston: Houghton Mifflin, 1951) and *A Way of Being* (Boston: Houghton Mifflin, 1981).

20. William Glasser, *Schools Without Failure* (New York: Harper & Row, 1968).

21. Ibid.

22. Stewart B. Shapiro, "Developing Models by 'Unpacking' Confluent Education." Occasional Paper no. 12, *Development and Research in Confluent Education* (Santa Barbara: University of California, 1972).

23. Refer to the cohort concept and model discussed in Chapter 2 of this text.

24. McNeil, *Curriculum: A Comprehensive Introduction,* p. 32.

25. Michael Apple, *Education and Power* (Boston: Routledge and Kegan Paul, 1982) and *Teachers and Texts: A Political Economy of Class and Gender Relations in Education* (New York: Routledge & Kegan, 1986).

26. Henry Giroux, *Critical Pedagogy, the State, and Cultural Struggle* (Albany: University of New York Press, 1989).

27. Jeannie Oakes, "Limiting Students' School Success and Life Chances: The Impact of Tracking," in *Contemporary Issues in Curriculum,* ed. Allan C. Ornstein and Linda Behar-Horenstein (Boston: Allyn & Bacon, 1999), pp. 227–234.

28. Harold Shane, *Educating for a New Millennium* (Bloomington IN: Phi Delta Kappan, 1981).

29. See Chapter 1 for a detailed discussion of transformational leadership.

30. The *hidden curriculum* refers to learning that takes place unintended from the formal curriculum.

31. McNeil, *Curriculum: A Comprehensive Introduction.*

32. E. Bridges and P. Hallinger, *Implementing Problem Based Learning in Leadership Development* (Eugene: University of Oregon, 1995), ERIC Clearinghouse on Educational Management.

33. J. A. Banks, "Multicultural Education: Historical Development, Dimensions, and Practice," in *Handbook of Research on Multicultural Education,* ed. J. A. Banks and C. A. Banks (New York: Macmillan, 1995), pp. 3–24.

34. Sonia Nieto, *The Light in Their Eyes: Creating Multicultural Learning Communities* (New York: Teachers College Press, 1999), pp. 100–109.

35. McNeil, *Curriculum: A Comprehensive Introduction,* p. 39.

36. M. Frances Klein, "Alternative Curriculum Conceptions and Designs," in *Contemporary Issues in Curriculum,* ed. Allan C. Ornstein and Linda Behar-Horenstein (Boston: Allyn & Bacon, 1999).

37. Linda Darling-Hammond, "Teacher Evaluation in the Organizational Context: A Review of the Literature," *Review of Educational Research 53,* no. 3 (Fall 1983): 285–328.

38. McNeil, *Curriculum: A Comprehensive Introduction,* p. 53.

39. Klein, "Alternative Curriculum Conceptions and Designs," p. 31.

40. Ibid.

41. McNeil, *Curriculum: A Comprehensive Introduction,* p. 70.

42. McNeil, *Curriculum: A Comprehensive Introduction.*

43. Paul Hirst, *Knowledge and the Curriculum* (London: Routledge & Kegan Paul, 1974).

44. Benjamin S. Bloom and others, *The Taxonomy of Educational Objectives: Effective and Cognitive Domains* (New York: David McKay, 1974).

45. W. Fredrick, "The Use of Classroom Time in High Schools Above or Below the Median Reading Score," *Urban Education 11* (January 1977): 459–464.

46. John A. Goodlad, *A Place Called School* (New York: McGraw-Hill, 1983).

SELECTED READINGS

Balfour, L., and A. MacKenzie. "Involving Teachers in Curriculum Change." *Principal (Reston, Va) 88,* no. 4 (2009): 48. Retrieved June 10, 2009 from Education Full Text database.

Eisner, Elliot. "The Art and Craft of Teaching," in *Contemporary Issues in Curriculum,* ed. Allan Ornstein and Linda Behar (Boston: Allyn & Bacon, 1999).

Eisner, Elliot. *The Educational Imagination* (3rd ed.). (New York: Macmillan, 1993).

Fitzharris, L. "Making All the Right Connections." *Journal of Staff Development 26* (2005): 24–28.

Gardner, Howard. *Frames of Mind: The Theory of Multiple Intelligences* (New York: Basic Books, 1983).

Goodlad, J. L. *A Place Called School* (New York: McGraw-Hill, 1984).

Greene, Maxine. "Philosophy and Teaching," in *Handbook of Research on Teaching* (3rd ed.), ed. Merlin C. Wittrock (New York: Macmillan, 1986).

Griffin, Gary A. "Leadership for Curriculum Improvement: The School Administrator's Role," in *Critical Issues in Curriculum: The 87th Yearbook of the National Society for the Study of Education,* ed. Laurel Tanner (Part I, pp. 244–266). (Chicago: University of Chicago Press, 1988.)

Hughes, Larry W. *The Principal as Leader* (New York: Macmillan, 1999).

Ingram, N., D. C. Virtue, and J. L. Wilson. in "Overcoming Obstacles to Curriculum Integration, L.E.S.S. Can Be More!" [Electronic Version]. *National Middle School Association Middle School Journal 40* (2009): 1–11

Jacobs, Heidi Hayes (Ed.). *Interdisciplinary Curriculum: Design and Implementation* (Arlington, VA: Association for Supervision and Curriculum Development, 1989).

Kozol, J. *Savage Inequalities: Children in America's Schools* (New York: Crown, 1991).

March, J. K., and K. H. Peters. "Curriculum Development and Instructional Design in the Effective Schools Process." *Phi Delta Kappan 83,* no. 5 (2002): 379–381.

Mathews, J. "Meeting the Challenge." *Principal Leadership (Middle School Ed.) 5,* no. 7 (2005): 22–26.

Mizelle, N. "Moving Out of Middle School." *Educational Leadership 62,* no. 7 (2005): 56–60.

Petrilli, P. "Closing the Reading Gap." *Principal 84,* no. 4 (2005): 32–35.

Popham, W. "Content Standards: The Undecided Conspirator." *Educational Leadership 64,* no. 1 (2006): 87–88.

Popham, W. J. "Who Should Make the Test?" *Educational Leadership 65,* no. 1 (2006): 80–82.

Saban, A. "Toward a More Intelligent School." *Educational Leadership 60* (2002): 71–73.

Sergiovanni, Thomas J. "The Roots of School Leadership." *Principal 74,* no. 2 (November 1994): 6–9.

Slavkin, M. "Engaging the Heart, Hand, Brain." *Principal Leadership 3* (2003): 20–25.

Sternberg, Robert, J. "A Three-Faced Model of Creativity," in *The Nature of Creativity,* ed. Robert J. Sternberg (New York: Cambridge University Press, 1988), pp. 125–147.

Wraga, W. G. "Toward a Connected Core Curriculum" [Electronic Version]. *Educational Horizons 87,* no. 2 (2009): 88–96.

7

Promoting Student Achievement

Quality comes not from inspection but from improvement of the process.

—W. EDWARDS DEMING[1]

A s educators, high student achievement is something we all desire. In recent years it has become both a state and national priority among political leaders as well. As a result, the landscape of education and the role of the principal have changed dramatically. Today, accountability, high-stakes testing, and student assessment are in the forefront of educators' thinking. Principals' and teachers' jobs are on the line if student test scores do not reach certain levels. And in extreme cases, even schools and districts are at risk of being taken over by state government if test scores fail to meet minimum standards.

ISLLC 2   The temptation for educators is to attempt the quick fix and to chase the test. Although there is something to be said for curriculum alignment and to be sure that all students learn how to take tests, these are only quick patches on the system and will produce only short-term gains. Students are not really learning more or developing better life skills but are only becoming better test takers or studying more directly what the test designers deem to be important. What does it really take to produce high student achievement in any school that can be sustained over time? This chapter focuses on issues of improved student learning as a sustainable and meaningful process of promoting student achievement.

Instruction and Learning

If *curriculum* can be defined most simply as what is taught in the school, then instruction is the *how*—the methods and techniques that support and aid students in their learning. The emphasis in instruction should be on student learning, not on teaching, but obviously both are significant.

Consideration of instruction as the process for providing content, or the *what,* to the learner presents several major problems to the thoughtful organizer of the school program. These can best be presented as a series of questions:

- What is the nature of the learner?
- How is learning going to be measured?
- How can students best be organized?
- What instructional processes are available to be used?
- How do these processes accommodate individual differences?
- What are the implications of these instructional processes for the other organizational components of the school?
- How can these processes be improved?

In this chapter we answer these questions through the lens of the curriculum discussed in the previous chapter. This orientation rests heavily on the academic and technological orientations to curriculum that assume a *discrepancy* view of teaching. Such a view suggests that one must first determine *what should be taught* and then plan accordingly. The true judgment of the effectiveness of that teaching will then determine *what is learned* based on what was intended.

Instruction is the lifeblood of the school. It is the process by which content, or curriculum, is transported to the student. Instruction, however, requires a learner who gains insight, acquires information, and forms values not only from the content of the curriculum but also through the processes by which the content is presented (i.e., instruction). Therefore, the entire learning environment of the school constantly provides content for learning. This entwining of curriculum and instruction forces school administrators to look very carefully not only at what they teach in the school but also at how they teach it, for the medium is truly the message.

Individual Differences among Children

Let us begin by looking at the learner. How different are children from each other? And what differences are important to consider when organizing a school? Differences can be found in children's intelligences, learning abilities, height, weight, age, gender, interests, needs, ethnic backgrounds, learning styles, achievements, and personalities. But before determining which differences matter in school organization, we should consider what these differences really are. Obviously, as children mature, differences increase. Many characteristics can be measured against accepted fixed scales and spoken of in fairly concrete terms. Items such as gender or ethnic background remain fixed and can usually be described in specific terms. However, factors such as abilities, interests, needs, learning styles, and personalities are far more difficult to assess, for they are far more complex, varied, and changeable. As a result, efforts to classify people become more dependent on other constructs for definition and therefore less exact. For example, rarely will a single continuum suffice in a description of ability or intelligence.[2] Ability or intelligence to do what? To be meaningful, ability descriptions must also be scaled in some way. Ability compared to what or to whom? Ability to do something or to do something better than someone else? Comparative information, then, is necessary in studying or determining differences in abilities because of the abstract nature of terms such as *ability*.

One reason for looking at individual differences is to determine the conditions they may set for organization. Individual differences obviously affect the way instruction and curriculum are organized. Contributing to these organizational decisions will be decisions relating to grouping children. *Achievement* is most often used as a basis for predicting *ability*. As a result, the two terms become inappropriately interchanged. Achievement relative to various intelligences can be measured with a fairly high degree of accuracy; in contrast, translating achievement into ability is fraught with danger because of the inability to always know of those factors contributing to a student's opportunity to achieve.

For example, a child may have the ability to be an excellent computer programmer, but if he or she has never had the opportunity to sit at a computer terminal, future performance is uncertain. Thus, to take past achievements with computers as a predictor of future success would be erroneous. More thought about the conditions or circumstances under which past achievement occurred needs to take place before making instructional decisions.

If one is going to look not at ability but at achievement as a determinant for organizing children for learning, what kind of differences should one expect to find in a school population? Studies done at the University of Minnesota in the early 1940s, that still hold today, established this simple rule of thumb to indicate an achievement range[3]: The achievement range of an age group of children is equal to approximately two-thirds of their chronological age. A group of 6-year-old children will have an achievement range of four years; a group of 9-year-olds will have an achievement range of six years. In other words, the slowest 9-year-old will be approximately equal to an average 6-year-old (three years below), and the fastest 9-year-old will be approximately equal to an average 12-year-old (three years above). Figure 7.1 illustrates the formula for school-age children. Note particularly the overlap of achievement over any three-year age span. A group of 6-year-olds, a group of 7-year-olds, and a group of 8- year-olds have a broad range of achievements in common. The extremes contribute only fractional differences across the several years.

School Accountability and Student Achievement

The variation in the children that arrive to school, plus the environmental factors that further compound individual differences, is tremendous. Despite overwhelming student diversity, educators are still responsible to maximize student learning for all and to be accountable. This certainly requires excellence in all school leaders' actions, but it also demands that the tools at hand are used wisely.

Federal Initiatives toward Testing and Accountability

On January 8, 2002, President George W. Bush signed into law the No Child Left Behind (NCLB) Act of 2001. The act was a major reform of the Elementary and Secondary Education Act (ESEA) that was first enacted in 1965. The NCLB Act redefined the federal role in K–12 education and was supposed to help close the achievement gap between disadvantaged and minority students and their peers. The act was based on four basic principles: stronger accountability for results, increased flexibility and local control, expanded options for parents, and an emphasis on teaching methods that have been proven to work.

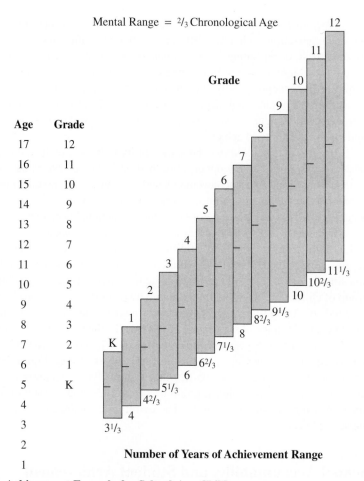

Mental Range = $^2/_3$ Chronological Age

Age	Grade
17	12
16	11
15	10
14	9
13	8
12	7
11	6
10	5
9	4
8	3
7	2
6	1
5	K
4	
3	
2	
1	

Number of Years of Achievement Range

FIGURE 7.1   Achievement Formula for School-Age Children

On the accountability theme, the NCLB Act was to strengthen Title I accountability by re-quiring states to implement statewide accountability systems covering all public schools and stu-dents. These accountability systems must be based on adopted state standards in reading and mathematics, *annual testing* for all students in grades 3 through 8, and annual statewide progress objectives designed to ensure that all groups of students reach proficiency within 12 years (2013). Assessment results and state progress objectives were to be broken out by poverty, race, ethnicity, disability, and limited English proficiency to ensure that no group is left behind. School districts and schools that fail to make adequate yearly progress (AYP) toward statewide profi-ciency goals will, over time, be subject to improvement, corrective action, and restructuring mea-sures aimed at getting them back on course to meet state standards. Schools that meet or exceed objectives or close achievement gaps were to be eligible for state academic achievement awards.[4]

The No Child Left Behind Act has resulted in the creation of assessments in each state that measure what children in grades 3 through 8 know and learn in reading and math. Student

ISLLC 6

progress and achievement have been measured according to tests that are given to every child, every year. The act provides parents, citizens, educators, administrators, and policymakers with data from those annual assessments available in annual report cards on school performance and on statewide progress. These yearly reports give parents information about the performance of their children's schools on these tests, the qualifications of teachers, and their children's progress in key subjects.

Norm-Referenced Tests

Two major types of achievement tests are used in schools: norm-referenced tests and criterion-referenced tests and both are used in NCLB assessments. Norm-referenced tests use the group as the basis for comparison; criterion-referenced tests are based on specific content or standards found in the curriculum.

Almost all schools rely heavily on the *norm-referenced achievement test,* or what is sometimes referred to as a *standardized achievement test,* for their student accountability systems. Norm-referenced tests compare each students or a collection of students (e.g., a classroom, school, or district), against the group (norm) to conduct their analysis. The norming group may be local, state, national, international, or some other specifically defined population. Test items are selected in the various subjects based on each item's ability to discriminate among the various respondents. According to test designers, a good test item is generally considered to be one that higher-achieving students get right and lower-achieving students get wrong. Items that most students can get right, do not often make good norm-referenced achievement test items—even though their content is taught in the school's curriculum—because they do not discriminate between high-achieving and low-achieving students. Don't forget: The purpose of these tests is to allow educators to compare groups or norms, not necessarily to measure what a student knows about a specific body of knowledge.

Comparisons to the norm group are made with several different types of derived or standardized scores. Remember, raw scores only identify the number of questions answered correctly on a test or subtest. Rarely, if ever, do educators use the raw score for any reporting purpose. Rather, they create a variety of *standard scores* that have been derived by comparing an individual student's raw score to the scores of the norming population.[5] Use of the phrase *the child is on grade level* or the term *grade-level equivalent* generally refers to student scores that met the average (or 50th percentile) of all the children of a particular age who took the test. It is not directly linked to any specific content. Looking back to Figure 7.1 in this chapter, the 50th percentile or midpoint on each bar represents this grade-level standard for each age group. A common misunderstanding is that test scores are usually tightly clustered around this "grade-level standard," when in fact the distribution of scores within a normal group of students will be relatively broad with a great deal of overlap across grade levels.

Other types of derived scores that are useful in analyzing student achievement are stanine scores, normal curve equivalent scores, and scaled scores. Scores based on a normal distribution are shown in Figure 7.2.

Stanines. The *stanine* score is useful for interpreting where a particular child performs relative to the group. It divides the normal distribution of scores onto only nine levels, thus simplifying the comparison for parents or for decisions regarding grouping of children.

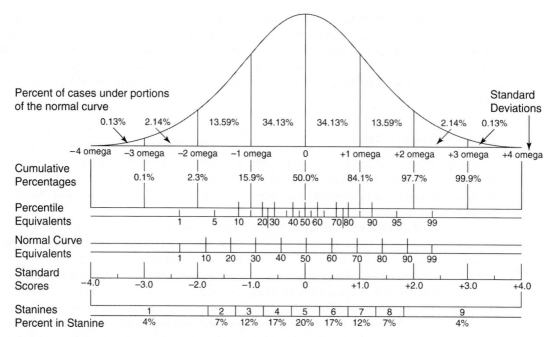

FIGURE 7.2   The Normal Curve, Percentiles, and Standard Scores

Source: Test Service Bulletin No. 48. Reproduced by permission. Copyright © 1955 by The Psychological Corporation.

Normal Curve Equivalent.   The *normal curve equivalent (NCE)* is another way of describing where a student's score falls along the normal curve. The numbers on the NCE line run from 1 to 99, similar to percentile ranks, which indicate an individual student's rank, or how many students out of 100 had a lower score. Normal curve equivalent scores have a major advantage over percentiles, however, in that they can be averaged. That is an important characteristic when studying overall school performance, and, in particular, in measuring schoolwide gains and losses in student achievement.

In a normally distributed population, if all students were to make exactly one year of progress after one year of instruction, their NCE scores would remain exactly the same and their NCE gain would be zero, even though their raw scores (i.e., the number of questions they answered correctly) increased. Some students will make more than a year's progress in that time and will have a net gain in the NCE score. This would indicate that those students have learned more, or at least have made more progress in the areas tested, than the general population. Other students, although making progress in their skills, may progress more slowly than the general population and will show a net loss in their NCE ranks. As with many other scales related to the normal curve, the average NCE, by definition, is 50.

Scaled Scores.   A *scaled score* is also a mathematical transformation of a raw score. Raw scores are limited in their measurement precision because of differences among test items and the number of items on each subtest. A scaled score takes into account the differences in the difficulty of items and is calculated to provide a more precise measure of the knowledge or skills tested. Through this calculation, an increase of one point at one place on the scale is described as being equal to a one-point increase anywhere else on the scale. Scaled scores are particularly useful for reporting changes over time. Scaled scores for individual students or groups of students within each content area should increase each year, because tests use a continuous scale from the lowest to the highest grade levels. Thus, the same child or group of children can be followed across their school career over time, creating gain scores for them year by year. Scaled scores can be compared within the same test, but not between two different tests. For example, the Stanford-9 scaled scores cannot be compared with the CTBS-5 scaled scores. Also, scaled scores should not be used to compare two different content areas, such as reading and mathematics, on the same test.

Gain Scores.   A *gain score* is a measure of how much a child's test scores have climbed the test scale from one administration of the test to the next, or across multiple administrations of the test potentially spanning the child's entire testing career. The gain score is calculated by noting the difference in scores for a particular child over time, generally the annual administrations of the test. Thus, if a child had a scaled score in reading of 420 the first year and a scaled score of 442 the next year, the gain would be 22 points. The collective gains of all the children in a particular classroom or all the children in a school can be averaged to get an estimate of the growth of that classroom or school. This is a valuable piece of information only if one also knows how all other children in some comparison group did. For example, you have a basis of comparison if you know that all children of similar age in your state scored an average increase over the year of 20 points and all children in the nation scored an average of 19 points. By using these group averages as target gains, you can determine that the 22-point gain is greater than the average. You can therefore conclude that that classroom or school is making better than average gain in their achievement scores. See Table 7.1.

Value-Added Assessments.   A *value-added assessment* is a statistical tool for gauging how much students gain in academic achievement in a given year. Stated another way, it reflects how much "value" has been added to the development of a child by his or her schooling. By aggregating pupil gain scores by school, value-added assessments can be used to evaluate schools, regardless of differences among entering students. By aggregating scores by teacher, value-added assessment can be used to identify which teachers' students are learning the most and which teachers' students are learning the least as measured by the selected standardized test.

Since a gain score is based on the annual gain of an individual student, it neutralizes the differences children bring to school with them from different environmental and family backgrounds or differing qualities of previous teachers. A gain score looks only at the difference or gain during the past year and is not a measure of the overall achievement score of the child. Thus, the gains can be largely attributed to the individual child's growth during the previous year. The gain score calculation based on norm-referenced achievement tests provides a detailed method of analysis of the delivery of the curriculum and instruction in a school compared to the progress of other schools. Tennessee was the first state to adopt a value-added assessment system. Dr. Bill Sanders, former professor at the University of Tennessee, developed the Tennessee Value Added Assessment System by adapting statistical procedures to control for many of the biases that often plague testing systems.[6] It has been used statewide since the early 1990s and is recognized as the most extensive model to calculate accurate value-added data.

TABLE 7.1   Computing Gains at the Classroom Level

GRADE 5		MATHEMATICS		NORMAL NORM GAIN=25
Teacher A				
STUDENT	**SS FOR 2009**	**SS FOR 2010**	**AVERAGE SS**	**2009–2010**
Aaron	783	782	783	−1
Aileen	734	774	754	+40
Adam	715	770	743	+55
Amanda	716	761	739	+45
Alan	721	743	732	+22
Amy	717	743	730	+26
Arnold	714	741	728	+27
				Average gain = +31
Teacher B				
Barbara	711	727	719	+16
Barry	699	736	718	+37
Betsy	719	713	716	−6
Benjamin	687	730	709	+43
Brenda	706	709	708	+3
				Average gain = +19
Teacher C				
Carl	674	731	703	+57
Caroline	678	724	701	+46
Charles	676	722	699	+46
Chloe	672	711	692	+39
Christopher	658	704	681	+46
Colleen	668	679	674	+11
				Average gain = +41

SS = scaled score.

Although value-added systems have school and teacher value-added scores as their core, more importantly, value-added assessments allow schools to conduct detailed analyses of their curriculum and instruction to find where their weaknesses lie. It can become immediately evident where lack of growth is occurring in particular grades, subjects, or classrooms. By disaggregating value-added scores by subgroup, pattern graphs for each grade and subject can show which subgroups are making the greatest or least gains, often with surprising results. For example, one school doing its own simpler form of value-added analysis looked to see which of their low-, middle-, or high-achieving students were making the greatest gains. Although it would seem natural to think of the high-achieving students as those likely to gain the most, what the school found was exactly the opposite. Its slowest students were producing greater gain scores than their students with the highest achievement scores. Conclusion? The school found its educators were working very hard with their slower students while ignoring the bright students, as-

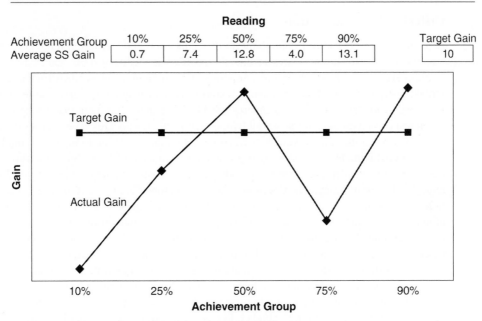

Sample School
Ms. Teacher
8th Grade
2010

Achievement Group: Children whose reading
achievement score falls within this range.

Target Gain: National norm gain—Scale Scores(SS).

Reading

Achievement Group	10%	25%	50%	75%	90%	Target Gain
Average SS Gain	0.7	7.4	12.8	4.0	13.1	10

FIGURE 7.3   **Gain Scores for Achievement Groups within a Classroom**

suming they could "get it on their own."[7] The value-added system allows schools to determine if they are placing equal emphasis on instruction for *all* its students and to determine in which subject areas the students are making the best and worst gains. See Figure 7.3.

What a value-added system does not reveal is *why* gain scores are low. Are low gain scores a result of lack of alignment between the test and the curriculum? In other words, teachers might not be teaching what the test measures. Or, is the problem one of not spending enough time on a particular subject? Or, does the school have teachers who, for whatever reason, are not doing a good job of instruction? This can sometimes be determined by comparing the results of several teachers in the same grade over several years. If one produces great gains and others do not, why?

The value-added system is an excellent tool to look for strengths and weaknesses in curriculum alignment, but it also has its dangers. What if your school has determined to teach knowledge areas within subjects other than what the test measures at a particular grade level? Or, what if your school has decided to include other subjects not measured into your curriculum, thus reducing the hours of instruction in the measured areas? Or, what if your school has decided to teach from a different philosophy of education than the test designers had in mind? Compared to other schools, you may not produce similar gains in the tested areas, but you may still be providing students with a rich, exciting learning experience. All of these test analysis tools assume there is agreement as to what is important for a child to know and be able to do. All large-scale testing, in its way, becomes "the tail that wags the dog," strongly influencing what teachers teach. When teachers teach what they test, it is imperative that they maintain a broad prospective about what children should learn.

Criterion-Referenced Tests

A second major type of test commonly used in education is the criterion-referenced or content-referenced test. This test measures a student's specific knowledge or skills against a criteria or curriculum standard. These criteria are generally the curriculum prescribed for the class-room, school, district, or state. Teacher-made or textbook tests are examples of criterion-referenced tests. As district and state curriculum standards have become more common, many schools are developing tests based on the criteria set out by these curriculum standards. Their scores have meaning in terms of what the student knows or can do, rather than in relation to the scores made by some norm group. Frequently, the meaning is given in terms of a cutoff score. Students who score above that point are considered to have scored adequately ("mastered" the material) or reached a minimum level of proficiency, whereas those who score below it are thought to have not reached proficiency. Schools are evaluated each year based on their adequate yearly progress (AYP) by determining the percentage of students who have reached a minimum proficiency on a specified test in each discipline. The minimum proficiency level must be reached for each designated subgroup based on poverty, race, disability, and so forth, for the school to have reached AYP.

Criterion-referenced tests are sometimes developed to determine if a child should advance to another level or be allowed to graduate; thus they become "gateway" tests through which students must pass before proceeding to their next level of education. Although these tests may be better measures of what an individual child has learned or what a teacher has taught relative to a particular curriculum, the problem is that they are not as useful in comparing a child, classroom, school, or district to the total group if the curriculum taught is not the same for all, nor are they of particular value in determining relative progress over time.

In recent years, designers of nationally sold norm-referenced tests have paid additional attention to including criterion-referenced-type items on their tests. For that to work effectively, however, a common curriculum is required for all taking that test. The expectations generated by these nationally used tests are largely the driving forces in curriculum alignment, causing school leaders to alter their curricular offerings to match the prescribed test. So, rather than selecting a test that measures the curriculum educators wish to teach, test designers have been allowed to become curriculum planners as professional educators chase after the holy grail of higher achievement scores.

Data-Driven Decision Making

ISLLC Standard 2 see Appendix B has performance indicators that suggest the importance of using a variety of sources of information regarding performance to make decisions. Student tests properly administered and recorded are one of the most valuable tools to measure not only the achievement of each child, but, more importantly, the progress of the entire school. This can be done, however, only after the playing field has been leveled. The important question for the school should never be "How high has this child scored?" Rather, the question should be "What has been the contribution of the school to this child's learning and how can we improve it?" As the quote opening this chapter says, "Quality comes not from inspection but from improvement of the process."

Grouping Students

Instruction in any normal school setting requires many decisions about the grouping of children. Basically, these decisions will relate to three variables: group size, group composition, and group flexibility. The basic purpose of grouping students is to bring about the highest quantity and quality of instruction possible. Grouping practices should be consistent with curricular decisions and should be compatible with each student's needs and interests. These lofty goals must be tempered by two factors.

The first factor is the variations of abilities within each learner, which makes homogeneous grouping very difficult. The second factor is the practical consideration of the cost of a particular organization design in comparison with its related effectiveness. For example, group size usually suggests certain staffing patterns that can be converted into dollar costs. A school might conclude that a staffing ratio of three-to-one would give the best quality and quantity of learning per student but that it would be too expensive. Instead, grouping designs must consider more economical staffing ratios, most likely in the range of 15 to 30 students per 1 staff member.

Group Size

Over the years, research studies on class size have produced mixed results. Two meta-analyses of class size, researched by Glass and Smith, published by the Far West Laboratory, have been widely interpreted as providing convincing evidence that smaller classes are better than larger ones. The basic finding of analyses on class size indicated that smaller classes resulted in increased achievement. However, the study showed that in classes ranging from 20 to 40 pupils, class size made little difference in achievement. The major benefits from reduced class size were obtained when size was reduced below 20 pupils.[8]

A Tennessee study[9] using more than 70 classrooms in a well-designed four-year project of primary classes (K–3), size 13 to 17, size 22 to 25, and size 22 to 25 with an aide, produced conclusive results. Students in the small classes made higher scores on both the achievement and criterion-referenced tests. The greatest gains were made in inner-city small classes. The highest scores were made in rural small classes. Teachers reported that they preferred small classes in order to identify student needs and provide more individual attention as well as to cover more material. The findings also suggest a cumulative and positive affect of small classes in later grades. Students in grade 4 who had previously been in the project's small classes demonstrated significant advantages on every achievement measure over students who had attended regular classes.

Teachers who had the smaller classes were observed to cover their basic instruction more quickly, thereby providing increased time for additional material. They used more supplemental texts and enrichment activities and more in-depth teaching of basic content took place. More frequent opportunities were available for children to engage in firsthand learning activities using concrete materials. In summary, teachers were better able to individualize instruction. Smaller classes allow for more personal attention to the student, which encourages a closer student–teacher relationship, as discussed in Chapter 6.

Group Composition

What should be the criteria for organizing children into groups? Obviously, efficient instruction requires groups; the needs of each student, however, should be the first consideration. This section will deal first with some of the more controversial grouping practices, such as homogeneous ability grouping and retention, and their accompanying problems. Then, on a more positive note, alternative grouping patterns based on interest, age, skill, and achievement, will be discussed, along with group flexibility and tenure.

Ability Grouping in the Elementary and Middle School.   A common practice is to organize or group students on the basis of their supposed ability, creating a tracking system with a two-, three-, or four-group continuum consisting of high-ability, average-ability, and low-ability students. The basic assumption underlying this pattern of student organization is that by subdividing children from the extremely broad-ability continuum found in any normal school population, teachers will be better able to focus instruction on the needs of the children in any particular group. Thus, ability groups supposedly narrow the range of abilities within any group and make it more possible for the teacher to organize and prepare materials for a narrower range of abilities.

Criteria used to determine group composition have included achievement test scores, IQ scores, previous grades, and teacher opinion. Serious problems develop when any of these criteria or combinations are used as the basis of organizing students on a permanent basis or for extended periods of time. This method of grouping is usually not effective. No common denominator can be found for long-term grouping across disciplines or even within disciplines. For example, interest can greatly change productivity within a discipline, overriding previous supposed ability measurements.

Children can be grouped successfully according to one factor to obtain a degree of homogeneity, but the group remains heterogeneous in all other aspects of curriculum and instruction. For example, homogeneity in mathematics can be obtained by placing in a group all children who know their multiplication tables through 12, but they remain a heterogeneous group for the rest of the curriculum, including other areas of mathematics.

When the descriptors of homogeneity are based on previous math achievements, an IQ test score, or all previous grades, almost all useful definition of homogeneity is lost. This is so because in almost any specific skill or knowledge, some children placed in the lowest group on one basis will exceed the knowledge level of other children placed in the highest group on another. Therefore, homogeneous grouping as a broad-based or permanent grouping design simply does not work, and the homogeneity is a figment of the imagination of the staff.

Many teachers and administrators have argued strenuously that ability grouping *does* work and that definite differences exist among students. Of course, differences can be seen, but the point is that the overlap in abilities is far greater from group to group than most imagine, and, most importantly, homogeneous grouping overlooks the individual child.

Several attitudinal factors must also be considered in a discussion of homogeneous grouping. The phenomenon of the *self-fulfilling prophecy* enters into the ultimate outcomes of ability grouping. This prophecy says that children become what others say they are or what they think they are.[10] Research about self-concept has shown that children's own attitudes toward themselves as people and their assessment of their own abilities represent major factors in their ultimate success or failure in school. Teacher attitudes, as well as the student's self-concept, contribute greatly to the child's ultimate success or failure in school. The placement of a child in a group on the basis of perceived ability can seem to prove itself correct by adjustments in productivity on the part of the child that in fact take place as a result of the placement, thus fulfilling the prophecy. There is also the question of "reproductive theory"—the idea that children at different academic levels have different access to quality education, thereby perpetuating a stratified social order.

Over the past 40 years, numerous research studies have considered ability grouping. A massive review of many of these studies was reported in 1973 with the following conclusions:

1. Homogeneous ability grouping as currently practiced shows no consistent positive values for helping students generally, or particular groups of students, to achieve more scholastically or to experience more effective learning conditions. Among the studies showing significant effects, evidence of slight gains favoring high-ability students is more than offset by evidence of unfavorable effects on the learning of students of average and below-average ability, particularly the latter.

2. The findings regarding the impact of homogeneous ability grouping on affective development are essentially unfavorable. Whatever the practice does to build or inflate the self-esteem of children in the high-ability groups is counterbalanced by evidence of the unfavorable effects of stigmatizing those placed in average- and below-average-ability groups as inferior and incapable of learning.

3. Homogeneous ability grouping, by design, is a separative educational policy, made ostensibly according to test performance ability but practically according to socioeconomic status and, to a lesser but still observable degree, according to ethnic status.

4. In cases where homogeneous or heterogeneous ability grouping is related to improved scholastic performance, the curriculum is subject to substantial modification of teaching methods, materials, and other variables that are intrinsic to the teaching/learning process. And that may well be the causative factor related to academic development, wholly apart from ability grouping per se. Similarly, with respect to social development, evidence that points to variables other than ability grouping tends to relate substantially to personal growth or lack of growth.[11]

High School Grouping. In high schools, ability grouping functions somewhat differently than in the lower grades. Deficit and average students do not seem affected by achievement grouping, but talented students achieve more and have better attitudes about subject matter when they are placed with others who are also talented. Ability grouping frequently occurs naturally in the selection of elective courses labeled "honors" or in advanced-placement courses. Advanced foreign language courses and higher-level mathematics courses also attract the more able students. Nevertheless, studies on grouping in the elementary school continue to support the position that heterogeneous grouping produces greater student learning than does homogeneous grouping.[12]

Retention

One form of ability grouping that is often overlooked is the result of the retention policies operating in many school districts. Retention places a child with a less intellectually and socially mature group based on the child's demonstrated low ability or achievement. Therefore, it is actually an instance of ability grouping—adjusting the placement of the child to fit a curriculum and instructional level thought more appropriate, rather than bringing the appropriate curriculum and instructional level to the child.

ISLLC 5

Retention is as ineffective an approach to the grouping of children as the previously discussed method. A poorly achieving fourth-grader is not more like a third-grader. The affective development of the student must be considered along with the cognitive development. That student is still more like his or her peers and will be more successful with them than if retained and placed with a younger group of children. At any grade level, the achievement range will spread over a number of grade levels. The Cook studies of the 1940s concluded:

> When pupils in the lower 10 percent of the classes are failed because of low achievement, they do not become better adjusted educationally or socially in the retarded position. The available evidence indicated that, on the average, they achieve as much or more by being given more regular promotions.

The study went on to point out:

> When attempts are made to reduce the range of abilities and achievement in a school by retarding slow learning pupils and accelerating fast learning pupils, there is an increase in the proportion of slow learning pupils in each grade. Average grade achievement is lowered.

Somewhat tongue in cheek, the study concluded:

> If the major concern of the teachers is to maintain grade level standards, the most effective way of increasing achievement standards in a school is to retard the bright and accelerate the dull pupils.[13]

Research on retention continues to show its inappropriateness as a means of adjusting for individual differences.[14] Nevertheless, it is a popular policy in many schools. Retention does not work as a method of maintaining standards, nor does it work as a means of threatening children to perform. Follow-up studies indicate that retained students are far more likely to drop out of school as high school students when their age-mates graduate. In Chapter 2 we discussed the concept of total quality management (TQM). Retention violates the TQM principle of not setting outcome goals. Children will learn more if a school uses instructional process solutions to adjust for individual differences of children.

Appropriate Bases for Grouping

Groups are necessary for school organization, but retention and homogeneous ability grouping as semipermanent forms of student organization are not effective. What should be the basis for grouping? The following principles and techniques for organizing students are sound:

- Regular classrooms and teams should be based on heterogeneous grouping. Some means should be taken to ensure that all teams have an equal portion of students on various achievement and ability levels.

ISLLC 2

- Achievement grouping for math and reading is appropriate, particularly if these subjects are taught from a skill continuum. However, achievement groupings should not result in tracking. Primary identity for a student should still be with the heterogeneous grouping pattern.
- The principal has the responsibility of sharing with teachers the research on retention and grouping practices. "Conventional wisdom" misleads in this case. The principal also needs

to be responsible for developing grouping patterns that serve the needs of the unique student population and should monitor teacher implementation of these grouping plans.

- Grouping patterns must be flexible and, as a result of individual student assessment, allow change in student placement as needed.
- Within each classroom setting, subgroupings should be kept small enough to ensure individual instruction.
- Children of various ages may be grouped together if some other appropriate criteria such as skill development is utilized.
- Particular care should be taken so that grouping practices do not become damaging to the self-concept of the child or create stereotypes in the eyes of other students or teachers toward particular children.

Group Flexibility

How long should an established group remain intact? When groups are reorganized, how extensive should that reorganization be? At what level within the organization should decisions for group reorganization take place? These questions relate directly to the ultimate flexibility that can be obtained for grouping within any school organization.

Groups should remain intact until they have accomplished their skills objective. Once the original purpose for the grouping has been achieved, the group must be reorganized. This may be after one hour of instruction in a skills group, or it might be after three years together as a heterogeneous, multiage group. Skill groups, interest groups, and achievement groups should be designed so they can be reorganized daily, if necessary.

Problems of Regrouping. The need for frequent regrouping in the school presents several problems in school organization. First, it is impractical to refer all grouping decisions to the principal, because the quantity and frequency of needed grouping decisions would overwhelm that office. More significantly, most of the information needed for intelligent grouping decisions is found at the level of teachers and students.

ISLLC 3

To give teachers and students an opportunity to make flexible grouping decisions, a school is best organized into learning communities consisting of two or more teachers, their students, and an extended time block. With this arrangement, students and teachers can group students. The unit design for school organization with a team of teachers, aides, and a group of 75 to 150 students is a good example of this organization.[15]

The important concept is that the principal has passed on the power of decision making regarding grouping directly to the teachers. Once the components of the group have been designated, the principal's role becomes one of giving advice to the teams for internal grouping decisions. The teachers, in turn, then organize the groups.

Grouping Guidelines

Student grouping is necessary for all school organizations. The following summarizes the grouping task:

- For purposes of assigning students to individual teachers or teams, a heterogeneous or mixed grouping plan is usually best.

- Homogeneous grouping should take place inside the classroom and should be done by teachers. The basis for internal class grouping can be interest, achievement, skill, age, or designed heterogeneity.
- Homogeneous grouping should be kept flexible with several different grouping patterns used each day. All homogeneous groups are usually of short duration. Flexibility is necessary because of the changing nature of groups and the problems of negative student self-concept or poor teacher attitudes that can develop from rigid homogeneous grouping patterns.
- Homogeneous groups should not be used for more than one-third of each school day.

Research on Teaching

How Children Learn

As the twenty-first century unfolds, school leaders' ideas of what kind of education is needed to be successful is changing. One hundred years ago, for many, education was limited to the three Rs—reading, writing, and 'rithmetic—and certain essential elements necessary to be a U.S. citizen. By the end of the twentieth century, the ability to think and read critically, to express oneself in a logical manner, and to solve complex problems had become the new standard. The meaning of *knowing* had shifted from being able to remember and recite information to having the skills needed to access and use it.[16] Furthermore, *knowing* requires that students be able to integrate school learning into the fabric of their own lives by personalizing the lessons they are taught at school. Researchers have found that if teachers design their lessons to connect the preexisting knowledge base of their students, they will most likely increase the level of learning of their students. A growing research base about how children learn supports this premise. The work of the National Research Council in their report on *How People Learn*[17] points out four specific areas of focus if educators are going to successfully connect with children's learning:

1. The greater the social and cultural distance between the school environment and the home and community environments, the more difficult it is for students to draw on their preexisting knowledge as they work to understand school lessons. The report suggests that teaching must be *learner centered,* such as lessons that draw from the local community or television. That is, teachers must use preexisting knowledge to construct new knowledge. Engaging parents and other caregivers as partners in their children's education is one obvious strategy to do this. Transfer from school knowledge to everyday life is the ultimate purpose of schooling.
2. Teaching must also be *knowledge centered* as well as learner centered. Thinking and problem solving require mastery of well-organized bodies of knowledge. The content, organization, and sequencing of the curriculum must be carefully constructed for the student to develop a deep understanding of the subject matter. Curriculum standards are often constructed to aid in this knowledge organization.
3. Learning environments should be *assessment centered.* Assessments are to be formative to provide teachers with timely information from which they can modify instructional planning to better accomplish learning objectives. The assessment must be to measure if the students are learning for understanding. Testing should be frequent (daily or weekly). The purpose of the tests should be to give feedback to both students and teachers.

ISLLC 2

4. Schools and classrooms should be *learning communities.* Students, teachers, school staff, parents, and other stakeholders should have a common commitment to learning to the extent that modeling the desired patterns of behavior in the school constantly reinforces a desire for learning.

Research regarding instruction and the development of a consistent view of teaching represents one of the major trends in education in the past decade. Education has made a major shift in its attention from focusing on teacher traits to focusing on instructional skills. Since the standard curriculum in today's schools centers heavily on academic and technological orientations, we discuss the methods that are particularly applicable to them. Certainly, the curriculum can, and should be, enriched by the addition of the other orientations and the methods more suited to their delivery. The research on effective teaching has produced a list of recommended instructional skills that, when implemented effectively by teachers, produces observable, measurable gains in student learning. This emphasis on a directive teaching model is, of course, consistent with the measured curriculum discussed in Chapter 6. It is *not* always the most appropriate style for other curriculum orientations. Summaries of the major teaching competencies, along with citations of their research, are presented next for teacher competencies in planning, lesson implementation, cooperative learning, student motivation, evaluative feedback, evaluation activities, grade assignment, time on task, and differential instruction instruction.

Effective Planning Skills

Research on teachers' planning indicates that if teachers (1) identify instructional objectives; (2) set an appropriate level of difficulty for mastery; (3) plan out matching instructional methods, procedures, materials, and student activities; and (4) use good formative and summative evaluation techniques, the resulting preparedness can increase the probability of improving student achievement as measured by test scores. Such planning also ensures teacher confidence, direction, and security.

Some of the success of this planning can certainly be attributed to the improved curricular alignment that occurs from the detailed planning around objectives drawn directly from a prescribed curriculum. However, the *planning* for instructional implementation is believed to be the major cause of the gain found in student test scores.

The research on planning also provides a clear understanding of the stumbling blocks to planning.[18] Teaching for mastery demands a well-developed statement of goals and instructional objectives as well as appropriate criterion-referenced tests.[19] Although this makes good sense to administrators and many teachers, it requires a tremendous amount of work for teachers. Most teachers, however, intuitively base their success in the classroom on student interest and attitudes and not on cognitive gain. Therefore, the teachers do not obtain the personal reinforcement from the results of the students' test gains.[20]

Effective Lesson Implementation

The effective implementation of a lesson planned by the teacher is as important as the planning itself. High-gain teachers use a variety of instructional methods, including drill, explanation, discussion, inquiry, role-playing, demonstration, and problem solving. One important element of good lesson implementation is the use of advanced organizers, which give the learner an overview of the lesson. Hunter's concept of an anticipatory set is an example of an advanced organizer.[21]

Other important elements of effective lesson implementation include asking relevant questions, giving explanations, and doing demonstrations, in conjunction with frequent feedback to the teacher regarding student understanding. Feedback techniques, such as signing (thumbs up, thumbs down) or "if you know the correct answer raise your hand," can provide this information to a teacher throughout the lesson.

Increased wait time, the amount of time a teacher waits after asking a question, also has shown positive effects on student performance. Untrained teachers often wait only one to two seconds after asking a question. A longer wait time produces longer, more complete student responses, more student confidence in their responses, increased factual evidence used by students in their responses, a greater number of slow students participating, and reduced teacher-centered presentations.[22]

Research also has produced surprising results about questioning techniques. Many teachers do not use questioning of students during discussion very much, but it has been demonstrated that the frequency of factual, single-answer questions is positively related to gains in achievement.[23]

Quizzing and reviewing also have been shown to be elements in successful lesson implementation. When teachers give regular quizzes one or more times a week, scores on final exams go up. Frequent testing influences study behavior positively.[24]

The most effective teachers also use homework to enhance study habits of students. Studies support the view that frequently assigned homework, in small amounts to provide independent practice on what has been learned during the instructional lesson, has a positive effect on achievement.[25]

Cooperative Learning

This instructional strategy delegates some control of the pacing and methods of learning to student groups, usually composed of two to six persons. Students in the groups work together on assignments, sometimes competing with other groups. Individuals in the group assume responsibility for sharing knowledge and tutoring each other. It is an active-learning approach and has been shown to offer great opportunity for the development of higher-order thinking skills in all participants.

Classrooms that are organized for cooperative motivation instead of competitiveness produce a better classroom climate. Competitive organization permits aggressiveness, cheating, lowered motivation, and failure-avoiding behaviors; whereas cooperative environments are linked to positive peer relationships, higher achievement, positive self-esteem, and interracial acceptance.[26]

Student Motivation

The suggestions in the previous sections can help educators focus on the correct direction for the curriculum, instruction, and climate of the school, but they do not deal with the motivations of the individual child. A growing body of research focuses on how teachers can develop in students the desire to learn and succeed. Some of the best work has been done by Dweck at

Columbia University[27] based on many years of research. The following are some of the major points from her work:

ISLLC 2

- There is no relationship between mastery-oriented qualities and intelligence. Being mastery oriented is about having the right mindset. Students who are mastery oriented think about learning, not proving how smart they are.
- Educators should focus on students' efforts and not on their abilities. Teachers need to help children value their effort and teach them to look for the challenge.
- Teachers must help children focus on the value of learning rather than on grades or some other external reward. Intrinsic rewards (the love and excitement of learning) are far better and longer lasting than extrinsic rewards. The love of learning is self-perpetuating, whereas the love of a grade is short-lived.
- Students can be taught that their intellectual skills can be grown and improved through their hard work by reading, studying, and confronting a challenge.
- Undue emphasis on testing can be harmful if it conveys the message to students that the whole point of school is to do well on tests. It is also harmful if students begin to believe that how well they do on tests sums up their intelligence or their worth as a student.
- A teacher who teaches students to equate their intelligence and their worth with performance will reduce their desire to learn and make them afraid of challenges.
- Across the years, motivation is often more important than a student's initial ability in determining success. Many creative geniuses were not born that way; rather, they were fairly ordinary people who became extraordinarily motivated.

These findings regarding motivation suggest several important considerations for school principals. There is a strong message to be cautious in how educators use assessment data, being careful not to use the data to label (group) children nor to use the data in an overt way in an attempt to motivate children.

Evaluative Feedback

This competency consists of several tasks, including providing written comments to students on their progress in addition to grades, returning tests as quickly as possible, holding individual conferences with students, and interpreting test results to students and parents. The research evidence is extensive regarding the importance of the frequency and timeliness of effective feedback to students. Formative feedback, done while the lesson and learning are in

ISLLC 2

progress, is best done orally rather than in writing. It is most beneficial when correcting wrong answers, both to correct the student and to allow the teacher to modify the lesson to cope with the problem.[28]

Feedback in the form of praise should be used extensively but within certain parameters. Low-achieving students may require more explicit recognition for their classroom participation; however, indiscriminate praise may not motivate learning. What is desired is real recognition for real achievement.[29] Feedback on tests and assignments also provides information both to the students on how their work is being evaluated and to the teacher on how successful the instruction has been.[30]

A high volume of feedback from the teacher is of value for reinforcement, as well as for its information content.[31] Research also shows that immediate feedback from the teacher is important, as is a high frequency of testing on content material in the classroom.[32]

Appropriate Evaluation Activities

The effective teacher begins instruction by making the methods of evaluation clear to students; basing the evaluation on specific goals, objectives, and content of the course; and using both pretests and posttests to measure student gain. Student progress is measured through a series of both formative and summative evaluation techniques.

Specific statements of instructional objectives, in measurable terms announced to the students, become the first step in projecting toward the evaluation. These objectives need to be closely aligned with the stated curriculum and should be reflective of some diversity, as shown by some classification system such as the work of Bloom (cognitive domain), Krathwohl (affective domain), or Samson (psychomotor domain).[33] Surveys have shown that teachers generally select most of their objectives from the cognitive domain and most from the lowest level (knowledge) of that domain.[34] Greater diversity of objectives is usually desirable.

Formative evaluation, while instruction is unfolding, should be frequent and have as its purpose monitoring and guiding students to the correct learning as well as providing the teacher with data for monitoring instructional effectiveness.[35] Summative evaluation should be used to determine if the student has achieved the objectives. Mastery learning is a graduated approach to summative evaluation. Here, instructional objectives are divided into small units with specific objectives whose mastery is essential for the mastery of the major objectives. In mastery learning, frequent testing and evaluation are crucial. Research indicates that mastery learning evaluation techniques produce superior student achievement, learning retention, transfer of learning, and positive affective outcomes.[36]

Grade Assignment

High-gain teachers recognize the importance of assigning grades and take the responsibility seriously. They keep in mind what parents want to learn from student report cards, and they use grades to accurately reflect student progress rather than as a form of behavior modification. Teachers must test often and consistently to achieve good reliability of evaluative data.[37]

Marking systems that use a maximum of five to nine discriminations are best understood by parents; therefore, a 5-point, letter-grade scale is probably a better communicator than is a 100-point scale.[38] Pass–fail grading systems appear to lead to lower achievement.[39]

Two general approaches are used by teachers in assigning grades. The first is grading students on their performance relative to their classmates. The second involves an absolute scale of some type based on a standard, such as a predetermined number of objectives to be achieved. The first type, that of relative scores compared to other students, is commonly called *grading on a curve*. Students' grades are either based on raw scores drawn from posttest data only or gain scores based on the difference between pretest and posttest data. Gain scores logically provide a better measure of student achievement under the instruction of that particular teacher. However, this type of relative comparison of student scores to one another is appropriate only if there are very large groups of students included, and the students are not tracked. This is rarely the case in the normal classroom setting.

The second type of grading, that of using an *absolute scale,* is common to criterion-referenced tests and to mastery learning. Proficiency tests with minimum acceptable levels of performance also use this logic. Grades are based on a predetermined level of achievement necessary to obtain a particular grade, such as 8 out of 10 correct for a B, or 9 out of 10 correct for an A.

Grading must reflect student performance and growth. When it reflects something other than academic achievement, it cannot be considered valid. High-gain teachers do not abuse the assigning of grades but consider it a significant part of their communication with both parents and students.

Time on Task

The high-gain teacher uses the time allocated for the class in a highly efficient manner. Classwork begins promptly at the beginning of each period, management time and transition time are kept to a minimum, and the teacher reinforces students who are spending time on task. Studies report that low-achieving students are off task in excess of 50 percent of the time, whereas high-achieving students are off task less than 25 percent of the time.[40] Another study, of junior high students, showed that low achievers had an engagement time of approximately 40 percent, whereas high achievers reached in excess of 85 percent engagement time.[41]

The research evidence demonstrates that time is a valuable resource in school, and when used efficiently, increases student performance.[42] The studies identify three levels of time used: allocated time—that assigned to a particular course or subject; engaged time—the amount of allocated time in which students actually are engaged in learning activities; and academic learning time (ALT)—a refinement of engaged time reflecting quality of learning. Factors included in the definition of *quality* are the appropriateness of instructional materials relative to the achievement level of the student, the best student's success ratio of learning (suggested is an 80 percent success ratio for most learners), and the amount of concentration the learner is actually contributing to the instructional process.[43]

The high-gain teacher is punctual and begins instruction for each class promptly, leaving management details until later in the hour, if possible. During seatwork time, the teacher monitors students closely, encouraging more time on task. It is suggested that at least 50 percent of each class period be devoted to active, direct instruction. This is significantly higher than what is found in most classes. For example, one study demonstrated that math teachers on the average used only 14 percent of their time for direct instruction, with 34 percent going for written work, 8 percent for review, and the balance assigned to off-task activities.[44]

Differentiated Instruction

Where does differentiated instruction fit, in light of all the research findings supporting direct instruction in the form of demonstration-practice-feedback? How does the finding of the need for whole-group instruction impact individualized methods?[45] Although direct instruction has shown great results for the acquisition of specific skills, it cannot do it all; in fact, for higher-order learning and thinking skills, direct instruction may be counterproductive.[46] An effective classroom must solicit student involvement in learning activities under appropriate conditions for mastery. This demands a proper climate and opportunity for the student to achieve success. These requisites demand that teachers provide appropriate opportunity for individual differences if maximum student productivity is to be maintained. Teachers can accommodate individual differences in a variety of ways:

- By varying the level of teaching internal to the class through adjusting the level of questioning and varying the length of wait time
- By providing varying amounts of allocated time to different students
- By grouping within or between classes, as has been discussed earlier in this chapter
- By consideration of different learning styles of children
- By selection of classroom organizational methods, including learning centers, tutors, and study groups[47]

Differential instruction is based on the philosophy that classrooms where students are active learner, decision makers, and problem solvers are more natural and effective than those in which students are served a one-size-fits-all bases. Collaborative work on authentic, real-world projects is a preferred instructional format. Problem-based or project-based learning (PBL) supports this objective. Learner-constructed knowledge from multiple information sources and experiences is a desired goal. New cooperative software solutions such as wiki software support team-developed projects.

Projects can vary consider this teacher-assigned, problem-answering project for elementary school children: Where are all the places you gather as a third-grader with other children your age? Make a list, explain why you meet, and provide a picture of the group meeting for each purpose. Produce a PowerPoint slide show and a team presentation with a minimum of 10 gathering events. Middle school teams of children might develop a project around the election of a president, while a team of high schoolers could develop projects focusing on a science theory or a theme of history or geography. Most projects include components that encourage students to apply their knowledge across disciplines. Projects like these can offer multiple options for gathering information, making sense of ideas, and expressing what has been learned. Team composition can range form teams based on interest to teams based on level of ability or mixed abilities.

Instructional Tools for Differentiation.   We have emphasized differentiated instruction and the need to provide a variety of instructional activities for students in order to make such a system functional. The logical question is how to organize or create materials for differentiated-instruction.

Excellent commercial materials are now available for different approaches to instruction, and more are becoming available each year. In areas such as reading and math, schools can purchase an entire system for a wide range of student achievement levels. Other materials can be organized and coordinated for instruction by teachers using those materials. Teachers, of course, should also continue to use their own materials.

The real problem, however, is organizing materials in a systematic way so that they are adequately available to students when they need them, adequately self-instructional so that teacher time can be appropriately balanced, and adequately organized to ensure proper instructional sequencing, recording, and evaluation. Today's computers can aid greatly in managing records for differentiated instruction. A number of methods of instruction have gained acceptance as ways to achieve differentiated instruction and to enhance learning. Among these are mastery learning, independent learning, and cooperative learning (discussed earlier).

Mastery Learning. Mastery learning, as described by Bloom,[48] has been a very successful form of individualized instruction.[49] This form of mastery instruction, as a means of obtaining individualization, has many benefits and has shown good success for certain types of learning, primarily skills development. Nevertheless, difficulties do exist[50]:

- Alternate instructional materials and tests are needed for those students required to recycle to achieve mastery.
- Management problems of the increasing spread of achievements are caused by early masters and the extended recycling of others.

Independent Learning. Two frequently stated goals for secondary student development are the development of independence and the development of purpose. Traditional approaches to organization of instruction tend to limit, restrict, or inhibit these desired goals, however. Instruction that is heavily teacher directed, although it may be best for basic skills development, tends to foster dependence rather than independence. If student interdependence and independence with purpose are desired, then instruction must be organized to achieve it.

A variety of types of learning experiences may be considered as independent learning activities. Students may participate in homework and in-depth projects, walkabout challenge projects, enrichment courses, regularly scheduled classes, informal discussion, and other activities that are consistent with the purposes of the independent learning phase of instruction.

Specific independent learning objectives for students include the following:

- Assume an increased responsibility for making decisions relative to his or her education.
- Develop an increased control over his or her impulse behavior.
- Become a more purposeful, independent learner by achieving a higher degree of interdependence, venturesomeness, resourcefulness, goal directedness, and persistence.
- Develop an increased capacity to solve problems and learn to use critical and creative thinking processes.
- Acquire relevant subject matter content.
- Develop an increased interest in learning.
- Achieve emotional independence of parents and other adults.
- Achieve more and more mature relationships with peers of both genders.
- Desire and achieve socially responsible behavior by becoming more self-disciplined.
- Acquire a set of values in an ethical system and a guide to behavior.

The implementation of an effective independent study program will be a new activity for many schools. Each student participating in advanced forms of independent study should sign an appropriate contract that states purpose, completion date, conference dates, and so on.

Summary

In conjunction with any instructional system must come a plan for organizing and grouping students. Grouping considerations include group size, composition, and flexibility. Extensive preparation is needed to develop a variety of learning goals, objectives, and activities, so that appropriate instructional plans can be developed for all students.

Research on teaching indicates the importance of each teacher having skills in lesson planning, lesson implementation, student motivation, evaluative feedback, evaluation activities, grade assignment, maintenance of high time on task, cooperative learning, and differentiated instruction. The principal must have an understanding of diversified instruction and exhibit an expectation of such instruction from the teachers.

ACTIVITIES

1. Review Case Studies 3, 4, 26, and 28 at the back of this book. Apply the instructional concepts expressed in this chapter. How might you proceed in addressing the problems cited in these cases? Set forth a strategy to overcome each problem.
2. Reflect on the instructional strategies and behaviors in your own school. Identify one or more areas where restructuring should take place. Why do you believe so? Apply the concepts of this chapter to your school. How would you proceed to restructure your school's instructional program? How might you use the concepts of

Chapter 9, Human Resources Development, to assist in your planning?
3. Turn to the ISLLC Standards found in Appendix B. Review the functions listed in Standard 2. Reflect on which of the standard items relate directly to the concepts of learning as presented in this chapter. How do the concepts of learning match Standard 2? Are there important concepts not included in the standard curriculum format? Identify one function to link directly to a concept or idea discussed in Chapter 7.

ENDNOTES

1. Mary Walton, *The Deming Management Method* (New York: Perigee Books, 1986), p. 60.
2. Howard Gardner, *Frames of Mind: The Theory of Multiple Intelligences* (New York: Basic Books, 1993). Gardner suggests at least five different forms of intelligence: linguistic, logical-mathematical, spatial, bodily-kinesthetic, and personal.
3. Walter W. Cook and Theodore Clymer, "Acceleration and Retardation," in *Individualized Instruction, 1962 Yearbook of the National Society for the Study of Education,* ed. Nelson B. Henry (Chicago: NSSE, 1962), pp. 179–208.
4. "The Facts about . . . Measuring Progress," from the Education Department's No Child Left Behind site, provides information on the federal goverment's plan for annual testing of students in grades 3 through 8. See also "Academic Assessment and Local Educational Agency and School Improvement," Section 1116 of the No Child Left Behind Act.
5. *Standard score* is a general term referring to scores that have been "transformed" for reasons of convenience, comparability, ease of interpretation, and so on. The basic type of standard score, known as a *z*-score, is an expression of the deviation of a score from the mean score of the group in relation to the standard deviation of the scores of the group. Most other standard score are linear tranformations of *z*-scores, with different means and standard deviations.

6. For more detailed information about the TVAAS system, go to www.ablongman.com or to this referenced site for a collection of materials: www.shearonforschools.com/TVAAS_index.html.
7. Go to www.ablongman.com for information on an Microsoft Excel template by Terry Roe to do your own simple version of value-added assessments-disaggregating by student subgroup.
8. Gene V. Glass and Mary Lee Smith, "Meta-Analysis of Research in the Relationships of Class Size and Achievement," in *The Class Size and Instruction Project,* Leonard S. Chaen, principal investigator (San Francisco: Far West Laboratory for Educational Research and Development, September 1978).
9. Helen Pate-Bain, C. M. Achilles, Jayne Boyd- Zaharias, and Bernard McKenna, "Class Size Does Make a Difference," *Phi Delta Kappan* (November 1992): 253–256.
10. A study by Rosenthal and Jacobson investigated the concept of the self-fulfilling prophecy and found that teacher attitudes and expectations about a child do have a direct bearing on the child's performance. Robert Rosenthal and Lenore Jacobson, *Pygmalion in the Classroom* (New York: Holt, Rinehart and Winston, 1968).
11. Dominick Esposito, "Homogeneous and Heterogeneous Ability Grouping," *AERA Journal* (Spring 1973): 163–179.

12. R. E. Slavin, "Grouping for Instruction in the Elementary School," *School and Classroom Organization* (Hillsdale, NJ: Lawrence Erlbaum, 1989).

13. Walter W. Cook, "Effective Ways of Doing It," in *Individualized Instruction, 1962 Yearbook of the National Society for the Study of Education,* ed. Nelson B. Henry (Chicago: NSSE, 1962), Chapter 3.

14. Margaret M. Dawson and Mary Ann Rafoth, "Why Student Retention Doesn't Work," *Streamlined Seminar, NAESP 9,* no. 3 (January 1991): 1–6.

15. *IGE Unit Operations and Roles* (Dayton, OH: Institute for Development of Educational Activities, 1970).

16. H. A. Simon, *The Sciences of the Artificial* (Cambridge, MA: MIT Press, 1996).

17. *How People Learn: Brain, Mind, Experience and School,* Committee of the Developments in the Science of Learning, ed. J. D. Bransford, A. L. Brown, R. R. Cocking, Commission on Behavioral and Social Sciences (Washington, DC: National Academy Press, 1998).

18. P. L. Peterson, R. W. Marx, and C. M. Clark, "Teacher Planning, Teacher Behavior, and Students' Achievement," *American Educational Research Journal 15* (1978): 417–432.

19. J. I. Goodlad, M. F. Klein, and associates, *Looking Behind the Classroom Door* (Worthington, OH: Charles A. Jones, 1974).

20. T. R. Mann, "The Practice of Planning: The Impact of Elementary School on Teachers' Curriculum Planning," *Dissertation Abstracts International 35* (1975): 3359A–3360A.

21. M. Hunter, *Mastery Teaching* (El Segundo, CA: TIP Publications, 1982).

22. M. R. Rowe, "Relation of Wait-time and Rewards to the Development of Language, Logic, and Fate Control: Part II—Rewards," *Journal of Research in Science Teaching 11* (1974): 291–308.

23. J. Stallings and D. Kaskowitz, *Follow-Through Classroom Observation Evaluation,* 1972–73 (Menlo Park, CA: Stanford Research Institute, Stanford University, 1974).

24. P. Peterson and H. Walberg (Eds.), *Research on Teaching* (Berkeley, CA: McCutchan, 1979).

25. J. D. Austin, *Homework Research in Mathematics 1900–1974.* Paper presented at the 1974 Annual Georgia Mathematics Education Conference at Rock Eagle, GA, 1974.

26. D. W. Johnson and R. T. Johnson, "Instructional Goal Structure: Cooperative, Comparative, and Individualistic," *Review of Educational Research 44* (1974): 213–240.

27. Carol S. Dweck, *Self-Theories: Their Role in Motivation, Personality, and Development* (Philadelphia: Psychology Press, 1999).

28. "Florida Beginning Teacher Program," Office of Teacher Education, Certification, and Inservice Staff Development, Tallahassee, FL, 1982. M. Mims and B. Gholson, "Effects of Type and Amount of Feedback upon Hypothesis Sampling Among 7–8 Year Old Children," *Journal of Experimental Child Psychology 24* (1977): 358–371. B. B. Hudgins et al., *Educational Psychology* (Itasca, IL: Peacock, 1983).

29. J. Brophy, "Teacher Praise: A Functional Analysis," *Review of Educational Research 51* (1981): 5–32. W. Brookover, C. Beady, P. Flood, J. Schweitzer, and J. Wisenbaker, *School Social Systems and Student Achievement: Schools Can Make a Difference* (New York: Praeger, 1979).

30. M. Hunter, *Appraising the Instructional Process.* Presentation for California Advisory Council on Educational Research, November 1973. Appears in *Resources in Education* (Washington, DC: ERIC Clearinghouse on Teacher Education, October 1977). B. Rosen-shine, *Teaching Functions in Instructional Programs,* Airlie House Paper (Washington, DC: NIE Conference, 1982).

31. R. Bardwell, "Feedback: How Well Does It Function?" *Journal of Experimental Education 50* (1981): 4–9.

32. Peterson and Walberg, *Research on Teaching.*

33. B. S. Bloom, M. B. Englehart, E. J. Furst, W. H. Hill, and D. R. Krathwohl, *Taxonomy of Educational Objectives: The Classification of Education Goals. Handbook I: Cognitive Domain* (New York: Longmans Green, 1956).

34. Good and Brophy, *Looking in Classrooms.*

35. Peterson, Marx, and Clark, "Teacher Planning."

36. J. H. Block, *Schools, Society and Mastery Learning* (New York: Holt, Rinehart and Winston, 1974).

37. Clinton I. Chase, *Measurement for Educational Research* (Reading, MA: Addison-Wesley, 1978).

38. G. A. Miller, "The Magic Number Seven, Plus or Minus Two: Some Limits on Our Capacity for Processing Information," *Psychological Review 63* (1956): 81–97.

39. L. A. Gatta, "An Analysis of the Pass-Fail Grading System as Compared to the Conventional System in High School Chemistry," *Journal of Research in Science Teaching 10* (1973): 3–12. W. L. Claiborn, "Expectancy Effects in the Classroom: A Failure to Replicate," *Journal of Educational Psychology 60* (1969): 377–383. W. M. Stallings and H. R. Smock, "The Pass-Fail Grading Option at a State University: A Five Semester Evaluation," *Journal of Educational Measurement 8* (1971): 153–160.

40. D. Powell and M. Eash, "Secondary School Cases," in *Evaluating Educational Performance,* ed. H. Walberg (Berkeley, CA: McCutchan, 1974), pp. 277–293.

41. C. Evertson, *Differences in Instruction Activities in High and Low Achieving Junior High Classes.* Paper presented at the Annual Meeting of the American Educational Research Association, Boston, 1980.

42. J. Stallings, "Allocated Academic Learning Time Revisited, or Beyond Time on Task," *Educational Researcher 9* (1980): 11–16. W. Frederick, "The Use of Classroom Time in High Schools Above or Below the

Median Reading Score," *Urban Education* (1977): 459–464. T. L. Good, "How Teachers' Expectations Affect Low Achieving Students," *American Educator* (December 1982): 22–32.

43. Peterson and Walberg, *Research on Teaching.*

44. J. Stallings and A. Robertson, "Factors Influencing Women's Decisions to Enroll in Elective Mathematics Classes in High School." Final Report to the National Institute of Education (Menlo Park, CA: SRI International, 1979).

45. W. R. Borg, "Time and School Learning," in *Time to Learn,* ed. C. Denham and A. Lieberman (Washington,

DC: The National Institute of Education, U.S. Department of Education, 1980).

46. P. L. Peterson, "Direct Instruction Reconsidered," in *Research on Teaching,* ed. P. L. Peterson and H. J. Walberg (Berkeley, CA: McCutchan, 1979).

47. Good and Brophy, *Looking in Classrooms.*

48. Bloom, *Human Characteristics.*

49. B. B. Hudgins et al., *Educational Psychology* (Itasca, IL: Peacock, 1983).

50. Peterson and Walberg, *Research on Teaching.*

SELECTED READINGS

Bernhardt, V. L. "Data Tools for School Improvement." *Educational Leadership 62* (2005): 66–69.

Brimijoin, K., E. Marquissee, and C. A. Tomlinson "Using Data to Differentiate Instruction." *Educational Leadership 60* (2003): 70–73.

Cooley, V. E., and J. Shen. "School Accountability and Professional Job Responsibilities: A Perspective from Secondary Principals." *NASSP Bulletin 87* (2003): 10–25.

Cunningham, W. G., and T. D. Sanzo. "Is High-Stakes Testing Harming Lower Socioeconomic Status Schools?" *NASSP Bulletin 86,* no. 631 (2002): 62–65.

Evans, R. "Reframing the Achievement Gap." *Phi Delta Kappan 86,* no. 8 (2005): 582–589.

Ferriter, Bill. "Learinig with Blogs and Wikis." *Education Leadership 66,* (2009): 34–38.

Firestone, W. A. "Accountability Nudges Districts into Changes in Culture." *Phi Delta Kappan 90,* no. 9 (2009): 670–676.

Gardner, Howard. *Frames of Mind: The Theory of Multiple Intelligences* (New York: BasicBooks, 1993).

Greenberg, P. "Bringing Home into the Classroom." *Scholastic Early Childhood Today 17,* no. 7 (2002): 32–40.

Grier, Terry, and Kent Peterson. "It's Cool to Succeed." *Educational Leadership 62* (2005): 65–68.

Hall, P. "Shifting Accountability from Subgroups to Students." *NAESP Principal* (March/April 2007): 26–31.

Hatrick, E. "A Climate for Success." *School Administrator 65,* no. 9 (2008): 54.

Holly, P. J. *Creating a Data-Driven System.* Data Driven School Improvement Series, Workbook 5 (Upper Saddle River, NJ: Pearson Education, 2003).

Kozol, J. "Standardized Testing: The Do-or-Die Agenda" [Electronic Version]. *Principal* (March/April 2006): 18–22.

National Research Council, Committee on Developments in the Science of Learning. *How People Learn: Brain,*

Mind, Experience, and School: Expanded Edition (Washington, DC: National Academy Press, 2000).

Pasi, R. "A Climate for Achievement." *Principal Leadership 2,* no. 4 (2001): 17–20.

Picciano, A. G. *Data Driven Decision Making for Effective School Leadership* (Upper Saddle River, NJ: Pearson Education, 2006).

Popham, W. J. "A Tale of Two Test Types" [Electronic Version] *Principal,* (March/April 2006): 12–16.

Prensky, Marc. "Turning on the Lights." *Educational Leadership 65* (2008): 40–45.

Saifer, S., and R. Barton. "Promoting Culturally Responsive Standards-Based Teaching" *Principal Leadership 8,* no. 1 (2007): 24–28.

Sanders, William L., and Sandra P. Horn. "Educational Assessment Reassessed: The Usefulness of Standardized and Alternative Measures of Student Achievement as Indicators for the Assessment of Educational Outcomes." *Educational Policy Assessment Archives 3,* no. 6 (March 1995).

Schniedewind, N., and E. Davidson. "Differentiation Cooperative Learning." *Educational Leadership 58,* (2000): 24–27.

Schweiker-Marra, K., and J. Pula. "The Effects of a Homogeneous Low-Tracked Program on Academic Performance of At-Risk Students." *The Delta Kappa Gamma Bulletin 71* (2005): 34–42.

Shellard, E. G. "How Assessment Data Can Improve Instruction." *Principal 84,* no. 3 (2005): 30–32.

Trimble, S. "Between Reform and Improvement in the Classroom." *Principal Leadership 4,* no. 1 (2003): 35–39.

U.S. Department of Education. "Academic Assessment and Local Educational Agency and School Improvement," Section 1116 of the No Child Left Behind Act (2001).

Woods-Wooton, P. "Breaking Down the Answers." *Principal Leadership 2* (2002): 38–40.

8 Special Students and Special Services

It was a wise man who said that there is no greater inequality than the equal treatment of unequals.

—FELIX FRANKFURTER[1]

The administration of special education services looms as one of the most complex and increasingly demanding responsibilities faced by the school principal. Student populations are more diverse than ever before in this nation's history, bringing a challenge to schools as they seek to identify, place, and properly deliver an appropriate continuum of services to those judged to be "exceptional." Researchers suggest a strong link between being at risk for special education services and a background marked by poverty and language/race barriers.[2] This gives reason for concern when considering estimates suggesting that "our nation's population will grow to 265 million by the year 2020, with the largest growth among minority groups."[3] In addition, "estimates are that the number of children in poverty will substantially increase from 14.7 million to 20.1 million."[4]

Not only does increased diversity pose its challenges, but so too do the demands for school restructuring. The days of teaching students with special needs in isolated settings are over. No longer are special education programs considered to be merely add-ons; rather, they are viewed as an integral part of the total school operation. Calls for school reform and restructuring demand a more systemic look at school organization. Schools must design programs to meet the needs of students rather than forcing students into "preset" programs that may or may not meet their needs.

At the same time, operational funds are short, available teachers are scarce, and parents are more adequately informed relative to their legal rights. Recent political mandates have added to the responsibilities faced by school personnel with the higher demands for accountability for all students. Certainly, it is not a time when the school principal can delegate the responsibility for administering special services to someone else! If ever the school principal should be an integral player in the process, it is *now!* The principal sets the tone for the special education services delivery system within the school. Likewise, he or she serves as the focal point for program structuring and determines just how the special education process will be administered. Nowhere is leadership more desperately needed than in this arena. As we discussed in Chapter 1, the way in which that leadership is enacted will depend in great measure on the ethical principles and values that shape the leader's administrative philosophy.

Ethics of Administration

ISLLC 5

Two ethics, the ethic of care[5] and the ethic of justice,[6] are extremely important for school principals to consider as they administer special education programs within their respective schools. Both ethics must be considered in dealing with the personal and legal implications of services to special education students, but principals often face ethical and moral dilemmas as they struggle to reconcile the two.

The ethic of justice is based on a sense of fairness and equality. Individuals are treated in a uniform manner; individual differences are not always considered. An ethic of justice places much emphasis on maintaining moral rules and on recognizing and respecting the rights of others. Relationships are reciprocal and mediated through rules, with rules becoming a means for minimizing hurt to others. Interpretation of rules and regulations is impersonal and objective.[7] In areas of legal compliance, the ethic of justice forms an important backdrop for guiding the legal requirements of special education services.

The ethic of care forms a protective network through which principals may articulate a more effective and personally relevant special education service delivery system. An ethic of care ensures that decisions are based on ethical consideration of relationships rather than merely on rules, regulations, and a sense of fairness advocated by a strict adherence to an ethic of justice.[8] Caring is based on connection and involves a personal responsiveness to the unique needs of others, resulting in feelings of concern and solicitude.[9] The ethic of care is viewed as both a practice and a disposition. It involves taking the concerns and needs of others as the basis of action and is directed toward four ethical elements:

1. *Attentiveness.* Recognizing the needs of others and not allowing personal needs to prevent one from taking appropriate action in response to the needs of others
2. *Responsibility.* Taking action out of genuine concern rather than on the basis of perceived obligation
3. *Competence.* Providing care and doing so with responsibility for the decisions made relative to that care
4. *Responsiveness.* Recognizing and responding positively to the vulnerability of those in one's care

Principals who attempt to balance the dual roles of legal administrator and child advocate help to set the tone of acceptance and community so vital to the successful implementation of special education services. It is important in this regard that principals recognize and encourage others to appreciate the four phases of caring:

1. *Caring About.* Recognizing that care is necessary
2. *Taking Care Of.* Assuming some responsibility for the identified need; providing a service to meet that need

3. *Care Giving.* Meeting the needs by taking an active part in the individual's care
4. *Care Receiving.* Recognizing that individuals respond to the care that is provided and being attentive to that response (i.e., have the individuals' needs been appropriately met?)[10]

It is important to note that as principals exercise a sense of care in the administration of special education programs, the individuals in need of care may extend far beyond the student. The needs of those who will deliver the needed care to students—parents and teachers—must also be considered. In meeting many of these needs, the principal will be responsible for responding with adequate parental and staff support programs. Extensive staff-development training will be necessary to enable those who serve the needs of others to do so in more effective ways. In so doing, the principal has fulfilled the highest level of care for the student as well as the caregiver.

Administration of Special Education Services

ISLLC 3

Special education is governed by a series of laws that together form an umbrella of compliance regulations that guide the school principal in the administration of quality legal services. A summary of each law is presented.

Family Educational Rights and Privacy Act

The Family Educational Rights and Privacy Act (FERPA),[11] enforced by the U.S. Department of Education, was passed in 1974 to protect the privacy of educational records. Although the law is not classified as special education legislation, it does impact all special education students along with the regular population of students. The law provides parents and eligible students (those 18 years or older or attending a postsecondary institution) the right to inspect and review their educational records (records directly related to the student and maintained by the district or institution). In addition, it gives those parents or eligible students the right to request that corrections be made to school records that are believed to be incorrect or in violation to privacy rights. The law requires the following:

- Written parental or eligible student permission for the release of student information
- Notification of parent and eligible student rights under FERPA
- Notification to parents and eligible students of previously distributed directory information

In interpreting this law, it is important that the school principal carefully distinguish between *directory* and *personal information.* Table 8.1 outlines the differences in these two information sources.

A second law that has implications for special education services is Section 504, which deals specifically with students who have disabilities.

Section 504: Nondiscrimination on the Basis of Handicap in Programs and Activities Receiving or Benefiting from Federal Financial Assistance

This law[12], currently scheduled for reauthorization, was designed to prevent discrimination toward any individual judged to have a handicap (i.e., disability). Crucial to the law is a clear

TABLE 8.1   Personally Identifiable Information versus Specific Directory Information

PERSONALLY IDENTIFIABLE INFORMATION	SPECIFIC DIRECTORY INFORMATION
Name	Name
Address	Names of parents and other family members
Telephone listing	Address of student or student's family members
Date and place of birth	
Major field of study	
Participation in officially recognized activities and sports	Social Security or student number
Weight and height of athletic team members	List of personal characteristics or other other identifiable information

definition of who is judged to be handicapped. The law defines *handicapped persons* as "any person who (i) has a physical or mental impairment which substantially limits one or more major life activities, (ii) has a record of such an impairment, or (iii) is regarded as having such an impairment."[13] The 1997 amendments include in that definition drug addicts and alcoholics as handicapped.

Section 504 prohibits exclusion of students with handicaps (disabilities) from aids, benefits, or services that are provided to students without handicaps; provides students with handicaps with equal opportunity to participate in those services, aids, or benefits; and requires that such services be "as effective as those provided to the non-handicapped."[14] Finally, the law prohibits different or separate services except "when necessary to provide equally effective benefits."[15]

This last provision is especially important, as it has been misinterpreted by many to mean that students with handicaps (disabilities) must *always* be placed in services identical to those provided for other children. This official interpretation of the amendments goes into great detail to discuss the concept of "equivalent" versus "identical" services and states specifically that "in order to meet the individual needs of handicapped persons to the same extent that the corresponding needs of non-handicapped persons are met, adjustments to regular programs or the provision of different programs may sometimes be necessary."[16] The interpretation states further, "It must be emphasized that, although separate services must be required in some instances, the provision of unnecessarily separate or different services is discriminatory."[17] These interpretations of the law reinforce the urgent need for principals to carefully orchestrate the placement process by thoughtfully considering the unique needs of each student with a handicap (disability) regardless of the label of certification. Certification of the student merely establishes the presence of a handicapping condition. Verification, through the Individual Educational Plan (IEP) team process, establishes that such student has specific educational needs that require special education services. At this point, the student's *unique* needs should be the focal point for any service delivery decision.

The final legal framework to be considered in this umbrella of provisions is the Individuals with Disabilities Education Act (IDEA) and its latest amendments.

Individuals with Disabilities Education Improvement Act (IDEIA)

ISLLC 3

This law, enacted in 1975 as Public Law 94-142, became effective in 1978. Originally, it was named the Education for All Handicapped Children's Act (EAHCA) and, in 1990, was renamed the Individuals with Disabilities Education Act (IDEA). The IDEA amendments of 1997 further clarified its provisions.[18] The amendments introduced significant changes in the services provided to special education students. Basically, these changes revolved around three main themes:

1. Strengthened parental participation in the educational process
2. Accountability for students' participation and success in the general education curriculum and mastery of IEP goals and objectives
3. Remediation and rehabilitation of behavior problems at school and in the classroom

The Individuals with Disabilities Education Act required that every participating state offer to all children with disabilities a "free and appropriate public education"[19] and that those children be educated with children who are not disabled "to the maximum extent appropriate."[20] Free appropriate public education (FAPE) must meet state standards, be provided at public expense, and include special education services specifically tailored through an individual educational plan to meet the unique needs of the individual. These services included any preschool, elementary, or secondary educational services provided to students without disabilities within the state. Related services were included as part of this requirement.

Not only did IDEA provide for the academic needs of students with disabilities, but it also gave attention to the behavioral dimensions of the students' education. As stated in the provisions, "When a child's behavior impedes his or her learning or that of others, the IEP team must consider positive behavioral interventions, strategies, and supports to address that behavior."[21]

The new provisions of the law focused strongly on the general curriculum and emphasized the importance of these main concepts:

- Identification and monitoring of each child's unique educational needs
- Involvement of all stakeholders in the child's education
- Transition and preparation of children with disabilities for employment and postsecondary education[22]

The new emphasis on the general curriculum raised several important questions that needed to be considered for each student:

- How does the student's disability affect his or her involvement and progress in the general curriculum?
- What particular goals and/or objectives will aim toward ensuring the student's involvement and progress within the general curriculum?
- What other educational needs result from the student's disability?
- What related services should be provided to enable the student to progress toward annual goals and make progress in the general curriculum?
- What specific monitoring procedures are in place to check the student's progress toward goal attainment?
- Has the IEP responded appropriately to student progress or failure to progress?[23]

The IDEA required school districts to provide a free appropriate public education, including special education and related services, in the least restrictive environment (LRE), as determined by an IEP team and written in an individual education plan. These services, mandatory for all children from age 3 to 21, could be certified by an appropriate specialist as having a disability or exceptionality and verified by a multidisciplinary team of educators as needing special education services. Exceptionalities included but were not limited to, the following:

Mental retardation	Emotional disturbance
Learning disabilities	Visual impairment
Hearing impairment	Other health impairment
Orthopedic impairment	Speech impairment
Autism	Deaf–blind
Multidisabled	Traumatic brain injury
Developmental delays	

The law required that certain due process procedures be followed, assuming the right of the parent and child to be fully informed and included in the decision making at all steps in identification, child evaluation, planning, programming, and program evaluation. (See Chapter 16 for a more complete review of the law regarding special students.)

A new reauthorization of IDEA was signed into law on December 3, 2004. The new statute, known as Individuals with Disabilities Education Improvement Act of 2004—IDEIA 04—went into effect on July 1, 2005. We will discuss the original IDEA (1990) and its steps of implementation. This discussion will be followed by an overview of the new provisions (2005).

Idea (1990)

Program Steps

Particular steps were to be followed in implementing a special education program. The schools were charged to proceed according to outlined steps. Since many of these steps are still operable, they will be presented in the present tense.

Step 1: Screening.   The school has the responsibility to monitor the development of each child in order to know as early as possible if any child is having problems with his or her school work. Screening checks are to be made for the child's medical health record as well as the child's progress in school. Medical screenings are usually scheduled by the district special education departments or appropriate health agencies. Educational checks are initially the responsibility of the regular classroom teacher to observe and identify children with potential disabilities. Vision and hearing screenings are part of this process.

Step 2: Prereferral Actions.   When a student presents a particularly unique problem, the classroom teacher often needs somewhere to turn for help. The problem may surface as a disciplinary problem, a learning difficulty, poor attendance, or what seems like a lack of interest in planned classroom activities. None of the strategies tried by the teacher has seemed to work. If the child is referred to special education, weeks can pass before a formal assessment is completed, and a staff meeting is held to recommend a plan. In some cases, a formal referral may identify a student as disabled and recommend placement in a special education instruction program. Other students may be identified as mildly disabled, but not in need of special education programming, and still others will not be identified as disabled at all. For these last two groups, the delay in providing immediate support to the teacher and student may not have been necessary at all.

Prereferral procedures should be developed that will allow for more immediate action and assistance in most cases and that would be less costly than the formal referral and assessment process. The prereferral procedure should begin with the collection and review of classroom data gathered by the teacher. Included should be attendance information, available standardized and classroom test data, teacher observations of student effort, attention, ability to follow directions, listening, social skills, self-confidence, peer relationships, and so on. Teaching strategies attempted should also be documented. Scientifically researched-based interventions must be implemented in the general education classroom. Progress monitoring should occur to determine the effectiveness of the interventions.

Step 3: Support Team Review. Each school should organize a school support team (S-team) to function as an intermediate step between the recognition of a problem by a classroom teacher and a formal referral for a comprehensive educational evaluation. For students who are obviously disabled, this support team review is bypassed and a formal referral is made immediately. On the other hand, the teacher who is experiencing less severe difficulty with a student should request the team's assistance. The information gathered through the prereferral action is received by this team. The team that meets regularly to discuss such cases considers the problem, generates possible remedial actions, and recommends specific intervention strategy. The S-team should be made up of experienced teachers qualified to teach that age child, possibly the special education teacher, and other appropriate staff members such as a Title I teacher or guidance counselor. One member should function as the S-team coordinator to schedule meetings, organize records, and ensure that the team's recommendations are implemented.

The S-team should be viewed as problem solvers, bringing to focus the expert resources of the school on those issues that fall just short of resulting in a formal special education referral. Those students deemed to have educational or emotional problems beyond the normal capability of the school staff and program to adequately address ultimately will be given a formal referral to the other education specialists for further evaluation.

Step 4: Formal Referral for a Comprehensive Evaluation. An evaluation is scheduled to specifically determine the severity of the child's deficits. An assessment team may include all or any of the following: school psychologist, occupational therapist, physical therapist, other special educators, physician, regular classroom teachers, parents, and/or medical specialists. Parents have the right to obtain an independent evaluation at their own expense if they so choose; however, depending on the nature of the events, the school must sometimes eventually assume these costs. Ultimately, the IEP team determines if the student is eligible for special education. Eligibility is based on the child meeting the certification requirements for a particular special education category, and a determination that their needs cannot be met in the general education setting without special education support services.

Step 5: The IEP Team. The IEP team, made up of a group of at least three school professionals and the parent/guardian, is responsible for developing an appropriate educational program for the student based on a careful review of all diagnostic data. The IEP team's responsibilities include (1) reviewing the present level of educational performance as derived from the assessment data, (2) developing the individualized educational program, and (3) making a recommendation for placement.

The IEP team approach is designed to ensure that decisions concerning a student's program will be made by a team of persons whose primary goal is to accommodate the interests, needs, learning styles, and abilities of that student. Careful consideration should be given to the selection of IEP team members who are most qualified to contribute to the development and implementation of the IEP. Individuals who must be part of the initial IEP team include the principal or his or her designee; the teacher who recently or currently has the student in class; the assessment specialist(s), such as the psychologist or audiologist, who conducted the assessments as part of the evaluation; the parent/guardian of the student; and the student, when appropriate.

The IEP team provides a written record of the decisions reached by the members at the IEP meeting. It sets forth in writing the commitment of resources necessary for the child who has disabilities, functions as a management tool to ensure services, is the compliance/monitoring document for government monitoring of the law, serves as the evaluation device in determining the child's progress, and functions as the communication document with the parent. The IEP must contain the following components:

1. Biographical information
2. Behavioral statement
3. The present level of educational performance
4. Statement of how the student's disability adversely affects participation in the general curriculum
5. Annual program goals and interim program objectives
6. Classroom participation and modifications
7. Special education placement and justification
8. Multidisciplinary team signatures of participants
9. Parent signature and statement of review/appeal rights
10. Indicated date for annual review

The Individuals with Disabilities Education Act required that the individual educational program developed by the IEP team be provided in the *least restrictive environment.* Today, that generally means inclusion. *Inclusion* differs from *mainstreaming* in that the latter term usually referred to integrating children with disabilities and children without disabilities for only a portion of the day, which may be during nonacademic times. In a fully inclusive model, students with disabilities, no matter how severe, are taught in the regular education classroom of their home school with their age and grade peers for the full day with support services provided within the classroom. In short, inclusion means bringing support services to the child rather than moving the child to a segregated setting to receive special services. This means that each child should be placed in a setting where he or she can be with noneligible children as much of the time as possible. The act allowed for 10 different placement options but demanded that the least restrictive option appropriate for the child be used. The act required that a continuum of service options be provided. A typical sequence of options would include the following:

1. Full time in the classroom with special supplies and/or equipment
2. Full time in the classroom with consultative services for the teacher

3. Full time in the classroom with additional instruction by a special education teacher in the classroom

4. Part time in the classroom (as much as is appropriate) and part time in a special *resource program* coordinated with the regular classroom activities

5. Full time in a special *comprehensive development classroom (CDC)* provided to meet the needs of the severely/profoundly involved students who require intensive planning and programming

6. Part time in the school program with a special education paraprofessional supervising the child with disabilities while in the classroom

7. Other related services, including transportation; speech pathology and audiology; psychological, physical, and occupational therapy; recreation; counseling; medical (for diagnostic and evaluation purposes); school health; social work; parent counseling and training; assistive technology devices and services; transition; nursing; interpreter; as well as others not specified

8. Ancillary services provided by agencies outside the school to provide services a minimum of four hours a day in order to maintain the child in the classroom

9. Residential services to provide for a child whose disabling conditions are so profound or complex that continuous intervention is required to meet his or her educational needs and no special education services offered in a CDC or self-contained program can meet these needs. Although these programs are very costly, if the IEP calls for this service, the school system is responsible for the total program

10. Home or hospital instruction provided to continue the educational advancement of eligible students who are unable to attend school

Step 6: Implementing the Plan. Options numbered 1 through 6 from the preceding list are often implemented in the school, whereas the services of options 7 through 10 are more often provided by school district staff, by special schools, or by contract with outside agencies. The concept of *least restrictive environment* has been applied to greater and greater numbers of special education children, bringing more low-functioning children and children with disabilities into contact with the education program. As a result, many more children with severe disabilities, previously served in segregated special schools, are part of the school and are spending at least a part of their day in classrooms, often accompanied by an attendant. In some cases, building instructional and material modifications are required.

Often, the initial reaction of the staff to students with severe disabilities in their classrooms is one of fear because of health concern for such a child and concern that he or she will disrupt the normal classroom environment. A good in-service training program for the staff frequently turns the fear of special students into a learning opportunity. This is especially true when classroom children are taught about the classmates who are joining them. Often, compassion and understanding develops in children that could not be taught as effectively any other way. Rather than children who are disabled detracting from the learning of other children, they often enrich it with the development of new values and understanding for all children.

The principal should take advantage of the opportunities provided by the special education program and its integration into the education activities and be very careful not to allow these to develop into separate programs.

Program and Assessment Reviews

Each special education student's IEP is reviewed annually by the IEP team for the purpose of determining the continuing appropriateness of the program placement, goals, and objectives. Progress reports are required to be sent home every six weeks, indicating the amount of progress being made to achieve mastery of the goals and objectives. Review dates must be monitored so that the annual reviews take place on schedule. The intent of the review should always be to move the child toward a less restrictive environment with less special education assistance if this is appropriate. The effort should be to try to move the child back toward the program whenever possible. The evaluation process for each special education student must be repeated every three years. A reevaluation summary must be completed to determine if additional assessments are required to continue eligibility. If additional assessments are needed, then a new assessment plan must be developed and carried out, recertification must take place, and the IEP team must once again develop a new IEP.

Safeguarding Special Education Records

Special education records must be maintained separate and apart from a student's school cumulative record folder. Access to the special education records is to be carefully controlled, with availability restricted to only those school personnel who have direct contact with the child or to whom the parents have given written permission for access, such as an outside psychologist. Sign-out sheets should be used and permission letters kept on file. Education records are not supposed to reference the existence of a special education file. The purpose of this regulation is to protect the special education student from later discrimination that might occur if it became known the child had some type of disability. Some schools code their cumulative folders with some special mark to indicate the existence of a separate special education folder.

Rights of Parents

The requirement of involvement of the parents of the potential or verified special education student has been noted through this entire section describing special education procedures. From the notification of the initial referral, through the assessment process, to the writing of the IEP, and finally to the approval for placement, as well as future access to their child's records, parents must give their informed consent as participants in the process. Failure to notify or obtain this consent is a violation of the rights of parents under the law. Parents have the right to revoke previous consent. In the event they choose to revoke a previous consent, they then are not entitled to all rights they were previously afforded.

Disciplining Students with Disabilities

Discipline of children in school is an important concern of all principals. In most situations, the day-to-day decisions regarding the control of children has been the prerogative of the principal supported by the staff. However, in the case of children with disabilities, intricate federal and state regulations govern the administration of punishment of these students; these regulations are based solely on federal court cases interpreting the laws.

Children who have attention deficit hyperactivity disorder (ADHD) may receive educational services and protection under Section 504 regulations. These children, by the nature of their disabling condition, often show up in the principal's office as discipline cases. Great care must be taken in establishing discipline procedures for these children because they often defy normal school behavior expectations. One cannot discipline children with disabilities in the unilateral fashion generally used for other students. In 1989, in *Honig* v. *Doe*,[24] the U.S. Supreme Court ruled that students with disabilities cannot be unilaterally suspended or expelled for more than 10 days a year without provision of due process. This case triggered an array of procedural restrictions on local schools. Table 8.2 summarizes basic disciplinary actions often used in school and indicates under what conditions they may or may not be used for children with disabilities.

TABLE 8.2 Conditions of Disciplinary Action for Children with Disabilities

DISCIPLINARY ACTION	CONDITIONS OF USE
Verbal reprimand	OK
Written warning	OK
Payment for damages	OK as long as the child's behavior does not suggest IEP changes
Time-out	OK
Detention (lunch, recess, after school)	OK
In-school suspension	OK if supervised by a certified special education teacher and/or the child's IEP is being carried out
Corporal punishment	Many states prohibit its use. If permitted, it must be administered fairly. It is not recommended for children with disabilities.
Aversive therapy/Devices*	Only if specified in IEP
Bus suspension	Counts as part of 10-day maximum if busing is included in child's IEP
Exclusion from extracurricular activities	OK as long as activities are not central to IEP goal
Suspension/Expulsion	OK for 10 school days per offense so long as "pattern of exclusion" does not exist.[†] For longer periods, the IEP team must determine the offense not to be related to the child's disability.
Alternate school placement	OK as long as the change is made through the regular IEP process.

Any disciplinary action must have no adverse effect on IEP goals and objectives and must not be applied in a discriminatory manner.

*Effective January 1, 2009, a new law governs this category. It is entitled Public Chapter 1063, the Special Education Isolation and Restraint Modernization and Positive Behavioral Support Act.

[†]In addition to the 10-day limitation imposed by *Honig* v. *Doe,* the Office of Civil Rights reminds districts that Section 504 requires a student reevaluation prior to every significant change in placement. Therefore, any change in placement, including a suspension/expulsion, for more than 10 days or any consecutive 10-day suspensions must be evaluated by the IEP team.

In understanding the disciplinary actions appropriate to the area of special education, it is important to consider the concept of *manifest determination*. The concept has been defined as "a *process* that looks at the child's disability, the functional basis for the behavior, behavior intervention plan if it exists, the behavior, and the child's program to determine if the behavior was caused by or was strongly linked to the disability."[25] If it is determined that the child's behavior is in fact connected to his or her disability, the IEP team must then develop a behavior intervention plan (BIP). Such a plan is defined as "a plan that is developed *after* the functional behavior assessment [FBA]. It uses the *FBA* to attempt to address the inappropriate behavior and to change the behavior by replacing the inappropriate behavior with appropriate behavior."[26]

IDEIA 04[27]

Major provisions of the reauthorization of IDEA, known as the Individuals with Disabilities Improvement Act of 2004 (IDEIA 04), make strong connections between the original IDEA and the No Child Left Behind Act. The connections include the provision for *highly qualified teachers* and the focus on the academic progress of students with disabilities. Specifically, the reauthorization makes major changes in the identification of students with learning disabilities by initiating a "Response to Intervention" procedure that allows the school district to disregard the identification of a learning disability based on a severe discrepancy between academic achievement and intellectual ability, if it can be demonstrated that the student responds appropriately to "scientific research-based intervention" as part of the evaluation procedure.

The reauthorization provides for coordinated interagency intervening services with particular emphasis on students in kindergarten through grade 3 who, although not identified as handicapped (disabled), show a need for additional academic or behavioral support. Along with this emphasis is an increased focus on literacy instruction.

Increased emphasis on academic achievement is also noted in the development of individual educational plans. All IEPs must include levels of academic achievement and a statement of measurable annual goals for academic and functional performance.

A final important change in the reauthorization has to do with discipline. The reauthorization establishes a new standard for manifestation determination. A review of the student's file must show that the violation of student conduct was caused by, or had a direct relationship to, the student's disability, or that it was the direct result of the school district's failure to implement the IEP. In determining placement, if in fact a manifest determination is shown, the IEP team must conduct a behavioral assessment, implement a behavioral plan, and return the student to his or her original placement (unless special circumstances, as identified in the statute, can be shown).

Dealing with Parents of Special Children

The identification of a child as a potential special education child is always stressful for parents, and the principal and staff must be prepared to deal with a variety of reactions from parents. The

parent may or may not have been aware for some time that a problem exists for his or her child. This knowledge may have been suppressed or the parent may already have a long history of dealing with the child and the school about the problems. There are at least four general patterns of parental reaction for which the school, the IEP team, and the principal, whether part of that IEP team or not, must be ready.

The Supportive Parent

This parent is understanding of his or her child's problems, is concerned about the child's education, and respects and appreciates the efforts of the school to develop an appropriate educational plan for the child. He or she generally is most supportive during IEP team meetings, attending faithfully and asking how he or she might best support the school's efforts at home. Some parents always accept the recommendations of the school staff without question, whereas others may begin to question the IEP team recommendations if they feel services are not adequate. This latter type may become a demanding parent if the school fails to carefully present a rationale for its recommendations.

The Denying Parent

This is the parent who is unaccepting of the possibility that his or her child has a disability. He or she is offended by the request for a referral, often initially refusing to sign the permission for testing and frequently demanding to submit outside independent evaluations to refute the school's claim that the child has a disability. In some cases, he or she begins to resist actions of the school by not attending meetings, by refusing to sign documents, and generally by becoming purposefully nonresponsive. The denial of the disability may be due to a feeling that the child's disability is a reflection on his or her own intelligence or on his or her ability as a parent to raise the child. In these cases, parent education must often be an additional consideration before meaningful assistance can be provided for the child.

The denying parent is often extremely frustrated with the child, and his or her demands of the child are often impossible, given the identified disability. It is sometimes helpful to counsel with the parent privately, reviewing assessment data and pointing out that disabling conditions know no social or intellectual bounds (Albert Einstein had a learning disability, the Kennedy family had a sister with mental disabilities, and President Franklin D. Roosevelt was confined to a wheelchair). Additional support needs to be provided to these families, because these feelings of denial die slowly and new strategies for dealing with the disability at home must be learned if the home is to be a supportive environment. Parent education and counseling is an appropriate consideration in the development of the IEP for these situations.

The Nonresponsive Parent

The problem of the nonresponsive parent is a difficult one. Notices are sent out, phone calls are attempted, and certified letters are sent in order to meet the due process, informed-consent legal requirement for parent notification. Some schools even attempt to arrange a home visit to elicit a parental response. In some cases, the work schedule of the parent interferes; in others, child care makes school visits difficult. If these are really the problem, the school should make every effort to arrange a schedule or situation that will allow the parent's participation. However, there are situations where there is little or no interest on the part of the parent in the child's schooling. In these cases, it is often appropriate to identify some other responsible adult to work with this child and to provide an adult advocate and educational support system outside the classroom environment.

The Belligerent, Demanding Parent

This parent is going to attempt to obtain more than the school (the IEP team) believes is necessary to provide appropriate options for program placement. He or she will question the assessments provided by the school staff to the point of demanding independent evaluation or bringing in his or her own psychologist. He or she will challenge the recommendations of the IEP team, and if his or her demands are not met, will threaten to or actually will bring his or her lawyer or advocate to the IEP team meeting.

As a principal, be prepared to participate fully in the IEP team process yourself. Don't leave your teachers to deal with situations without strong support. If you can see that a particular staffing is going to be very difficult or complicated, request that someone from the district-level special education office join the IEP team. Remember: You must keep in mind the best interests of the child, tempered by the needs of the parents, staff, administration, and other children in the school. Your goal is to provide each child with an appropriate educational program in the least restrictive environment possible, given that child's disabling conditions.

The Role of the Principal

For the principal, the IEP team represents a visible form of involvement with the special education program and the special needs children in the school. Although it is possible for the principal to designate a representative to serve on IEP teams, direct participation by the principal in the IEP team process signals an interest in this program to students, teachers, and parents. It also provides to the principal direct feedback regarding the adequacy of the special education program in meeting the needs of the children in the school and provides an opportunity for leadership in improving the program where needed.

`ISLLC 1`

The Role of the Classroom Teacher

Many students with special needs are in classrooms. The teachers in these classrooms have certain responsibilities for these children, including the following:

`ISLLC 2`

- Identifying and referring children who are potentially disabled
- Taking part in due process and IEP team procedures
- Collecting assessment data about children with disabilities
- Assisting children with disabilities with special equipment
- Participating in a team effort with special education staff
- Helping all children work and play together
- Communicating with parents
- Providing accommodations and modifications based on the IEP

Whenever a child with disabilities is placed in the classroom, the responsibility of the classroom teacher for that child is the same as for any other child in the room. Because all children differ with respect to the amount, rate, and style of learning, minor modifications in methodology, curriculum, or environment are often necessary for children, disabled or not. When a child's IEP specifies modifications in methodology, curriculum, or environment from the class, the development of such specially designed instruction is the responsibility of *special educators*. Classroom educators are responsible for assisting in carrying out the program. Overall classroom management remains the responsibility of the classroom educator.

Educating children who are severely disabled in the classroom can often be difficult. It is here where problems sometime arise. Given the requirement of the law for providing programs in the least restrictive environment and inclusion, more children with severe disabling conditions are now being educated in the regular school setting, both in the classroom as well as in the special education classroom but housed in the neighborhood school.

Children with mental disabilities challenge many teachers. Many of the learning disabilities, though mild in a sense, cause great difficulty for the child and require great understanding and skill on the part of the teacher. Some children used to be referred to as discipline problems and sent to the office; others were regarded as lazy and not motivated to do their work. Educators now know that many of these students actually have a type of learning disability such as attention deficit disorder, dyslexia, dysnomia, or one of a host of others. In many cases, the problem has gone undiagnosed for many years and becomes compounded by the repeated failure to succeed on the part of the student who now has advanced to middle or even high school. Many teachers have not been trained either to diagnose these problems or know how to deal with them properly when they are known. Additionally, many teachers feel overwhelmed by the number of children and problems they face daily in the classroom.

Most school faculties need good staff-development activities in many aspects of working with children with special needs. Training in diagnosing and treating learning disabilities can be a help to virtually every classroom teacher. Knowledge in the use of supplementary aids and services such as brailled worksheets for students who are blind, provision of tape recorders or word processors for children who cannot write, or the operation of physical aids such as wheelchairs, walkers, and hearing aids is helpful. Skills in the use of cooperative learning techniques in conjunction with special educators and in the management of disabilities in the classroom need to be learned.

Most needed of all, perhaps, is training for teachers to help them understand and deal with their own fears and biases concerning people who are disabled—and how to help children in their classes to do the same. Finally, teachers need to be trained about their role in state and national special education policies, referrals, evaluations, IEP development, due process, working with parents, and working with special educators regarding such things as student grading, scheduling, and record keeping.

Outside Public Agencies

A variety of public agencies in every community have direct access to the school. Local states and communities have different names for these agencies and offer somewhat different services, but each school must recognize the demand and need to interact with these services. The three

ISLLC 4, 6

that are common to almost every school are public welfare or human services departments, public health agencies, and judicial systems (usually represented by police departments and juvenile court systems). Each of these agencies has certain legal responsibilities and authority. The authority of each of these agencies transcends the walls of the school, and the school principal is not always "master of the house." It is important not to get into a turf battle with the representatives of these agencies, but rather to develop a supportive network with them to serve the children of the community better. Consider these was: The police come to pick up or question a child regarding a local crime; the principal is summoned to juvenile court to testify on a matter dealing with one of the school's children; a representative of the protective services unit of the local welfare department comes to investigate a child abuse case. In situations such as these, not only is it important for the principal to know his or her rights and the rights of the children but also to have a good working relationship with the representatives of these agencies so that all can work for the benefit of the children and the community.

The development of a network of contacts with private agencies and other public agencies is also important. Who should be in a principal's network depends somewhat on the nature of the local student clientele. Important network contacts for many schools would include groups that can provide clothing or food on an emergency basis, both emergency and nonemergency medical treatment, and both public and private mental health professionals.

Public Welfare or Human Services Agencies

Child abuse cases are one of the most common school-related involvements with public welfare or human services agencies today. A problem that a few years ago was normally considered "only a family matter" now is recognized as an area of responsibility for our society. Most states now require schools to report suspected child abuse cases to the appropriate authority for investigation. The classroom teacher who notices heavy bruising on a child or a pattern of absences along with extreme emotional behavior on the part of a child is required by law to report it. The school is, in fact, the one place outside the home where a child can take some refuge from an abusive home environment. Confidentiality regarding the reporter of abuse is generally guaranteed. However, it is this confidentiality issue, along with the sensitive nature of child abuse investigations, that sometimes causes some difficulty.

Child abuse investigators often consider the school to be an appropriate, safe location to conduct initial interviews. The school is a safe place to contact a child without alerting a suspected abuser, and it is a place where the child is more comfortable and perhaps willing to discuss the problem. Such interviews, though, can disrupt the ongoing instruction in the school. The intrusion into the school by an outside investigator can also be taken as an interference in the school's domain.

Most state laws give authority to child abuse investigators from public agencies outside the school to interview children on school premises and, in some cases, to take them into their custody. These investigators also have the authority to conduct the interviews in private with no school official present, and generally they do not have to reveal the content of an interview after it is concluded. For some principals, this procedure contradicts what they consider to be their responsibilities for their children. The first reaction may be not to want to take a child out of class, and second, not to want to let an "outsider" conduct a private interview with a child for whom the principal is responsible. The laws of most states, however, give the public social services agency this authority if it chooses to use it. The following suggestions are appropriate ways to manage requests from outside investigators:

- Always ask to see credentials.
- Attempt to convince investigators of the importance of having a school representative present during any interview. Some workers will allow you to be present.
- Control the time and place for the conference. You are generally allowed to protect instructional time.
- Document the conference, noting date, place, names of persons present, and length of the conference.
- Refuse to give access to student records without a signed release from the parent, guardian, or a court order.

In almost all cases, it is to the school's long-range advantage to develop a good working relationship with these outside agencies. They have a job to do and are also trying to safeguard the well-being of the children. Most often, you need each other.

Law Enforcement Agencies

The major school involvement with law enforcement agencies will be requests by officers to interview children while they are at school. The basic suggestions listed for investigator procedures also apply to police officers who are often employed security guards for school activities. Developing a good working relationship with police officers who work in the school zone can be most helpful to both the school and the police. The occasional informal discussion with them can sometimes cut bureaucratic paperwork and procedures and solve a problem where formal procedures could not.

The school principal will also be called on to testify in juvenile court in conjunction with children from his or her school. Every community has a juvenile court system ranging in size from a part-time judge in smaller communities to large buildings and multiple judges in larger communities. School children may be brought into juvenile court for three different types of situations. The first is for felony or misdemeanor charges similar to charges brought against an adult. However, juvenile court handles the disposition of a case somewhat differently: Publicity of juvenile crimes is kept at a minimum and prescribed treatment has rehabilitation as its purpose rather than punishment.

Status offenses, the second category, make up the largest number of cases that involve school officials. *Status offenses* can be defined as actions that are considered violations of laws for children but not adults. Nonattendance at school (truancy) and running away from home are the most common. For school officials, instigating truancy charges becomes the last resort among efforts to obtain regular attendance from a child. In many cases, the real problem is the parents. Juvenile courts have the power to order certain action from the parents to improve or control their child's behavior, such as requiring the parent to ensure the child's presence at school each day or be held in contempt of court. A contempt charge against the parent could result in the parent being jailed. Once again, a good working relationship between the school principal and the juvenile court can be most helpful in solving such problems.

The third type of case dealt with by the juvenile court involves the problems of neglected and/or abused children. In these cases, the children are the victims rather than the offenders. School employees are often reporters of suspected child abuse and may be called on to testify in juvenile court regarding their observations. Testifying in these situations can be particularly traumatic. Reporting child abuse is generally kept confidential, or at least confidentiality is attempted. However, when the accused are the parents or someone else closely associated with the school, testifying can be difficult.

Outside Agencies and Closed Records.   In an effort to protect the reputation of children and their families, many of the agencies that work with children are required by law to maintain strict confidentiality of the records they develop and maintain. This is true, for example, with the special education records maintained by the school. When a child has been in the custody of the juvenile court or has been a ward of the welfare department's children's protective services unit and is then returned to or placed in your school, it is extremely difficult and not impossible to get any information about the child's recent history. In some cases, this makes it extremely difficult to know how to deal with a child or even if the safety of other children should be a concern. Some local areas have developed coordinating councils for the several children's agencies in an effort to improve communication among them. The individual principal will probably find his or her efforts to develop an informal network among the workers of the various agencies to be a very useful communication link to information not available through the formal channels.

Services of Outside Social Welfare Agencies

Mental health agencies, chemical abuse agencies, civic clubs, local churches, and so on, all have an interest and a role to play in the welfare of school children. Networking once again becomes the byword for the principal and staff. Situations always develop that fall short of eligibility for one or more of the formal service agencies to the school. It may be a parent who becomes aware that his or her child is doing drugs, or it may be the child who appears to be suffering from severe depression; however, until children take some overt act to harm themselves, there is no regular agency support available. In these situations, it is important for principals to have contacts with professionals from other agencies from whom they can get advice and learn where the school or the parents might turn for help.

Public Health Departments and Local Schools

The services provided by public health agencies directly to school children vary greatly throughout the country. In some states, the only contact may be to monitor immunization records to ensure the health of the general public; in other areas, services may include provision for public health personnel to provide direct services to children in the school. Nurses stationed in the school, health presentations in classrooms, dental services, immunizations, and some emergency medical care may be provided. Once again, there may be more services available for the asking than the average school receives. It is up to the principal to make the contact, develop the relationship, and add these professionals to his or her network of available persons to be called on when needed.

Summary

Schools have many special children with various special needs. The quality of school life depends on the collective satisfaction of the needs of all the children. The principal cannot personally meet the needs of each and every child, but he or she can set the tone, develop the network of contacts who can assist in providing for the children's needs, and be a facilitator of resources for achievement of needs. The symbolic leadership of the principal in showing concern for all children demonstrates to the staff the significance and importance of their efforts.

ACTIVITIES

1. Review Case Studies 2, 7, 8, and 25 at the end of this book. Analyze the problems presented and apply the special services concepts developed in this chapter. What approach would you use in addressing the problems? Set forth a strategy to overcome the difficulties faced by the school as well as ways to deal with the individuals involved.

2. What are some ways the services required by special education laws can be implemented while minimizing the time required of the classroom teacher for special education activities?

3. What are the agencies in your community that provide services to children? In what networks does your school participate to help link together these services?

4. Turn to the ISLLC standards found in Appendix B. Review the functions listed in Standard 2. Reflect on which of the standard items relate directly to the needs of special students. How do the concepts of special education and special needs children match Standard 2? What other standards speak to the needs of special students? Identify one function to link directly to a concept or idea discussed in Chapter 8.

ENDNOTES

1. Juducial opinion, 1949.
2. L. Baca and E. Almanza, *Language Minority Students with Disabilities* (Reston, VA: Council for Exceptional Children, 1991).
3. C. A. Utley and S. L. Mortweet, "The Challenge of Diversity" in *Inclusion: The Integration of Students with Disabilities,* ed. M. J. Coutino and A. Repp (Belmont, CA: Wadsworth, 1999), p. 61.
4. Ibid.
5. Carol Gilligan, *In a Different Voice: Psychological Theory and Women's Development* (Cambridge, MA: Harvard University Press, 1982).
6. L. Kohlberg, *The Philosophy of Moral Development: Moral Stages and the Idea of Justice* (Cambridge, MA: Harper & Row, 1981).
7. L. Ballering, *Practicing Administrators' Attitudes toward the Ethic of Care.* Doctoral dissertation, University of Houston, 1997.
8. Ibid.
9. F. C. Power and T. A. Makogon, "The Just-Community Approach to Care," *Journal for a Just and Caring Education 2,* no. 1 (1997): 9–24.
10. Ballering, *Practicing Administrators' Attitudes toward the Ethic of Care.*
11. Family Educational Rights and Privacy Act (FERPA), 34 C.F.R. Part 99, Subpart A—General.
12. Analysis of Final Regulations Under Section 504 of the Rehabilitation Act [45 FR 30936 (May 9, 1980): amended at 55 FR 52141 (Dec 19, 1990)].
13. Part Three: Section 504 Regulations. Unannotated Version: Nondiscrimination on the Basis of Handicap in Programs and Activities Receiving or Benefiting from Federal Financial Assistance (Sup.1—10/9), p. 148.
14. Analysis of Final Regulations for 504, p. 5
15. Ibid., p. 6.
16. Ibid., p. 5.
17. Ibid., p. 6.
18. L. Bartlett, G. Weisenstein, and S. Etscheidt (Eds.), *Successful Inclusion for Educational Leaders* (Upper Saddle River, NJ: Merrill Prentice-Hall, 2002).
19. Americans with Disabilities Act of 1990, 42 U.S.C. 1401 *et. seq.*
20. Ibid.
21. Dr. John McCook, class lecture, University of Tennessee, November 2002.
22. Ibid.
23. G. Zelin, Conference Presentation, *What Is Appropriate Educational Progress and How Do We Prove It?* Presented to Tennessee Association of Administrators of Special Education, Fall Legal Conference, Gatlinburg, TN, 2002.
24. *Honig* v. *Doe,* EHLR 559:231 (U.S. 1988).
25. McCook, 2002.
26. Ibid.
27. Reauthorization IDEIA 04.

SELECTED READINGS

Bartlett, Larry D., Greg R. Weisenstein, and Susan Etscheidt. *Successful Inclusion for Educational Leaders* (Upper Saddle River, NJ: Merrill Prentice-Hall, 2002).

Bubaj, S. "Making Everything Fit." *Principal Leadership 5* (2005): 21–23.

Crisman, B. W. "Inclusive Programming for Students with Autism" [Electronic Version]. *Principal 88* (November/December 2008): 28–32.

Curtis, Steven. "Parents and Litigation: Insights from a Special Education Law Clinic." *Phi Delta Kappan 86* (2005): 510–514.

Delmore, P. "Pulling the Plug on 'Pull-Outs.' " *Principal Leadership 4* (2003): 35–36.

Fenion, A. "Hiring an Effective Special Education Teacher" [Electronic Version]. *Principal 88* (November/December 2008): 24–27.

Gittins, N. "Uneasy Alliance." *Principal Leadership 6* (2005): 59–61.

Green, J. "Collaborating with Special Education Administrators." *Principal (Reston, Va) 88,* no. 2 (2008): 12–15.

Hardman, B. "The Pumpkin Project." *Phi Delta Kappan 86,* no. 7 (2005): 522–524.

Jones, R., P. Zirkel, and R. Barrack, "Special Education and Regular Education: Achieving High School Success with the NCLB and the IDEA" *Catalyst for Change 35,* no. 2 (2008): 19–24.

Lambert, Joan. "Easing the Transition to High School." *Educational Leadership 7* (2005): 61–63.

Levinson, E. M., and E. J. Palmer. "Preparing Students with Disabilities for School-to-Work Transition and Post-School Life." *Principal Leadership 5* (2005): 11–15.

Merritt, S. "Clearing the Hurdles of Inclusion." *Educational Leadership 59* (2001): 67–70.

Reynolds, B. H. "Are Principals Ready to Welcome Children with Disabilities?" [Electronic Version]. *Principal 88* (November/December 2008): 16–19.

Ryan, J., A., Katsiyannis, R., Peterson, and R. Chmelar, "IDEA 2004 and Disciplining Students with Disabilities" *NASSP Bulletin 91,* no. 2 (June 1, 2007): 130–140. (ERIC Document Rep-roduction Service No. EJ763161)

Sailor, W., and B. Roger "Rethinking Inclusion: Schoolwide Applications." *Phi Delta Kappan 86,* no. 5 (2005): 503–509.

Shapon-Shevin, M. "Inclusion: A Matter of Social Justice." *Educational Leadership 61,* no. 2 (2003): 25–28.

Sorrentino, A., and P. Zirkel. "Is NCLB Leaving Special Education Students Behind?" *Principal 83,* no. 5 (2004): 26–29.

Warnemuede, C. "Helping Parents Help the Slow Learner." *Principal 87* (January/February 2008): 32–35.

Yell, M., A. Katsiyannis, and R. Bradley. "A Special Role." *Principal Leadership 4,* no. 2 (2003): 22–28.

Yell, M., J. Shriner. and A. Katsiyannis "Individuals with Disabilities Education Improvement Act of 2004 and IDEA Regulations of 2006: Implications for Educators, Administators, and Teacher Trainers" *Focus on Exceptional Children 39,* no. 1 (2006): 1. (ERIC Document Reproduction Service No. EJ54722)

9 Human Resources Development

If schools want to enhance their organizational capacity to boost student learning, they should work on building a professional community that is characterized by shared purpose, collaborative activity, and collective responsibility among staff.

—F. NEWMANN AND G. WEHLAGE[1]

Human resources development is both a concept and a process. As a concept, it is concerned with the full development and utilization of an organization's most valuable resources—its human ones. As a process, it is an integrated continuous flow of functions that make up a dimension of principal responsibility known as *personnel administration*. The various functions are integrated through the philosophy, policies, procedures, and practices involved in the human resources development (HRD) process. We address two of those functions in this chapter: professional development and personnel evaluation.

Although most educational leaders espouse a dedication to the enhancement of individual potential, organizational practices may, in fact, be counterproductive to the fullest development of its human resources. In this chapter, we discuss integration of the individual and the organization, explore various teacher differences that impact the design of professional development, investigate the nature of professional development and its various delivery models, and examine the relationship between professional development, personnel evaluation, and school improvement.

Integration of the Individual and the Organization

The work of Schein[2] provides much insight into the complex process of integrating the individual and the organization in ways that will effectively meet the goals and needs of both. Schein views this integration process in three stages: entry, socialization, and mutual acceptance.

During the *entry* stage, the individual endeavors to make the right career choice, train for the occupation, and search for the appropriate position. It is a time, as well, when the organization is determining the nature of the job that is needed, identifying the skills that the individual will need to possess, recruiting a pool of candidates, and ultimately making an appropriate selection of the best person to fit the job. The thoughtfulness and skill with which both parties approach this stage will be a determining factor for the next stage: socialization.

The *socialization* stage marks a point at which "the individual builds a picture of the organization and his or her future in it."[3] At the same time, the organization comes to view the individual in terms of his or her future role within the organization. Although both parties may have viewed their union with high expectations for success, the realities of the situation are often far different from what they seemed initially for either or both parties. Often, the disenchantment has to do with the employee's lack of competence or unclear performance expectations set by the organization. At other times, it may be strong differences related to the values held by the organization or the individual. At the point of disenchantment, the organization has two choices. It can either sever its relationship with the new employee or it can commit its resources to the improvement of the person *the organization* chose for the position.

The individual in a similar situation also has choices. Obviously, the person can leave the organization or stay and rebel. Not so obvious is another choice, which is to stay and conform to the values and expectations of the group. The individual's last choice, and one that enables the growth and development of the organization, is to stay and try to make a difference in the conditions and/or values that exist.[4]

The final stage, *mutual acceptance,* is a time for granting full membership to the individual through such rites of passage as special privileges, increased responsibilities, and a type of "psychological contract." As Schein suggests, "All that has been established is that there is enough of a match between what the individual needs and expects and what the organization needs and expects to continue the career in the organization."[5] What happens beyond this point depends greatly on the opportunities for growth that the organization provides to the individual.

Teacher Empowerment

In considering the need for personal and professional development within school settings, it is time that teachers are "seen in a new way."[6] McLaughlin and Yee[7] help put this notion into perspective by distinguishing between two views of a teacher's career: an institutional view and an individual view. Although the institutional view of a career is the all too common view, it is the responsibility of leaders to ensure that conditions are present that will enable teachers to view their careers from an individual, or more intrinsic perspective. In the following discussion, these views are considered.

ISLLC 2

Institutional versus Individual View of a Career

The *institutional view of a career* is one in which effectiveness in the profession is judged by self and/or others as a measure of one's ability to climb various rungs of the bureaucratic ladder. Reflective of the machine metaphor, it allows the bureaucratic hierarchy to become the measurement of excellence in the profession. The institutional view places the teacher in a subservient role and reinforces compliance and followership. The hierarchy becomes the measure of achievement, and the value of "teacher" is viewed as secondary to that of an administrator. It is an externally imposed measure of competence that carries with it the ultimate goal of getting out of the classroom as quickly as one can move ahead. Moving ahead means basically conforming to a set pattern designed by someone higher in authority who is perceived to be more knowledgeable than the teacher in matters of teaching and learning. Years ago, Argyris[8] cautioned organizations against such a perspective; he suggested that the pathway to adult maturity is greatly hampered in bureaucratic organizations that foster this orientation. Organizations, he maintained, keep individuals in an immature state by not allowing them the freedom to exercise their abilities and to make their own decisions.

In contrast, the *individual view of a career* is intrinsically motivating and encourages the teacher to seek developmental opportunities that will maximize potential for its own sake—to become the most effective and contributing teacher that one is capable of becoming. This view creates a joy in teaching and a far greater benefit to the profession than does the institutional view. The tendency toward *institutionalizing effectiveness* through the hierarchy has been demonstrated by efforts to recognize, support, and reward excellent performance in the classroom through such efforts as teacher career ladders and merit pay. This alone, however, will not change teachers' attitudes. The real efforts toward motivation must take place at the building level. Principals must recognize and encourage teacher potential and provide opportunities for growth and self-discovery. McLaughlin and Yee[9] suggested that individual effectiveness, satisfaction, and growth are cultivated by two factors: level of opportunity and level of capacity.

Level of opportunity is the real determiner of the degree to which individuals can develop their highest level of professional competence. Three factors are especially important in encouraging this development. The first of these factors is *stimulation.* Research paints the picture of the typical classroom teacher to be one of loneliness, isolation, and despair.[10] Little chance is provided for meaningful interchange of ideas, for camaraderie, or for cultivating a sense of belonging and contribution. The sense of collegiality is missing; the opportunity for collaboration is nonexistent. Through professional learning communities, principals can help eliminate many of the conditions that create such disengagement for teachers.

Second, it is important that teachers receive *challenge.* It is not enough that teachers master a set of minimum competencies and then rest on their laurels. They need to be provided a chance to maximize their potential. Refining their strengths and developing artistry in their profession should become the focus. Often, these opportunities come by contributing to the growth of others through peer coaching or mentoring or by serving as a team leader. In any case, teachers are given opportunities that excite them and motivate their need for self-actualization. Certainly, the research by Maslow,[11] Herzberg,[12] Alderfer, and others suggests that it is the higher levels of need that motivate.

Third, teachers need *feedback.* Confirmation of their successes reinforces not only their enthusiasm but also the refinement of their skills. Awareness of areas needing improvement provides teachers with information necessary to focus their efforts more successfully in later attempts. Often, principals have little time for intensive feedback sessions with teachers; therefore, they must provide opportunities for others within the school to assist. Professional development and teacher growth then become a joint responsibility.

Although it is imperative that teachers be given levels of opportunity to increase their individual effectiveness, satisfaction, and growth, they also must be provided similar opportunities to increase their *level of capacity.* In other words, they must be given *power.* Such power includes not only their access to resources but also their ability to mobilize and utilize them, as well as the capability to influence the goals and directions of their institutions.[13] As McLaughlin and Yee stated, "Teachers with a sense of capacity tend to pursue effectiveness in the classroom, express commitment to the organization and career, and report a high level of professional satisfaction."[14]

Individual and Group Needs

Individual uniqueness has major implications for the work that principals must do in the area of human resources development. Teaching, evaluation, and staff development are all affected by the individuality of teachers.

Teachers vary in their readiness levels and in their motivational needs; principals should consider these variables when determining teachers' development needs. As the research suggests, "The circumstances most suitable for one person's professional development may be quite different from those that promote another individual's growth"[15]

Three very important variables determine level of need: teacher age, years of teaching experience, and readiness or maturity level. Certainly, interests and learning/personality styles are additional factors that play a part. Teachers collectively, as adult learners, also have certain needs that should be considered when designing any professional-development programs. Perhaps the most appropriate place to start in this discussion is with the needs of teachers as a group.

The Adult Learner

Knowles[16] provided a thoughtful perspective to the area of adult learning. His work suggests that as adults, teachers learn best under these conditions:

ISLLC 2

- They have opportunities to plan and design their own learning/development opportunities.
- There is relevance to the learning experience.
- Learning is problem centered rather than content centered.
- Past experience can be incorporated in experiential learning settings.

Although there are needs that teachers do have as a group, there are also unique differences among teachers based on their years of teaching experience and their developmental levels. Let us consider the research of Huberman[17] as a beginning point in understanding these differences among teachers.

Teacher Needs Determined by Experience

Huberman[18] classified teachers into five stages of development based on their years of teaching experience. Although the model is based primarily on research of secondary teachers with little or no administrative experience, it does suggest a *process* through which teachers are likely to progress in their career. Principals should not assume that all teachers progress through these stages in exactly the same sequence. As Huberman suggested, some may develop in a linear fashion while others may exhibit "plateaus, regressions, dead-ins, or spurts."[19] The model is helpful to principals as they work with teachers, however, for it allows them to understand more fully the impact that individuals and groups have on each other. It also assists principals in planning professional development that is more suited to teacher need. In the following section, each teacher career stage is considered.

Survival and Discovery Stage (1–3 Years).   In the first career stage, survival and discovery coexist; ironically it "is discovery that allows the novice teacher to tolerate survival." [20] Although this career stage is dotted with reality shock and self-preoccupation, it is also a time when teachers are excited about their first classroom and are elated by feelings of being a "colleague among peers."[21] During this time it is important for teachers to be guided in ways that help them see teaching from a broader perspective. They need to arrange fragmented tasks of method and strategy into a large context. Teachers have learned many skills from their university preparation programs at this point, but they have had little opportunity so far in their development to integrate those skills and apply them to their own teaching. Supervisors and principals can guide them in making connections between the theories they have recently been taught and their actual practice in the classroom. Holland and Weise[22] provide useful suggestions to guide principals in working with novice teachers.

Stabilization Stage (4–6 Years).   Teachers take on the mantle of "teacher" and take major steps toward professionalism during the stabilization stage. Not only do they assume responsibility for their immediate classrooms but also for the profession of teaching. Teachers begin to feel comfortable in their basic knowledge of good teaching (most have moved from probationary to tenured status), and they are ready to experiment and create their own teaching styles. At this time, teachers should be provided more opportunities for *capacity building.*[23] As they make more decisions related to their own teaching and professional development, they move more toward teacher empowerment and an individual view of their career. (See Chapter 2 for a more complete discussion of this concept.)

Experimentation and Activism (7–18 Years).   Teachers begin to experiment at this time, for they have gained skill and competence in their teaching. They have established a comfortable knowledge base about good teaching and are eager to experiment with new ideas that they hope will maximize their impact on student learning. This stage is a natural time for involvement, contribution, and challenge, as well as a time when teachers want a greater voice in those things that impact their teaching. It is a time for accepting new responsibilities; however, it is a period for many when they begin to question their professional choice. Some wonder if they truly want to remain in the profession, and disenchantment occurs for many, resulting in either a search for new responsibilities or a complete job change.

Serenity/Relational Distance and Conservatism (19–30 Years).   At this time many teachers who have previously been innovative and dynamic in their instructional methods begin to shift to a more mechanical response. Teachers no longer exhibit the energy and enthusiasm previously exhibited. Although they do have increased serenity and self-confidence, this is also a time marked by "relational distance from students."[24] The age gap between teacher and student widens, and there is less connection than before. Often teachers at this stage become reluctant to embark on anything new or innovative and seem greatly concerned with maintaining the status quo.

Principals need to be aware of this tendency toward the line of least resistance and withdrawal and look for ways to involve these teachers in meaningful activities. At this important time in the lives, many teachers need real leadership and inspiration to raise their levels of values consciousness,[25] inspiring them to continue contributing to the organization in productive ways. In Chapter 1 we discussed the importance of a school leader working to transform not only the organization but also the individuals who serve within that setting.

Disengagement (31–40 Years).   This stage is distinguished by either serenity or bitterness. There is increased withdrawal and internalization—a gradual disengagement and absorption in one's own interests is evidenced. Teachers also feel of pressure to move over for younger employees and fresher ideas. Many teachers in this stage still have much talent and expertise that they could contribute to the organization if they were properly challenged and encouraged. Often teachers can become revitalized during this stage by having opportunities to contribute to the growth of others in such activities as mentoring and peer coaching.

The important idea to remember from Huberman's research is that teachers will have different needs at various times during their careers. This fact has significant implications for school principals and suggests that professional development must be tailored to meet teachers' differing needs. A model similar to Huberman's, although not connected to defined years of experience, is discussed in the next section.

Maturity and Readiness Levels

De Moulin and Guyton[26] identified four levels of teacher maturity or stages of development: provisional, developmental, transitional, and decelerating. Their study suggested that the age factor does not necessarily determine a teacher's level of growth in the profession. For instance, some teachers might remain in the developmental level for most of their career. In contrast, the transitional and decelerating levels might include teachers represented by various age levels. These stages will be briefly discussed as a way of supporting the concept of developmental phases for teachers.

Provisional.   Provisional teachers experience great stress based on their uncertainty in the teaching situation. Their inexperience and limited knowledge of child psychology contribute to a trial-and-error approach to performance. As these teachers gain experience, their comfort and confidence increase. This stage is quite similar to Huberman's survival and discovery stage; however, it does not relate necessarily to the number of years that the teacher has taught, as other factors may compound the situation. Teachers at this stage, regardless of their years of experience, should be provided with the *levels of opportunity*[27] necessary to build skill and confidence. Matching these teachers with a mentor reinforces their skill acquisition and provides them with opportunities to receive the important feedback necessary for learning transfer. The concept of collegiality and collaboration, discussed at length in Chapter 2, has tremendous implications for meeting the needs of teachers at this level.

Developmental.   At this stage, teachers exhibit self-confidence, direction, and structure. A great deal of satisfaction and sense of direction is balanced by curiosity and refinement of instructional practice. This is a wonderful time for exploration and growth! Teachers enjoy the opportunities provided through peer coaching, teamwork, study groups, and action-based re-search. It is ironic that although the majority of the teaching staff in most schools tend to be at this level, the bulk of time spent in professional development is spent in "training programs" pro-vided through traditional in-service education!

Transitional. Teachers at this stage begin to decline in classroom effectiveness. Many begin to question their desire to remain in the teaching profession. There is little desire to participate in professional development, and most are content to operate from a day-to-day perspective. Many of these teachers have reached a plateau in their careers where there seems to be nothing chal-lenging and inspiring. These teachers need to be inspired to look for opportunities for personal and professional growth that have previously been unrecognized. There is much overlap between this stage of development and the Huberman stage of disengagement.

Decelerating. At this stage, teachers have little motivation for work and exhibit a clock-watching perspective. Burnout is a classic symptom, with more traditional methods being the choice for instructional format. Again, competent teachers must become reengaged in the educational process. Finding a way to inspire their contributions and continued growth is a major challenge for today's school leader.

Professional Development

What part does staff development play in helping to meet the emerging developmental needs of teachers? How does teacher development, individually and collectively, contribute to the in-creased effectiveness of the school's educational program? These are important questions to con-sider as we view the nature and scope of staff development. A working definition of *professional development* is necessary to begin. For the purposes of this chapter, we will use the terms *professional development* and *staff development* synonymously.

Staff development has been called many things, including *in-service training, professional development,* and *human resources development.* In all cases, it has been considered to be some-thing "done to" teachers in a compressed period of time (e.g., a fall workshop or special confer-ence) that makes them more content and effective in the classroom setting. A major paradigm shift concerning staff development, however, has been brought about by three major ideas: (1) results-driven education, (2) systems thinking, and (3) constructivism. Each of these, individ-ually and collectively, is causing school principals to view staff development much differently than they did in past years.[28]

- *Results-Driven Education.* Just as accountability has become the emphasis for the class-room, so too has it impacted the nature of staff development. The true measurement of the effectiveness of any staff-development program is currently being judged by how it affects the instructional behavior of teachers in a positive way that benefits the learner.
- *Systems Thinking.* What happens in one part of the organization has an effect on all other parts of the organization and on the organization as a whole. Staff development now en-courages a broader view of the impact that changes in any one aspect of curriculum, in-struction, or assessment might have on all aspects of the organization.

- *Constructivism.* The emphasis has shifted from the nature of learners as passive receivers of information to one in which learners are actively involved in making sense of their own learning. The need to provide learners with the necessary skills to build their own knowledge structures has caused staff development to be viewed in a similar fashion. Teachers, viewed as adult learners, collaborate with peers, students, and others to share knowledge and to construct new knowledge based on collective understanding.

Table 9.1 outlines the major shifts that have occurred because of the three trends suggested. We will explore these paradigm shifts and examine their impact on the design and delivery of staff development.

Models of Staff Development

A current review of the literature related to staff development suggests that it must become multifaceted in its delivery. Sparks and Loucks-Horsley[29] have suggested that five models of staff development are currently being delivered. Principals need to understand these models and their applications to the professional development of teachers. They also should be able to appropriately apply the models to match the needs of individual teachers. These five staff-development models are discussed next.

TABLE 9.1   Paradigm Shift in Staff Development

FROM	TO
Individual development	Individual and organizational development
District-centered approaches	School-centered approaches
Fragmented, piecemeal efforts	Improvements based on school improvement plans toward change
Focus on adult needs	Focus on student needs and learning outcomes
Externally delivered training	Comprehensive, multifaceted staff-development models incorporating the talents and resources of staff
Staff development provided by one or two departments	Staff development as a critical function and major responsibility performed by all administrators and teacher leaders
The transmission of knowledge and skills by "experts"	The study by teachers of the teaching and learning process
A focus on generic teaching skills	A combined focus on generic and content-specific skills
Staff development as a "frill" dependent on an availability of financial resources	Staff development as an essential component of the educational process

Source: Adapted from D. Sparks, "A Paradigm Shift in Staff Development," *The ERIC Review 3,* no. 3 (1994): 2–4.

Individually Guided Staff Development.   This model, based on the assumption that teachers can best determine their own developmental needs and that they are motivated to direct their own learning experiences, casts teachers as self-motivated individuals who learn best when they can guide the relevancy of their own experiences. The model consists of several phases: **(1)** identification of a need, **(2)** development of a plan to meet that need, **(3)** activities outlined to accomplish the plan, and **(4)** evaluation of the plan. Examples of the individually guided model include individual study of an issue of special interest, development of a special project, curriculum-improvement activities, and other activities tied to a teacher's particular interest.

Observation and Assessment.   As previously discussed, feedback is a major component leading to the development of an *individualized view* of one's teaching career. Without directed feedback, a major link to motivation is lost. The observation and assessment model provides opportunities for teachers to provide the feedback to each other that may not always be available from the principal. The model is based on the assumptions that reflection and analysis are critical avenues that facilitate professional growth and that teaching can be improved by observation and feedback from another. Not only does the reflection benefit the targeted teacher, but the observation and analysis of the teaching act is mutually beneficial to both teacher and observer. When teachers are given positive feedback, their efforts are reinforced and motivation increases.[30] Examples of observation and assessment that might be included in a school setting are peer coaching, team building and collaboration, and clinical supervision. In peer coaching, teachers alternate visits to each other's classrooms, gather and analyze data, and give feedback. Both teacher and observer are targets for improved classroom performance, as reflection is mutually occurring.[31]

Involvement in a Development/Improvement Process.   This model takes the form of curriculum improvement and development. It relates directly to school improvement projects designed to improve classroom instruction or to solve a specific problem related to school effectiveness. The model is based on the assumption that teachers, as adult learners, want to be engaged in the resolution of problems in which they have a direct professional interest. It assumes, also, that teachers are in a position to best identify the issues that need resolution. In this approach, teachers become researchers, independent learners, and shapers of solutions to their own curriculum/instructional problems. The model proceeds according to the following steps:

1. *Problem Identification.* Either the individual or a small group of teachers identify a need.
2. *Response Formulation.* The individual teacher or the group brainstorm possible alternatives to consider in resolving the issue.
3. *Information Gathering.* The need for further study or investigation of the issue is determined and study is completed.
4. *Plan Formulation.* Based on the information gathered, a plan or program is developed.
5. *Plan Assessment.* Data are gathered to determine the effectiveness of the plan. Information gleaned from the assessment is used to further refine or modify the existing plan.

Training.   Long the most common form of staff development, the training model is synonymous in the minds of many with the entire concept of staff development. In addition to its familiarity, it is the most cost-effective of all models in terms of initial delivery. A major caution in its use, however, is the notion of *transfer of learning.* Modifications of the external, or visible, teaching behaviors of staff are desirable and tend to be the major focus of initial training. There is an underlying, more important purpose with any staff-development effort, however, and that is to change the *thinking* of teachers. The important issue with training, then, is how to enable the transfer of the learned skill to the classroom setting. Any training must be reinforced with other follow-up procedures, such as mentoring or peer coaching, to ensure that learning transfers to the teacher's classroom.[32]

Inquiry.   In the inquiry approach, the teacher, either individually or in a small group, inquires into an issue of concern relative to classroom instruction or a related school problem. The inquiry may be either a formal or informal process in which valid questions are formulated and researched. This model allows for collective study by a group of teachers and encourages the combined analysis of many individuals pooling their ideas and resources. It is based on the assumption that teachers do question their own practices and search for valid answers to their problems. It assumes, as well, that teachers can develop new understandings and practices based on the discoveries made. The model, often referred to as *action-based research,* has been made popular through the Japanese concept of quality circles and total quality management (TQM), which was discussed in Chapter 2.

Matching Teacher Differences and Staff-Development Opportunities

These five models of staff development have great potential for providing a synthesized approach to total professional development within a school setting. The models also capitalize on the unique needs that teachers have based on experience or developmental level.

Because of their different areas of emphasis and method, these staff-development models, become fertile ground for professional development opportunities for teaching staff, based on the unique needs discussed in the second section of this chapter. It is one thing to know *how* to help a teacher through development; it is quite another to identify the needs that should be addressed. It is important, then, to understand the nature and design of personnel evaluation and supervision.

Personnel Evaluation and Supervision

What is *judged* from the results of personnel evaluation? What *purpose* does the evaluation serve? We will consider these questions through a discussion of merit and worth.

Merit and Worth

Merit and worth—and their relationship to one another—are part of the evaluation process. In the evaluation of personnel for decision-making purposes, both are applied.[33]

ISLLC 2

Merit, which is the more common of the two concepts, is concerned with measuring the effectiveness of the individual's performance within a given setting, such as a teacher in the classroom performing job-related tasks. When a comparison of an individual's performance is made against a standard, or in many cases a comparison of the individual's performance against the performance of others in similar roles, then the individual's merit within the position has been judged.

Worth, on the other hand, is a determination of how valuable that teacher's particular position is to the rest of the organization and to the fulfillment of the organization's mission. It is an assessment of that value based on need. As Scriven stated, "Worth must be determined by comparing resources in education with needs in education."[34] It is possible, therefore, for a teacher, or other staff member, to be judged as having merit but to be in a position of little worth to the organization. It is not possible, however, for any position to have worth without the presence of merit. Very little merit also implies very little worth. Judgments of performance are based on both concepts, and this can sometimes cause conflict. Because of scarcity of resources or changes in organizational need, teachers can lose their positions even though they have great merit. It also happens that at times teachers who are less than meritorious are allowed to continue in positions that have value or worth to the organization. The question then becomes: At what point does lower merit affect position value? These are troublesome issues that face principals as they attempt to evaluate teacher performance.

Merit and worth are important concepts to consider, as well, when evaluating teachers as a group. As societal resources become scarce, there is an increasing need to justify the cost of education to the public. Performance evaluation becomes one way of substantiating teachers' merit to suggest the worth of education. Herein lies one of the greatest challenges of personnel evaluation: How does one justify accountability to the public and at the same time maintain the trust and cooperation of individuals within the school setting that will enable the performance one so desires? How can an evaluation occur in both a summative and formative manner without neglecting one of the stated purposes? How does one foster change once the problems have been identified?[35]

Summative and Formative Evaluation

Personnel evaluation has two purposes: summative and formative. The *summative process,* often called *teacher appraisal,* is designed to provide a basic foundation for making decisions that can be justified. It is used to make a judgment relative to the *merit* of an individual's performance. Since it is administrative in nature, it is usually the predominate responsibility of the principal and/or the principal's designee. Decisions based on summative evaluation might include any or all of the following:

- Should the teacher be hired for a particular position?
- Should the teacher be dismissed?
- Should the teacher be placed on tenure?
- Does the performance of the teacher justify merit pay?

Because these are important decisions that affect the lives and careers of individuals, the assessment instrument, procedures used, and practices applied in the process need to stand the scrutiny of legal challenge. We deal with these issues in Chapter 16. Note here that these legal issues are relevant only in the case of summative evaluation or teacher appraisal.

In recent years, many states have mandated forms and processes by which teacher appraisal will take place. Many of these mandates have resulted in standardized rating scales and designed checklists. Care must be used in basing an entire appraisal system on this or any other specific model. There is danger that the criteria will become too narrow to encompass the teaching of subjects that incorporate higher-order thinking skills or that require a high level of creativity on the part of students.

Tom McGreal has proposed alternatives to the rating scales for appraisals to make them more useful as a clinical tool.[36] He has suggested that an appropriate appraisal be based on a cooperative goal-setting model and that the appraiser and the teacher identify specific instructional improvement goals on which to work together. In working together, the techniques of clinical supervision are used, and a supportive environment is established. Appraisal, thus, is the basis for staff development. The collaborative goal setting based on the formal appraisal that ensues at the postobservation and later conferences is critical to the development process. These changes suggest some important ways, then, in which the two purposed of evaluation may differ.

Formative evaluation is concerned primarily with professional growth and development. It is administered much more frequently than summative evaluation, and because it does not concern itself with administrative judgments for decision making, it can be, and most often is, a joint responsibility shared among teachers. Formative evaluation is often termed *clinical supervision,* although this is only one of the many forms that formative evaluation can take.

Clinical Supervision

Clinical supervision is a collaborative process. The term *clinical supervision* gained national prominence in the 1960s through the writings of Robert Goldhammer and Morris Cogen.[37] Originally, the model was proposed for use with student teachers. Its applicability in the formative evaluation of practicing teachers was soon recognized.

Five steps compose the model. Each step helps both the supervisor and the teacher in focusing on the teaching/learning process. An examination is made of the strengths and weaknesses of a lesson; then the process involves identifying specific activities to improve future lessons or teaching practices. The final step is formal feedback to the teacher.

Step 1: The Preobservation Conference. The purpose of the preobservation conference is to provide focus to the upcoming observation. The teacher outlines for the principal the plans for the lesson and helps identify specific aspects to which attention will be directed during the observation. The teacher's plan is expected to contain learner objectives, introductions, teaching strategies to be employed, resources to be used, evaluation plans, and lesson closure.

During this discussion, there is opportunity for the principal to clarify the various components of the lesson and to offer suggestions about other possible approaches. The discussion about the initial observation should focus on specific areas of interest or concern to the teacher rather than areas or concerns of the principal. Later observations and discussions will provide ample opportunity to address concerns, of the principal.

It is important for the teacher to understand the purpose of each step in the clinical model. The teacher needs to know that the principal or other observer will be taking notes during the observation for the purpose of giving accurate feedback. Before the conclusion of the preobservation conference, both a time for the classroom visit and a time for the postobservation conference should be established.

Step 2: The Classroom Observation.   The teacher's task is to teach the lesson as planned. The observer's task is to record those items specifically identified in the preobservation conference as well as the events surrounding the lesson. Specific happenings should be scripted and in the language of the teacher. Activities relating to the lesson—student verbal and nonverbal behavior, for example—should be noted. Opinion and summary statements need to be avoided; the language of the participants and specific events are what the principal needs to provide useful feedback. The observer should be on time and stay for the entire lesson.

Step 3: Analysis of the Lesson.   To prepare for the postobservation conference, script notes need to be analyzed. Were the objectives obtained? How did the various intended teaching strategies work? What unusual circumstances were observed? What seemed to work? What didn't? What comments can be made about the teacher's verbal and nonverbal (physical) behavior? How about student verbal and nonverbal behavior? What did the teacher do well? What specific aspects might be improved? What should the teacher work on for the next observation?

Step 4: The Postobservation Conference.   The conference needs to take place in a comfortable and private location. The teacher's classroom itself is often appropriate. A good opening line, after the amenities, is this: "What do you think went well?" Then, the teacher should be asked to clarify the objectives of the lesson, review what happened, and assess whether the objectives were attained and to what degree. At this point, the principal will relate some of his or her specific observations supported by the notes that were taken. Successes will be discussed.

Agreement should be reached about what went on. Together, the teacher and the principal should decide on some strategies that might be worth trying. Information should be solicited from the teacher. Every conference should conclude with some growth objectives and some agreed-upon plans for improving any deficiencies.

Step 5: Postconference Analysis.   The final step in the clinical model is an evaluation of the process and the outcome. Information is solicited from the teacher. How could the process be improved? Are the growth objectives clear? What assistance is available to the teacher? After the teacher leaves, the principal needs to reflect on the process and his or her own behavior and skill. Did the conference go well? Why or why not? The process is intended to promote both improved instruction and supportive relationships. One likely will not occur without the other.

As previously mentioned, staff evaluation has two basic purposes: (1) to improve the performance and provide direction for the continued development of present staff and (2) to provide a sound basis for personnel decisions such as awarding of tenure, promotions, transfers, or dismissals. These two purposes create a dilemma for many administrators even though both support quality education. Staff improvement is largely a helping relationship, most effectively carried out when built on trust between the teacher and the principal. Personnel decisions are judgmental in nature and can cause teacher apprehension.

Several authors[38] have suggested that supervision and teacher appraisal styles become situationally specific; that is, make situational factors determine the approach used by the principal in working with each staff member. This situational approach is similar to situational leadership models proposed by Blanchard[39] and Glatthorn.[40] A differentiated system of situational supervision has four levels:

1. *Clinical supervision,* as described in the previous section
2. *Collaborative professional development,* as a collegial process in which a small number of teachers work together for professional growth (the quality circle idea from TQM integrates well with this approach)
3. *Self-direction,* in which the teacher prepares an individual development plan (IDP) with the assistance of the principal who serves as a resource person
4. *Administrative monitoring,* where the principal makes a series of brief, usually announced, visits as "quality control" assurance

The fourth approach, commonly used by administrators, should not be considered a supervisory method because it does not provide improvement opportunities to the teacher being observed. Nevertheless, each of these approaches has its appropriate place in certain circumstances, depending on the maturity and needs of the teacher. Table 9.2 points up many of the differences in the three supervisory approaches from the preceding list.

Staff development and evaluation are essential activities of the school principal. Just as a teacher manages student learning by using a diagnostic prescriptive model, so too can the principal direct staff development using staff evaluation as a diagnostic tool and an evaluation-by-objectives approach as a prescriptive tool. For proper staff development and evaluation, the principal must take an initiating, rather than reacting, role, and the comprehensive plan for staff evaluation must be based on a sound rationale.

TABLE 9.2   Situational Models of Supervision

	CLINICAL	COLLABORATIVE	SELF-DIRECTED
Teacher initiative	Low	Moderate	High
Supervisor initiative	High	Moderate	Low
Approach	Formal, systematic	Collaborative	Self-directed
Goal of learning	Create rationality/order	Problem solving	Goal directed
Knowledge	Predefined set of life-survival skills	Concrete results that "work" for individuals	That which is discovered
Learning	Condition individual by outer environment	Outcome of learner–environment interaction	Unfolding process within learner
Foundation	Behaviorist	Cognitivist	Humanist
Learning theory	Conditioning	Experimentation	Self-discovery
Teacher risk	Low	Moderate to high	Moderate to high

Source: Adapted from A. A. Glatthorn, *Differentiated Supervision* (Alexandria, VA: Association for Supervision and Curriculum Development, 1984).

The Staff Evaluation Cycle

Staff evaluation and development is a cyclical process. The evaluation leads to a development prescription that is checked once again through evaluation. Seven basic steps in the staff evaluation cycle focus on the ultimate purpose of improving instruction. The cycle begins when the teacher and principal plan goals and targets for the year and include other people in the evaluation process during the year. The seven steps of the evaluation cycle are as follows:

1. Prepare an individual development plan.
2. Select specific objectives or activities for observation or review.
3. Determine the observation method, time, and place.
4. Observe and collect data.
5. Analyze data and provide feedback.
6. Summarize and interpret collective observational data.
7. Report evaluation results, target achievement, and make recommendations for individual and staff development at an annual conference.

Individual Development Plans

An IDP is a written schedule of experiences designed to meet a person's particular goals for development. It is a method of systematically planning for training and other experiences to develop necessary skills and knowledge. Rather than haphazardly chancing time and money on what may not be a useful learning experience, the IDP gives both staff member and administrator an opportunity to set reasonable objectives and then plan experiences that support those objectives.

The IDP is realistic and feasible because its construction includes both administrator and staff member perspectives. The staff member's personal and professional goals are considered insofar as these are organizationally feasible. The staff member gets information and feedback so that goals can be set that are organizationally necessary and reasonably achievable.

Individual development is a joint responsibility of the administrator and the staff member. As such, it is a logical extension of the clinical supervision and appraisal process. The principal's responsibility is to arrange the work environment to capitalize on the skills and interests of the staff so that the important tasks get accomplished in the most efficient and effective way. To do so requires that the principal and staff member work together to identify skills deficiencies (developmental needs), strengths, and professional and organizational goals. The IDP is a joint commitment to address these issues.

The IDP includes first a self-assessment. The individual staff member reviews his or her professional qualifications, skills, and interests. A personal judgment is made about how these skills may be capitalized on in the organizational setting and how any skill deficiency can be best addressed. The second step in this process is for the individual to think about his or her professional career and begin to establish long-term career goals.

The responsibility of the principal is to conduct an analysis of the staff member's strengths and weaknesses as well. This analysis is always conducted from the perspective of what is good for the school. Frequently an individual's self-assessment will overlook important organizational demands and skills needs.

ISLLC 2

ISLLC 3

After the two analyses, a development conference is held and the IDP begins to take specific form. Important information is exchanged at this conference; the two parties may not see all things similarly. Congruence is never likely to be achieved without a discourse about job-related expectations. At this time, the principal becomes aware of the goals of the staff member and, where possible and feasible, may provide assistance through establishment of a mentoring process.

Mentoring

The focus to this point has been the relationship between the principal as supervisor and individual staff members. Mentoring proposes a relationship between peers—however, generally not peers of equal stature and experience. Mentoring is often used to assist in the orientation of new employees.

The term *mentor* comes from Greek mythology. Mentor was the friend and counselor to whom Ulysses entrusted his son when Ulysses set off on a 10-year odyssey. It was a complex role: Mentor was protector, advisor, teacher, and father-figure to the inexperienced boy. The relationship was one of trust and affection.

In today's organizational setting, a formalized mentor program typically involves a relationship between a veteran employee of some stature and a younger inexperienced colleague. Often, the practice is reserved to those who have been identified early as fast-trackers or potential leaders. However, the concept is easily applied at the building level, albeit perhaps not quite as formally, but nevertheless to good effect. Mentoring can substantially improve the clinical approach to supervision and become a very sophisticated *peer* supervision program.

Careful matching of individuals is essential. The administrator should develop an initial list of potential mentors before considering the process further. Factors that result in a good mentor include willingness to act as a mentor, personal commitment to helping others develop, commitment to the school, extensive knowledge and insight about how things get done in the organization, solid experience, good professional relationships beyond the immediate building or system, and a proven record of success.

Fundamental to a long-term relationship is an early orientation to the program at which the involved parties can, within a school system and school building policy, work through role definitions and expectations of each other. This process will clarify initial commitments to help foster the climate of trust and openness important to success. The establishment of a regular feedback and monitoring system is essential and must be encouraged and supported by organizational mechanisms.

The role of the principal in human resources and organizational development is a crucial one. Whether the aspect of the human resources development program that is being addressed is individual in nature or is focused on the work group, there is a need for administrative support, an appropriate structure, and a monitoring system. Administrative support begins with needs assessment one continues when the expectations are established. It is buttressed by a willingness to engage others in the planning of the development efforts and a willingness to secure time and dollar resources to support the effort.

Positive Reinforcement

Learning and development—whether adult, adolescent, or child—are facilitated by positive reinforcement. Among a number of findings reported in a research synthesis about effective school practices was the following characteristic of leaders in these schools:

> Leaders set up systems of incentives and rewards to encourage excellence in student and teacher performance; they act as figureheads in delivering awards and highlighting the importance of excellence.[41]

These findings highly correlate with those about successful management in the private sector:

> The excellent companies have a deeply ingrained philosophy that says, in effect, "respect the individual," "make people winners," "let them stand out," "treat people as adults." [42]

In sum, then, there are four implications for the principal who wants a well-developed, highly motivated staff:

1. Development needs of the staff must be accurately assessed. Self-assessment is a starting point, but the principal must also conduct an investigation, using clinical observations in classrooms, student data, and current and foreseeable school and community concerns, among other data sources.
2. High standards of performance must be established and advertised. Setting performance standards in cooperation with staff members has been revealed to be the most effective practice.
3. Human resources development systems require careful planning and a variety of approaches. IDPs as well as group development events must focus on recognized needs and be regularly monitored.
4. Positive reinforcement techniques need to be consistently and continually employed. Public pats on the back, award ceremonies, private thank yous, bonuses for jobs well done—what Peters and Waterman call "hoopla"[43]—all serve to keep people congruent with the needs of the organization and productively motivated.

Summary

Negative responses to organized efforts in the name of staff development are the result of a history of bad experiences with activities that have gone on in the name of in-service training. However well-intended such activities may have been, too frequently they have not addressed either the needs of the individual staff members or the needs of the organization.

Better approaches exist, and these approaches issue from a model of human resources development that recognizes the varied needs of individual organization members; the needs of the organization; the nature of adult learners; the time and effort required, depending on the nature of the knowledge, skill, or attitude to be acquired; and the impact that individuals have on the very nature and culture of the workplace.

A C T I V I T I E S

1. Review Case Studies 4 and 14 at this end of this book. Apply the goal-setting and strategic planning concepts of Chapter 4 and the human resources development concepts expressed in this chapter. How might you proceed in addressing the problems cited in these cases? Set forth a strategy to overcome the problem.

2. Review Case Studies 22 and 30. Analyze the problems presented and apply the concepts of human resources development presented in this chapter. What approach would you use in addressing the problems? Set forth a strategy to overcome the difficulties faced by the schools in these cases.

3. Turn to the ISLLC standards found in Appendix B. Review the functions listed in Standard 3. Which of these best support the human resources concepts discussed in this chapter? What weakness do you find in your school's human resources management? How would you go about correcting them?

E N D N O T E S

1. F. Newmann and G. Wehlage, *Successful School Restructuring: A Report to the Public and Educators by the Center for Restructuring Schools* (Madison, WI: University of Wisconsin, 1995).

2. Edgar Schein, *Career Dynamics: Matching Individual and Organizational Needs* (Reading, MA: Addison-Wesley, 1978).

3. Ibid.

4. Ibid.

5. Ibid.

6. Gene Maeroff, "A Blueprint for Empowering Teachers," *Phi Delta Kappan 69* (March 1988): 473.

7. Milbrey McLaughlin and Sylvia Yee, "School as a Place to Have a Career," in *Building a Professional Culture in Schools,* ed. Ann Liberman (New York: Teachers College Press, 1988).

8. Chris Argyris, *Personality and Organizations* (New York: Harper & Row, 1957).

9. McLaughlin and Yee, "School as a Place to Have a Career."

10. Dan Lortie, *Schoolteacher* (Chicago: University of Chicago Press, 1975).

11. A. Maslow, "Toward a Psychology of Being," in *The Creativity Question,* ed. A. Rothenburg and C. Houseman (Durham NC: Duke University Press, 1976), pp. 296–305.

12. Frederick Herzberg, Bernard Mausner, and Barbara Bloch Snyderman, *The Motivation to Work* (New York: John Wiley & Sons, 1959).

13. McLaughlin and Yee, "School as a Place to Have a Career."

14. Ibid.

15. Dennis Sparks and Susan Loucks-Horsley, "Five Models of Staff Development in Teachers," *Journal of Staff Development 10,* no. 4 (Fall, 1989): 40–57.

16. M. Knowles, *The Modern Practice of Adult Education* (Chicago: Association/Follett Press, 1980).

17. Michael Huberman, "The Professional Life Cycle of Teachers," *Teachers College Record 91,* no. 1 (Fall 1989): 32–57.

18. Ibid.

19. Huberman, "The Professional Life Cycle of Teachers," p. 131.

20. Ibid.

21. Ibid.

22. Patricia Holland and Kaye Weise, "Helping Novice Teachers," in *Principal as Leader,* ed. Larry W. Hughes (Upper Saddle River, NJ: Merrill, 1999).

23. McLaughlin and Yee, "Schools as a Place to Have a Career."

24. Huberman, "The Professional Life Cycle of Teachers," p. 134.

25. This concept was discussed in Chapter 1. Part of the role of the principal is to provide opportunities for organizational members to develop the means necessary for moving to higher levels of values awareness.

26. Donald De Moulin and John Guyton, "An Analysis of Career Development to Enhance Individualized Staff Development," *National Forum of Educational Administration and Supervision Journal 7,* no. 3 (1990).

27. McLaughlin and Yee, "School as a Place to Have a Career." These authors discuss the need to provide teachers with two opportunities that will inspire their development as professionals: *level of capacity* and *level of opportunity.*

28. Sparks and Loucks-Horsley, "Five Models of Staff Development in Teachers."

29. Ibid.

30. Beverley Showers, *Peer Coaching: A Strategy for Facilitating Transfer of Training* (Eugene, OR: Center for Educational Policy and Management, University of Oregon, 1984).

31. B. Showers, B. Joyce, and B. Bennett, "Synthesis of Research on Staff Development: A Framework for Future Study and a State-of-Art Analysis," *Educational Leadership 45,* no. 3 (1987): 77–87.

32. Beverly Joyce and Beverly Showers, "The Coaching of Teaching," *Educational Leadership 40,* no. 1 (1982): 4–10.

33. Michael Scriven, "A Unified Approach to Teacher Evaluation," *Toward a Unified Model: The Foundations of*

Educational Personnel Evaluation (Center for Research on Educational Accountability and Teacher Evaluation: Western Michigan University, 1994), pp. 2–15.

34. Ibid., p. 1.

35. Linda Darling-Hammond, Arthur Wise, and Sara Pease, "Teacher Evaluation in the Organizational Context," *Review of Educational Research 53,* no. 1 (1983): 285–328.

36. Ronald Brandt, "On Teacher Evaluation: A Conversation with Tom McGreal," *Educational Leadership 4,* no. 7 (July 1987): 20–24.

37. See Robert Goldhammer, *Clinical Supervision* (New York: Holt, Rinehart and Winston, 1969); and Morris Cogen, *Clinical Supervision* (New York: Houghton Mifflin, 1973).

38. A. A. Glatthorn, *Differentiated Supervision* (Alexandria, VA: Association for Supervision and Curriculum

Development, 1984); and Carl D. Glickman, *Developmental Supervision* (Alexandria, VA: Association for Supervision and Curriculum Development, 1981).

39. K. Blanchard, D. Zigarmi, and P. Zagarmi, "Situational Leadership: 'Different Strokes for Different Folks,'" *Principal 66,* no. 4 (March 1987): 12–16.

40. Glatthorn, *Differentiated Supervision.*

41. Northwest Regional Educational Laboratory, *Effective Schooling Practices: A Research Synthesis* (Portland, OR: The Laboratory, 1984), p. 8.

42. T. J. Peters and R. H. Waterman, *In Search of Excellence: Lessons from America's Best Run Companies* (New York: Warner Books, 1982).

43. Ibid.

SELECTED READINGS

Arnau, L., J. Kahrs, and B. Kruskamp. "Peer Coaching: Veteran High School Teachers Take the Lead on Learning." *NASSP Bulletin 88,* no. 639 (2004): 26–41.

Bernstein, E. "What Teacher Evaluation Should Know and Be Able to Do: A Commentary." *NASSP Bulletin 88* (2004): 80–88.

Danielson, Charlotte. "The Many Faces of Leadership." *Educational Leadership 65,* no.1 (2007): 14–19.

Darling-Hammond, L. "The Quiet Revolution: Rethinking Teacher Development." *Educational Leadership 53,* no. 6 (March 1996): 4–10.

Davis, J. "A Principal's Plan for Mentoring Novice Teachers" *Principal 87,* no. 5 (2008): 55.

Flannagan; J. S., and N. Kelly. "Differentiated support." *Principal Leadership (Middle Sch Ed) 9,* no. 7 (2009): 28–30.

Glatthorn, Allan. *Supervisory Leadership* (Glenview, IL: Scott, Foresman, 1990).

Glickman, Carl D. *Supervision of Instruction* (Boston: Allyn & Bacon, 1989).

Goldstein, Irwin L. *Training in Organizations: Needs Assessment, Development and Evaluation* (2nd ed.) (Monterey, CA: Brooks/Cole, 1996).

Guskey, T. R. "Analyzing Lists of the Characteristics of Effective Professional Development to Promote Visionary Leadership." *NASSP Bulletin 87* (2003): 4–20.

Harris, Ben M. *Supervisory Behavior in Education* (Englewood Cliffs, NJ: Prentice-Hall, 1985).

Hollaway, John H. "Mentoring New Leaders." *Educational Leadership 61,* no. 7 (2004): 87–88.

Hunter, M. "Knowing, Teaching, and Supervising." In *Using What We Know About Teaching,* ed. P. L. Hosford (Alexandria, VA: Association for Supervision and Curriculum Development, 1984), pp. 169–192.

Lieberman, J. M. "National Board Certification: Bringing Out the Best in Teachers." *Principal 83* (2004): 45–47.

Minarik, M. M., B. Thornton, and G. Perreault. "Systems Thinking Can Improve Teacher Retention." *The Clearing House 76,* no. 5 (2003): 230–234.

Nieto, S. "From Striving to Thriving" [Electronic Version]. *Educational Leadership 66,* no. 5 (2009): 8–13.

Renard, L. "Setting New Teachers Up for Failure or Success." *Educational Leadership 60* (2003): 62–64.

Rooney, J. "Who Owns Teacher Growth? "*Educational Leadership 64,* no. 7 (2007): 87–88.

Ruder, R. "What to Do When the Brightest Begin to Dim." *Principal Leadership 5,* no. 8 (2005): 28–29.

Sparks, Dennis. "The Looming Danger of a Two-Tiered Professional Development System." *Phi Delta Kappan 86* (2004): 304–306.

Wasburn-Moses, L. "How to Keep Your Special Education Teachers." Principal Leadership 5 (2005): 35–38.

Zimmerman, S., and M. Deckert-Pelton. "Evaluating the Evaluators: Teachers' Perceptions of the Principal's Role in Professional Evaluation." *NASSP Bulletin 87* (2005): 28–37.

Managing the Organization

T he school leaders of the twenty-first century must have knowledge and understanding of theories and models of organizations and principles of organizational development, operational procedures at the school and district level, principles and issues relating to school safety and security, human resources management and development, principles and issues relating to fiscal operations of school management, principles and issues relating to school facilities and use of space, legal issues impacting school operations, and current technologies that support management functions. They should also believe in, value, and be committed to making management decisions to enhance learning and teaching; taking risks to improve schools; trusting people and their judgments; accepting responsibility; having high-quality standards, expectations, and performances; involving stakeholders in management processes; and assuring a safe environment. The Educational Leadership Policy Standard: ISLLC 2008 Standard 3 supports these characteristics.

Standard 3: An education leader promotes the success of every student by ensuring management of the organization, operation, and resources for a safe, efficient, and effective learning environment.

Part Three addresses this standard and the functions that accompany it.

CHAPTER

10

Staffing the School

Recruitment, Selection, and Termination Processes

Selecting quality teachers may be the single most important thing you do as an administrator. A beginning high school teacher who stays in the classroom for a 30-year career can have had almost 5,000 students under his or her instruction by the time of retirement.

—G. C. UBBEN[1]

Recruitment and selection policies of school districts vary. The local school's involvement in the recruitment and selection process will depend on how the school district administrators perceive their role. If the machine metaphor is used—where the efficiency of the organization is best served with a centralized approach to personnel administration—then the central office for the school district is likely to play the major role in the recruitment, selection, and placement of new and transferring employees. The principal becomes the gatekeeper for the local school, with the role of confirming or objecting to the decisions of the central office. On the other hand, if the brain metaphor is applied with a learning organization as the preferred model, the local school—teachers, principal, parents, and even students—become the decision makers in the selection process, with the central office playing a supporting role.

Organizational tension created from personnel decisions exists in many organizations because the issue of *locus of control* has not been carefully delineated. Central personnel offices operating from the machine metaphor wish to play a major hand in personnel decisions to ensure efficiency as well as compliance with the law. This model suggests a highly centralized decision process.

Principals wishing to use the learning organization concept prefer to follow the brain metaphor, reserving personnel decisions for the members of local learning community. This is a highly decentralized model. This chapter takes the position that the learning organization model is preferred, with most of the personnel decisions made by stakeholders at the building level. However, the chapter also points out many of the tension points that occur with this approach.

Determining Staffing Needs

When staff vacancies occur through staff attrition or school growth, it is always an opportunity to stand back and review staffing needs across the entire school. If an English teacher resigns or a second-grade teacher retires, do not look only to fill the vacancy that has just occurred; rather, use the opportunity to review the entire staffing structure of the school. Two questions will get you started. First, if you were not allowed to fill the vacancy, how would you fulfill the instructional need created by the loss of a teacher? For example, do you have other teachers certified in English who could change assignments to cover the vacancy, or would you place more students in the other English sections to cover the load? For the second-grade position, a similar thought

ISLLC 3

process might be used. Would you place more students in other second-grade sections, or would you do a combined second and third grade, or would you move to some other multiage configuration? What are the projected enrollments for the next several years? Is there a greater pending need at another grade level?

The second question asks you to review your school improvement plan. Do you have proposed improvements that suggest new personnel or a different staffing pattern than the existing one? If you proposed a team-based, multiage classroom organization how could you best utilize staff? If at the secondary level you proposed to add more electives to the curriculum, how would you staff them? Here is your opportunity to create a new position and hire a new staff member with the best credentials to carry it out or to move a qualified existing staff member and then fill his or her old position. All of these questions must be weighed against each other. It is really a chess game, and it's your move. Make it the right one! When the answers to such questions have been sorted out, you can then create a position and person description to fill your newly designed staffing need.

Recruitment

The major recruitment efforts by the school begin with good position and person descriptions. Figures 10.1 and 10.2 depict sample person and position descriptions. If the school finds it difficult to locate appropriate candidates, central office personnel should be contacted to review the recruitment process. For example, if the principal, in an effort to diversify the staff, has asked for a teacher from somewhere other than the local college, and the personnel office has not posted vacancies at other colleges, the recruitment drive will be ineffective. The principal must assume responsibility for seeing that recruitment policies are broad enough to meet personnel needs.

The selection of personnel should be a cooperative effort between the district personnel office and the local school. The role of central office should be to screen applicants and to send those best matching the position descriptions to the school for final selection. In some large school districts, a personnel office may employ teachers unassigned to specific buildings, but even in this case, the building principal and staff should have the final decision regarding who works in the building.

FIGURE 10.1   Person Description

Lakeview Schools

219 Lakeview Ave.

Lake City

Person Description

Position: Elementary Teacher

Sex: Prefer male

Teaching Experience Necessary: None

Training Requirements: BS; prefer graduates from other than local college

Certification: Elementary, K–3

Teaching Strength: Strong reading training; interest in social studies

Other Skills: Prefer someone with training or experience with team teaching or cooperative learning

Other Interests: Prefer someone with a vocational interests that would appeal to young boys such as camping, hiking, model-airplane making, and so on

Source: Larry W. Hughes and Gerald C. Ubben, *The Elementary Principal's Handbook: A Guide to Effective Action,* 4th ed. Boston: Allyn & Bacon, 1994, p. 238. Used with permission.

FIGURE 10.2   Position Description

Lakeview Schools

219 Lakeview Ave.

Lake City

Position Description

Position Title: Teacher (team) grade-level elementary 1–3

Purpose of Position: To plan, organize, and instruct primary children

Starting Date:

Salary Range: Beginning teacher,   B.S.—$33,000
                                        M.S.—$37,000

Principal Duties: The teacher will be a member of a four-teacher team working with 6- to 8-year-old children. Instruction is organized on an interdisciplinary basis with cooperative planning units. The team has four assigned classrooms and schedules children in a flexible manner into these spaces. Major instructional responsibilities will include reading and mathematics as well as participation in the integration of other subjects.

Performance Responsibilities:

I. Instructional Skills
   A. Knowledge and Training
      1. Is academically competent in assigned teaching areas.
      2. Keeps abreast of new findings and current trends in the field.
      3. Remains open-minded and willing to grow and change.
      4. Provides opportunities for all students to experience success.

(continued)

FIGURE 10.2   Position Description (*continued*)

B. Classroom Environment and Management
   1. Maintains a classroom environment conducive to learning (by using special interest areas, learning centers, units, themes, furniture arrangements, proper lighting, heating, ventilation, and structured rules and regulations understood and accepted by all).
   2. Monitors individual pupil progress and adapts the pace of instruction accordingly.
   3. Uses democratic procedures that show consideration for the rights of others.
C. Methods and Techniques
   1. Uses a variety of stimulating instructional techniques (such as the lecture method, demonstration, self-directed activities, both small and large group activities [drill and rote activities], and community resources, audiovisual aids and individualized programs).
   2. Demonstrates and fosters the growth of communication skills.
   3. Presents subject matter in a functional manner.
   4. Makes homework assignments for meaningful instructional purposes.
D. Planning
   1. Establishes short- and long-range goals with well-defined objectives and identifies appropriate procedures to accomplish them. (Example: A minimum competency and curriculum guide.)
   2. Provides opportunities for all students to experience success.
   3. Has a well-defined alternative plan for substitute teachers.
E. Evaluation
   1. Provides feedback to students on their accomplishments and progress with positive and effective reinforcements.
   2. Uses instruments based on activity, objective, or goal-oriented criteria.
   3. Guides students toward self-motivation, self-evaluation, and self-direction.
II. Student Attitudes and Performance
   A. Demonstrates consistency, firmness, and impartiality in dealing with students in a professional manner.
   B. Appreciates individuality.
   C. Shows positive attitudes toward students by helping all children experience success, possibly through the use of tutorial and counseling activities.
   D. Promotes desirable standards of work and behavior within the classroom.
III. Personal Qualities
   A. Demonstrates a positive and enthusiastic attitude and a genuine interest in students, colleagues, curriculum, and the education field in general.
   B. Recognizes and capitalizes on his or her own assets, thereby projecting a good model for students in dress, demeanor, and speech.
   C. Is able to profit from constructive criticism.
   D. Shows qualities that reflect the importance of punctuality, efficiency, dependability, accuracy, and congeniality.
IV. Professional Growth and Development
   A. Participates in enrichment activities, including such activities as study in his or her field and/or travel.
   B. Actively pursues avenues of personal and professional growth through workshops, classes, professional organizations, and seminars.
   C. Establishes personal goals for professional development.
V. Teacher Relationships
   A. Teacher/Parent
   1. Establishes an effective line of communication between home and school via notes, conferences, written reports, work samples, telephone conversations, and meetings of groups such as the PTO that stress discussion of students' strengths and weaknesses.

   2. Encourages parents to form a partnership with the teacher in the total education of their child—mentally, emotionally, physically, and spiritually.
 B. Teacher/Community
   1. Works effectively with legitimate community organizations and identifies and utilizes community resources to augment the educational opportunities of the children.
   2. Projects a positive image of the total school program to the community; liaison function is served.
 C. Teacher/Teacher
   1. Cooperates fully with colleagues in shared responsibilities.
   2. Shows tolerance for peer differences.
   3. Shares experiences, ideas, and knowledge with peers.
   4. Communicates effectively with other teachers who have shared or will share the same students for the purpose of developing smooth continuity between grade levels and subject matter.
 D. Teacher/Administrator/Supervisor
   1. Understands and adheres to the chain of command.
   2. Participates in decision making when appropriate.
   3. Demonstrates cooperation in performing both classroom and extra duties.
   4. Seeks advice and counsel when needed.
   5. Forms a partnership to develop good public relations in the school district.
 E. Teacher/Student
   1. Recognizes the uniqueness of all students.
   2. Guides and encourages students in a friendly, constructive, and impartial manner.
   3. Initiates procedures that will invite regular feedback for students.
   4. Maintains a classroom atmosphere conducive to mutual respect, one that adequately establishes appropriate roles.

Source: Larry W. Hughes and Gerald C. Ubben, *The Elementary Principal's Handbook: A Guide to Effective Action,* 4th ed. Boston: Allyn & Bacon, 1994, pp. 238–240. Used with permission.

The greatest problem in the selection of new staff members often comes from the need of the central office to place "transfers." These are generally tenured employees who must be moved from a previous assignment in the district. Because they are tenured, the school district must place them ahead of any new hires. Although there may be many legitimate reasons for the transfer of employees within a school district, some school districts have a bad habit of playing "pass the trash." This is the practice of allowing the transfer of poor or incompetent teachers from school to school rather than going through the process of dismissal. Once again, the principal must evaluate each candidate for a position in the school on the basis of what he or she thinks is best for the school.

The principles of learning organizations and the concepts of teacher empowerment strengthen the principal's position in employing new staff members. Involving the leadership team in setting policies for the selection of new staff members, and involving members of the teaching staff in the interview and selection process, will increase the principal's power base in resisting undesirable placements of staff by a central personnel office.

Federal Regulations to Prevent Employment Discrimination

Care must always be taken to abide by the federal laws regarding recruitment and selection of staff. The Civil Rights Act of 1964 and the Equal Employment Opportunity Act of 1972 and

ISLLC 6

their several amendments as well as the Americans with Disabilities Act (ADA) of 1990 make it unlawful to discriminate on the basis of race, color, religion, gender, age, national origin, or disabling condition.

Equal Employment Opportunity Commission (EEOC) Act.   In order to reduce the risk for discrimination during the process of selecting new employees, the EEOC has made it unlawful to ask about the following on either a written application or during an interview:

- Complexion or color of skin
- The applicant's religious denomination, affiliation, church, parish, pastor, or religious holidays observed
- The applicant's gender, marital status, name of or other information about spouse, or ages of children if any
- Whether the applicant has a disability or has been treated for any of certain diseases. However, you may ask if the applicant has any physical impairments that would affect the ability to perform the job for which the applicant has applied.
- If the applicant has ever been arrested. You may ask if the applicant has been convicted of a crime.
- Any previous name that the applicant has used. You may ask if he or she worked for your organization under a different name (e.g., a maiden name).
- Birthplace or birthplace of the applicant's parents or spouse; birthdate or certificate of naturalization papers, and so on
- Submission of the applicant's photograph before hiring
- Whether the applicant or a relative is a citizen of a foreign country. You may ask if the applicant is a U.S. citizen, intends to become one, or has a legal right to be in the United States.
- The applicant's native language. You may ask which languages the applicant speaks and writes.
- Questions or information about the applicant's relatives. Prior to employment, you may not even ask the name of a person to contact in case of emergency.
- The clubs, societies, and lodges to which the applicant belongs. You may ask the applicant to list organizations he or she believes to be pertinent to the job.

After the individual has been employed, many of these items of information can then legally be asked on an employee information form.

Americans with Disabilities Act (ADA).   The Americans with Disabilities Act prohibits employers, public and private, from discriminating against any individual with a disability. The law covers the full range of employment activities, including recruiting and hiring, termination, compensation, job assignment and advancement, and training. The law requires that employers make reasonable accommodation in the workplace to enable the individual to perform fundamental job duties of a position. This may require providing properly positioned whiteboards and new technology to allow the person to function successfully. Often, the workplace itself is more of a barrier to the physically challenged than job skills and knowledge. Care must be shown not to exclude anyone from consideration for employment because of his or her disabling condition if he or she is capable of performing the essential functions called for by that position.

The Selection Process

The selection process for the employment of new staff members has several steps or stages.

Screening

The first step is application clarification. Before an interview, the principal should carefully review the candidate's application file, comparing the application with the personal description. Few candidates will possess all the qualifications that have been specified, but the principal should try to find candidates with most of them.

Discrepancy Analysis

The second step in the selection process should be a discrepancy analysis of the application materials. Remember, applicants usually present themselves in the best manner possible, minimizing weak points. One technique used to uncover discrepancies is to search the file for missing information. Common problem areas are (1) efforts to conceal unfavorable past activities by excluding dates and (2) not listing appropriate reference sources. Other things to check for include health and legal problems.

The reviewer should look particularly at references from previous employers to make sure each employment situation is represented. Read between the lines on health records. Look for gaps in employment or school records. The interviewer can request more detailed explanations about areas where possible discrepancies have been identified. Most often, candidates will give perfectly acceptable explanations regarding the discrepancies, but occasionally interviews uncover serious problems by a discrepancy review.

Reference Check

If the job candidate has had previous teaching experience and is one of the final candidates being considered for the position, a personal telephone contact with the previous principal or some other school administrator who is acquainted with the candidate is usually helpful. Often, an interviewer can obtain more information during a phone call than from a written reference.

Care must be taken, however, in the manner in which questions are asked. Similarly, one must be careful in answering any questions regarding a previous employee. The courts have held that in cases of employee nonreemployment where no charges have been officially brought and where no dismissal hearing has been held, an employer is restricted in the negative comments he or she may make about a previous employee. This ruling is based on the concept that such comments could limit the opportunity of that former employee to obtain employment elsewhere and therefore place a limit on that former employee's "liberty," a right that is protected under the amendments to the federal Constitution.[2] Therefore, employers must use care in stating opinions regarding former employees' performance.

These court decisions, however, do not prevent one from asking for references or answering questions. Nevertheless, they do signal that one must stick to the facts rather than delving into opinion or gossip. Similarly, when asking for information from a previous employer, recognize that this individual is under the same limitation and should hesitate in answering questions of a speculative nature. Ask for factual information about the previous employee. One very telling question that the former employer can answer is this: "If the person in question would seek a job in your school again, would you rehire him or her?" If the answer is anything but extremely positive, it should raise a caution flag for the interviewer.

The Job Interview

The job interview has several basic functions. It provides an opportunity for the candidate to clarify any apparent discrepancies found in the written job application. The job interview, however, goes beyond the written application by allowing the principal and staff to gather information in greater depth than can be obtained from written materials only.

The interview also allows the principal and staff to gain insights into the personality and interpersonal skills of the applicant. Teaching is a "people" business, and teachers must be able to relate well to other adults and children. Research has shown that good verbal skills are particularly significant in determining the quality of a teacher. These skills can best be assessed through an interview. Whenever possible, an employment recommendation should be based on group interaction with the principal and the existing staff.

Interviews should be arranged to involve teachers, department heads, and team members in the process. This is one additional way to empower teachers. Some will argue that under the concept of site-based management, your local site board should also be involved. We believe that staff selection is a task to be delegated to the professional staff based on policy set by the local site board, but that board members should not be involved directly in the selection process. The one exception to this might be if the central office continues to dictate personnel placements for the school. Then the clout of the site-based management board might be needed to veto unwanted placements.

When staff members are asked to participate in the interview process, they also are obligated to follow the EEOC guidelines regarding appropriate questions. It is usually wise to hold a short refresher course before staff members interview candidates to remind them of appropriate and inappropriate questions.

Interviews can be conducted using a variety of different formats. Here is an interview agenda that is well accepted:

1. *Establish the atmosphere.* Open the interview slowly and try to create a warm, pleasant, relaxed atmosphere that will reduce the candidate's anxiety.
2. *Ask focused questions.* Such questions will elicit the knowledge and information needed about the candidate. The principal and staff want to learn of his or her perceptions of personal strengths and weaknesses, his or her understanding and philosophy of education, his or her verbal fluency, and his or her ability to project enthusiasm. The use of what-if questions often works well to get the candidate indirectly to share these beliefs and attitudes.
3. *Be an active listener.* Ask open-ended questions rather than yes–no questions. Support the candidate verbally with "uh-huhs," or "tell me more." The candidate should be contributing about 70 percent of the conversation to the interviewers' 30 percent during the interview.

4. *Share school information with the candidate.* Remember the candidate also has a decision to make ("Do I want to come to work for you?"). Tell the candidate about the specific job vacancy; with whom he or she may be working, particularly if those individuals met the candidate; the kinds of children enrolled in the school; particular programs that the school may have; and information about the school community if the candidate is not from that area.

5. *Close the interview.* Thank the candidate for his or her time and openness. Share the next steps in the selection process, including when he or she might expect to hear from the school or how he or she might keep up with the decision process.

6. *Write out your notes.* Gather information from the others who participated in the interview process. Often a team discussion works well. If several candidates are to be interviewed before a decision is made, the use of a checklist or some formatted method of recording perceptions is wise so that later comparison can be more objective.

Employee Probationary Status

The selection process for staff continues through the probationary phase for new employees. Most states have a one- to three-year probationary period during which the employee is on a continuing contract before receiving tenured employment. During this period, the principal and staff must reaffirm the original decision to employ a particular staff member. Usually, the contract renews automatically around April 15 unless notification is given to the teacher for nonrenewal. Through the continuation of the orientation phase and evaluation of instructional competence, which is discussed in more detail in a subsequent chapter, the emphasis for staff development is on improving the quality of teaching. The selection process is usually considered complete only when tenure is granted. During this probationary period, the principal must consider the possibility of termination or nonrenewal of the contract when there is reason to suspect that the original selection was not wise.

Orientation and Development of New Teachers

The No Child Left Behind legislation of 2002 requires a *highly qualified* teacher in every classroom, yet more than one-third of all new teachers leave the classroom within the first three years of employment as a teacher. Hiring highly qualified teachers is only one part of the process. Keeping qualified teachers and helping them develop into highly qualified professionals is as important. A major role of a principal is to teach new teachers to be good teachers. The word *principal* is really a shortened version of *principal teacher,* or the lead teacher. The principal is to be a teacher of teachers. When hiring a brand-new teacher, the principal is often correct in assuming that the new teacher probably does not know how to teach. New graduates were smart enough to get a college degree and to have survived the college classroom exposure to pedagogy, but they have not had an opportunity to really become familiar with the expectations and challenges of schools. That's where the principal comes in. It is the principal's job to teach these individuals how to survive and thrive in the school setting and to keep them as successful teachers and not lose them to attrition or failure. Remember from the previous chapter, most new teachers are at the survival and discovery stage.[3] Build a support system for all new staff members, even if there is only one new teacher or transfer teacher; follow these guidelines:

1. Provide each new teacher with a teacher support system through a teacher mentor. Chapter 9 has an overview section on mentoring.

2. Provide an administrator support system also. This is the principal's teaching opportunity. The support system needs to begin the day the new staff member is hired even if it is in the middle of the summer. Don't wait until school starts. Remember, the new teacher is excited about his or her new career and is anxious to get started.

   a. Begin with a welcome letter and provide the new teacher with as much information as possible as early as possible. Class schedules, room assignments, calendar dates, and student lists are all welcome bits of information.

   b. Fight the school culture that suggests giving the new teacher the leftovers. Try to develop a school culture that eases the burden on a new teacher by giving him or her the better-behaved children, the nicer classroom, the newer books—even if this violates the culture of "seniority" that exists in most schools.

   c. Last year's school yearbook makes an excellent orientation document for a new teacher. In it he or she will be able to find names and faces of returning staff and students. Much of the school culture is portrayed via clubs, sports teams, and special groups.

   d. As early as possible, give the new teacher the teacher editions of textbooks he or she will be using so that some lessons can be organized before school starts.

   e. Provide the new teacher with a "how to get started" session several days before the first day of school. In this session suggest how he or she might greet the children the first day, how to get the children organized, and tips for first lessons.

   f. Point out the importance of early classroom management and how it sets the tone for the year. Give specific suggestions as to how the new staff member might establish desirable behaviors the first few days.

   g. Give basic starter tips, such as suggesting the teacher not fill out grade books or distribute texts until the enrollment has stabilized after a few days.

   h. Once school has begun, continue to meet with the new teacher about once a week for at least the first marking period (six to nine weeks) in a voluntary session before or after school. Identify issues the teacher would like to discuss, such as ideas on how often to give tests, what to do with a misbehaving child, how to assign report card grades, procedures for marking report cards, how to respond to parent concerns, teacher evaluation and supervision, and so on. For many of the teacher's suggested topics, the principal should be able to handle them well. For others, it will be best to bring in a seasoned staff member or special expert such as a guidance counselor.

   i. Support the new faculty member with frequent classroom visits—not long formal visits, but a series of short visits so the teacher will become comfortable with the principal's presence. Use these visits mainly for observation to gain insight for other discussion ideas for weekly sessions with the new staff member. Remember, the most important responsibility of the principal is instructional leadership.

   j. Continue these "new faculty" sessions on a less frequent basis throughout the entire first year. During the second and third years of a new teacher's career, the topics can shift more to issues of quality teaching techniques and methods. Bringing high-quality teachers into the sessions, followed by an opportunity to observe the veteran teachers in the classroom, is often a good approach.

These orientation and development sessions for new teachers are the principal's major avenue to mold new teachers into the skilled, dedicated professionals that all schools so desperately need. If these sessions do well, the new teacher can be proudly recommended for tenure when the probationary period is over.

Teacher Tenure

ISLLC 6

One of the most misunderstood concepts in education is tenure. It is not, as often believed, a guarantee of a job from which dismissal is all but impossible. Rather, in most states, tenure is simply a statement of the guarantee of due process assuring exercise of academic freedom for the teacher by allowing dismissal only for specific causes listed in the tenure law. Tenure does not guarantee the right to a job. If the job is abolished or if a teacher is found to be incompetent, insubordinate, or guilty of a variety of professionally unacceptable behaviors, that teacher can be dismissed, with proper due process.

In the past few years, federal courts have broadened their decisions regarding due process and human rights to the point that due process guarantees, including many of the guarantees found in the tenure laws, have been extended to most employees. As a result, probationary teachers are now guaranteed many of the same due process rights afforded tenured teachers in the past.[4]

Involuntary Termination

An extremely poor or incompetent teacher should never be kept on the staff of a school simply because dismissal is difficult. The law establishes definite rights for employer and employee.

ISLLC 6

Procedural due process is guaranteed, but due process does not mean that teachers cannot be dismissed. What it means is that teachers have specific rights, such as the right to a hearing, the right to be treated in a fair and nondiscriminatory fashion, and the right to require that just cause be shown for a dismissal action. The law may be more specific about the causes and process of dismissal for teachers under tenure, but dismissal can still be accomplished.

Every step in a dismissal action should be carried out on the assumption that it will ultimately go to court. Adopting this attitude is the best way to prevent court action. Rarely will an attorney engaged by a dismissed teacher or provided by a teacher association take a case to court if the school district has prepared its action carefully. When the courts reject the dismissal and order reinstatement of a teacher, it is most often because of improper procedure on the part of the school district and less likely due to teacher behavior.

Preparation for Dismissal

Dismissal decisions should not be made quickly. A tentative decision not to rehire a first-year teacher for the following year should be contemplated three to four months before the deadline

ISLLC 3

for contract renewal. For a tenured teacher, often two or three years are needed to build a case defensible in court to reverse earlier recommendations that were positive enough to have resulted in tenure even though the earlier recommendations may have been a mistake. Unfortunately, poor personnel records and poor evaluation procedures are common in school districts.

The defense attorney will often demand to see the entire personnel file for a teacher being dismissed. If positive evaluations have been given in the past, even though they were unjustified, a greater collection of data of a negative nature is required to offset them. Evidence that the teacher received specific notice of inadequacy and was offered help is important.

In a hearing, the courts will try to answer the following questions: Was procedural due process used? Is the evidence appropriate and supportive of the case? Was the employee discriminated against? Were efforts made to help the employee? Did the employee have prior knowledge that his or her work was unsatisfactory? Was the employee provided time and the opportunity to improve or correct whatever deficiencies existed?

Due Process

Teachers must be given timely notice of the decision not to rehire. If contract renewal comes on April 15, with a two-week hearing notice deadline, employees should be notified by April 1. A certified letter is the best way of assuring a record of such notification. Employees must be informed that they have the opportunity for and the right to a hearing. The hearing time, date, and place should be stated in the letter. If the teacher is tenured, the letter should also include the specific causes or charges for dismissal. Recent due process decisions from the courts in some cases make it highly advisable to provide this opportunity for a hearing to nontenured teachers as well as to those who have tenure.[5–6]

Appropriateness of Evidence

Evidence should be firsthand, factual, and documented accurately with appropriate dates. If the offense is cumulative in nature, the collection of data should also be cumulative. Descriptive notes of supervisory meetings and conferences—for example, expressing agreed-upon outcomes and a statement describing the extent of the implementation or the lack thereof on the part of the teacher—should be included. The statements should be objective. Rather than stating, "This teacher did a poor job of teaching today," the note should state, "In presenting a lesson on the Civil War, the teacher did not hold the interest of the class, the students did not understand the lesson as presented, and the class became unruly while under the teacher's direction." Include the date; the time; the events that led up to the conference, such as the previous involvement of a supervisor; and any immediate follow-up action that was taken. A note might simply read, "Mr. Smith arrived at school at 8:30 on December 2, 3, and 4. His designated time of arrival is 8:00. He has been notified of this deficiency." This is not a judgmental statement but a simple statement of fact. Such items, properly collected, can be used to support a claim of incompetence, neglect of duty, or insubordination. Remember to record facts, not opinions, and do this in a timely fashion.

Equal Rights

Was the employee treated in a fair and nondiscriminatory manner? Was anything done to or for this employee that was not done or available to other employees? Was the assignment unfair?

Was the teacher asked to do more or less than the rest of the staff? Was supervision uniform? A grossly unequal schedule for supervision, for example, can be construed to be harassment. When problems arise, however, it is not unreasonable for supervision to increase as long as the time sequence can be demonstrated. Supervisory appointments and documentation included only in the file of the teacher being dismissed, with no evidence of supervision included in the files of the other members of the staff, however, will often be looked on as discriminatory action by the courts.

Efforts to Help the Teacher

The courts will want to know what was done to make this individual an effective employee. Was adequate supervision of a helping nature developed? Was adequate time given for the improvement effort? If not, the courts may not uphold the dismissal action but may reinstate the employee, suggesting that the supervisory staff provide assistance.

Most often, when the principal is well prepared and has central-office support, teacher dismissal, while serious, will take place quietly. A teacher who knows that school officials are well prepared most often will not request a hearing and will simply resign. Most cases resulting in the failure to dismiss are a result of poor preparation and improper procedure on the part of the school district. See Figure 10.3 for a flowchart for employee dismissal procedures.

Reduction in Force

Reduction in force (RIF) is the term given to a mandatory reduction in the number of employees in your school. It is one of the most gut-wrenching actions you may ever have to take as a school administrator. Decisions regarding who is going to loose their jobs are often totally out of your hands; rather, school board policy and teacher contracts dictate decisions. Criteria for determination of which employees are going to be eliminated are generally spelled out in these documents. Frequently the criteria are based on program elimination, seniority, and credentials, with junior members of the staff at the highest risk of losing their jobs. Depending on school district policy, transfer rights of positions within a building and or transfer rights across buildings within the district can drastically affect the makeup of your staff.

As teachers or other staff members are identified to loose their positions, a huge morale problem often develops. Both the departing employees and those staying are affected. Recognize that this crisis creates the need of special assistance to aid in the transition. You may wish to give special recognition to the departing staff members who through no fault of their own are leaving. You and your staff might help them look for other employment. Certainly invite them to substitute in your building and reapply for jobs in your school when times get better.

The impact of an RIF on the programs in your school can be significant depending on how many positions are lost, what programs have been eliminated, and how many teaching positions are now held by different people. The loss of regular classroom teachers almost always results in larger class sizes. At the elementary level, instead of class sizes of 20 they may go to 25. When programs such as art or music are eliminated, regular classroom teachers may need to incorporate these activities into their classrooms. At the secondary level, fewer teachers means fewer class sections available—probably eliminating some of the curricular offerings that are smaller in enrollments. Transferred staff members, while experienced, are new to your school, so team

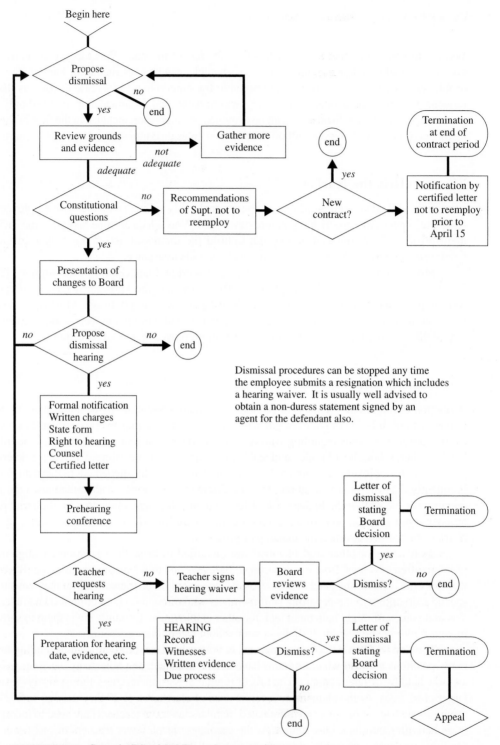

Begin here

Propose dismissal — no → end
yes ↓

Review grounds and evidence — not adequate → Gather more evidence
adequate ↓

Constitutional questions — no → Recommendations of Supt. not to reemploy → New contract? — yes → end
yes ↓   no ↓

Presentation of changes to Board

Notification by certified letter not to reemploy prior to April 15

Termination at end of contract period

Propose dismissal hearing — no → end
no (left loop)
yes ↓

Formal notification
Written charges
State form
Right to hearing
Counsel
Certified letter

Dismissal procedures can be stopped any time the employee submits a resignation which includes a hearing waiver. It is usually well advised to obtain a non-duress statement signed by an agent for the defendant also.

Prehearing conference
↓

Teacher requests hearing — no → Teacher signs hearing waiver → Board reviews evidence → Dismiss? — no → end
yes ↓   yes ↑

Preparation for hearing date, evidence, etc. → HEARING
Record
Witnesses
Written evidence
Due process → Dismiss? — yes → Letter of dismissal stating Board decision → Termination → Appeal
no ↓
end

Letter of dismissal stating Board decision → Termination

FIGURE 10.3   Steps in Dismissal Procedures

Source: Larry W. Hughes and Gerald C. Ubben, *The Elementary Principal's Handbook: A Guide to Effective Action,* 4th ed. Boston: Allyn & Bacon, 1994, p. 248. Used with permission.

building activities are in order to reestablish the learning community atmosphere that every good school needs.

Voluntary Termination

Each year staff members will resign from a school for a variety of reasons: retirement, transfers, better jobs, starting a family, going back to school, and incompetence. In every case the principal should hold a termination interview before that person departs. Several basic purposes exist for such an interview. Of primary concern is the help the school might offer the individual in adjusting to a new life situation.

The interview should also be an opportunity to investigate the perceptions of the departing employee regarding the operation of the school. At times, principals have difficulty getting good information about the operation of the school and the existing climate within the staff. Often, departing employees will be candid about their perceptions concerning existing problems. They may even identify some previously hidden reason for leaving.

Finally, the interview can be useful in identifying prospects for substitute, part-time, volunteer, and future employment when the departing employee is planning to remain in the community. Retired teachers, or those who are staying home to rear a family, are particularly good candidates for part-time employment or volunteer positions.

Summary

The search for and the employment of new staff members is one of the most important tasks of a school administrator. The process begins with the determination of staff needs—including recruitment, selection, orientation, and staff development—and culminates with the placement of the employee on tenure.

Termination of employees, voluntarily or involuntarily, occurs in most schools every year. The principal needs to conduct exit interviews with all terminating employees. Involuntary termination is usually a difficult, but sometimes necessary, task. An important point in staff dismissal is following due process and ensuring that the employee's rights have not been violated.

ACTIVITIES

1. Review Case Studies 11, 14, 18, and 23 at the end of this book. Analyze the problems presented and apply the concepts of staff evaluation developed in this chapter. What approach would you use in addressing the problems? Set forth a strategy to overcome the difficulties faced by the individuals in these cases.

2. Develop a plan for the evaluation of the staff in your school. Over what portion of the year should it run? How much of your time will it take to conduct an evaluation of your faculty members? Should you evaluate all teachers each year? If not, which teachers get priority evaluations? What about other nonteaching staff members? What is your responsibility for their evaluation? How much of your time will this take?

3. Turn to the ISLLC standards found in Appendix B. Review the performances listed in Standard 3. Which of the functions best support the human resources concepts discussed in this chapter? What weakness do you find in your school's human resources management? How would you go about correcting them?

ENDNOTES

1. G. C. Ubben, class lecture, University of Tennessee, Knoxville, October 1995.
2. *Board of Regents* v. *Roth,* 92 S. Ct. 2701 (1972). This case dealt with the nonreemployment of a nontenured teacher who had difficulty obtaining another job because of comments made by the administrators of the nonreemploying school. The teacher charged that his right to "liberty" was violated by his inability to obtain other employment because of his lack of opportunity to defend himself against unheard charges. The Supreme Court found that his due process rights were violated and ordered that he be given a hearing and back pay.
3. Michael Huberman, "The Professional Life Cycle of Teachers," *Teachers College Record 91,* no. 1 (Fall 1989): 131.
4. See Chapter 16 for information about the steps in procedural due process.
5. Cases Related to Due Process—Teacher Dismissal
    a. *Board of Regents* v. *Roth,* 92 S. Ct. 2701 (1972) and *Perry* v. *Sunderman,* 928 Ct. 2694 (1972). These are the precedent-setting cases regarding due process just as *Brown* v. *Board of Education* set the precedent for discrimination cases.
    b. *Paul* v. *Davis,* 424 U.S. 693 (1976); *Bishop* v. *Wood,* 246 U.S. 341 (1976); and *Meachum* v. *Fano,* 427 U.S. 215 (1970).

    c. 7th Cir., the Court of Appeals in *Confederation of Police* v. *City of Chicago,* 547 F. 2d 375 (1977).
    d. *Codd* v. *Velger,* 97 S. Ct. 882 (1977).
    e. *Arnet* v. *Kennedy,* 416 U.S. 134 (1974).
    f. *Peacock* v. *Board of Regents,* 510 F 2d 1324 (9th Cir.)
    g. *Withrow* v. *Larken,* 421 U.S. 35 (1975).
    h. Hortonville 96S Ct. 2308.
    i. *Mt. Healthy City School District* v. *Doyle,* 97 S. Ct. 568 (1977).
6. Although most state tenure laws and continuing contract laws in and of themselves do not require a hearing for non-tenured staff, the federal Constitution and the Civil Rights Act of 1964 might. According to a series of court decisions over recent years, a teacher is considered to have certain rights under the First and Fourteenth Amendments to the Constitution. Although nonrenewal of a contract does not require a hearing, dismissal does. If a denial-of-freedom-of-speech claim is made, a hearing is advisable, and if the case is receiving much publicity so as to endanger the individual's opportunity for other employment, a hearing should be held. Also, if discrimination is charged, a hearing should be held. If an opportunity for a hearing is not granted, the teacher may later file a complaint charging violation of due process.

SELECTED READINGS

Berry, B. "Recruiting and Retaining Highly Qualified Teachers for Hard to Staff Schools" *NASSP Bulletin 88,* no. 638 (2004): 5–27.

Boreen, Jean, Mary K. Johnson, Donna Niday, and Joe Potts. *Mentoring Beginning Teachers: Guiding, Reflecting, Coaching* (2nd ed.) (Portland, ME: Stenhouse Publishers, 2009).

Clement, M., W. Kistner, and W. Moran. "A Question of Experience." *Principal Leadership 5,* no. 6 (2005).

Clement, M. C. "Help Wanted: How to Hire the Best Teachers." *Principal Leadership (Middle School Ed.) 3,* no. 1 (2002): 16–21.

Clement, M. "Improving Teacher Selection with Behavior-Based Interviewing" *Principal 87,* no. 3 (2008): 44–47.

Cowdrey, J. "Getting It Right: Nurturing an Environment for Teacher-Learners." *Kappa Delta Pi Record 40,* no. 3 (2004): 128–131.

Gorky, D. "Recruiting Minority Teachers." *American Teacher 86* (2002): 10–11.

Jacob, B. A. "The Challenges of Staffing Urban School with Effective Teachers" [Electronic Version]. *The Future of Children 17,* no. 1 (2007): 129–153.

Jorgenson, O., and C. Moon. "Grow Your Own Teachers!" *Principal Leadership 2,* no. 9 (2002): 35–38.

Kaplan, L. S. "The Politics of Teacher Quality: Implications for Principals." *NASSP Bulletin 86* (2002): 22–41.

Kelehear, Z. "Mentoring the Organization: Helping Principals Bring Schools to Higher Levels of Effectiveness." *NASSP Bulletin 87* (2003): 35–47.

Longo, G. "Applying Credibility to Teacher Hiring." *School Administrator 60* (2003): 35.

Munoz M., P. Winter, and N. Ronau. "Finding the Right Fit." *American School Board Journal 190* (2003): 42–43.

Reeves, D. "New Ways to Hire Educators." *Educational Leadership 64,* no. 8 (2007): 83–84.

Ruder, R. "What to Do When the Brightest Begin to Dim." *Principal Leadership 5,* no. 8 (2005).

Sargent, B. "Finding Good Teachers and Keeping Them." *Educational Leadership 60,* no. 8 (2003): 44–47.

St. Maurice, H., and P. Shaw. "Teacher Portfolios Come of Age: A Preliminary Study." *NASSP Bulletin 88,* no. 639 (2004): 15–25.

Scherer, M. "All Teachers Can Learn." *Educational Leadership 66,* no. 5 (2009): 7–8.

Washburn-Moses, L. "How to Keep Your Special Education Teachers." *Principal Leadership 5,* no. 5 (2005): 35–38.

11 Restructuring the Deployment of Instructional Personnel

Inherent in any good staffing design is optimal utilization of staff. Staff planning must take into account the present needs and functions of the members of the organization, as well as the school's long-range goals and plans that might modify hiring practices in the future.

—J. Lloyd Trump[1]

ISLLC 3

One of the greatest responsibilities assigned to a principal is organizing and assigning staff in the school. Included in normal staffing respsonsibilities is the deployment of all employees and volunteer workers to the instructional program and service functions of the school. Central-office administrators and supervisors often have a hand in these assignments, but especially with the advent of site-based management, the responsibility, and particularly the final decision, rest with the principal and staff.

Professional employees in school organizations usually have great insight and excellent ideas of how a school could be improved. They also have the need for both personal development and professional growth through interaction with other professionals in the school. School organization, however, often works against this opportunity for interaction because of self-contained classrooms that isolate teachers for up to six hours each day. The development and vitality of the school as a learning community depends on the opportunity and ability of the school staff to interact with each other. One way for school professionals to interact is to participate in building-level management decisions that affect the school's curriculum and instruction.

Empowerment

ISLLC 2

Ultimately, what is wanted of teachers is quality instruction and learning that takes place between teachers and students. Many functions within the school organization must be properly balanced for this to be maximized. On the one hand, too little attention on the part of administration regarding what goes on in each classroom can lead to lack of coordination of the curriculum, great variation in the quality of teaching, and great variation in the motivation of teachers. On the other hand, too much control or structure over teachers or centralization of authority over the classroom might produce some uniformity but take away teachers' autonomy, thereby negatively affecting teacher motivation and reducing the quality of instruction among the better teachers.

Only a fine balance can adequately empower teachers to exercise appropriate professional judgment while ensuring the coordination of the curriculum and supervision of instruction. The appropriate empowerment of teachers must lie in the amount of authority granted, methods of accountability used to ensure responsibility, and the organizational structures created to maintain the proper communication flow necessary to carry out these tasks.[2]

Professional Learning Communities

ISLLC 1

The organization of the staff within the school and the opportunities faculty members have to interact with other faculty members in shared responsibilities are important to the growth and development of the school as a learning community. The organization of the faculty may enhance or inhibit communication among staff members and the development of shared values and beliefs. In his writing on learning organizations, Peter Senge[3] suggested that systems thinking needs to be employed for improvement and growth to take place within organizations. Sergiovanni[4] further expanded the idea in his writing on learning communities. He described a preferred school learning community to include parents, students, teachers, and administrators who have shared values, purpose, and commitments and to bond together around a common cause.

Learning community norms become major motivational forces for determining the best strategies for improving the systems of teaching and learning. To create an environment within the school that enhances the nurturing of learning communities, principals must practice a very different kind of leadership behavior than is typically found in traditional corporate top-down organizational structures. The norms of the group give meaning to the community life. The norms become motivators and guide the group together as colleagues. The role of the leader becomes one of facilitating group conversation and helping guide the members of the learning community to an acceptable set of values and beliefs. Teachers become leaders and in turn work to instill the values of a learning organization in their students and parents.

Organizing for Professional Learning Community Development

A staff cannot be ordered to be a learning community. It must be grown as a culture, with common values, beliefs, vision, and mission. This growth and maturation takes time. A culture can be enhanced, however, as one would enhance a biological culture by creating an environment that encourages growth. The development of the culture of the school can be accelerated or retarded by the way the school is organized.

Traditionally, staffing has been by simple unit-classroom structure; that is, one teacher, one group of students, one room, sometimes one instructional format, and sometimes one subject. Staffing plans have been built and modified from year to year using this basic classroom unit. Such a pattern is very restrictive for learning community development, particularly when used in conjunction with some of the curricular, instructional, and grouping ideas presented in previous chapters. Organizing teachers into teaching teams offers several desirable alternatives to single classroom units and creates the opportunity for professional learning community development.

Staffing Patterns for Elementary and Middle Schools

An elementary or middle school staff can be organized in a variety of ways depending on its desired results. We favor learning communities that utilize teams of teachers with responsibility for a common group of students. The integrated contributions of several teachers, the teacher growth enhanced by common planning and quality circles, and the collective team concern for the growth of the students generate a synergism that is difficult to match in the traditional self-contained classroom.

Variations in Staff Assignments

Different staffing options are possible for a given student population, ranging from the traditional self-contained classroom under the direction of one teacher to a variety of learning community models involving regular classroom teachers, specialists, instructional assistants, parent volunteers, student helpers, and others.

For our example, we are going to tell the story of Ubben Elementary School, which has a student population of more than 500 students. The school is located in a small industrial town on the edge of a larger city. Its families are made up of middle-class commuters to the larger city, farm families from the outlying area, a growing Hispanic population of construction and factory workers who currently enroll 147 children in the school, and a small African American population of largely service workers who send a total of 23 children. The school includes grades K–5 and has recently added about 40 preschool children from families eligible for free or reduced-cost lunch. State laws as well as local school district regulations require that class size not exceed an average of 20 students per class in the primary grades and 25 in the intermediate grades and that no class exceed these maximums by more than 10 percent. Twenty-seven teaching positions are allocated for the K–5 enrollment.

Supplemental teaching positions are also provided for the school. Fifty-two children from the total enrollment are certified special education (special ed) students with a variety of disabling conditions—earning the school two special education teachers. Approximately 45 percent of the enrollment is eligible for free or reduced-cost lunch—earning the school the equivalent of two Title I teaching positions. One teaching position is provided for the growing enrollment of English language learners (ELLs). Some of the children are both special education certified and Title I eligible. The school district provides one physical education (PE) teacher, one librarian/technology teacher, one art teacher, and one music teacher. There is some money available for instructional aides from special education and Title I funds. The administration consists of one principal and one assistant.

TABLE 11.1   Ubben Elementary School Traditional Staffing

GRADE	ENROLLMENT	TEACHERS	AVERAGE CLASS SIZE
PreK	38	2	19
K	75	4	19
1	80	4 (or 5)	20 (or 16)
2	95	5	19
3	85	5	17
4	100	5	20
5	90	4	23
Physical education		1	
Librarian/technology		1	
Art		1 (or 1/2)	
Music		1 (or 1/2)	
Special education		2	
Title I		2	
English Language Learner (ELL)		1	
Guidance		1	
Administration		1 principal	
		1 assisstant principal	
Total	563	41	

Instructional assistants for special education, Title I, and ELL are also available.

Grade enrollments are as follows: PreK—38 students, K—75, grade 1—80, grade 2—95, grade 3—85, grade 4—100, grade 5—90. Total enrollment is 563. Possible staff assignments are shown in Table 11.1.

The number of students in each grade almost never works out uniformly. If a single-grade-level structure is to be used, one simply does the best one can to keep the numbers low and class sizes relatively equal. Class size research discussed in Chapter 7 points out the importance of keeping class size in the primary grades to a student-to-teacher ratio of under 20 to 1, preferably closer to 15 to 1. Ubben Elementary, would like to have five teachers in grade 1, thereby reducing the student-to-teacher ratio to 16 to 1. This would provide a little growth room if there is an enrollment increase during the year. If it is not possible to have five teachers, first grade will be the first place to assign available instructional aides.

Almost all school staffing arrangements are the result of compromises. In the case of Ubben Elementary, the staff felt it was extremely important to keep the first-grade classroom as small as possible to ensure that all children received as much attention as possible in this first-grade year. To do this, the decision was made to reduce both the music and art positions to half-time positions.

This allowed for the addition of one more first-grade classroom, which reduced the overall student-to-teacher ratio to 16 to 1.

Elementary School Teacher Specialists

The next concern for Ubben Elementary was how to most effectively use teacher specialists, that is, maximizing their effectiveness by minimizing the disruptiveness of a pullout program where individual students are excused from their regular class to receive special instruction. The decision was made to use the teacher specialists in two different ways. First, for teacher specialists who see all students (i.e., music, art, library/technology, PE, and guidance): If this position is available, a parallel-schedules team approach will be used, collectively taking all the students from the same grade at the same time everyday. (See Chapter 12 for the details of designing parallel schedules.) This allows the grade-level team planning time each day while their students are with the subject-area specialists.

Special Education, Title I, and ELL Staff

Second, for the other specialists, those assigned to only a specific portion of the students (i.e., special education, Title I, and ELL), two basic choices were available. (1) Pull these students from the regular classroom to attend the classes of the specialists. The huge disadvantage of this approach is that these students miss instruction in the regular classroom while they are away with the specialist. Also, the pullout approach locks up the schedule for everyone else, allowing little deviation from the standard schedule because of the pullout schedule for the specialist. (2) The second approach applies the concept of *inclusion* in an attempt to integrate into the regular classroom the work and talents of the specialists in a coordinated, planned, team approach to instruction.

Ubben Elementary School chose the second approach. With four or five teachers per grade level working at Ubben Elementary, it is virtually impossible for two special education teachers or two Title I teachers to visit 23 classrooms (grades 1–5) everyday, even with the help of instructional assistants. So students must be organized and grouped in some way to reduce the number of classes visited by the specialists. To do this, all four or five teachers at a grade level must work as a learning community, sharing responsibilities and sometimes sharing students.

Here is how the principal and teachers at each grade level grouped the students. The staff wanted to follow the instructional philosophy of inclusion by placing as many as possible of the special education students in regular classrooms for as much of the day as possible. They recognized that they would still need to maintain a comprehensive development class (CDC) or resource room for some of the students. With a total of 52 special education students spread across grades 1–5, there were approximately 10 special education students per grade (with a variety of disabling conditions). The 10 students in a grade were divided between *only two* of the regular classrooms at each grade level in order to concentrate this population in fewer classrooms. The special education staff could then focus on just two classrooms per grade level rather than five.

Each special education teacher and assistant have an average of one-half hour per day to devote to each individual classroom of grades 1–5, in addition to their responsibilities in the resource room. With the grade-level team functioning as a learning community, the two regular classroom teachers work with the special education teacher and assistant to determine how to best integrate instruction for the special education students on that team.

The drawback of concentrating all 10 special education students in only two classrooms in the extra burden an inclusion approach can create—even with the added assistance. In some cases of a severe disabling condition, a full-time assistant was assigned to a student. For other students, time was divided between the regular classroom and the resource room, which partially reduced the enrollment in the regular and special education classrooms. The other offset for Ubben Elementary was that with this design all Title I students, other than those who were also special education students, were placed with the other grade-level teachers. All Title-I-eligible

ISLLC 2, 3

students not in special education at each grade level were divided up among two or three of the remaining members of the grade-level team, with the Title I reading and math specialists and instructional assistants working with them. With approximately 45 percent of the students Title I eligible and a few of those also special education students, this left approximately 30 to 35 students at each grade who needed Title I reading and/or math instruction. Once again, these students were served in only two classrooms per grade, reducing the schedule conflicts and better concentrating the efforts of the Title I specialists.

Distribution of English language learners was similar. The 26 ELLs at Ubben Elementary, or about 5 per grade including preschool and kindergarten, were concentrated in one of the classrooms at each grade level. Many of these students were eligible for other special services; therefore, they would be best served in one of the Title I classrooms by the ELL teacher as an integral member of that team.

For the concentrated use of specialists at Ubben Elementary School to work, several other matters had to be checked out. First, the principal arranged a meeting to discuss the plan with both the special education and Title I supervisors serving Ubben Elementary to be sure they understood and approved the plan and to help establish parameters for its operation. Second, great care had to be taken in assigning students who were not special education or Title I students to the classrooms to rebalance the overall achievement levels of each of the classrooms and to re-create heterogeneity in the classrooms. The outcome was a relatively normal, balanced distribution of achievement levels in each classroom. However, as the new school year began, several of the grade-level teams did move a few students when they thought placement could be better.

With this staffing design in place for Ubben Elementary, the special education and Title I teachers were able to focus on only two classrooms at each grade level rather than on four or five. The learning community at each grade level began to concentrate on delivering instruction in the classroom. Each grade-level team—one of the special education teachers, the Title I teachers, instructional assistants, and the ELL teacher—began to plan to coordinate the instructional program among themselves. For the hours that the specialists joined the teams, classroom grouping of students for specific instruction was adjusted to include an assigned group for each participating specialist. The specialists met with each team in a planning meeting every week. Table 11.2 shows the staffing assignments.

Multiyear Staffing Assignments

Looping.   Looping is a multiyear teaching assignment in which the teacher stays with the same group of children for more than one year and then loops back to guide another group through.

ISLLC 3

Looping promotes the concept of community by extending the relationship with the teacher and student group for two or more years. In a study of elementary learning communities, Little[5]

TABLE 11.2 **Concentrated Use of Special Education and Title I Teacher Specialists at Ubben Elementary School**

GRADE	TEACHER A	TEACHER B	TEACHER C	TEACHER D	TEACHER E
PreK	19 students				19 students ELL students
Kindergarten	19 students	19 students		19 students	19 students including ELL students
Grade 1	5 Special ed 11 Regular ed	5 Special ed 11 Regular ed	16 Regular ed	16 Title I and Regular ed	16 Title I and Regular ed ELL students
Grade 2	5 Special ed 14 Regular ed	5 Special ed 14 Regular ed	19 Regular ed	19 Title I and Regular ed	19 Title I and Regular ed ELL students
Grade 3	5 Special ed 12 Regular ed	5 Special ed 12 Regular ed	17 Regular ed	17 Title I and Regular ed	17 Title I and Regular ed ELL students
Grade 4	5 Special ed 15 Regular ed	5 Special ed 15 Regular ed	20 Regular ed	20 Title I and Regular ed	20 Title I and Regular ed ELL students
Grade 5	5 Special ed 18 Regular ed	5 Special ed 18 Regular ed		23 Title I and Regular ed	23 Title I and Regular ed ELL students

suggests looping promotes pride in belonging, celebration of individual strengths and differences, and appreciation for building strong ties between students and teachers. The curriculum in a looping arrangement remains standard for the grade level with the looped teacher being responsible for the two-year sequence as the children mature.

Although looping is most common in the primary grades, some schools use it throughout the elementary grades with a K–1 loop, a 2–3 loop, and a 4–5 loop. Teachers involved with looping suggest they get off to a much quicker start with instruction the second year because they know the children as a result of their previous year's experience with them. On the other hand, teachers often do not want to trade classrooms each year. They much prefer to stay in the same room, exchanging instructional materials and furniture if necessary.

Multiage Grouping. A variation on looping is the creation of multiage groups where students stay in a group for two or more years but the children in the group consist of two or more age groups. Figure 11.1 If it is a three-year group, one-third of the group will be new each year and remain with the teacher or teacher team for three years in what can develop into a close-knit community atmosphere. Over the three-year span a child is with the teachers, in the first year the child will be in the youngest group, the next year in the middle, and finally in the oldest group, experiencing different relationships each year (see Figure 11.1). Curriculum is handled somewhat differently than with looping. For skill subjects such as reading and math, children are diagnosed and placed on their appropriate skill level. Children of different ages may be in the same group depending on their development levels. For other subjects that are generally organized around topics or projects, the curriculum is often rotated on a two- or three-year cycle depending on the multiage span. For example, a unit on Living Things as part of a science curriculum would

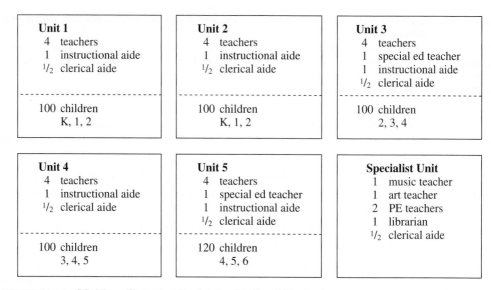

FIGURE 11.1   Multiage Grouping Design for Staff and Students

be taught to all ages in the group only once each three years, so some of the children might receive it as 8-year-olds, some when they are 9 years old, and some not until they are age 10, but all children in the classroom learn it together regardless of their ages that year.

Other schools keep the curriculum closely aligned with the child's age group in order to keep a certain sequence or alignment with a standardized test. This approach requires more lesson preparation and presentation by the teacher(s) in a multiage environment and allows less integration of the ages.

Middle School Staffing Patterns

In elementary classrooms, a single teacher will teach most of the core subjects. Middle school teachers often begin to specialize; they focus on one or two disciplines because of the growing sophistication of course content. Students generally will have a different teacher for each of their middle school subjects. Preferred middle school staffing patterns call for a team of teachers to share a common group of students and to coordinate their instruction as a learning community. Anfara Middle School is our example here.

Anfara Middle School, which includes grades 6, 7, and 8, has 671 students and serves a suburban community near a larger city. Although it has a Hispanic enrollment of 40 students and an African American population of 25, most of the students are from white, middle-class homes in which both parents work. In the total student population, there are 67 special education students and 132 students who receive free or reduced-cost lunch.

The school staff consists of six language arts teachers, six social studies teachers, six math teachers, and six science teachers. The staff also includes a full-time art teacher, a band instructor, a chorus teacher, two PE teachers, a health teacher, and a technology teacher. In addition, there are two full-time guidance counselors, a librarian, a school nurse, a principal, and

TABLE 11.3   Anfara Middle School Staff

SUBJECT	STAFF
Language arts	6 teachers
Social studies	6 teachers
Math	6 teachers
Science	6 teachers
Art	1 teacher
Music	1 band director
	1 chorus teacher
Physical education	2 teachers
Health	1 teacher
Technology	1 teacher
Guidance	2 counselors
Library	1 librarian
School nurse	1 nurse
Special education	3 teachers
	3 instructional assistants
Title I	6 instructional assistants
Administration	1 principal
	2 assistant principals
Certified staff total	41
Instructional assistants	9

two assistant principals. The school has three special education teachers. Anfara Middle School employs six regular instructional assistants who are paid from Title I funds and three special education assistants as shown in Table 11.3.

Middle School Learning Communities

Anfara Middle School staff is divided into two learning communities at each grade level, for a total of six learning communities, each with a language arts, math, science, and social studies teacher. A group of approximately 110 students is assigned to each of the communities, or teams. One of the instructional assistants is assigned to each team. All of the special education students who are in the regular classrooms are assigned to one of the teams at each grade level. The other grade-level team has most of the Title I students who are not in special education. The overall staffing pattern for Anfara Middle School is shown in Table 11.4.

ISLLC 3

TABLE 11.4   Anfara Middle School Staffing

GRADE	TEAM A	TEAM B	SPECIAL TEAM
Grade 6	Language arts teacher Math teacher Science teacher Social studies teacher Instructional assistant Special education inclusion Special ed assistant 114 students including special ed	Language arts teacher Math teacher Science teacher Social studies teacher Instructional assistant Title I assistant 112 students	Art PE (2 teachers) Technology Guidance (class) Chorus (all students unless in band) Band Library
Grade 7	Language arts teacher Math teacher Science teacher Social studies teacher Special education inclusion Instructional assistant Special ed assistant 113 students including special ed	Language arts teacher Math teacher Science teacher Social studies teacher Instructional assistant Title I assistant 112 students	Above team serves grade 7.
Grade 8	Language arts teacher Math teacher Science teacher Social studies teacher Special education inclusion Instructional assistant Special ed assistant 109 students including special ed	Language arts teacher Math teacher Science teacher Social studies teacher Instructional assistant Title I assistant 111 students	Above team serves grade 8.

Middle School Advisor Staffing

Anfara Middle School has an advisor program in which a staff member works several times a week with a small group of student-advisees in a planned guidance program. In order to reduce the advisor-to-advisee ratio, each of the six learning teams is supported by two additional staff members drawn from the ranks of the specialists and administration. Two teachers from art, music, PE, health, and technology are each assigned to one of the grade-level learning communities; the special education teachers, librariaen, guidance counselor, and administration are also part of each community. These additional staff members reduce the number of students assigned to each advisor to fewer than 20 advisees. Schedule suggestions for advisor systems can be found in Chapter 12.

Staffing Patterns for Secondary Schools

General ideas have been presented for staffing design, curricular arrangements, and instructional strategies in elementary and middle schools. How does a high school operating in a traditional mode begin to make the transition to incorporate some of these strategies into its operating model and gain benefits from a learning community model? We begin with an existing high school with a staff of 67 professionals and 1,260 students and consider a number of staffing alternatives. Each staffing pattern takes into account some of the ideas previously discussed in the chapters on curriculum, instruction, and grouping of students. The first model shows how the school might be organized at the present time in a traditional departmental staff organization.

Departmental Staff Organization

The standard departmental staffing arrangement shown in Figure 11.2 divides the high school into nine departments: language arts; social studies; science; math; foreign language; physical education, health, and driver education; fine arts; vocational education; and special services. The school is a comprehensive high school with a large vocational program. The special services department is somewhat unique. It includes guidance counselors, one vocational rehabilitation counselor, one special education coordinator, two instructional media specialists, and one person to coordinate both the independent study program and action learning program. The three principals share the school's

ISLLC 3

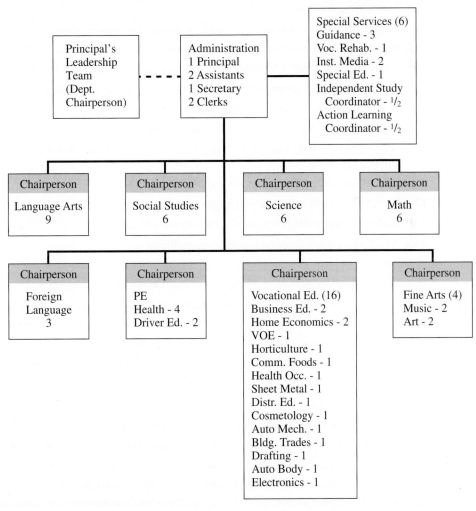

FIGURE 11.2   Standard Departmental High School Staffing Pattern

administration, with one of the assistants responsible for buildings, grounds, lunchroom, transportation, office management, and some discipline. The other assistant's major responsibility is the curricular and instructional program and the coordination of volunteer services.

A department head coordinates the activities of each department and serves as a member of the principal's leadership team. Figure 11.3 lists possible department head responsibilities.

FIGURE 11.3   Department Head Responsibilities

Job Description—High School Department Head

1. Coordinate the inventory of textbooks and audiovisual materials.
2. Coordinate the development of an instructional budget for the department.
3. Provide the department staff with information regarding advances in subject matter and promising instructional materials.
4. Coordinate the placement and supervision of student teachers and interns in the department.
5. Recommend special resources and personnel needed to aid the department's instructional staff.
6. Direct department staff in selecting or preparing appropriate objectives for each curricular area.
7. Seek the advice of a counselor or principal in handling special department problems.
8. Assume responsibility for completing routine reports.
9. Participate in the development of the school's in-service teacher education program.
10. Observe on request the instructional presentations of department staff and provide feedback aimed at improving instruction.
11. Provide individual assistance to new and beginning teachers.
12. Hold the staff accountable for student achievement.
13. Evaluate paraprofessionals assigned to the department.
14. Attend all meetings of the principal's leadership team.
15. Schedule and chair department meetings.
16. Channel information from a variety of sources to the department teachers.
17. Conduct demonstration lessons for department staff members using new materials and procedures.
18. Coordinate the assessment of students and the department based on individual objectives.
19. Plan with appropriate personnel to research activities for the department.
20. Schedule department meetings for goal setting, problem solving, and evaluation.
21. Coordinate the assessment of students' characteristics prior to any grouping.
22. Cooperate with other department chairpersons in coordinating schoolwide facilities and resources.
23. Confer informally with department staff members to discuss ways of improving instruction.
24. Facilitate communication between central-office personnel, consultants, and department staff.
25. Participate in the selection of professional staff assigned to the department.
26. Participate in the evaluation of professional staff assigned to the department.

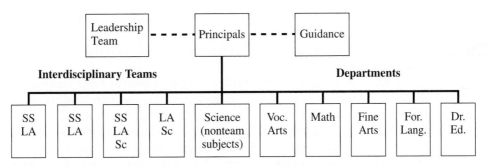

FIGURE 11.4   Interdisciplinary Team Staffing for Fluid Block Schedules

Learning Community Staffing Patterns

The basic staff of a typical high school, as shown in Figure 11.4, can be used to create numerous variations in team arrangements. Appropriate team designs, however, must provide a good relationship with a planned curricular design, good instructional strategies, and desirable patterns for student grouping. A summary of previous information concerning good design for curriculum, instruction, grouping, and staffing includes the following: team members from two or more disciplines; a differentiated staff including a team leader, team members, aides, and clerks; and a group of 75 to 150 students in a block of time appropriate in length to the number of subjects included in the team. The interdisciplinary team allows for the best options in integrating the curriculum, ease of schooling, flexibility in grouping, and student control.

Interdisciplinary teams can be organized in a variety of ways. One high school organized a series of two-subject, four-teacher teams, consisting of two language arts teachers and two social studies teachers in a three-hour block of time coordinated with a free-floating elective. Each team met with one group of approximately 120 students in the morning and worked with another block of students during the afternoon. The other half of the students' day involved participating in a regular elective program.[6]

Using the staff outlined in Figure 11.4, the fluid block design organized language arts, social studies, and science teams. One of the main advantages of the fluid block design is its allowance for three basic styles of instruction, ranging from traditional, to team approaches, to individually paced labs.[7] Most of the teachers in the basic required subjects of language arts, social studies, and possibly science must be willing to work in a team arrangement for a fluid block schedule to work. Teachers in other subject areas may join teams, may wish to set up their instruction as an individually paced laboratory (typing, art, foreign languages, and certain math courses lend themselves nicely to individualized labs), or may operate in a traditional-type schedule as in the past.

Specialized Thematic or School-within-a-School High School

Although large high schools have the advantage of being able to offer many different subjects, they lack the intimacy and closeness among faculty and students that a small school can create. One solution to the size problem is to create several small schools inside a large school by

ISLLC 2

clustering students, staff members, and a special curriculum by giving them a common schedule and preferably common spaces within the school building. These *school-within-a-school* designs often are promoted around a particular theme or specialization that is then emphasized in every subject taught within the program.

For example, Hardin Valley Academy, a high school of 1,642 students (grades 9–12) has divided the school into four separate learning communities, each focusing on a different theme. The Science, Technology, Engineering, and Mathematics Academy (STEM), the Law, Business, and Public Affairs Academy, the Health Sciences Academy, and the Liberal Arts Academy. The academies do not have equal enrollment because some are more popular with the students than others. The curriculum in each academy follows state standards for each subject, but applications and examples provided by the faculty follow the theme of that particular academy. Electives contribute to a student's specialization in the theme of the chosen academy. Faculty members are assigned to one academy, so each academy has its own faculty for most subjects. Students take almost all of their core subjects in their chosen academy and venture out only when a chosen elective is available only from another academy. For example, world languages are only taught in the Liberal Arts Academy but available to students from other academies. Although the school is designed for students to follow one academy throughout their high school career, students are not bound to one academy. They are allowed to request from guidance counselors a transfer to another academy any semester in their high school career. Most students remain with their original selection. The 16 to 35 faculty members within each academy plan their curriculum together for their four-year program. Both disciplinary and interdisciplinary teams operate within each academy as illustrated in Table 11.5.

TABLE 11.5 High School Thematic Academies (School within a School)

ACADEMY THEME	STAFF SPECIALTIES	STAFF SPECIALTIES
Science, Technology, Engineering, Math (grades 9–12)	English, social studies, math, science, business/computer, technology, engineering	Beyond the individual disciplines are the specific application of each discipline to the theme.
Law, Business, Public Affairs (grades 9–12)	English, social studies, math, science, business/computer, criminal justice, leadership, speech, finance/economics	Instructors with experience in applied professional specializations are desired—law, finance, engineering, medicine, business, graphic design, computers, etc.
Health Sciences (grades 9–12)	English, social studies, math, science— anatomy/physiology, health sciences, nursing, forensic science, medical therapeutics, world languages	If full-time instructors cannot be found in specific applied disciplines, *practitioner partners* are sometimes hired to coteach with regular staff.
Liberal Arts (grades 9–12)	English, social studies, math, science, business/computer, world languages, fine arts	These may be professionals in their field such as medical doctors, judges, engineers, technicians, writers, mechanics, business people, artists, etc.

Learning Community Planning

Learning communities suggest the active participation of staff members in decisions that affect their own areas of responsibility. This includes an expanded role in curriculum and instructional decisions, evaluation decisions, and day-by-day organizing and scheduling functions. These tasks are most effectively carried out on a team or learning community basis.

One of the most crucial factors in a successful team operation is adequate planning time and efficient utilization of that time. If at all possible, team planning should occur during the regular school day. Planning should be regularly scheduled; at least two hours per week are needed in a minimum of one-hour blocks. Building an agenda for team meetings needs to be an opportunity for all team members to share in the planning for the team. One good procedure is to place an agenda planning sheet in a central location for the team to list items they wish to discuss at the next scheduled meeting. Some principals have the teams prepare their agenda so that copies can be quickly reproduced and distributed to team members, as well as to other key people such as the librarian, special education teacher, or the principal, all of whom may want to attend the team meeting. Each meeting should have a designated chairperson, and a secretary for the team should keep minutes of the meeting. Figure 11.5 is an example of a form to be used for agenda building.

Team Planning Tasks

A variety of planning tasks of both a long- and short-term nature need to be carried out by each team. Effective use of planning time can usually be enhanced by focusing on a particular purpose during a meeting. The following five types of planning meetings are suggested, with recommendations regarding frequency:

1. *Goal-Setting Meeting.* One goal-setting meeting should be held each semester to look at the philosophy of the school, the curriculum guidelines existing for its direction, and the identification of goals for the particular group of students for whom the team is responsible. Goals should be long range in nature—things to work toward over a semester or year.
2. *Design Meeting.* A design meeting is a planning meeting to select instructional topics and develop instructional units. Principles and objectives as well as general ideas for the unit are considered. After the topic has been selected, one team member is usually assigned the responsibility of drafting the unit. When the draft is ready, the team modifies and builds on the design. Specific objectives are listed, overall responsibility for each member of the team is outlined, and the calendar of events is developed with specific target dates. Methods of student evaluation are also planned. One of these meetings is necessary for each new unit, and a minimum of one each quarter or marking period is essential.
3. *Grouping or Scheduling Meeting.* This planning meeting outlines activities for the next week or two, defining specific instructional plans, organizing students into appropriate groups, and constructing the weekly calendar and daily schedule. One of these meetings is needed at least once every two weeks, if not weekly.
4. *Situational Meeting.* This meeting focuses on individual children. Various children within the group are discussed by the members of the team to coordinate information and develop plans for learning activities for that child. The teacher advisor for the particular child has

Team: _____4 - A_____   Date of Meeting: _____10/14_____

I. Students

Name	Person Presenting	Concern	Est. Time Needed
Bill Fox	Mary	attendance	5 m.
Nancy York	Jane	uncomp. assign.	5 m.

II. Program Development

Area	Person Presenting	Est. Time Needed
Unit—election	Gary	20 m.
Unit—health	Mary	to next time

III. Staff Development

Area	Person Presenting	Est. Time Needed
accelerated learning	Pat	20 m.

IV. Administrative

Area	Person Presenting	Est. Time Needed
lunchtime	Pat	5 m.
Friday's assembly	Pat	5 m.

FIGURE 11.5   Form for Agenda Building

the responsibility of carrying out team decisions. These meetings should probably be held each week, with each teacher advisor determining which children need to be discussed by the team.

5. *Evaluation Meeting.* The major focus of this meeting should be evaluation of the instructional program and units. Questions to be asked are these: Did we achieve our goals? What were our strengths? What were our shortcomings? How well did we function together as a team? One of these meetings should be held each quarter immediately after the close of the quarter or immediately after the completion of a major unit.

Team Meeting Schedule

Assuming a planning schedule that allows for two planning meetings per team each week in a six-week instructional period, a schedule of team meetings for the period might look like Figure 11.6.

FIGURE 11.6 Schedule of Team Meetings

Two team meetings should be held each week.

Prior to school year	• Goal setting for the semester • Design of units for the first grading period • Initial grouping and scheduling of students assigned to team
Week 1	• Situational meeting • Grouping and scheduling meeting
Week 2	• Situational meeting • Grouping and scheduling meeting
Week 3	• Situational meeting • Grouping and scheduling meeting
Week 4	• Situational meeting • Design meeting—plans for the next period meeting
Week 5	• Situational meeting • Design meeting
Week 6	• Situational meeting • Evaluation meeting (of teaching)
Week 7 (repeats Week 1)	• Situational meeting • Grouping and scheduling meeting

Extra grouping and scheduling meetings as well as situational meetings are scheduled early in the year to work through changes in enrollment and to place children better as more data are available.

The School as a Learning Community

This chapter has focused on the small clusters of teachers and staff linked with students and parents as the nucleus of a learning community. In practice, however, the entire school should be one large learning community linked with common values, beliefs, vision, and goals working across departments, grade levels, or interdisciplinary teams. Leadership teams or schoolwide councils become a way of establishing communication links to help in the development of *community* across the school.

A learning community, to function successfully, requires greatly increased participation in school decisions on the part of staff members. An excellent way to involve the faculty is through the formation of a leadership team to improve the school's curricular and instructional program. If the school has a multiunit learning community design, as described in this chapter, this leadership team should be made up of the head of each learning community and the principal (see Figure 11.7); otherwise, department heads or grade-level chairpersons would be appropriate. Topics for consideration by this leadership team include virtually any significant decision that will require staff cooperation and is in their field of expertise. A quality circle approach is appropriate for some of leadership team activities.

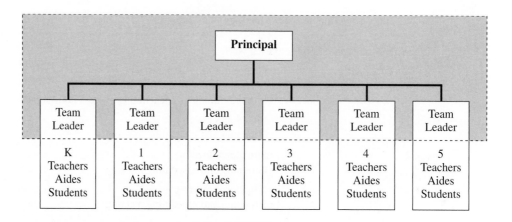

The staff within the dotted line makes up the leadership team.

FIGURE 11.7   Leadership Team

Matrix Management

In a similar fashion to the leadership team, special coordinating committees should be organized to deal with curricular areas such as reading, math, social studies, or any area that requires cross-unit coordination. These committees may be permanent or temporary in nature, depending on the assignment.

If a multiunit staffing design is used, these committees can best be formed with one teacher from each team (Figure 11.8). The curriculum committee, thus formed, provides representation from each of the teams as well as communication back to each team. Each staff member also shares in the schoolwide efforts to provide community and thrust to the curricular and instructional program. The major line of responsibility (vertical) in the matrix still rests with each team. The curriculum committees (horizontal) function only to coordinate the overall school program and to provide articulation across the grades.

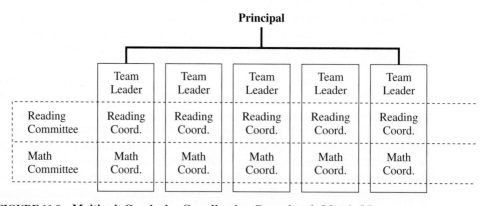

FIGURE 11.8   Multiunit Curricular Coordinating Committee's Matrix Management

Parent Involvement in Learning Communities

Parents or other community volunteers, properly organized, can provide valuable support staff to the paid employees in the school. Most schools can use more help. Tasks such as clerical duties or instructional support (e.g., listening to a child read) require time but do not necessarily require professional-level skills. The concept of the learning community encompasses the participation of parents. The interest of parents in their children's education is a known major factor in the effectiveness of a child's education.

Cavarretta,[8] for example, suggested that parents can assist the school in many ways: conduct surveys and gather data, attend professional conferences and become familiar with the language of education, work on school committees that choose textbooks, evaluate curriculum design, create technology programs, and cultivate new expectations for parent–teacher conferences.

In many schools the parents are willing and eager to be involved, particularly in elementary schools and middle-class communities. However, for many middle and high schools, as well as in lower socioeconomic communities, the problem is often one of motivating parents to come to the school or of scheduling activities for them when they are available. A study by Pena[9] concerning the involvement of minority parents found that language, parent cliques, parents' education, attitudes of the school staff, cultural influences, and family issues were all factors in determining parental involvement.

For each school community where parental involvement is low, the first step must be to identify the reasons and then work to develop communication and positive attitudes that will encourage parent participation. The problems and solutions for each community and each set of grades will be different. For elementary schools, parent involvement is usually the greatest but still must be encouraged and developed into a positive learning influence. For middle and high schools, the situation is more difficult. Children often like to keep their two worlds separated and discourage their parents from participating. Nevertheless, it is more important than ever that the school–home link is maintained.

Student performances are the typical way to entice parents to the school, but there must be strategies in place to keep them involved. Organizing all of the stakeholders in the school into a learning community with a series of specific, needed roles is one good strategy. The school needs their help. They have an important contribution to make to the school. And, not just a few professional parents but all of them should be involved, K–12. Every family in the school participating in some aspect of the learning community should be the goal.

Parenting is a learned skill. Some parents had good role models but many parents did not and now are having difficulty with their children. The more we as educators can help our students' parents develop good parenting skills, the better performance we will see from the children in school. Just as we provide staff-development activities for our teachers, we should provide parent-development activities for our families. The learning community provides the natural vehicle for this responsibility. As you find new tasks for your students' parents at school, be sure to arrange learning experiences for them so they can function more effectively as learning community members.

Summary

The principal has many plans to make regarding how best to utilize the staff. Many of these plans rest on earlier decisions regarding curriculum, instructional formats, and grouping of students. Teaching teams organized as learning communities offer maximum flexibility for instructional

ISLLC 4

programming, but attention must be given to good team planning for this approach to work. The appropriate use of specialists must also be considered in elementary and middle school staffing. Secondary school staffing patterns can be designed with flexibility in mind as well. A variety of staffing patterns can be used to facilitate learning communities with teaching teams or departmental units. Schoolwide learning community structures for overall management should take several forms, including a school management council and curriculum or grade-level committees.

ACTIVITIES

1. How would you proceed to restructure your school's staff deployment? Why would it be important to integrate your plans on instructional and curriculum restructuring with your plans on staff restructuring?

2. Review Case Studies 7, 13, 15, and 17 at the end of this book. Analyze the problems presented and apply the staff deployment concepts developed in this chapter. What approach would you use in addressing the problems? Set forth a strategy to overcome the difficulties

faced by the school as well as ways to deal with individual teachers.

3. Turn to the ISLLC standards found in Appendix B. Review the functions listed in Standard 3. Which of the functions best support the learning community concepts proposed in this chapter? How could you better organize your school's staff to facilitate learning community development?

ENDNOTES

1. J. Lloyd Trump, *Images of the Future,* Experimental Study of the Utilization of Staff in the Secondary Schools and the National Association of Secondary School Principals, 1959.

2. Gene I. Maeroff, "A Blueprint for Empowering Teachers," *Phi Delta Kappan 69,* no. 7 (March 1988): 472–477.

3. Peter M. Senge, *The Fifth Discipline: The Art and Practice of the Learning Organization* (New York: Doubleday/Currency, 1990).

4. Thomas J. Sergiovanni, *Moral Leadership: Getting to the Heart of School Improvement* (San Francisco: Jossey-Bass, 1992).

5. Thomas S. Little and L. Little, "Looping: Creating Elementary School Communities," *Phi Delta Kappa Fastbacks* no. 478 (2001).

6. Gerald C. Ubben, "A Fluid Block Schedule," *NASSP Bulletin 60* (February 1976): 104–111.

7. See the section in Chapter 12 on block schedules.

8. J. Cavarretta, "Parents Are a School's Best Friend," *Educational Leadership 55,* no. 8 (1998): 12–15.

9. D. C. Pena, "Parent Involvement: Influencing factors and implications," *Journal of Educational Research 94,* no. 1 (2000): 45–54.

SELECTED READINGS

Barnes, P. "A Team Effort." *Teaching PreK–8 34* (2003): 18.

Bracey, Gerald W. "Going Loopy over Looping." *Phi Delta Kappan 81,* no. 2 (October 1999): 169.

Chirichello, Michael, and Carol Chirichello. "A Standing Ovation for Looping: The Critics Respond." *Childhood Education 78,* no. 1 (Fall 2001): 2–9.

DuFour, R. "What Is a Professional Learning Community?" *Educational Leadership 61,* no. 8 (2004): 6–11.

DuFour, R. "Functioning as a Learning Community Enables Schools to Focus on Student Achievement." *Journal of Staff Development 18* (1997): 56–57.

Erb, Thomas O. "Meeting the Needs of Young Adolescents on Interdisciplinary Teams: The Growing Research Base." *Childhood Education 73,* no. 5 (1997): 309–311.

Fullan, M. G., and A. Hargreaves. *What's Worth Fighting For: Working Together for Your School* (Andover, MA: Regional Laboratory of the Northeast and Islands, 1991).

Giangreco, M. "Working with Paraprofessionals." *Educational Leadership 61,* no. 2 (2003): 50–53.

Haberman, M. "Can Star Teachers Create Learning Communities?" *Educational Leadership 61,* no. 8 (2004): 52–56.

Hackman, D. G., V. N. Petzko, J. W. Valentine, D. C. Clark, J. R. Nori, and S. E. Lucas. "Beyond Interdisciplinary Teaming: Findings and Implications of the NASSP National Middle Level Study." *NASSP Bulletin 86,* no. 632 (2002): 33–47.

Henry, B. "Combating the Four-wall Syndrome." *Principal Leadership 5* (2005): 30–34.

Hinkle, T., and P. Kinney. "Collective Wisdom." *Principal Leadership (Middle School Ed.) 9,* no. 2 (2008): 30–33.

Hord, S. M. "Professional Learning Communities." *Journal of Staff Development 30,* no. 1 (2009): 40–43.

Hord, S. M., and S. A. Hirsh. "The Principal's Role in Supporting Learning Communities" [Electronic Version]. *Educational Leadership 66,* no. 5 (2009): 22–23.

Knackendoffel, E. Ann. "Collaborative Teaming in the Secondary School." *Focus on Exceptional Children 40,* no. 4 (December 2007): 1–20.

Little, Thomas S., and L. Little. "Looping: Creating Elementary School Communities," *Phi Delta Kappa Fastbacks* no. 478 (2001).

McCowen, Claire, and Scott Sherman. "Looping for Better Performance in Middle School." *Middle School Journal 33,* no. 4 (March 2002): 17–21.

McGoogan, G. "The Bear Den: An Elementary Teaching Team." *Educational Leadership 59* (2002): 30–32.

Pandini, P. "The Slowdown of the Multiage Classroom." *School Administrator 62* (2005): 22–30.

Protheroe, N. "Professional Learning Communities." *Principal 83,* no. 5 (2004): 39–42.

Rea, P., and J. Connell. "A Guide to Coteaching." *Principal Leadership 5* (2005): 36–41.

Senge, Peter M. *The Fifth Discipline: The Art and Practice of the Learning Organization* (New York: Doubleday/ Currency, 1990).

Sergiovanni, Thomas J. *Moral Leadership: Getting to the Heart of School Improvement* (San Francisco: Jossey-Bass, 1992).

Taylor, R. T. "Shaping the Culture of Learning Communities." *Principal Leadership (High School Ed) 3,* no. 4 (2002): 42–45.

Turk, R. L., K. Wolff, C. Waterbury, and J. Zumalt. "What Principals Should Know about Building and Maintaining Teams." *NASSP Bulletin 86,* no. 630 (2002): 15–23.

Wade, C., and B. Ferriter. "Will You Help Me Lead?" *Educational Leadership 65,* no. 1 (2007): 65–68.

Wild, M. D., A. S. Mayeaux, and K. P. Edmonds. "Collaborative Teaching: The Best Response to a Rigid Curriculum." *Education Week* (May 21, 2008): 26–27.

12

Restructuring Time
Scheduling

The school schedule is considered by many to be the command performance of the principal. It is here that the ability to conceptualize, to organize, and to carry out detailed planning is most visible. If well done, the schedule will strongly support the instructional and curricular program of the school. On the other hand, if poorly designed, the schedule will be a roadblock to a balanced curriculum and instructional flexibility.

—L. W. HUGHES AND G. C. UBBEN[1]

*S*cheduling can be defined as the plan to bring together people, materials, and curriculum at a designated time and place for the purpose of instruction. Its basic purpose is to coordinate the requirements laid down by previously reached decisions regarding curriculum, instruction, grouping, and staffing.

The effective schools research has much to say about the use of time in school. The concept of academic learning time (ALT), discussed in earlier chapters, describes scheduled time as its umbrella component from which the "actual" instructional time and "engaged" time are achieved. It is, therefore, imperative that scheduled time be maximized so that ultimately high amounts of instructional and engaged time can also be obtained.[2] Academic learning time studies indicate that increasing the amount of time devoted to a particular subject increases the learning opportunities for that subject. In other words, if you wish to increase student reading scores, devote more time to teaching reading. Of course, given a finite amount of time in a school day, that means some other subject or discipline will have its learning time reduced.

Several important concepts in scheduling should be reviewed before actually beginning the construction of a schedule. The concepts are equally important for elementary, middle, and high school schedules. These include the flexibility, simplicity, and complexity of the schedule; the decision level at which schedule changes are made; efficiency in the use of time; and the timeliness of the schedule. Other concepts to consider are previously made decisions concerning the design of curriculum and instruction; staffing and grouping patterns; and space availability and utilization.

Schedule Flexibility

The schedule should have either the potential of being legitimately changed with great frequency or the internal elasticity of meeting a variety of curricular and instructional requests within its regular structure. For example, the teacher who would like to take a group of children on a half-day field trip should be able to do so without disrupting the entire school schedule. Likewise, the group that needs an extra hour to complete a project should be able to have that hour with an easy adjustment in the schedule.

Simplicity and Complexity

The schedule needs simplicity to prevent interdependence of the components of the schedule; the modification of one component should not require the modification of several others. Complexity, on the other hand, is also needed to meet the demands of individual differences of students. Intricate schedule designs must be constructed to meet individual differences. This

ISLLC 2

seeming paradox, is about another application of the loosely coupled/tightly coupled concept of organization. An analogy that seems fitting to describe this relationship is found in modularized electronics. The complexity of their circuitry is an amazing example of modern-day technology. On the other hand, this complex design is constructed in such a way that if a failure occurs, or a modification is desired, a circuit board can be removed and replaced very quickly once the trouble spot has been identified or the desired modification determined—without having to disassemble the entire set. So it is with schedules: A good schedule must permit the complex construction required for individual differences while maintaining simplicity to allow easy changes.

Efficiency and the Use of Time

The effective schools research points out the need for time efficiency. There are many ways greater efficiency can be obtained within the schedule; several specific suggestions follow:

ISLLC 3

■ Minimize the use of nonspecific study time during school hours. This means the reduction— or better yet, the elimination—of study halls. Too often students at the high school level who cannot get into scheduled classes are put in study halls. This is a reflection of the principal's inability or unwillingness to design a tight, efficient schedule. In a good schedule, study halls are virtually eliminated. At the elementary and middle school levels, activity periods must be carefully designed so they do not also become holding areas for children otherwise not engaged in a supervised learning activity. Similarly, in schools that use block schedules with 90-minute classes, to teach for 60 minutes followed by a 30-minute study period is not a good use of time. Rather, several different instructional strategies should make use of the full 90 minutes of class time.

- Minimize the time used for movement from classroom to classroom. Techniques will vary greatly depending on building arrangements and instructional design. Specifics might include the use of two- or three-hour blocks of time with no student passage required, as well as clustering of classrooms and lockers to minimize travel on the part of students for the development of efficient hall traffic patterns and the reduction of the time between classes.
- Enhance available instructional time with the development and implementation of an efficient policy regarding the use of the intercom system. Within the school, restrict its use to the first and last few minutes of the day so as not to interrupt potential instructional time.

Other efficiencies can be implemented in the use of teacher and student time in school: (1) good use of lunchtime (including a duty-free lunch for teachers and the opportunity for students to relax as well) and (2) effective use of before and after school waiting time on the part of students (waiting for buses, parents, etc.). Every minute of the school day counts. The rule must always be "What is the best possible use of this time?"

Timeliness of Scheduling Decisions.   Timeliness is part of flexibility. Schedules must be designed so that daily and weekly instructional and curricular needs can be met as they occur. Consider these two examples: A teacher who is a member of a five-teacher team in a middle school finds that a video is going to run about five minutes into the next period, so she asks her team teachers to hold their classes for a few extra minutes. A teacher wants his students to participate in a webinar that is scheduled to run across several class periods; he and his teammates adjust the schedules to accommodate the time demands of the webinar schedule. (A webinar is Web-based seminar.)

Scheduling Decision Level—Loosely Coupled

The decision level is the point in the hierarchy of an organization where decisions are made. A basic rule for good decision making in most organizations is that decisions should be made at the lowest level within the organization where adequate information exists for that decision (loosely coupled). The application of this rule to scheduling suggests that students and teachers should have maximum involvement in scheduling decisions. At the building level, scheduling should be kept as simple as possible so that the various components can be changed without disrupting the entire school. Also, each building should have maximum control over its schedule and not be frequently subjected to the schedules of other schools in the school system. Some traditional areas of conflict such as coordinating bus schedules between schools or scheduling shared teacher specialists require higher-level decisions. The major conflicts will arise over making up specialists' schedules within the school, in coordinating special areas such as gymnasiums and music rooms, and in scheduling schoolwide programs such as lunch.

Schedule Design

There are several approaches to achieving a good schedule. Although the details of scheduling certainly differ among elementary, middle, and high school, the basic tenets are largely the same. One of the best methods is to provide relatively large blocks of time unencumbered by outside influences to teams of teachers and groups of students so they can develop a detailed daily schedule to meet curricular and instructional needs. Such a schedule must accommodate a few special activities such as lunch, physical education, or music (see Figure 12.1).

ISLLC 2

Inside these large blocks of time, the team of teachers and students functioning as a learning community plans all of the learning activities. These internal schedules can differ from one day to the next as plans are made by the team reflecting the instructional format, curriculum, groupings, and staffing assignments. Because each of these instructional blocks stands alone, changes within them do not affect the remainder of the school. Only the parallel schedule of the PE and music specialists is fixed.

Figure 12.2 illustrates a simple form of scheduling within the block of time that can be used by a team of four teachers following a basic rotating design. In this schedule, each teacher has access to each group of children operating in a semi-departmentalized school-within-a-school design. The schedule does not meet all of the curricular, instructional, and grouping recommendations made in the previous chapter, but neither does it preclude further development to meet the additional criteria. The team has a high degree of autonomy to plan its schedule as it sees fit and can modify it as frequently as every day if it chooses.

Numerous schedule variations can be created from this basic design. It offers an excellent opportunity to create groups that vary in size as well as the ability to group students according to a variety of special interests and skills patterns.

At the elementary level, a team might create small groups for reading instruction by assigning children to instructional groups on a skills basis. Each team member can teach a small group of children by sharing activities and placing children in several different learning activities. To have reading groups of a reasonable size, three teachers of a four-member team can each

	Team A	Team B	Team C	Team D
Morning	Team Scheduled Block	Team Scheduled Block	TSB	PE MUSIC
			PE MUSIC	TSB
	LUNCH	LUNCH	LUNCH	LUNCH
Afternoon	Team Scheduled Block	PE MUSIC	Team Scheduled Block	Team Scheduled Block
		Team Scheduled Block		
	PE MUSIC			

FIGURE 12.1   Team Scheduled Block (TSB)
Note: Teams can arrange their own internal schedule. Only lunch and PE/music are fixed.

Period	Student Group A	Student Group B	Student Group C	Student Group D
1	R	SS	SC	M
2	SS	SC	M	R
3	SC	M	R	SS
L	L	L	L	L
4	M	R	SS	SC
5	PE	PE	Music Alternate Days	

R Reading
SS Social Studies
SC Science   Four teachers responsible
L Lunch   for groups A–D
M Math

FIGURE 12.2   Block Rotating Schedule

take 10 children in their reading group while the fourth teacher supervises the other children in some form of teacher-planned instructional activity (see Table 12.1). Sharing responsibility among teachers within a schedule permits the group variation necessary for good instruction. During additional periods, the schedule can shift so that each teacher has some large-group direct instruction time as well as small reading groups for skills instruction. An instructional aide could assist in supervising computer centers and independent study activities while the regular staff does direct instruction.

Grouping patterns can remain flexible. As the learning community's planning develops, the internal schedule can change as frequently as needed. Variations for math, the addition of

TABLE 12.1   Reading(R) Skills Group Schedule

	TEACHER A	TEACHER B	TEACHER C	TEACHER D	AIDE
9:30–10	R1 10 children	R2 10 children	Directed instruction, 30 children	R3 10 children	Learning centers, 20 children
10–10:30	R4 10 children	Directed instruction, 30 children	R5 10 children	R6 10 children	Learning centers, 20 children
10:30–11	Directed instruction, 30 children	R7 10 children	R8 10 children	R9 10 children	Learning centers, 20 children

Nine groups receive 30 minutes of directed instruction.

science, social studies, or language arts activities (including independent study work), and the scheduling of field trips can be built in and designed by teachers without requesting approval from an outside authority. Only when special teachers, facilities, and services for these activities are needed must the team consult and coordinate with the principal at the building level.

Ultimately, how the block schedule is to be used depends on the decisions regarding curriculum, instruction, grouping, and staffing. If teachers are organized in teams, the curriculum has a broad base of subjects, the instructional program is individualized, and the grouping is designed to allow change frequently, then the block schedule may be designed to accommodate those needs with ease.

Learning Community Planning Time

One of the most important features of any schedule involving a team of teachers working as a learning community is the provision of adequate team planning time. Every teacher should have a minimum of five hours each week for planning and materials preparation. Much of this time should be in common with other members of the team. Teachers usually prefer to arrange this time in several large blocks rather than divide it into many small segments. Teachers and aides can occasionally alternate supervision, giving each team member some time for planning or materials preparation. However, extended planning sessions where all team members are present is also a must.

Parallel Scheduling

Team planning can usually be best arranged on a schoolwide basis using parallel scheduling. A parallel schedule is one where the teacher specialists (e.g., art, music, PE library) take responsibility for all of the children that are assigned to a particular learning community during a given period. This frees all of the regular learning community members at the same time, giving them a common planning time.

Parallel scheduling can provide large blocks of planning time through the use of specialists. The elementary school or middle school staff must include three or four full-time specialists such as music teachers, art teachers, and PE teachers. These teachers are scheduled in a design paralleling that of the regular teaching staff so the specialists can replace the regular learning community, freeing them from all of the children in their learning community for a given block of time. The specialists then work in rotation with these children from one team for a period of one or more hours (see Figure 12.3). Specialists can handle additional children if there are more specialists available or if an aide can work with a specialist and increase group size. The specialists work with each group of children so that within a one- or two-day period, they replace each team (the team organization used here is the one shown in Figure 12.3).

These examples of schedules are meant only to be suggestions to generate ideas. Many variations can be developed from these different models. Each school and each team must develop a schedule of its own, tailored to meet its individual needs. It is important to let the schedule follow the demands of the curricular and instructional program and the student grouping and staffing patterns and not to allow the schedule to dictate the rest of the program.

ISLLC 2

	Monday	Tuesday	Wednesday	Thursday	Friday
Morning	Specialists Replace Team A	Replace Team C	Replace Team E or Specialist Planning	Replace Team B	Replace Team D
Afternoon	Replace Team B	Replace Team D	Replace Team A	Replace Team C	Replace Team E or Specialist Planning*

FIGURE 12.3   Team Parallel Schedule

*In a five-team school, the specialists use an extended, duty-free lunch for planning.

Elementary School Schedules

Although some schools have created classroom teaching teams for all elementary grades, the self-contained primary and intermediate classrooms where one teacher teaches all of the core subjects is still the predominant staffing pattern in elementary schools. The most common approach is to include specialists in the classroom to work with special needs children rather than to use pullout programs that remove children from the regular classroom. Specialists focus on reading and math special education, English language learner (ELL) programs, and response-to-intervention (RTI) programs. The learning community exists to help teachers plan and coordinate the many and varied instructional activities and participate in professional development. The parallel schedule gives them common planning time to accomplish these tasks. Particularly for the lower grades, it is very important to keep class sizes small.[3]

Middle School Schedules

Middle schools have unique problems in scheduling students and staff. Greater subject area specialization on the part of teachers is required than is generally the case in elementary schools. However, it is preferred that each student have a limited number of teacher contacts. This means that each teacher must be capable of teaching several subjects, and this has become particularly difficult with the additional requirements of No Child Left Behind regarding the "highly qualified" expectations for middle school teachers in each subject area taught.

The range of differences in the achievement levels of middle school children is also greater than in elementary school. Therefore, to meet the individual skills needs of the children, greater efforts must be made to differentiate instruction either through skills grouping, cooperative learning, or some other technique. Care must also be taken with homogeneous grouping because of its detrimental effects on student attitudes and achievement when overused.

The block schedule shown in Figure 12.2 is probably the best design for a schoolwide schedule in the middle school, along with the following ideas for the internal team schedule.

Achievement grouping is recommended for use in reading and math instruction because of the relatively large span of abilities in the middle school. Curriculum tends to be organized

Teacher Period	A	B	C	D
1	Reading Groups A & E	Reading Groups B & F	Reading Groups C & G	Reading Groups D & H
2	Math 1	Science	Social Studies	Language Arts
3	Math 2	Science	Social Studies	Language Arts
4	Math 3	Science	Social Studies	Language Arts
5	Math 4	Science	Social Studies	Language Arts

FIGURE 12.4   Middle School Team Schedule with Tracking

according to skill levels in these two subjects, which makes them the best candidates for this technique. Most other areas of the curriculum should use heterogeneous grouping.

Homogeneous achievement grouping is more successful in improving learning when the curriculum is modified for the homogeneous grouping. When homogeneous grouping is used, the criteria for grouping must specifically match the curricular area (e.g., total reading scores for reading groups and math scores for math groups). Grouping on the basis of an annual achievement test, for example, is much too general and should not be done.

From a scheduling standpoint it is almost impossible to group more than two subjects if each teacher teaches a separate subject. The schedule shown in Figure 12.4 will allow homogeneous grouping in reading with good flexibility in assigning and moving students because all four teachers will be teaching reading at the same time. In this schedule, the math teacher homogeneously groups students during periods 2 through 5 into four or eight levels for mathematics. However, this schedule fails to meet the specification of heterogeneity for social studies, science, and language arts because the math grouping spills over into these subjects. So the good math students stay together in science, period 3; social studies, period 4; and language arts, period 5. Therefore, this is a poor schedule!

Additional refinements to the schedule can help solve the problem of homogeneous grouping carrying over. In order to create heterogeneity, a matrix must be designed that will undo the grouping created by a subject such as math that runs parallel to social studies, science, and language arts. The matrix must reassign the math groups to bring about the desired heterogeneity. This can be done by assigning each of the math classes a series of scheduling numbers and placing students in groups of four or five (called *modules*). These subgroups for the math grouping can then be dispersed through the other classes in an orderly manner.

The first column (math) of Figure 12.5 assigns each succeeding group of five math students a number. The top-five math students are assigned number 1. The lowest-five math

Home Base: Heterogeneous groups   2 subjects each teacher
Reading: Skill groups—8 groups
Math: Skill groups—each math module contains 5 students—120 total
Other Subject: Heterogeneous groups

Teacher Period	Home Base Heterogeneous	Home Base Heterogeneous	Home Base Heterogeneous	Home Base Heterogeneous
1	(Heterogeneous groups are created by rank ordering on reading scores with each home base receiving every fourth card.)			
2	Reading Skill Groups A,E	Reading Skill Groups B,F	Reading Skill Groups C,G	Reading Skill Groups D,H
3	Math Homogeneous Groups 1 4 2 5 3 6	Language Arts 7 16 10 19 13 22	Science 8 17 11 20 14 23	Social Studies 9 18 12 21 15 24
4	Math 7 10 8 11 9 12	Language Arts 15 24 18 3 21 6	Science 13 22 16 1 19 4	Social Studies 14 23 17 2 20 5
5	Math 13 16 14 17 15 18	Language Arts 20 5 23 8 2 11	Science 21 6 24 9 3 12	Social Studies 19 4 22 7 1 10
6	Math 19 22 20 23 21 24	Language Arts 1 12 4 15 9 17	Science 2 10 5 14 7 18	Social Studies 3 11 6 13 8 16

7, 8 Lunch-activity period—Art—Music—PE—Health—Guidance—etc.

FIGURE 12.5   Middle School Team Schedule: Four-Teacher Team—Homogeneous and Heterogeneous Groupings

Note: These numbers are based on the math groupings of five students each and are used to re-create the heterogeneity for language arts, science, and social studies.

students are given number 24. This number assigned to students in math class is then used to disperse them, thus creating heterogeneous grouping in the other three subjects.

A schedule for a four-teacher middle school team might carry the following specifications; many variations of these assignments are possible, however:

- All teachers teach reading—reading is divided into eight skill levels.
- One teacher teaches math—math is divided into four or more skill levels.
- One teacher teaches social studies. ⎫ These classes are to be grouped hetero-
- One teacher teaches science.　　　　⎬ geneously and not reflect either the math
- One teacher teaches language arts. ⎭ or reading grouping.

Secondary School Schedules

Secondary school schedules, although somewhat more complex, can often be viewed as extensions of elementary or middle school schedules. Different types of secondary school schedules are discussed next under the following headings: group schedules, block schedules, and mosaic schedules, including both cafeteria-style schedules and schedules based on student course requests. Each of these designs offers variations that are reflections of decisions previously made about curriculum, instruction, grouping of students, staffing, and facility usage. Most well-designed secondary school schedules are quiet complex and can be very labor intensive to build. Therefore, the last part of this section is devoted to the steps necessary to produce a quality schedule and the computer tools available to aid in the process.

Group Schedules

A group schedule of single subjects is most often used to place in groups students who are registered for the same subjects and where the elective offerings are very few. Students are scheduled into classroom-sized groups and stay together through the day. Only two steps are required for this scheduling procedure: (1) Determine the number of students taking the same subjects and identify how many sections are needed; and (2) arrange the classes into a schedule according to their groups, rotating through the subjects in a similar fashion to Figure 12.2. Only physical education and music or some other elective might rotate on an alternate-day basis.

This schedule works well for a group size of 100 to 150 students who will stay together for four to five classes each day. It is typical of junior high schools but in recent years has become popular in high schools using a school-within-a-school design.

Block Schedules—Middle and High School

Block schedules are a form of mosaic schedule that assign a longer period of time for classes and reduce the frequency of meeting times. The traditional six- or seven-hour schedule of the typical middle or high school creates a hectic, fast-moving, disruptive day for most teachers and students. Frequent class changes constantly disrupt available academic learning time (ALT). An excellent alternative to the traditional six- or seven-period day is block scheduling. Block schedules generally increase the length of a class by doubling it and reduce the number of classes a student and teacher participate in on a given day, usually by half. To achieve this one-half reduction, classes generally meet every other day or are one semester in length.

Block schedules offer a number of distinct advantages over traditional schedules. They reduce the number of class changes that students must make during any one school day. They reduce the number of students for whom a teacher must prepare each day and/or term. They also reduce the number of assignments, tests, and projects that the student must address at the same time and decrease the fragmentation inherent in single-period schedules. Block schedules also provide teachers with blocks of time that allow and encourage the use of a variety of teaching strategies. Students have extended amounts of time for learning. In addition, block schedules provide the opportunity for interdisciplinary teaching, which is a much sought after curriculum goal of the middle school.

Academic learning time is also enhanced with the use of block scheduling. Chapter 10 discussed the ALT concept and the importance of reducing the amount of start-up and close-down time at the beginning and end of each lesson. Two-period classes reduce by more than one-half the lost time by eliminating a class change. Block schedules are also relatively easy to implement. They do not require student assignment procedures much different from those already on place for a six- or seven-period schedule. Only the relative changes of hours and days that classes meet must be modified.

Alternate-Day Schedules.   Alternate-day block schedules may be adopted to meet the needs of schools that offer six, seven, or eight courses per year. In schools where six or eight classes have been taught, half of the classes are taught every other day. Classes might have a Monday–Wednesday–Friday schedule one week and a Tuesday–Thursday schedule the next; or Monday could be maintained with single-period classes and double-period classes operate on Tuesday–Thursday and Wednesday–Friday. The seven-course block schedule uses six courses that meet in double periods while one course meets as a singleton. Often, the singleton is scheduled in conjunction with the lunch hour. Tables 12.2 and 12.3 illustrate the six- and seven-course alternate-day block schedules.

The 4/4 Semester Plan.   In the block schedule semester plan, the school day is divided into four instructional blocks of approximately 90 minutes each and the school year is divided into two semesters. Each semester, students are enrolled into four courses that meet daily for a full 90-minute period. Instruction that was previously stretched out over 180 days is now taught in 90 days. The

TABLE 12.2   Alternate-Day Six-Course Block Schedule for Five-Day Schedule

PERIOD	MONDAY	TUESDAY	WEDNESDAY	THURSDAY	FRIDAY
1	1	2	1	2	1
2	2	2	1	2	1
3	3	4	3	4	3
4	4	4	3	4	3
5	5	6	5	6	5
6	6	6	5	6	5

TABLE 12.3   Alternate-Day Seven-Course Block Schedule for Six-Day Rotation

PERIOD	DAY 1	DAY 2	DAY 3	DAY 4	DAY 5	DAY 6
1	1	2	1	2	1	2
2	1	2	1	2	1	2
3	3	4	3	4	3	4
4	3	4	3	4	3	4
5*	5	5	5	5	5	5
6	7	6	7	6	7	6
7	7	6	7	6	7	6

* Period 5 is held constant each day to simplify the lunch schedule and to provide for an even number of periods to pair.

two-period block reduces the lost academic learning time more than enough to make up for shorter assigned minutes of instruction. In fact, some argue that more instructional time is really available under this 90-minute, one-semester plan than the traditional two-semester, one-period schedule.[4] Table 12.4 illustrates the basic 4/4 model. Proponents of the 4/4 semester plan suggest that the plan has the following advantages:

- Teachers have to work with only 50 to 90 students at a time.
- Teachers have only three classes and maybe fewer preparations.
- Students are responsible for only three or four subjects at one time.
- Students failing a course may have the opportunity to repeat it immediately the next semester.
- Students have opportunities to accelerate their study in specialty fields.
- More elective opportunities exist for high school students who now have as many as 32 choices over a four-year period of time.
- As many minutes of instruction (ALT) can be built into the schedule as single-period schedules.

Variations in block schedules are many. Lunch schedules, single-schedule needs for subjects that need to meet for the entire year, vocational programs that require blocks of time for

TABLE 12.4   The Basic 4/4 Two-Semester Block Schedule

PERIOD	SEMESTER 1	SEMESTER 2
1	Course 1	Course 5
2	Course 1	Course 5
3	Course 2	Course 6
4	Course 2	Course 6
5	Course 3	Course 7
6	Course 3	Course 7
7	Course 4	Course 8
8	Course 4	Course 8

school-to-work activities—all of these represent special impacts to the schedule. There is no space in this chapter to provide the answers to each of these variables. An excellent resource, however, is the work of Canady and Rettig,[5] who provide a great number of schedule adaptations in illustrating their book on block schedules.

Additional graduation requirements in many states are placing pressures on available time slots for school electives. Many schools have moved to block schedules, in part, to create more elective options. Block schedules using either alternate-day or semester-length courses often have four periods a day but eight periods a year. Through the four-year journey, a student has eight course options each year for a total of 32 courses, as opposed to the 24 courses of a six-period day or 28 courses of a seven-period day. For scheduling purposes, an eight-period day is designed. Periods one through four become the first semester and periods five through eight become the second semester. If an alternate-day block schedule is used, then periods one through four become the day 1 schedule and periods five through eight become day 2.

Mosaic Schedules

The most commonly used form of secondary school scheduling, mosaic scheduling, is designed to allow the scheduling of a large number of student electives. The term *mosaic* comes from the method of schedule construction. Each course to be offered is written on a small card or tile and moved about on a scheduling board so that it can be assigned a teacher, a time, and a room that is free of conflicts from other parts of the schedule. When the board becomes full of these small squares, it resembles a mosaic.

Block schedules are a form of mosaic schedule that use a longer period of time for classes and reduce the frequency of meeting times. Similarly, school-within-a-school schedules, are generally based on mosaic designs.

Cafeteria-style mosaic schedules.   Cafeteria-style schedules have students select their courses including choice of time and sometimes teacher, after a schedule is fully designed. Usually schedules are designed based on the previous year's schedules and what is known to have worked in the past for a particular school. Students are asked to sign up for each specific class and section they wish to take the coming year. This is often done by preparing enrollment cards for every available seat in all scheduled classes, placing them on tables with advisors in a large room, and asking students to request a card for each course they wish to take—selecting their elective courses first. Thus the name, *cafeteria-style schedule*. When the maximum enrollment for each section is reached, that section is closed and students must make other choices. This might entail choosing another time slot or may require the student to select another elective. Students who are last on the list to register may find it difficult to get the courses they need to take.

The advantage of cafeteria-style scheduling is its ease of construction from the administrative standpoint. Construction decisions are based on availability of curriculum offerings, the number of sections needed, availability of staff, rooms, and time. Individual student requests are adjusted to fit the schedule.

The problem with cafeteria-style schedules is that students are often unable to get the courses they need because of closed sections or conflicts in their schedule. A conflict occurs when two desired courses are only available the same period, forcing the student to choose one or the other. The courses may both be single-section courses, or perhaps a needed section has been closed because it is full. Even in well-designed cafeteria-style schedules, upward of 25 percent of the students may be forced to make second and third choices to fill out their schedules. Guidance counselors frequently spend the first week of school trying to juggle class rosters to get students into courses they must have to graduate.

Mosaic schedules based on student requests. A preferred way to design a mosaic schedule, although more difficult, is to first gather data about student course requests and then design a schedule taking each individual student request into consideration as part of the schedule design. This method, when properly done, greatly reduces the number of irresolvable conflicts about student course requests. A well-designed mosaic schedule may reduce these conflicts such that only 2 percent of student schedules require selecting different electives.

Schedules for student course requests can be constructed manually for a small high school, but more often they are created with the assistance of a computer scheduling program. A number of computer programs on the market can aid in this task of creating a mosaic schedule built on individual student requests. Chapter 14 discusses how scheduling software and school information systems can be integrated. Nevertheless, whether done manually or with the aid of computer software, the steps are basically the same.

Building a High School Mosaic Schedule

Although computer software programs are available that will actually generate a computer-designed schedule, many principals prefer to do the design phase manually. They find there a too many subtle decisions to be made that extend beyond the capability of computer logic. For example, making sure that Mr. Jones has a first-period class because of his tendency to show up late or trying to give certain coaches the last period of the day as a preparation period so they can get an early start on practice, or giving Smith and Johnson the same basic schedule because they have been trying to do some team teaching.

Computer-assisted scheduling procedures can save hours of clerical time by electronically loading student data into a manually planned master schedule. Excellent scheduling software is also available that will actually construct a master schedule.[6] However, a particular advantage of using only computer loading is the opportunity for the scheduler to maintain greater control over the schedule design. Trial runs can be processed with computer printouts indicating any problem with student requests that cannot be scheduled. These student conflicts can be reviewed by the schedule designer and result in additional scheduling modifications to avoid previously overlooked conflicts. All schedule modifications are to the draft master schedule only. Until the master schedule is close to perfect, no individual student schedules should be changed. Unsolvable conflicts are reviewed later.

A good master schedule should result in required student-schedule changes on an individual basis for no more than about 2 percent of the students. A number of draft runs of the schedule can be made with additional schedule modifications each time. This method will gradually produce schedules with fewer and fewer conflicts.

Computer scheduling packages also include study hall control; common course scheduling (the same students in more than one class); simulated runs; alternate course schedules in case of conflicts; balanced class enrollments as to size; and class lists of students for each teacher for each hour of the day, as well as generation of the master schedule itself. Costs of these software programs range from several hundred many thousand dollars. Nevertheless, it is generally believed that, the clerical and administrative time saved by the use of a software program more than offsets the cost.

Student and teacher schedules can be electronically transferred directly into the student record database each year, saving the clerical time necessary for data entry (see Chapter 14). The individual student schedules can be printed in multiple copies on paper as well as on cardstock, providing one copy to the student, one for the office, and additional copies for school files such as attendance, counseling, and the like. Individual schedules can also be printed with home addresses for summer mailing if this is desired (see Figure 12.6).

13939 WILBURN ANGLIA R			10	F	01–05		MARYVILLE	
STUDENT NAME			GRADE	SEX	NUMBER		HIGH SCHOOL	
PERIOD	SUBJECT NUMBER	SUBJECT	ROOM NUMBER	SEM.#	TEACHER		028	
							HOME ROOM	TELEPHONE
1	121	ENG 2 COL PR	014	3	014			
2	606	GEN BUS 1/2	013	1	117			
2	605	PERS COM 1/2	017	2	117			
3	925	PHYS ED 1/2	025	1	106			
3	929	DR ED SFM 2	105	2	105			
4	821	HOME ECON 2	001	3	001			
5	211	ALGEBRA 1	020	3	020			
6	311	BIOLOGY	023	3	023			

13940 WILBURN DAVID M			10	M	01–05		MARYVILLE	
STUDENT NAME			GRADE	SEX	NUMBER		HIGH SCHOOL	
PERIOD	SUBJECT NUMBER	SUBJECT	ROOM NUMBER	SEM.#	TEACHER		028	
							HOME ROOM	TELEPHONE
1	211	ALGEBRA 1	020	3	020			
2	925	PHYS ED 1/2	025	1	104			
2	929	DR ED SEM 2	005	2	205			
3	121	ENG 2 COL PR	014	3	014			
4	311	BIOLOGY	023	3	023			
5	491	LATIN 2	015	3	115			
6	021	BAND	026	3	026			

FIGURE 12.6   Computer-Printed Student Schedule

The steps in building a mosaic type schedule, whether done manually, or with computer assistance, are as follows:

1. Determine the educational offerings of the school. Each year, a needs assessment is conducted to determine what the curricular offerings for the following school year should be. New courses may be proposed by new district or state requirements or by the requests from students and staff. The initial list should consist of courses that are desired and for which there is some probability that they can be taught. With computer scheduling, all possible courses can initially be put on request.

2. Provide an appropriate means for students and parents to review the curricular offering and to select courses for students to take with appropriate guidance from teachers and counselors. A booklet listing all courses with a brief description can be prepared. The booklet can also list requirements for graduation and suggested courses of study. Planning worksheets for each year of a student's school career may also appear in the booklet so that tentative four-year programs can be worked out. Figure 12.7 shows a sample planning sheet for individual high school course

FIGURE 12.7   Senior High School Course Guide

Instructions: Use this form to plan your three years in high school. Circle the courses that you tentatively plan to take each of your three years in high school. Record next year's courses on the registration form and return this sheet to your homeroom teacher.

SOPHOMORE	JUNIOR	SENIOR
English 10 (Required)	English 11 (Required)	English 12 (Required)
American History (Required)	World History (Required)	Creative Writing
World Geography	World Geography	Social Studies (Required)
Physical Education (Required)	Elementary Algebra	World Geography
Elementary Algebra	Integrated Mathematics	Humanities
Integrated Mathematics	Plane Geometry	Elementary Algebra
Plane Geometry	Higher Algebra	Integrated Mathematics
Biology	Biology	Plane Geometry
French I, II, III	Chemistry	Higher Algebra
German, I, II, III	French I, II, III, IV	Trigonometry/Advanced Algebra
Latin I, II	German I, II, III	Advanced Mathematics
Russian I	Latin I, II, III	Biology
Spanish I, II, III	Russian I, II	Chemistry
	Spanish I, II, III, IV	Physics
		French II, III, IV
		German II, III, IV
		Latin II, III, IV
		Russian II, III
		Spanish II, III, IV

(continued)

FIGURE 12.7   Senior High School Course Guide (*Continued*)

SOPHOMORE	JUNIOR	SENIOR
Art I	Applied Physical Science	General Mathematics
Commercial Art I	Art I	Applied Physical Science
Keyboarding	Art II	Art I
Beginning Business	Commercial Art I, II	Art II
Electricity I	Keyboarding	Commercial Art I, II
General Metals	Office Skills	Keyboarding
Power I	Secretarial Skills	Office Skills
Wood I	Computer I	Secretarial Skills
General Graphic Arts	Bookkeeping & Accounting	Sales and Merchandising II
Home Economics I, II, III, IV	Architectural Drawing	Office Education
Journalism	Electricity I, II	Computer II
Speech	General Metals	Bookkeeping and Accounting
Gym & Choir (Alt. Days)	General Graphic Arts	Law/Sales
Gym & Band (Alt. Days)	Machine Drawing I	Architectural Drawing
Gym & Study (Alt. Days)	Machine Shop I	Electricity II, III
Orchestra	Power I, II	Machine Drawing I, II
	Wood I, II	Machine Shop I, II
	Home Economics I, II, III, IV	Power II
	Journalism	Wood II, III
	Speech	Home Economics I, II, III, IV
	Band	Journalism
	Choir	Speech
	Orchestra	Drama
	Boys' Physical Education	Band
	Girls' Physical Education	Choir
	Sales and Merchandising I	Orchestra
		Boys' Physical Education
		Girls' Physical Education

GRADUATION REQUIREMENTS

1. English 10, 11, 12
2. American History
3. World History
4. Social Studies
5. Two mathematics courses
6. Two science courses
7. Passing grade in 10th grade phys. ed.
8. Total of 14 credits plus 10th grade phys. ed.

FIGURE 12.8   Registration Code Sheet and Teacher's Tally Sheet

STUDENT COURSE REQUESTS

Student's Name:

Directions: Encircle the code number, *in red,* of all subjects for your next year's schedule as approved on your Proposed Program of Studies sheet. Recheck for accuracy. The homeroom teacher may reserve the responsibility of checking those subjects where ability grouping is involved.

MISCELLANEOUS	MATHEMATICS	BUSINESS EDUCATION
___060 Unassigned	___321 Alg. 2R	___604 Keyboarding (1/2)
___065 Driver Education	___330 Analysis A	___605 Office Practice
___067 Library Training	___331 Analysis R	___606 Pers. Use Computing (1/2)
	___351 Analy. Geom. (1/2)	___608 Voc. Off. Ed.—Jr.
Work Periods	___352 Probability (1/2)	___610 Computer I
___071 First	___354 Comp. Prog. (1/2)	___611 Computer II
___072 Second	___355 Comp. Prog. (1)	___612 Voc. Off. Ed.—Lab.
___073 Third	___356 Comp. App. (1/2)	___613 Voc. Off. Oc.—Coop
___074 Fourth	___358 Trig. (1/2)	___620 Acct. 1
___075 Fifth	___360 Calculus	___621 Adv. Acct.
___076 Sixth	___361 Calculus AP	___631 Bus. Law (1/2)
___077 Seventh		___632 Graphic Design (1/2)
	Science	___641 Bus. Arith.
Special Education	___400 Spec. Ed. Biol.	___642 Cons. Ed. (1/2)
___081 & 082 Spec. Educ.	___430 BSCS Biol. A (1/2)	___643 Bus Comm.
___083 Individual Acceler. Prog.	___431 BSCS Biol. B (1/2)	___099 Cl. Off. Aide
	___435 Botany (1/2)	
Coop. Voc. Training	___440 Biol. 2A (1/2)	*Homemaking*
___091 Job not yet assigned	___441 Biol. 2B (1/2)	___681 Homemaking 1A (1/2)
___092 Dist. Ed. (assigned)	___445 Radiation Biology (1/2)	___682 Homemaking 1B (1/2)
___093 Ind. Coop. (assigned)	___430 BSCS Biol. A (1/2)	___683 Homemaking 2A (1/2)
___094 Ind. Coop., Part G	___450 Chemistry A (1/2)	___684 Homemaking 2B (1/2)
	___451 Chemistry B (1/2)	___685 Homemaking 3A (1/2)
	___454 Chemistry 11 A	___686 Homemaking 3B (1/2)
	___455 Chemistry 11 B	___687 Chef's Course (1/2)
	___461 Physics A	
	___462 Physics B	

planning. Student requests should be gathered on a standard registration sheet that allows for easy tallying. A form such as the one in Figure 12.8 can be used for either manual or computer-assisted scheduling.

3. Tabulate student choices by subject to determine the number of students in each subject as a basis for the needed number of sections in each subject. The tabulating can be done by hand, placing the tallies on a sheet similar to the ones the students have used for registration, or by preparing input data for the computer indicating the student's request. Scheduling software can provide an accurate total listing of all subjects and the number of student requests for each subject.

4. Determine the number of sections needed for each subject. This can be done by selecting a maximum class size for each subject and dividing the total students by that number. In the case of small enrollments, a determination must be made of adequate staff numbers to offer all requested courses. For example, can you afford to offer a French 4 class if you have only six requests? In some cases, small requested enrollments may require dropping some electives and asking those students to select another option. Computer feedback can aid the principal in rapidly determining the enrollment feasibility of offering a particular course. The number of small-enrollment electives that can be offered is ultimately determined by the total student-to-staff ratio.

5. Determine the teaching staff needed and compare with the teaching staff believed to be available, considering areas of certification, budget, and so on. Teaching staff available can be determined roughly by multiplying the number of classes taught by each full-time teacher plus the number of sections taught by part-time personnel. Then compare the result to the number of sections indicated as being needed in the course tallies calculated in step 4.

Sections needed based on student requests 350
Teacher sections available based on total staff 335
Sections that must be cut from student request tabulations or
   provided for by the employment of three additional teachers 15

Now a more detailed analysis must be carried out to properly match teacher assignment requests and certification areas to student course tabulations. This is done by comparing specific subject section needs with available staff. Some flexibility is usually available in determining staff assignments where additional positions are to be filled or staff turnover exists. Table 12.5 shown a matching of teacher specialties and student requests.

Teacher assignments may need to be moved around in order for all subjects to be matched with qualified staff. In some instances, modifications may be made based on appropriate assignments for staff yet to be hired or yet to be employed by putting together logical assignments for new faculty (i.e., math–science, social studies–physical education–coaching, etc.). Ultimately, job descriptions for new staff can be formulated from these data.

6. Determine the number and length of class periods and the time for extracurricular activities. The number of periods in the school day should now be determined. Six or seven periods is typical for mosaic-type schedules. Additional school periods over and above the number of classes taken by the average student usually become study halls or early dismissal opportunities. In most cases, experience has shown that unless students are on work assignments of some type, study hall or early release hours are not used productively. Therefore, we suggest that the number of periods in the school day match fairly closely the number of courses for which each student registers. It is somewhat more difficult to build a no-study-hall or limited-study-hall schedule requiring students to take courses each hour, but the productivity for a student is usually improved; thus, such tightly organized schedules are worthwhile.

TABLE 12.5   Teacher Assignment Worksheet

STAFF ROSTER	DESIRED ASSIGNMENT	AREAS OF CERTIFICATION	PROPOSED ASSIGNMENT
Bailes, Cris	English 10–11	LA	LA 3–10, 2–11
Bray, Gail	SS 10	SS, LA	5–10th
Brewer, Max	Sc 11–12	Sc, Math	2–Chem 1—Phys 1–Biol
Crockett, Reba	Keyb, Bkk	Business Ed	4–Keyb 1–Bkk
Dietz, Pat	SS 10–11	SS, PE	SS 5–11
Edison, Freda	Algebra	Math, Spanish	Alg–4 Spanish–1

Extracurricular activities are most often scheduled after the regular school day. This works well when the students either walk to school or provide their own transportation. When a large number of students ride school buses, an after-school activity period greatly restricts the number of students who can participate. Some schools have had success in establishing midday activity periods during the early afternoon. All students are expected to select and participate in an activity, club, or intramural program, or they may use the period as a study period if no other opportunities are available.

7. Make a conflict chart to determine the subjects that must not be scheduled at the same time if students are to have the program they have selected. Subjects, for which only one section is offered, that are placed in the schedule at the same time prevent students from taking more than one such course. Therefore, in order for single-section subjects not to conflict, they must be scheduled at different hours of the day. Two-way conflicts can also frequently occur. This happens when two single-section offerings are matched with a request for a double-section course offered the same hours as the singles. Three-way conflicts are also possible, but the probability is relatively low (see Table 12.6).

The underlying philosophy of a good mosaic schedule is to design a schedule that is capable of honoring all student requests and to then build a schedule that eliminates all possible conflicts. The smaller the number of unsolvable conflicts within the schedule, the more perfect the schedule is considered to be.

A well-designed mosaic schedule should be able to reduce unsolvable conflicts to around 2 percent of the total student population. An *unsolvable conflict* is defined as a set of student course requests that cannot be honored because of conflicts within the schedule and that requires the student to select one or more alternate courses in order to complete a program.

A conflict chart sets up a matrix of the single-, double-, and triple-section offerings and shows how many students have signed up for the various possible combinations. The conflict matrix in Table 12.6 shows that three students want to take both courses 107 and 111.

TABLE 12.6   Conflict Matrix

COURSE NO.	107	111	121	142	451	455	621	697	704
107		3*	2	78	17	17	2	9	0
111			1	0	2	0	12	22	0
121				1	2	7	9	4	0
142					8	0	0	1	
451						3	2	0	
455							54	14	
621								0	12
697									2
704									

*Note that three students want to take course 107 and course 111. These two courses, 107 and 111, must be offered during different periods for these three students not to have a conflict.

Although a conflict matrix is a vital part of the mosaic scheduling procedure, it is also an extremely time-consuming task if done by hand—particularly in a large school. It is accomplished by taking each student course request and comparing it to the other courses also requested by that student. The comparison is indicated by placing a tally mark on the matrix at the bisecting point. Up to 15 comparisons could be required for six course requests from one student if they were all single subjects. On the other hand, computer-assisted scheduling will produce a complete conflict matrix for all subjects generated from the same data that were used to determine student tallies.

8. Assign classes to the master schedule in terms of the conflict matrix. Unless a computer-generated schedule is to be produced, this is a necessary manual task. A small card, approximately one-inch square, should be prepared for each section of each subject to be offered in the schedule. It is often desirable to color code the card by predominant grade levels, reserving an additional color for classes that draw heavily from all or several grades. The mosaic cards should contain the course title and the section designation such as 1–1, 1–2, or 2–3, indicting which section the card represents in the number of sections of that course, for example, English 10. The mosaic cards are then placed on a scheduling grid, listing all proposed teacher positions and the periods of the day.

Some of the scheduling software programs provide a columns and rows spreadsheet with rows representing hours and columns representing either teachers or rooms for principals to place the courses. Some principals prefer to use a magnet board set up with an hour and room grid naming the teacher and course on each mosaic tile. The process begins with the preparation of an entry for each course section to be scheduled.

The following order is usually helpful in constructing the schedule with a minimum of conflicts. Use the conflict chart for all decisions.

a. Assign twelfth-grade sections and proceed downward in grade order. This is desirable because the greatest number of singletons are often twelfth-grade courses. Also, it is thought desirable to design the twelfth-grade schedule first to ensure no conflicts since it is the seniors' final year in high school.

b. Assign subjects having only one section, scattering them throughout the school day. The scattering will reduce conflicts. Next, using the conflict matrix, check each single-section course against other single sections offered during that hour to ensure no conflicts. If some exist, move sections until all are free of conflict.

c. Be careful not to assign two or more classes to the same teacher during the same period.

d. Next assign classes having double or triple periods. Included are the core classes, vocational classes, team-taught block classes, and so on. Because of the larger block of time for these subjects, fewer options exist for scheduling; therefore, it is necessary to place them in the schedule early.

e. Next schedule subjects having only two or three sections; check each placement against the conflict matrix. By now, some moving of earlier placed sections will probably be necessary. Be sure to follow each through an analysis on the conflict matrix with other sections offered that hour.

f. Finally, fill in multiple-section subjects, taking care to properly balance teacher load. Try to assure reasonable balance each hour for teacher preparation time, as well as to ensure adequate availability of staff for teaching purposes. Each time a previously placed mosaic is moved, care must be taken to check out all other ramifications of that move on the conflict matrix. Consideration must also be given to available special facilities each hour, such as music rooms, science rooms, computer labs, and so on.

9. Prepare a room assignment sheet to prevent the assignment of two or more classes to the same room the same hour. A chart can be used simply by replacing the top row of teachers' names with classroom numbers and entering each room assignment on the appropriate mosaic of the master schedule.

10. Now tentatively assign students to the classes of the proposed master schedule. The computer software will load students into their courses and balance class size. As each student is assigned to a class, the information is recorded on the student's individual assignment sheet, as well as on the separate class tally worksheet in order to balance class size. Each student must be scheduled individually for each of his or her course requests. Previously undetected conflicts may now come to light if the information from the conflict matrix was not completely adhered to or if certain conflicts were overlooked.

A good scheduling software program will indicate the number of scheduling conflicts this master schedule has produced and where the major conflicts occur. Based on this information, the principal can readjust course locations to eliminate conflicts, giving more students a complete schedule. After each attempt to load student requests into the schedule and check conflicts, additional modifications in the proposed schedule can be made until a draft is produced with the fewest possible conflicts. When, in the principal's best judgment, the best possible draft producing the least number of conflicts has been achieved, the final steps may begin.

11. Print a final master schedule along with individual schedules for each student, teacher, and room. The master schedule may be posted on an open school website available for all to view. Individual teacher and student schedules can also be posted on the Web, but on a restricted or secure site available only to each individual to whom a schedule applies. FERPA requires strict privacy for posted student schedules.

12. Enlist the help of the guidance department to contact immediately the students who still have unresolved conflicts in their schedule to assist them in making other course choices that will be compatible with the final schedule. When the requested changes have been made, courses are again tallied to produce a final class count as well as a student class roster by period for each teacher.

13. Print first-day rosters are for each class or post them on the Web for each teacher to download, recognizing that additional course changes will be necessary through the first few days of school. Some of these changes will come from new students enrolling in the school. Others will be necessary because of no-shows and as the result of guidance-counselor-approved modifications in student schedules.

14. Sometime after the first week of school, post the master schedule, student schedules, and teacher assignments to the *school information system* to be available for reference throughout the school year.

Year-Round Schools

Another dimension of time deals with the length of the school year and the school calendar. Although U.S. schools traditionally have 180- to 200-day school years, many other calendar options are possible. Knowing that academic learning time is a critical element for student achievement, simply lengthening the school year would, in most cases, improve achievement scores. However, budget limitations and traditions get in the way. In a publication about year-round education, Ballinger stated:

> If year-round education were the traditional school calendar and had been so for 100 years or more, and if someone came along to suggest a "new" calendar wherein students were to be educated for only nine months each year with another three months free from organized instruction, would the American public allow, or even consider, such a calendar?[7]

Lengthening the school year has an immediate impact on student achievement both by providing more time for learning and by shortening the summer so allowing less time for forgetting. Schools devote a significant amount of instructional time each fall to the review of material taught the previous year because students forget over the summer. Some schools have modified the school calendar not by increasing the number of school days but by shortening the summer and providing longer vacation periods during the school year.

One common time organization is the 45-15 day plan. In this plan, students attend school in cycles of 45 days on, 15 days off. Such a plan allows for a six-week break in the summer. Some schools elect to extend the time in school with special intersessions during the off weeks. Other schedule arrangements are a 60-20 day plan and a 90-30 day plan.

Once the sequence of days is decided, the school must determine if all students will start and stop at the same time or if there will be a staggered form of attendance. Staggered attendance is usually used in schools where space is a critical issue. This plan allows the school to use the classrooms during vacation times for other groups of students still in attendance.

The advantages of year-round programs include continuity of learning, better flow and retention of learning, intersession opportunities for tutoring and/or enrichment activities, reduction in student retentions in grade, and less teacher stress/burnout because of the more frequent breaks in schedule. Stated disadvantages include family conflicts from children in different schools who may be on different schedules, difficulty for teachers to get extra training in the summer, interference with summer jobs and summer camps, and potentially higher costs of keeping the building open all year.

Summary

Scheduling has as its basic purpose the bringing together of curriculum, staff, and students for the purpose of instruction. It must be kept flexible, allowing for changes in group size and instructional time. Schedules must also provide for adequate staff planning and allow major scheduling decisions to be made by the team. Block-of-time schedules assigned to the team and parallel scheduling for team planning offer good solutions to scheduling demands.

In this chapter we considered several different concepts of scheduling a high school, from a simple group schedule to the complex modular schedule of some of the more experimental institutions. Complexity is not always best, however. More traditional mosaic schedules, when properly constructed, are most functional. When all aspects of school organization are considered—staffing, student grouping, curriculum, instruction, and student advisement and control—the block schedule must be given a high rating.

Under all circumstances, scheduling is a major determinant of the school program. Although schedules should not control, they must be designed in such a way as to not limit the desired instructional program for the school.

ACTIVITIES

1. Reflect on the use of time and the schedule in your own school. Can you identify areas where restructuring should take place? Why do you believe so? Why is it important to consider the planned decisions for curriculum, instruction, and staffing along with rescheduling decisions? Apply the concepts of this chapter to your school. How would you proceed to restructure your school's use of time?

2. Review Case Studies 1, 17, and 29 at the end of this book. Analyze the problems presented and apply the concepts of restructuring time developed in this chapter. What approach would you use in addressing the problems? Set forth a strategy to overcome the difficulties faced by the schools in these cases.

3. Turn to the ISLLC standards found in Appendix B. Review the functions listed with Standard 2. One of these states to "maximize time spent on quality instruction." What are your school's organizational goals relative to the use of time? How are these goals being met?

4. Another ISLLC Standard 2 function states "promote the use of effective and appropriate technologies to support teaching and learning." Does your school use computer technology to schedule students or to manage student records? If so, what does it do and what software is used?

ENDNOTES

1. L. W. Hughes and G. C. Ubben, *The Secondary Principal's Handbook* (Boston: Allyn & Bacon, 1980), p. 173.

2. J. Aronson, J. Zimmerman, and L. Carlos, "Improving Student Achievement by Extending School: Is It Just a Matter of Time?" Retrieved on June 19, 2006 from WestEd: www.wested.org/online_pubs/timeandlearning/TAL_PV.html.

3. Elizabeth Ward et al., "Student/Teacher Achievement Ratio (STAR)," *Tennessee's K–3 Class Size Study 1985–1990* (Nashville: Tennessee State Department of Education, 1990).

4. See Chapter 2 of Robert Lynn Canady and Michael D. Rettig, *Block Scheduling: A Catalyst for Change in High School Scheduling* (Princeton, NJ: Eye On Education, 1995). Canady and Rettig present an interesting rationale for longer classes providing more than twice the academic learning time of that provided by 50-minute classes.

5. Ibid., p. 300.

6. An Internet Google search of high school scheduling provides an extensive list.

7. Charles Ballinger, "Specializing in Time and Learning," The National Association for Year-Round Education (1999). Go to www.nayre.org.

SELECTED READINGS

Biesinger, K. D., K. J. Crippen, and K. R. Muis. "The Impact of Block Scheduling on Student Motivation and Classroom Practice in Mathematics" [Electronic Version]. *NASSP Bulletin 92,* no. 3 (2008): 191–2008.

Bloom, B. S. "Time and Learning." *American Psychologist 29* (May 1974): 682–688.

Black, K. "Changing Time: The 4 + 1 School Week." *Catalyst for Change 32* (2002): 8–9.

Bugaj, S. "Making Everything Fit." *Principal Leadership 5,* no. 5 (2005).

Canady, Robert Lynn, and Joanne M. Reina. "Parallel Block Scheduling: An Alternative Structure." *Principal* (January 1993).

Canady, Robert Lynn, and Michael D. Rettig. *Block Scheduling: A Catalyst for Change in High School Scheduling* (Princeton, NJ: Eye On Education, 1995), p. 300.

Canady, Robert Lynn, and Michael D. Rettig. "The Power of Innovative Scheduling." *Educational Leadership 53,* no. 3 (November 1995).

Flynn, L., F. Lawernz, and M. J. Schultz. "Block Scheduling and Mathematics: Enhancing Standards-Based Instruction?" *NASSP Bulletin 89* (March 2005): 14–23.

Gullat, D. E. "Block Scheduling: The Effects on Curriculum and Student Productivity" [Electronic Version]. *NASSP Bulleting 90,* no. 3 (2006): 250–266.

Hackmann, D. G. "Constructivism and Block Scheduling: Making the Connection." *Phi Delta Kappan 85,* no. 9 (2004): 697–702.

Haser, S. G., and I. Nasser. "Teacher Job Satisfaction in a Year Round School." *Educational Leadership 60* (2003): 65–67.

Lumsden, L. "After School Programs." *Clearing House on Educational Management 20,* no. 1 (2003).

McKinney, Regina, Beverly Titlow, and Geoerganne Young. "The Academic Enrichment Block." *NASSP Bulletin 83* (May 1999): 79–81.

Murray, S. "FlexMod Scheduling Redux." *Principal Leadership 8,* no. 7 (2008): 42–46.

Myers, N. "Block Scheduling. *NAESP Principal* (November/December 2008): 20–23.

Queen, J. Allen. "First Year Teachers and 4X4 Block Scheduling." *NASSP Bulletin 83,* no. 603 (January 1999).

Regnier, P. "Turnaround Times Twenty." *Principal 84* (2004): 24–26.

Retting, M, and R. Canady. "Block Scheduling's Missteps, Successes and Variables." *School Administrator 60,* no. 9 (2004): 26–31.

Veldman, R. "The Best of Both Schedules." *Principal Leadership 3,* no. 3 (2002): 36–38.

Wahlstrom, K. "Changing Times: Findings from the First Longitudinal Study of Later High School Start Times." *NASSP Bulletin 86,* no. 633 (2002): 3–21.

Wolfson, A. R., and M. A. Carskadon. "A Survey of Factors Influencing High School Start Times." *NASSP Bulletin 89* (March 2005): 47–66.

13 Fiscal Accounting, Budgeting, and Building Management

The procedures are clear from the system office and the state auditor and we follow them religiously. There are many procedures and rules. We follow every rule and sometimes it hurts because we have few funds we can use for teacher "perks."

—MARTHA JEAN BRATTON[1]

I t's a busy morning. You are sitting in your office preparing for a walk around the building when individual staff members, in turn seemingly, rush into your office in various states of concern.

- *Your head custodian:* "Joe Davis, the afternoon cleanup guy just called in. He can't come to work today. This is the second time this week!"
- *Your assistant principal:* "The toilets in the girls' restroom on 2 are overflowing, again!"
- *Ms. Albright, the English chairperson:* "My request for supplemental readers has been denied by the superintendent's office. We need these for our slow readers."
- *Tina Reyes, your physical education teacher:* "We need a bus for the field trip tomorrow. I forgot to get a requisition last week."
- *Two interacting department heads:* "Why should his department get the extra money? My budget clearly indicates a greater need!"

And, so it goes. Building maintenance issues, absent workers, no requisitions, denied fund requests, arguments about the use of available funds—among any number of other related issues that have to do with proper management of budget and building—cause daily confrontations and require decisions.

Fiscal accounting, budgeting instructional funds, and overseeing the general management of the building are functions of the principalship. To be sure, many of the activities associated with these functions may be delegated. Nevertheless, the ultimate burden for a proper budget, for a fiscal system that withstands audit, and for a building that is clean, safe, and well equipped is the responsibility of the chief executive of the building—the principal.

The principal does not, of course, have total control over who determines the monetary needs of all the instructional units, or who fixes the toilets, and the program in general; this falls to the central office, the state, and, sometimes, the federal government. But, it remains the principal's role to see that all of these things occur in a timely and efficient manner.

Where Does the Money Come From?

There are five sources of funds to help schools: local, state, federal, public and private foundations, and the sales of products such as soft drinks, snacks, and various other merchandise that the school sponsors. (These sales are major sources for the "activity accounts" that most schools maintain for "extra" expenses.)

Local and state public sources are primary. All of the states provide some operating funds and some capital for new buildings and renovations. How much is a matter of state legislative action and funding formulas that vary from state to state. The basic principle here is to provide for a standard of assistance that will meet the so-called basic needs of children in the state, regardless of where they live in that state. State support is never adequate to meet this principle and local taxes will vary widely depending on the value of the property in the local community. Local units, sometimes, but not always, with the same boundaries as certain civil units, such as cities or townships, provide support for the schools through property taxation. There will be a taxation standard that all communities in the state must meet. (Some states—Texas, for example—have school system units that are independent of other civil units. These "independent school districts" have their own taxing authority.)

Private and public foundations will support special projects that an alert principal and professional staff often can make use of to fund school programs of interest to the foundation. Often, an individual or agency in the central office keeps track of local, state, and national foundations that can be tapped for special projects. Universities, with research and grants offices, may provide assistance here, as will some state departments or agencies of education. Size of school makes no difference, and for the "right" projects, grants of $5,000 to as high as $50,000 or more have been awarded to teachers and departments for innovative or supplemental programs. Some awards are especially targeted for an identified special societal need, such as after-school tutorials or Saturday college preparatory seminars for low-income students, just to identify two popular programs.

Activity funds have various means of support.[2] These are not "regular" district funds and may, in some districts, not even been subject to audit. Some schools support a vast array of activities from marketing products. The sponsored materials that parents or others might be persuaded to buy are many: from soft-drink machines, from the school store of instructional supplies, from candy and snack machines, from T-shirt sales—whatever young people might want or need to purchase. Snack foods and soft-drink sales are coming under fire because of an increasing concern about the obesity of children and their poor dietary habits.

Another source of money that the principal must generally manage the bookkeeping of are those special accounts generated by school classes, booster clubs, and parent/teacher organizations.

This money is kept separate from the activity accounts and is often separately managed by the various treasurers of the groups. But beware! It is real money and the organizations are school related, no matter for what purpose the funds are raised. Organizational personnel may change and some treasurers are more competent than others. The school bookkeeper and the principal need to be vigilant and oversee these dollars in a manner that will sustain audit.

The availability and munificence of these funding sources varies considerably among schools. (PTA A and private sector A may be much different from PTA B and private sector B.) More affluent school communities are able to provide much more support.

> At Sarah's school, with PTA funds the principal pays for the staff Christmas party at $30 a pop. That would never happen here. The PTA earned $24,000 at their fall festival. We earned $400. I seek other sources for extra things. I can beg but it is easier to beg for student items than for teacher perks.[3]

The Building and Grounds

Research about first-rate schools has shown two things about resource and facility management. In first-rate schools, resources are allocated to maximally support instructional and curricular improvement. Also, good schools are invariably clean and safe and physically attractive both inside and outside. The schools may not be new or even recently built but they are well maintained. Good financial planning and budget are apparent and so is an obvious attention to the impact the physical environment has on school outcomes.

So, two major tasks confront the principal: The first is making sure that funds secured from a variety of sources and for a variety of outcomes are properly accounted for and properly used. The second is ensuring that the building is managed in such a way that it is well equipped and an attractive place for students and staff. This chapter is about both tasks and comprises four parts. In the first part, important concepts about financial planning and budgeting are discussed. Much attention is given to ways to engage the staff in fiscal planning that has an impact on the instructional program. In the second part, good accounting and record-keeping practices are examined. The focus of the third part is supplies and equipment management. The chapter concludes with a discussion about the care of the school plant, including a review of custodial schedules.

The Planning and Budgeting Process

There are four sequential steps to the budget development and budget implementation process: program planning and tentative allocation of resources by category; analysis and adoption of a final budget; administration and coordination of the budget, including record keeping; and review and appraisal of budget implementation with regard to the instructional goals of the school program. The budget process is continuous and cyclical. Figure 13.1 depicts this process.

Responsible financial planning rests on good program planning. It requires, as well, a substantial database about the nature of the student body; population projections and housing patterns; estimates of personnel needs; and historical information about average daily attendance (ADA) or average daily membership (ADM), whichever is the basis for the state reimbursement program, and reasonable projections thereof, among other information that would help determine the financial demands of the next fiscal period.

ISLLC 3

ISLLC 3

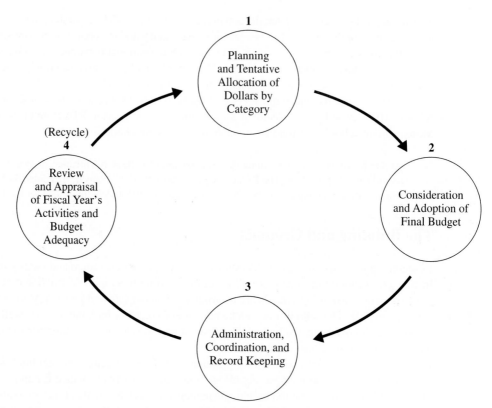

FIGURE 13.1   The Cyclical Nature of the Budgeting Process

Three Common Budgeting Processes

In site-based decision making, the budgeting process takes on critical importance. Three major techniques for budget development have emerged over the years, any of which may be employed at the site. Two of these clearly are conducive to much staff participation in budget development and implementation. One is such a "mechanical" approach that only minimal staff participation would seems needed.

Incremental Budgeting.   Incremental budgeting begins with the current year's budget, and in its pure form it is largely an "add-on" (or "subtract-from") process. It assumes stasis: stasis in the nature of the needs of the student body, stasis in curriculum organization, and stasis among line items. Within line items there may be shifts in proposed expenditures, to be sure, and staff decisions with regard to this one encouraged.

Fundamentally, however, the next school year is assumed to be very much like the current year. Certain fixed charges that can be anticipated may be excluded from building-level planning. That is, the district may do its own projections with regard to such things, for example, as utility bills and uniform maintenance. These will likely remain centralized and accounted for in the district business office.

At the school site, however, the principal will be expected to project needs for the next year on a formula that most often is based on the number of students anticipated to be enrolled. This becomes the primary factor for anticipating the number of teachers needed, supplies required, support staff permitted, among other expenses that go along with an increased or a decreased enrollment. Frequently, the student enrollment figure is based on average daily attendance or average daily membership for the current year and any changes that might be anticipated—for example, new housing starts.

Special requests such as needed building repair or special facilities for special programs and specialized projects housed in the building are usually considered separately. For example, programs funded by outside sources such as the federal government—"Title" programs, vocational programs, lunch programs, and the like—are handled separately.

When the totals are calculated, preliminary decisions are made with regard to the appropriation for the school for the next year. This is budget development at its simplest. It is also budget development at its most inadequate, because it assumes that what exists is working well enough. Incremental budgeting does not take into consideration any changes in the nature of the students to be served or changes in instructional technology, for example. It is status-quo driven, and structural, curricular, and instructional innovations are less encouraged than would be desirable. The amount of money to be spent is viewed as finite and dependent on the school allocation.

Zero-Based Budgeting.   At the other end of the budget development continuum is zero-based budgeting. In its purest form, this technique assumes a new year, every year. The school organization is divided into program or budget units. The mere fact that a program was funded during the current year or in previous years is no assurance that it will be funded in subsequent years. The program unit and ultimately program heads are expected to justify their program and the dollars needed to support that program on an annual basis. The budget is "zero" until this is done.

Justifications are made on the basis of curriculum evaluations, demographic realities, research about instructional technology, shifting priorities, identified needs, performance on state tests, and the established school and program goals. One important advantage of zero-based budgeting is that it forces continuous reevaluation of program objectives and needed resources and the establishment of new priorities or reestablishment of existing priorities. A downside is the time-consuming nature of the process, which does not recognize that any school has certain fundamental requirements. Everything is up for grabs. Beware, neophyte principal.

Planning, Programming, Budgeting System.   There is a better alternative to either of the two processes just described. At its best, the planning, programming, budgeting system (PPBS) recognizes that there are needs for a consistent base of support and that a per-pupil allotment may best provide for a baseline. That is, there is enough experience in the district to know that irrespective of individual learner needs, demographic realities, changes in instructional technology, and curriculum revisions, certain per-pupil costs of an education can be anticipated.

Beyond this, however, PPBS begins to take on the elements of zero-based budgeting. Some planners and analysts insert an *E* between the *B* and the *S* to stand for *evaluation*. The PPBES approach explicitly emphasizes that the goals and processes used to address these goals are subjected to evaluation. We believe this is implicit in a PPBS approach, but if it makes the point more telling, that's all the better.

The PPBS technique requires the establishment of specific program goals and processes to achieve these goals; projections of needs—students to be served, new technology, and so on; the generation, analysis, and projection of data about program element costs; alternative processes to achieve the goals; other sources of funding; and any additional personnel or additional facilities needed and their costs.

Implementing a Planning, Programming, Budgeting System

At its simplest, PPBS involves five steps:

1. Establishing the general goals to be achieved
2. Identifying the specific objectives that define this goal
3. Developing the program and processes that it is believed will achieve the objectives and goals
4. Establishing the formative and summative evaluation practices
5. Implementing a review and recycle procedure that indicates whether or not, or the degree to which, the program and processes resulted in the achievement of the objectives and the goals, and, if not, helping to determine other procedures, processes, and programs

The PPBS approach is designed to help the school staff decide specifically what is to be accomplished and how to go about it. The focus is on goal accomplishment. When sensitively and sensibly applied, an efficient expenditure of money results.

Too often, educational planning primarily has been concerned with the "inputs" of education. PPBS differs substantively from other budget-building procedures because PPBS focuses on desired "outputs" of the effort (goals and objectives) and afterwards considers the numbers of staff, books, equipment, and buildings that must be engaged to obtain the desired end.

There are other values to a PPBS plan, however. The process provides much opportunity for staff involvement and staff development about an issue that many may be interested in and all are affected by. At the initial stages, individual departments, teaching teams, grade levels—however, the building is operationally organized—essentially will be engaged in a "GII" decision process. Later, as tough decisions need to be made—initial budget proposals almost always outstrip available funds—the principal may find the "CI" or "CII" process more appropriate. Although even here, and perhaps especially here, GII decision processing may be the most effective. In any of these instances, good use has been made of the collective wisdom and subject matter expertise of staff to arrive at a budget which all will work hard to implement.[4]

Moreover, as PPBS is implemented, data are being collected about the productivity of distinct elements of the program. As the school enterprise has become more complex and more diversified, and more demanding of public funds, personnel, and time investments, there has been a resultant anxiety about results. There is a pressing desire on the part of the various publics to know more precisely what this investment is producing and where changes should be made. The PPBS technique helps provide this important information and forms a solid basis for gaining public support. Among the outcomes of such a budget development process are a concern for the future and a continuous assessment of current curricular and instructional practices.

Step 1: The Five-Year Plan

The planning process begins with the development of a five-year plan well in advance of any specific budget proposals for the next fiscal year. This is not a document that is developed quickly. The process does provide a good basis for in-service seminars with staff and lends a substantive focus to faculty meetings and workshops held throughout the school year.

The process may begin by organizing the pre-school seminars to focus on planning for the future. Several schoolwide or department sessions are held, at which time the topics to be addressed are often stated: "what a student at the end of grade 6 should know", "what this school needs is", "what the outcomes of the 7–12 social studies program should be," or any number of other topics that are generative of ideas that focus on curricular or student outcomes.

ISLLC 1, 3

After the idea gathering, staff members convert the product of these sessions into a series of goals and objectives by a process of synthesizing, summarizing, and combining. Once the staff has refined the statements of objectives and goals, they identify the processes, materials, and personnel that will be necessary to implement these goals and objectives over the next five years. The tentative five-year plan has four major components:

1. A written description of the current state of the discipline. The staff simply describes, briefly, where the department, or subject matter, or curricular field is at the present time in relation to what the literature and research reveal is the ideal state.
2. Statement of goals, objectives, and the indicators that will be accepted as evidence of achievement of objectives for the department. Although is important to establish objective indicators of achievement, this does not have to be done at this time; it can be done later. A staff could bog down at this point and become fatigued at developing long lists of performance objectives based on lower-level cognitive achievement. The five-year plan is subject to modifications through the formative evaluation that will occur as it unfolds.
3. A list of processes to implement the objectives.
4. A statement of needed equipment, materials, personnel, and other resources supportive of the processes

Component 4 is the culmination of the five-year plan development. The plan is subjected to refinement and modification and is ultimately submitted for executive review and discussion. It does not contain any dollar figures at this point. Although care should be taken not to hurry the process, definite time lines must be established for the completion of this process. Otherwise, it may become a cumbersome intellectual exercise that never gets completed.

Step 2: The One-Year Plan

Whereas the five-year plan for the school plots a general direction, the one-year building plan provides budgetary substance. The one-year plan is a proposal that specifically identifies what needs to happen next year if the five-year plan is to be realized. Figure 13.2 provides a suggested format for the one-year plan.

The one-year plan describes equipment needs, supplies, supplementary materials, immediate changes of personnel or addition of personnel, remodeling, and other needed resources. Justification for each specific item is available in the one-year document. This justification need not be elaborate; it is a brief statement about how the budget proposal is consistent with the five-year plan. An additional feature is that the departments or grade levels are asked to list needs in order of priority. If it is necessary to reduce budgets because of insufficient dollars, such cutting begins with lowest priority items in each of the proposals.

Subsequent Steps

The next steps involve submitting the budget and the curriculum proposals of the department or unit to the principal and the administrative staff for approval or return for clarification or modification. Ultimately, the preparation of a total school budget in summary form is made by the principal and

Department (or Grade Level): _____

Fiscal Year: _____

Prepared by: _____

Amount Requested: _____

Amount Allocated: _____

Request (indicate after each item which long-term objective it supports)	Estimated Cost	Suggested Source of Supply	Suggested Source of Funds (federal funds, local funds, donation, state experimental funds, etc.)
1. Needed personnel			
2. Needed equipment and materials			
3. Needed other resources (e.g., travel monies, consultants, etc.) N.B.: list above in descending order of priority			
Total Requested _____			

4. Attach a brief statement describing how this proposed budget is consistent with and supportive of the five-year plan.

FIGURE 13.2   The One-Year Plan

the staff for submission to the central office. Following this, there are negotiations and approvals of the individual school budgets in some form by the ultimate fiscal authority in the school district.

Eventually, an approved budget is returned by the principal to each department or unit—a budget from which requisitions throughout the year will be submitted to the principal and purchase orders issued. Each month a recapitulation of purchases to date is returned to the department.

Expectations and Product

Involvement of instructional staff in budget building does not make the principal's job any easier. In fact, after going through the initial process, team leaders, department heads, and other instructional staff can be expected to develop formidable and well-conceived arguments in defense of their budgets. Needless to say, however, the principal will be supplied with much of the data needed in order to go to the superintendent or the board of education to justify an adequate budget. Moreover, the central office and the school board will be well informed as to outgo and the reasons behind the outgo.

The budget-building process just described attempts to accomplish three things. First, it gives the appropriate personnel a large measure of authority for initial budget preparation in their areas of instructional expertise. Second, it causes foresighted curriculum planning. Third, it provides substantiation to the central office, school board, and the community that tax dollars are being spent in an efficient and effective manner.

Accounting for Financial Resources and Expenditures

Once the budget is built and accepted, good management is required to ensure that the money is spent in a way that is legal and ethical and sustains audit. Three general categories are part of the dollar allocations: capital outlay, long-term and short-term debt payment and interest, and current expenses. These are separate categories and generally cannot be "mixed." For example, one cannot spend debt service monies for general operating expenses, no matter how great the respective need may be.

The latter category, current expenses, is of greatest concern to the principal, although certain items that appear in a capital outlay account also require consideration. What goes into each of these accounts?

- *Capital Outlay.* An item with a life expectancy of more than a year generally goes into a capital outlay account. The account will therefore contain equipment and all permanent additions to the buildings and school site. Plant and site maintenance expenditures are not reported here—only those expenditures that represent an extension to the existing school building and site. Relative permanence is the key determinant.
- *Debt Service.* All short- and long-term loans and the repayment of those, including the interest payments, are reported in these accounts.
- *Current Expenses.* Current expenses include all expenditures made for things that are consumable during a single fiscal year. These include such expenses as textbooks, supplies, and salaries—known as *operating expenses.* Most often, these expenses can be found in the district budget classified under four categories: *instruction,* which includes all of the programs—regular, special, and adult; *support services,* which includes transportation, food service, student services, and student activities; *nonprogrammed charges,* which include any payments to other governmental agencies for services, including rentals; and *community services,* which include recreation programs and nonpublic school services.

ISLLC 3

Accounting for Financial Resources at the School Site

Once the budget is developed and approved, it becomes the responsibility of the principal to see that it is managed properly. Schools are big businesses. In many communities, the school system is the single largest employer of personnel and the largest industry in terms of capital flow. School districts receive and disburse huge amounts of money for a variety of services and materials during the period of a year.

Similarly, at the individual school buildings, principals have the responsibility for administering sizable financial resources—resources that come from the central district office as a result of local, state, and federal support programs, as well as much smaller sums that come from places such as parent–teacher organizations (PTOs), school clubs, plays, and so on. Managing financial resources is a major responsibility of most school principals.

All school systems have a prescribed accounting procedure, and a principal needs to be familiar with it in order to properly oversee income and expenditures. Figure 13.3 displays a

FIGURE 13.3   Outline of Typical Accounts for a Secondary School

General Activity Fund Restricted

INSTRUCTIONAL FEE	Combined Studies
Towel Fee	Debate Club
INSTRUCTIONAL FEE: ART	DECA
INSTRUCTIONAL SHOP	French Club
Auto Mechanics	German Club
Machine Shop	Gymnastics
Wood Shop	Home Economics
OTHER INSTRUCTIONAL	International Relations Club
Music	Key Club
Band Uniforms	Leaders' Club
MERCHANDISING SERVICE	Leo Club
Bus Tickets	Literary
PROFIT EARNING	Magazine
Coke Fund	Masquers
Concessions	Music: Band
SPECIAL PURPOSE	Music: Choir
Hospitality	Musical Production
Library	National Honor Society
College Credit Course	Oak Leaf
Sports Camp	Oak Log
Senior Trip	Pep Club
Scholarship	Red Cross
Science	Ski Club
Training & Technology	Spanish Club
STUDENT ORGANIZATIONS	Student Council
Anchor Club	Tennis Club
Bridge Club	TOEC
Class, Junior	VICA
Class, Senior	

typical array of accounts for a secondary school, and Figure 13.4 is a similar display for an elementary school.

In general, school principals need to keep a journal of receipts and disbursements and provide proper monitoring of these (see Figure 13.5). The principal may also have federally funded projects located in the building and will be expected to maintain appropriate records for these. Certainly, too, the principal will be responsible for securing supplies and materials, either by requisition from a central warehouse, perhaps using a system of transfer vouchers, or directly from a supplier. Probably most, if not all, of the principal's accounting responsibilities will occur in

FIGURE 13.4   Outline of Typical Internal Ledger Accounts for an Elementary School

MERCHANDISING SERVICE
  Bus Tickets
  Insurance
  Workbooks
PROFIT EARNING
  Coke Machine
  Pictures
  School Store
SPECIAL PURPOSE
  Field Trips
  Assemblies
  Hospitality
  Instructional Supplies
ORGANIZATIONS
  Faculty Club
  Student Council
  PTO
  Intramural Program
  All-School Chorus

the operations (supplies, equipment, etc.) part of the budget. Figure 13.6 displays a purchase requisition flowchart in common use in schools. (Principals usually are not required to account for capital income and expenditures. These accounts are commonly handled in the central office.) In most schools, there will be a clerk on whom will rest the responsibility for keeping the books. Under the principal's direction, this person will generally make the journal entries and keep the records in order. This does not relieve the principal of executive responsibility, however. Regular review is essential, and we recommend an annual independent audit of all records.

For the first few months on the job, the principal is best advised to be involved directly in the accounting process to learn intimately the business side of the enterprise. Proper accounting and budget procedures are essential to a well-managed school. The accounting system exists in order that the school may expend its funds efficiently and in accordance with the plan incorporated in the budget document. It also provides a history of spending and may be used to evaluate how the plan developed in the budget document is proceeding.

Financial resources are always in short supply, and it is not likely that all of the budgetary requests in support of the instructional objectives and school goals can be met in any one year. Thus, it becomes most important for the principal to keep a close record of outgo, making sure that outgo is consistent with the budget plan and that sufficient funds remain for the purchase of high-priority items throughout the school year. It is a sad fact that improper accounting procedures have too frequently resulted in an inadequate amount of money in April for the purchase of routine supplies

FIGURE 13.5   Monthly Report Form

Statement of Receipts and Disbursements

Report for _____ 20 _____   Prepared by _____

                                                                                  Central Treasurer

ACCOUNT	CASH ON HAND 1ST OF MONTH	RECEIPTS THIS MONTH	TOTAL	DISBURSEMENTS	BALANCE END OF MONTH
TOTAL	$_____	$_____	$_____	$_____	$_____

Reconciliation of Bank Statement

Bank balance as of _____ $_____
Plus deposits not shown on statement _____ $_____
Plus others _____ $_____
Minus outstanding checks _____   TOTAL $_____
_____ $_____
Book balance as of_____ $_____
_____ $_____

necessary to complete the school year. Under such a system, teachers tend to overpurchase and hoard supplies in their rooms. These practices are neither healthy nor necessary in a well-ordered school.

Most school districts use an accrual accounting system, which means that as soon as a purchase order is initiated or a requisition for anything is approved, it is encumbered in the account book. Through such a process, the principal knows immediately how much money remains to be expended in any particular account. Under such a system, it is not likely that financial obligations will be made beyond the actual amount of money available.

Naturally, all faculty and nonacademic personnel will not understand the intricacies of the accounting system, and sometimes individuals on the faculty may view the entire process as a hindrance to the instructional program. Thus, the wise principal will spend some time in faculty and staff meetings generally informing the staff about the reasons why good record-keeping and accounting procedures are important to an instructional program.

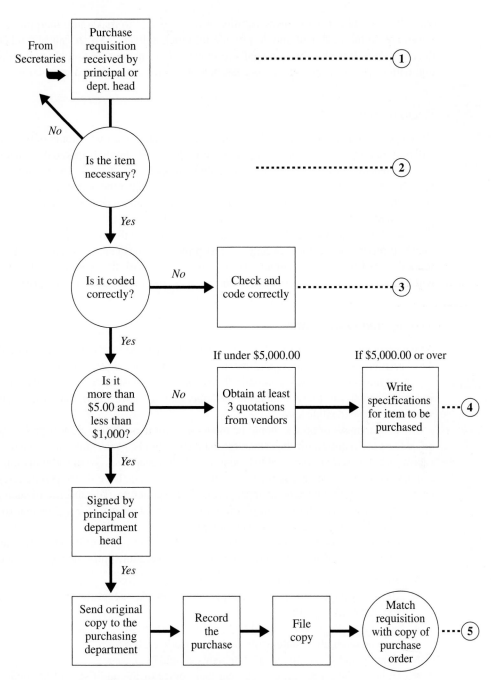

FIGURE 13.6   Purchase Requisition Flowchart for Principals and Department Heads

Beyond this, it is the responsibility of the principal to make sure the practices being followed are, in fact, efficient and do provide for quick delivery of materials and other services to the classroom. It is also the principal's responsibility to make sure that his or her decision making, with respect to expenditures, is consistent with the preestablished instructional budget.

Regular Review

Once systemized, the accounting procedures need not absorb a vast amount of time; instead, they will require only regular monitoring by the principal. Care should be taken that materials ordered are received and properly inventoried. Keeping a separate set of books for district funds will provide the principal with a good check on expenditures against the accounts of the school that are kept in the central business office. Mistakes do get made and when this occurs, it is to the principal's advantage to be aware of the error and be able to rectify it.

In many school systems, the central business office will supply the principal with periodic financial reports in the form of ledger sheet printouts. These can be easily checked against the school's set of books for accuracy. After reconciliation with the school's books, these printouts will provide sufficient record of the financial aspect of the educational enterprise.

Activity and Other Funds

ISLLC 3

As we previously noted, most schools receive and distribute funds other than those disbursed by the district office. Such sources and accounts commonly include PTO funds, classroom accounts, insurance monies, candy sales, athletic funds, club treasuries, petty cash, funds from charity drives, gifts, and so on. Individually, the accounts may be quite small, but collectively they often amount to a considerable sum.

A separate set of books should be maintained for these funds. No less precise bookkeeping procedures are required for these than for the district funds. Many states have passed special legislative acts that require the establishment of orderly procedures for the administration of school activity funds. Some states, as well as local school districts, have developed policies and procedures to guide individual schools in such financial accounting. The absence of such policies and guidance in any particular school district is no excuse, however, for a principal to be any less careful—to the contrary, more care is required.

In general, specific procedures must be established to control the collection and disbursement of the variety of activity funds. The following procedures provide a good guide:

- Official receipts should be issued for all money received.
- All money expended should be expended by check, except for small cash purchases paid from the petty cash fund.
- Supporting documents should be kept for all expenditures made.
- Bank reconciliation statements should be made each month.
- Monthly and yearly financial statements should be prepared.
- An audit should be made each year and copies of the audit should be filed with persons having administrative authority for the school.

Consistent with good financial practice, each group having an account that the school is administering should file a simplified budget indicating anticipated income, anticipated expenditures, and persons designated to approve money to be expended from the account. Further, all school employees who are responsible for handling funds should be bonded, the amount of the bond to be determined by an estimate of the amount of money that the school will manage. Many school districts provide a bond covering all employees in the school system who are responsible for such funds. Whether this is so in any particular district should be verified by the principal.

In some school districts, the principal is required to make a monthly report about the state of the internal funds in the school. Such a report commonly contains specific and general conditions of the accounts and expenditures. Regardless of whether this is required by district policy, it is an important procedure to be carried out by the principal and appropriately filed. It provides substantiation of the careful expenditure of funds and will assist in the annual audit. Figure 13.7 illustrates a monthly reporting procedure for an activity account.

School _____   Report for month of _____

Bank Reconciliation

Bank _____

Balance per bank statement _____ $ _____
                                    Date

Add
   Deposits in transit   _____
   Other (specify)   _____
Total $ _____
Deduct
   Outstanding checks

                                                           $ _____

Balance per general ledger _____ $ _____
                                    Date

_____   _____   _____
        Principal   School Treasurer   Date

FIGURE 13.7   Monthly Financial Report of the School Activity Fund

The Audit

The internal account books should be audited annually by an external accountant. The product of this audit should be filed with the district office. Do not misunderstand the purpose of the audit— it is not an attack on anyone's integrity. An audit has two primary purposes: It provides good information for improving accounting procedures, and it protects all of those who have been responsible for handling school funds.

Before accepting the position, the incoming principal should insist on an audit of all funds as a means of being informed about current practices and improving on these as necessary. The audit also establishes the state of the accounts before a person has responsibility for them. It red-lines the accounts, and the new principal starts with clean fiscal air. This is essential.

Supplies and Equipment Management

A major responsibility of the principal is securing, making an inventory, and allocating supplies and equipment necessary to the educational program. It is important that adequate quantities of soft goods (supplies) and the appropriate kinds of hard goods (equipment) be provided and available ahead of educational needs and secured in the most economical manner possible. It is

ISLLC 3

equally important that a management system be established that will not require an inordinate amount of supervisory time.

If the school is operating under a budget-development system as described earlier in this chapter, the selection and purchase of needed supplies and equipment in support of educational goals is easily routinized. At most, the task should require a regular review to see that anticipated needs are being met on schedule; estimated costs are remaining within budget; advantage is being taken of the appropriate discounts allowed by suppliers; inventories are adequate; and equipment is being appropriately tagged, recorded, conveniently stored, and used.

Storage and Inventory Control

The daily needs of instructional staff are such that amounts of common educational supplies (art paper, chalk, etc.) can be predicted and kept in sufficient reserve to meet needs for a period of a few months. Responsibility for ensuring that appropriate amounts of day-to-day supplies are available can become that of the school clerk or another designated person. This task need not and should not require much attention by the principal. An inventory control procedure set up by the principal working with a designated individual will permit routine replenishment of supplies. Adequate inventories of educational materials and supplies unique to special aspects of the program can be maintained by the person who is responsible for that special aspect of the program.

Things break and wear out and disappear. Equipment must be kept in good repair, and staff members should be made aware of their responsibility to report immediately any malfunction of equipment so that necessary action can be taken. Routine ways need to be established to address these realities so that teachers are able to teach and learners are able to learn unencumbered by malfunctioning or missing equipment. The form depicted in Figure 13.8 uses a light touch to get the job done and done quickly.

HI!
CLAMOR HERE,
YOUR MAINTENANCE MOLLUSK

It's my task to hammer away at any jobs that need fixing in your room. Is there anything that requires attention?

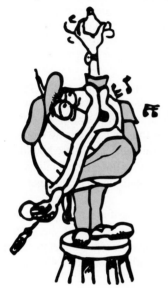

Don't clam up now.
We want a smooth-sailing ship.

Please fill out this form and leave at the custodial desk for quick service.

Room: _____

Service Required: _____

_____

_____

_____

_____

For immediate needs, please call the office.

White: office
Pink: staff

FIGURE 13.8   Maintenance Form

Central Warehousing

The responsibilities for supply management in school systems are frequently handled at the central-office level. Even if the principal has a considerable amount of responsibility with respect to supply management, large systems will have a central warehouse from which most supplies and equipment are secured. There is considerable advantage to this because systems can develop standardized lists of materials, with precise specifications.

Certain kinds of educational materials may also be housed centrally in the school district. Materials such as film, filmstrips, audiotapes and videotapes, compact disks, and so on, which have use throughout the system but are not required in any individual unit of study except on an infrequent basis, are often cataloged and housed centrally in the school district. Where this is the case, teachers must understand the need for more lead time in requisitioning and securing these for classroom use. This is not to say that last-minute requests should not be acted on to the degree possible. It is an unhealthy school system that is not responsive to an unplanned "teaching moment," but in general staff should try to anticipate the need for educational materials that are centrally housed.

Care of the School Plant

> One thing I always did to encourage a learner-receptive building was to provide for the display of student work—artistic and scholarly—around the building. Another excellent way was to have our head custodian attend staff meetings. He became an important part of the management team and both offered and received many suggestions that really helped everyone provide a humane physical environment for students and for staff.[5]

Properly housing the educational program and equipping the school presents some management priorities for the principal. Innovative programs can be housed in traditionally designed buildings. Whether the building represents the latest in school design or reflects architectural thinking in the 1970s, the principal's responsibility is the same: to ensure the maximum efficient use of the school plant for the educational program. An inefficiently used building, a poorly kept building, a building with unpleasant, colorless rooms, or a poorly maintained site all inhibit the development of a good educational program. These conditions have a negative impact on staff and student morale and productivity.

ISLLC 3

The principal has two important support groups: classified employees who are assigned to the building (custodians, cleaning personnel, cooks, kitchen personnel, etc.) and the districtwide maintenance department personnel. Working with nonacademic personnel to help them to do their jobs better requires the same kinds of human relations skills as working with academic staff.

Maintenance and Custodial Schedules

The building and grounds require much attention to create an attractive, safe, learning–living–working environment for students and staff. Many large districts have a director of maintenance and operations whose overall responsibility is to see that skilled persons are employed and deployed to respond to refurbishment and major maintenance needs of all the buildings in the district. However, it is the responsibility of the principal, working with the custodial staff, to identify major needs and to ensure that those are systematically attended to. The day-to-day custodial and light maintenance functions will, even in larger districts, fall to the building custodial staff.

Effective supervision of building maintenance programs need not require an inordinate amount of time and can be regularized through the use of a simple checklist. Such a checklist is shown in Figure 13.9.

The principal and the custodial staff should give particular attention to common internal building flaws: inadequate lighting fixtures, roof or wall leaks, dirt in the corners, broken windows, torn sashes, and so on. The entire staff, including instructional personnel, should assist in identifying maintenance needs and reporting them immediately to the office for attention. Many times, annoying maintenance defects are allowed to continue simply because a teacher or another staff member has not reported them, and they have gone unnoticed by the custodial staff. "Call for Clamor" needs to be a part of in-service instruction.

Description of Service

School: _____

Name: _____

Description of Service	7:00–8:45	8:45–9:00	9:00–9:15	9:15–10:00	10:00–10:15	10:15–10:30	10:30–11:00	11:00–1:30	1:30–2:00	2:00–2:15	2:15–3:30
Unlock building and turn off alarm	■										
Sweep all entrances and put out mats	■										
Police entire building	■										
Police all restrooms and flush out commodes	■										
Drop cafeteria tables down		■									
Dust-mop cafeteria, front and back hall			■								
Break				■							
Clean glass				■							
Set up for lunch					■						
Repolice restrooms before lunch						■					
Lunch							■				
Cafeteria duty								■			
Dust-mop back and front halls								■			
Recheck restrooms and clean wash areas									■		
Break										■	
Clean downstairs lounge											■
Clean upstairs lounge											■
Recheck restrooms and clean wash areas											■
Clean drinking fountain in cafeteria											■

FIGURE 13.9 Day Schedule, Head Custodian: Elementary School

Grounds and Playgrounds.   The school site needs to be attractively maintained. The high cost of land often is reflected in small school sites and inadequate play areas. This is true especially in urban areas where children are often most in need of wide open spaces in which to play and experience nature. Size of site need not deter the latter, however. With a little ingenuity, arboreta and nature walks can be constructed in the most constricted of places. Effective design will often provide adequate play space. In both instances, however, attention needs to be directed to making the available space attractive and safe.

Frequent inspections are key. Debris-strewn school sites are inexcusable, and unsafe equipment is both unconscionable and an issue for litigation in the instance of student or staff injury.

Three types of equipment account for a huge percent of all student injuries: swings and swing sets, climbing bars, and slides. Children are exuberant and like to show their prowess on such things. Most injuries occur from falls from this sort of equipment. The answer? Close supervision and equipment that is in good repair.

Evaluating the Appearance of the Building and Site

Routine work schedules and well-understood expectations are important to the maintenance of the school plant. Time lines and systematic planning for the completion of major maintenance and repair projects need to be supplemented with daily and weekly time schedules to ensure that routine custodial and maintenance tasks get done.

> As for creative use of facilities or use of older buildings—we ask principals annually to tell us what needs to be renovated or built. The renovation funding may come from the district or the campus, and sometimes the funds will be a partnership between the two. Our maintenance department is blessed with skilled craftsmen who can renovate, and through bond funds, we earmark major new construction—whether it's a new fine arts wing or a new floor on the gym.[6]

Regular evaluation of the building's appearance is important. An example of one district's evaluation survey can be seen in Figure 13.10. Such survey forms are best developed in concert with the staff so that expectations are clear and standards well understood.

Working with Classified Personnel

Custodians, maintenance personnel, cooks, aides, and secretaries all have important parts to play in the development of the productive learning climate. Frequently, the contributions of these people are not fully recognized. Unless attention is directed to the needs and contributions of support personnel, the risk is that, at best, a wary truce will exist between these personnel and the professional staff.

Evidence of such a situation will be revealed in the not-so-sly digs each will direct at the other in private meetings and in less-than-adequate services being rendered. Paper towel dispensers that always seem to be out of towels; corners of the cafeteria left unswept; inordinately long waits for equipment to be delivered or repaired; and any number of other examples that

ISLLC 3, 5

Principal: _____ School: _____ Custodian: _____ Date: _____

Entrances:	S	G	A	P
Walks:				
Floor mats:				
Door facings:				
Glass:				
Transoms:				
Door tracks:				
Offices:				
Doors:				
Facings:				
Walls:				
Floors:				
Furniture:				
Windows:				
Fixtures:				
Trash:				
Hallways:				
Floors:				
Walls:				
Lights:				
Water fountains:				
Learning Centers:				
Shelves:				
Floor:				
Furniture:				
Glass:				
Door:				
Classrooms:				
Door facings:				
Walls:				
Lights:				
Floors:				
Boards:				

Windows:	S	G	A	P
Furniture:				
Fixtures:				
Teacher's station:				
Cafetorium:				
Floors:				
Windows:				
Fixtures:				
Lights:				
Fountains:				
Machines:				
Doors:				
Fixtures:				
Storerooms:				
Walls:				
Tool racks:				
Supplies:				
Equipment:				
Restrooms:				
Floors:				
Walls:				
Partitions:				
Windows:				
Commodes:				
Urinals:				
Wash basins:				
Mirrors:				
Floor drains:				
Ventilation:				
Lights:				
Furniture:				
Garbage Area:				
Incinerator:				

COMMENTS:

S — Superior
G — Good
A — Average
P — Poor

FIGURE 13.10   Custodian–Maintenance Survey: Building Inspection Checklist

any reader of this book could supply—these occurrences are indicators that all is not well. In some instances, of course, the cause may be a lack of skill or a lack of clear understanding about organizational expectations. If so, the remedy should be quick—either on-the-job training or replacement.

Engaging support personnel in the same kinds of goal-setting and problem-solving activities that have been suggested for the professional staff is necessary. Administration by edict works no better with custodians and maintenance personnel than it does with the certificated staff. At the beginning of each school year, the principal needs to meet with the custodial staff to chart long-range objectives for building maintenance for the year and to work out a systematic plan for addressing these. Many of the custodial activities will be routine and daily or weekly in nature, of course. Some will not be. Also, the performance of even the routine custodial functions will be affected by such things as special events and even the time of day. Cooperative development of the work schedule is desirable and will result in the important things getting done, getting done well, and in a timely manner.

Selection and Retention of Classified Personnel

The selection, training, and appraisal of support persons are an important managerial task. Yet this has received little attention in professional literature. Improperly trained workers or workers who are unsure of their responsibility—whether in the cafeteria, in the boiler room, or in the principal's office—are a liability. Similarly, the nonacademic staff member who does not understand or particularly like children, while perhaps not common, is also a liability that a school cannot afford.

Personnel policies for the employment, in-service growth, and retention of good nonacademic personnel should be developed. Job descriptions, adequate compensation, and other benefits must reflect the school's interest in maintaining a nonacademic work force of the highest quality.

The standards of employment should not only evidence an interest in appropriate technical competence, but also a realization that most of these personnel will be working with children in some way or another. The latter simply suggests that appropriate attitudes and understandings about young people may be one of the most important employment and retention criteria. Evaluation of performance is essential.

Summary

The subject of this chapter has been threefold: financial support, financial management, and the management of buildings and grounds, including working with noncertificated staff. The allocation of finances, regardless of the source—federal, state, local, or foundation—requires careful planning. Budget development should involve the entire staff and funds allocated to those areas of decided need.

After decisions have been made about the use of available money, it becomes the responsibility of the principal to ensure that proper accounting is maintained. Attention must be directed not only to regular district funds but also to the activity fund, privately collected money earned by various school groups, and from the sale of goods such as soft drinks, snacks, supplies, and so on. There should be regular independent audits of all funds.

How the school looks and how the school is equipped contributes mightily to the attitudes of students and staff. The physical environment of the school grounds influences the learning and teaching environment. The school real not be new—most schools are not—but the school should be clean and all equipment in good repair. Graffiti must be removed and playgrounds must be inspected daily. Children (and teachers) can be taught to pick up litter. Custodians and other maintenance and service staff need all the help they can get—and the good principal sees that they get it. Great things will happen when they do.

ACTIVITIES

1. Case Studies 3, 6, 9, 20, and 29 have financial implications for the principal. Select two of these cases and set forth the processes for resolving the issues in a manner consistent with the concepts expressed in this chapter.

2. Issues of school security permeate Case Studies 10 and 21. What actions do you propose to resolve both issues in (a) the short term and (b) the long term?

3. Professional staff complaints about school maintenance continue to reach your desk. These range from classroom cleanliness to malfunctioning toilets. The custodial staff complains that teachers leave their rooms in a disorderly mess at the end of the school day. Address these issues. What steps will you take to reduce the implications these complaints have? What might you do to avoid being blindsided by such things?

4. Review the ISLLC standards in Appendix B, especially the functions listed in Standard 3. Which of the standards items relate to the material presented in this chapter? Identify one function that links directly to a concept expressed in Chapter 13.

ENDNOTES

1. Dr. Bratton is the principal of Christianberry Elementary School, Knoxville (TN) Public Schools.

2. A good source of ideas is John C. Pijanowsik and David H. Monk, "Alternative School Revenues," *School Business Affairs* (1996): 4–10.

3. Bratton, Ibid.

4. See Chapter 3 for a discussion of the GII, CII, CI, AII, and AI decision processes.

5. Dr. Susan Wey, former elementary school principal and now central office administrator, Fort Bend (TX) Independent School District.

6. Dr. James Cain, superintendent, Klein (TX) Independent School District.

SELECTED READINGS

Clover, M. W., E. B. Jones, W. Bailey, and B. Griffin. "Budget Priorities of Selected Principals: Relocation of State Funds." *NASSP Bulletin 88* (September 2004): 69–82.

Kedro, M. "Controlling the Purse Strings." *Principal Leadership 3,* no. 5 (2003): 19–23.

Kennedy, M. "Maintenance" *American School & University 80*, no. 6 (2008): 16.

Mabry, V. "The Principal's Role in School Fundraising." *Principal 84* (2005): 51–54.

McNeil, M. "Budgeting, Tax Trims in Conflict." *Education Week 27,* no. 22 (2008): 1.

Owing, W. A., and L. S. Kaplan. "School Finance as Investment in Human Capital." *NASSP Bulletin 88,* no. 640 (2004): 12–28.

Reyes, Augustina, and Gloria M. Rodriguez. "School Finance: The Russian Novel," in *Current Issues in School Leadership,* ed. Larry W. Hughes (Mahwah, NJ: Erlbaum, 2005).

Snider, J. "Democratize School Budget Data." *Education Week 28,* no. 32 (2009): 22–23. Retrieved June 23, 2009, from Education Full Text database.

Sorenson, Richardson D., and Lloyd M. Goldsmith. *The Principal's Guide to School Budgeting* (Los Angeles: Corwin Press, 2006).

14 Technology Applications for School Management

Moore's Law: "Computing capacity, as measured by the speed of microprocessors, doubles on the average of every eighteen months." Metcalf's Law: "The value of a network increases in direct proportion to the square of the number of machines that are on it."

—THOMAS M. SIEBEL AND PAT HOUSE[1]

As Jim sat down at his desk, he touched his computer keyboard to activate the screen. It had become almost as automatic as turning on the lights, except his computer stayed on all the time, except weekends. Jim first checked his e-mail for important messages. Although he belonged to a number of professional listservs, the filter on his e-mail program filed them automatically so they did not clutter up his incoming e-mail. He reviewed his incoming central-office e-mail, noted that the new budget proposals for next year were to be sent today, and looked to see if any of his staff members had contacted him. He then sent several notes to his secretary to include in the daily e-mail bulletin to teachers. Notices to students were posted on the school Web calendar that appeared on monitors throughout the school but had the added advantage of being accessible to students and parents from home.

Jim next reached into his shirt pocket and pulled out his BlackBerry smart cell phone and added the budget reminder as item 8 to those previously listed. Touching another key, his daily appointments appeared, and Jim noted that his 8:30 appointment was with the parents of Dan Hoglund. Realizing he needed to review Dan's case, he returned to his computer, entered the student database, entered his password, and requested the discipline file for Hoglund. He printed out the dates of incidents of the past year from Dan's discipline file as well as the detailed reports that had been entered by the counselor at Dan's suspension several days earlier.

In his few remaining minutes while waiting for the 8:30 conference, Jim made several edits on the screen to rough drafts of letters his secretary had typed for him the previous day. He did not work this way much anymore, but rather found that for many shorter letters he could compose more quickly at the keyboard than on his old "yellow pad."

Later, after his conference with the Hoglunds, Jim returned to his computer and entered into the discipline record a short note indicating the result of Dan's conference. Jim next loaded his electronic spreadsheet into the computer on which he had been preparing his new budget. He entered the several changes he had been contemplating, checked his updated totals, and printed a copy of the revised budget document to share with his department heads in his afternoon meeting.

Continuing his preparation for his afternoon department heads' meeting, Jim loaded his presentation graphics and spreadsheet programs. He quickly created four bulleted slides to outline his points and found the spreadsheet that contained the data he needed to support his positon. He highlighted the critical numbers and generated several graphs to illustrate findings. He saved them in a file that he could access from the conference room on the interactive whiteboard via the school computer wireless network.

The initial tasks completed, Jim turned to a review of the final draft of the new student handbook. This edition will be published as a Web document, saving the cost of paper printing, making the handbook available to students, parents, and staff at any time, and allowing for more frequent updates when desired. Paper-printed copies will be printed from computer printers on an as needed basis.

Do Jim's activities go beyond what you are doing as a teacher or administrator? Every one of the functions identified during Jim's busy morning on his computer and BlackBerry is in common use by administrators today. Electronic mail as a part of a local area network (LAN), word processing, desktop publishing, Smart-cell-phone-based daily reminders and calendars, student record systems, spreadsheets, and Web applications, as well as many more useful applications, are available for school principals. And the cost of software and hardware is not high. The potential saving in time can be great, and the access to more information for more effective administration is tremendous.

National Educational Technology Standards

The International Society for Technology in Education (ISTE) released its new National Educational Technology Standards (NETS) for Administrators in 2009. These standards are designed to help guide educational leaders in making wise decisions regarding technology and how it is used in schools. The standards are broadly stated and effectively lay out five areas of concern*:

1. *Visionary Leadership.* Inspire and lead development and implementation of a shared vision for comprehensive integration of technology to promote excellence and support transformation throughout the organization
2. *Digital-Age Learning Culture.* Create and sustain a dynamic, digital-age learning culture that provides a rigorous, relevant education for all students.

*Used with permission of ISTE.

3. *Excellence in Professional Practice.* Promote an environment of professional learning and innovation that empowers educators to enhance student learning through the infusion of contemporary technologies and digital resources.

4. *Systemic Transformation.* Provide leadership and management to continuously improve the organization through the effective use of information and technology resources.

5. *Digital Citizenship.* Model and facilitate understanding of social, ethical and legal issues and responsibilities related to an evolving digital culture.[2]

This chapter considers these technology standards as a framework for action and suggests actions and cautions to be considered by the school administrator.

Technology Plans

As a visionary educational leader, one of your responsibilities as principal will be the development of a technology plan with your staff and community. The plan should maximize the use of technology in meeting the administrative needs of your school as well as the curricular and instructional needs.

ISLLC 1

Technology planning must be a part of the overall school improvement plans; it is not a stand-alone area. It should be based on a vision of what the school community wants the school to be in the future and include a specific set of basic beliefs that have been agreed upon by the school faculty and staff. Figure 14.1 shows a set of basic beliefs from a technology plan for a K–8 elementary school.

Plans should be developed to span a number of years. Five-year plans, annually updated, are commonly used time frames. Topics may include these:

- Technology integration into the curriculum
- Technology integration into school management
- Teacher, student, and staff training in technology utilization
- Expected student technology competencies

Technology Culture

What is the culture of your school regarding the use of technology? What values and beliefs are expressed by your faculty through their use of technology? Is technology enthusiastically embraced by almost all your faculty? Maybe not. Is it resisted or ignored by most of your faculty?

ISLLC 2

Let's hope not. The second NETS standard suggests your job is to create "a digital-age learning culture" in your school.

One of the ways to begin to influence a culture is to model the desired behavior and values you wish to be adopted. An educational administrator needs to use the latest technology in front of the staff and encourage them in appropriate use of technology. For principals who are not "techies," ask a technology coordinator in the school or district to provide some assistance or have a teacher—or in some cases a student—be your technology coach. As in the scenario introducing this chapter, learn to use the technology you wish your teachers to use. In the process, you will find many efficiencies of operation for your own administrative tasks.

Here are some suggestions. School administrators must encourage the use of efficient technologies in the operation of school's administrative offices. Office workers as well as teachers

FIGURE 14.1 Pi Beta Phi's Five-Year Technology Plan: Basic Beliefs

In order to accomplish the goal of providing "diverse opportunities for students to learn to live in a rapidly changing and increasingly complex, multicultural society," technological resources must be utilized. Students must learn how to use the tools of the present to participate effectively in the economy of the future. Our school must identify important technological skills and make certain that our curriculum and instruction allow students to learn and practice those skills, while at the same time learning and practicing traditional academics. Technology provides the current tools that allow people to work, create, and communicate. Pi Beta Phi's responsibility is to integrate those tools into the larger web of math, language arts, science, social studies, visual arts, music, health, and physical education.

- The first step in this process is to develop how to most effectively use technology in teaching the rest of the curriculum.

- The second step is to determine what resources are necessary to accomplish that aim. In the selection and adoption of these resources, the following beliefs will serve as our guide.

  — Curriculum and instruction must be continually assessed.

  — Technology supports opportunities for significant student achievement.

  — All teachers and students need access to computer workstations.

  — All students must develop technological competencies.

  — All teachers need to utilize appropriate technologies for management and for instruction.

  — Students and teachers adapt to change at different rates.

  — Technological training should be ongoing in response to assessed individual needs and interests as well as to the identified needs of the school.

  — Effective use of worldwide educational resources requires utilization of current and appropriate technology.

- Expected faculty and staff technology competencies

- Specifications for hardware acquisitions

- Specifications for software acquisitions

- Source of funds for computer acquisitions

need to have frequent opportunities for development in the use of the latest technology. This means it is important to provide recent computer models for all administrators, office staff, and teachers, models capable of being networked together from a common server or webtop[3] for ease of file sharing and transfer. All users should have access to a good office suite of software such as *Microsoft Office*[4] or webtop software such as Google Docs or its equivalent. These office programs include software for word processing, presentation graphics, and spreadsheet capability. A program such as Microsoft's OneNote[5] is a tool to help principals and teachers stay organized.

Communication Using Technology

Technology has dramatically changed our ability to communicate with each other. As school administrators, we have opportunities to stay in touch with parents, students, community, and other professional educators like never before. This section of the chapter identifies many of the tools available—e-mail, webpages, telephone message systems, texting, social networks, blogs, and podcasts—to enhance principals' communication efforts with teachers, students, parents, and community.

School Website

A school website provides an opportunity to present a positive image of the school to the local community and to provide a solid information link to the parents of the children served by the school. It is the face of the school to the outside world; see Figure 14.2.

A good school website can contain a variety of semipermanent items, such as the school's mission statement; policies, rules, and regulations for the school; and names of the building administrators and staff members, including e-mail addresses and phone numbers. Similar information can be provided for key district administrators. Information can also be listed about school clubs and other school-related organizations. Parents can be encouraged to communicate with teachers and administrators via e-mail. A principal's newsletter published on the website on a weekly basis is an excellent way for the principal to keep parents and students informed.[6] Remember, however, that not all families have access to the Web, so other communication links must also be used. When putting children's pictures on a website, be sure to have parents sign a release form.

The part of the website that contains the following items should be expected to change frequently: school calendar of events for the week, month, and year; classroom news and announcements, including planned activities and homework assignments for each class; special school or classroom projects; breakfast and lunch menus; and educational links that provide resources for students and parents at home. A special page might celebrate school and student successes. Be sure to carefully consider in the school's technology policy any limits that need to be placed on children's identities in Web publications.

A faculty member or technology coordinator should be in charge of developing and maintaining the webpage. This person is often called the webmaster. However, all teachers should be taught webpage construction so they can maintain a presence for their classroom, club, or activity. Any materials they develop can be forwarded to the webmaster to integrate into the school site. Special software is available to aid in the construction of multiple-page sites.

The school website can also be maintained by a local service provider specializing in school website design and service. Using a standard school template, many companies charge only a small fee to design and maintain a website for a school. These services also bundle podcasting abilities, blog management, translation services, and other options. The school staff needs only to provide the content.

E-mail

E-mail is a very convenient communication tool for searching individuals as well as large groups of people both inside and outside the school. Many school announcements to teachers and staff can be quickly and efficiently sent using a listserv (a selected list of e-mail addresses to whom a message can be sent simultaneously). Members of the school community should be able to send e-mails to each other, but their e-mail addresses need to remain private and not be accessible from outside, if at all possible. On the other hand, each teacher and administrator needs to have a public e-mail address that is available to parents and community members.

FIGURE 14.2   Greeneville High School Website. Used by permission.

 HOME  CONTACT  DIRECTIONS  PARENT INFORMATION  STAFF ONLY

News & Events
  Latest News
  Calendar
  Principal's Corner
  About The School
  Handbook
  School Publications
  School Staff
  Forms
  Spotlight

Academics
  Daily Schedule
  Fine Arts
  Library

Community
  We R GHS
  Clubs & Organizations
  Guidance
  Community Services
  State Report Card
  ParentConnect
  My School Cast Login

Athletics
  Sports

Alumni
  Alumni

Staff Resources
  Munis
  NetTrekker
  Call Track
  Gaggle
  Install TekNet
  Web Mail
  United Streaming
  Instructional Technology

Teacher Resources
  Virtual Field Trips
  Free Audio Books
  Stories and Essays in MP3
  Google Lit Trips
  LibriVox

Latest News
  Last Day
  Graduation Info
  Soccer
  Student council Representatives
  Senior Banquet
  Summer School
  Locker Clean Out
  State Track Meet
  Student of the Day
  Class Rings

District News
  Greenville City Schools Annual Report and
  Five Year Plan
  2nd Annual Foothills Film Festival!
  Only the Best! May 2009
  2009 Upper East Tennessee Science Fair
  Cell Phones in the Classrrom
  2009 Character Education Awards

This Week At A Glance

School Events

5/20/2009
• Tennis: State Tournament
• Track TSSAA State Meet

5/21/2009
• Track TSSAA State Meet
• Tennis: State Tournament
• Credit Recovery Day

5/22/2009
• Tennis: State Tournament
• Track TSSAA State Meet
• Graduation Practice
  Time: 10:00 A.M.
• Graduation
  Time: 7:00 P.M.
• GHS Graduation–Hal Henard
  Time: 7:00 P.M.

Source: Greeneville High School Website.

For e-mail messages to be sent by the school to a portion or all of its community, the school information system(SIS) should include e-mail addresses for all. A well-designed, in-school e-mail program can tell the system to send a message to all teachers in the middle school or all parents of third-graders—and the system will know exactly who should receive the message.

School administrators also need the ability to terminate a user's access to the school directory when and if necessary, and the school should be able to choose what information is displayed in the school directory. If student e-mail is not part of a well-designed SIS, stand-alone student e-mail systems are available that provide a collection of filtering and monitoring devices to monitor content. Gaggle is a good example of such software.[7]

Telephone Message Delivery Systems

A telephone message delivery system that can rapidly "push out" school messages to parents is a valuable tool that gives all parents access to important information via the telephone. Such a system can help families stay informed about school events and can even make a difference in their child's education, increase attendance, and improve grades. Telephone message delivery systems serve a great variety of school communication needs:

ISLLC 4, 6

- School cancellation
- Bus delay announcements
- Volunteer opportunities
- Attendance messages
- Customized messages
- Emergency messages such as snow days
- Reminder of report cards being sent home
- Reminder for standardized testing day
- Athletic event announcement
- Announcements of PTA/PTO meetings
- Announcements of back-to-school night
- Rumor abatement
- Reminder for field trip permission slip
- Reminder for free or reduced cost lunch eligibility
- Reminder for parent–teacher conferences

In some schools, many parents are not connected to the Internet or if they are connected, they do not use it. So even though the Internet and school websites are a quick and easy way to make information available, they need to be supplemented by other communication to reach everyone. Telephone message delivery systems can make sure that everyone gets the message; they add a communication link to the Internet and printed material sent home. Parents are thus informed regardless of their personal situation.

A number of companies known as application service providers (ASPs) market telephone delivery systems for schools. The ones that seem to be providing the better service are those that are Internet based.[8] These services are able to push out thousands of phone calls in only a few minutes from their computerized call centers and multiple phone lines. Some of the services they provide include these:

- Select calling based on information provided by the school district (e.g., Ms. Jone's fifth-grade class or the families of the boys on the football team)
- Message translation services for multiple-language transmissions based on the language information provided by the school
- Two-way communication, by providing response message boxes for faculty and staff
- Customizable surveys with telephone keypad responses
- Calls based on a parent-selected time schedule for hard to reach parents
- Multiple attempts for phones not answered or messages received by answering devices

Instant Messaging (Texting)

The use of the cell phone to send typed messages instead of voice messages has grown greatly. Texting is a quick and efficient way to send brief messages or to carry on a conversation with someone where voice contact is not always appropriate. Young people have become so attracted to texting that its misuse has become a discipline concern in many schools. Student use and control of cell phones is discussed later in this chapter.

As a communication tool, texting offers another legitimate avenue to reach parents and others interested in what is happening in school. For example, Twitter[9] is becoming a networking tool for the school to use as a parent or community contact. It can be used in this way: A verified Twitter account is opened in the name of the school and announced on the school webpage. Parents are encouraged to join as friends (similar to joining a social network such as Facebook) who will receive all school announcements (tweets in the language of Twitter) on their cell phone or computer. Messages are sent in a text form and can be no more than 140 characters in length. Twitter is quick and free way to send short announcements and emergency messages to all who have joined. In this way, it is similar to the push-out voice message services discussed earlier. Multiple accounts can be opened to reach special groups. For example, open an account with only teachers and staff as members to use as a school emergency communication.

Telephone and Web-Based School Surveys

Every school administrator needs to know what parents or the local school community thinks about a variety of school issues: It may be a proposed change in the school calendar, it may be a suggested change in the report card, or it may be a question to the parents of eighth-graders about a proposed school trip. A number of software products and services are available to quickly ask and receive answers to such questions. Some are automated telephone surveys that are sent out through a telephone messaging service like the ones described in the previous section. A survey can be sent out to an audience selected by the school administrator from the school database of phone numbers of parents or other community members. Responses to the questions are sent by touching certain numbers on the phone keypad; responses are recorded and tallied. Obviously the questions for telephone surveys must be simple and short with simple answers. Most of telephone service companies provide this survey option along with their messaging service.

ISLLC 4, 6

Web-based surveys also provide a way to collect information. Using e-mail addresses of your intended target respondents, software such as InstantSurvey, SurveyMonkey, Phonelink, or your own SIS can broadcast, receive, and tabulate survey data.[10]

Social and Professional Networks

The development of professional and community networks contributes to the success of every school administrator. Traditionally, administrators did this by collecting business cards and setting up a contact list, but today there are better ways. Electronic social networks such as Facebook, Twitter, TeacherTube, and LinkedIn offer tools to the school administrator to reach out for information and support in ways not previously available.[11] These networks, with members worldwide or local, provide the school administrator with a way to keep in touch with close friends but also to reach out to contacts not otherwise readily available. For example, LinkedIn, a favorite because it is largely a network of professionals, works like this. When you join, you create a profile that summarizes your professional expertise and accomplishments. The next step is to begin to form connections by inviting trusted contacts to join LinkedIn and connect to you. Your network consists of your connections, your connections' connections, and the people they know—linking you to a vast number of qualified professionals and experts. Facebook works in a similar way to LinkedIn, whereas Twitter functions more like texting to all your friends at the same time on a cell phone or computer.

Administrator Education Blogs

A *blog* (a contraction of the term *weblog*) is a type of website or part of a website that is usually maintained by an individual with regular entries of commentary, descriptions of events, or other material such as graphics or video. Entries are commonly displayed in reverse chronological order.[12] Many administrators choose a blog format to communicate with their stakeholders: daily announcements to teachers under a principal-to-teacher blog, daily announcements to students posted on a principal-to-student blog, and announcements to parents and other community members on a principal-to-parent blog. These blogs can then be posted on the school webpage for the day and archived for future reference. The blog can reference with a hyperlink other published activities to which the principal wishes to draw attention. For example, the principal may wish to draw attention to audio or video recordings of school events posted as podcasts on the school website or can include a hyperlink embedded in the blog. A number of Internet sites provide the software to help set up and administer a blog.[13]

Blogs are also extremely beneficial to the administrator as a source of information. A daily scan of several major blogs will keep the principal current on the day's news and discussions. Several of the major education news sources provide lists of education blogs, each focusing on a particular theme of current interest to educators. Two current sources of on going blogs are ASCD and This Week in Education.[14]

Podcasts

Podcasts are either audio records or audio/video records (video podcasts) that are posted on the Web to be downloaded for viewing or listening. There are thousands of educational podcasts posted on the Web and available to be downloaded. Many podcasts can be useful for teachers in their classrooms; almost any school subject at every grade level can be found. In addition, many podcasts are excellent staff-development tools to help improve teaching techniques.[15]

Locally produced podcasts are of equal or greater value than these produced elsewhere. They have many useful purposes in schools when posted on the school's or teacher's website. Classroom uses might include teacher lectures recorded for later review by students, student presentations to be viewed by other students or parents, and guest lectures presented to one class and then made available to others.

On the administrative side, podcasts might include performances by student groups, which can be made available to parents and others; the principal's announcements to teachers; good teacher practices to be shared with other teachers in the building; and professional development events recorded for later reference. All of these are examples of locally recorded events that can be placed on the website for later viewing or listening.

Many of the website software packages have a podcast component built in. Also, there are a number of free Internet sites that provide software and guidance to produce quality podcast products.[16]

Education Electronic Newsletters

Important sources of current information useful to school administrators are the electronic newsletters sent out several times each week by professional education organizations These publications generally scan all of the major education news sources in the United States as well as other English-speaking countries of the world. Articles are selected from these sources and are presented as a brief summary of contents a hyperlink takes you to the original publication. ASCD SmartBriefs, Education Week Update, and NASSP Principal's Update are examples of these services.[17]

ISLLC 4

Cell Phones

Administrator Smart Phones

The smart phone is fast becoming a useful aid to the busy administrator. Its capabilities as a data source, time saver, and convenience tool for the administrator are virtually unmatched by any other electronic device. Besides being a mobile phone, the smart phone is capable of doing so much more for the administrator who is frequently on the move and not stationed, at a desk for much of the day. Several of the school information systems discussed in the following section have mobile applications that allow for the downloading of many forms of local school information directly onto a smart phone. For example, the principal should have immediately available the school calendar as well as his or her personal calendar. The database with staff and student information, including student pictures, can also be available on the smart phone. E-mail communication is immediately available as is access to the Web.

Student Cell Phones

Every student has a handheld computer provided by the student's parents at no cost to the school— a dream? No. For most of us it is already a reality. Cell phones labeled as 3G (third generation)

FIGURE 14.3   Greeneville High School Cell Phone Policy. Used by permission.

Greeneville High School Cell Phone Policy

1. Students are not permitted to use or have cell phones in sight from the time they arrive at school until 2:40 P.M.

2. Students are allowed to use their cell phone for reasonable communication purposes in or out of the building after 2:40, unless otherwise designated at specific school functions.

3. The taking of photos or the recording of videos, whether by cell phone or any other device, in places where privacy is a reasonable expectation is strictly prohibited. An incident of this nature could result in a sexual harassment violation.

4. Using cell phone cameras to record altercations on school grounds or at school events is prohibited. In such cases, phones may be confiscated as evidence.

5. Students are allowed to use the cell phones in the classrooms for educational purposes only and must be under the direct supervision of their teacher.

6. Under teacher direction, cell phones are to be placed on student desks in the "off" or "quiet" mode at the beginning of each class period.

Consequences for Cell Phone Policy Violations

1. Violation of the above policy with result in the student's cell phone being confiscated for seven days.

2. Students may choose to have their cell phone returned before the end of the seven days by paying a twenty dollar (cash only) fine at the end of the school day in the main office.

3. An administrator will be contacted if the student refuses to give up the phone for a violation, or if student turns in a "dummy" phone. The student's insubordination will result in a level 2 offense.

Source: Greeneville High School Website.

phones or later are, in fact, small computers with more capacity than many laptops. The question is, how are we going to treat them? Do we see them as an opportunity or do we see them as a problem? They are in fact both. In the hands of students they need to be controlled, but they also are great instructional tools. Each school must have a cell phone policy to lay out the framework for their use in and around the school.[18] Figure 14.3 illustrates one high school's student cell phone policy.

Note items 5 and 6 in Figure 14.3. This school actively encourages the appropriate uses cell phones in many classrooms as learning aids. Remember, cell phones can be used to make calls, text, e-mail, connect with the Internet, take pictures, and make videos. All have instructional value. The Greenville High School endnote lists some valuable Web locations—ranging from mobile search services from Google and ChaCha to cell phone applications that allow groups of individuals to vote in user-generated polls using mobile phone texting capabilities and an active website posting results. The cell phone becomes an audience response system (ARS), with the phone acting as the clicker device.[19] For students who do not have personal cell phones, some schools have negotiated with the district provider of staff cell phones to provide the school with several classroom sets of the latest phone technology so that phones are available for classroom use.

School Information Systems

For many schools, little aggregation of student data takes place. Information from different parts of the school organization is often kept in separate files, redundant, and difficult to share. Schools generally maintain huge amounts of information in areas such as student records, teacher assignment information, student assessment data, transportation information, food service records, library records, school financial data, special education records, and so on. The technologies used to manage these data are often incompatible, even within the same school or school district. This prevents anyone from really looking at the "big picture" across all the datasets that are part of schools. Software to support a newer concept of file storage and file sharing, called *data warehousing,* has emerged to aggregate previously stored data from separate data systems using software designed to connect all information and technologies. This new methodology of data warehousing, along with school information systems, is making it possible for schools to develop new analyses and reports that draw from several databases.

A well-designed school information system (SIS) integrates a wide range of information needs and sources for administrators, teachers, students, and parents. Features can include many of the following: school scheduling, calendars, e-mail, file management, teacher records, medical clinic records, report cards, and customized reports. SIS software systems available range from very complex, large-school commercial systems to very inexpensive or free open-access, stand-alone systems.[20]

An SIS should provide school administrators access to data that are current, and the system should be simple to manage. It should give users ways to self-manage their own data and tasks, which relieve the burden on school administrators and information technology (IT) personnel. A good system should eliminate redundant data entry and other tasks by automating and expediting repetitive processes.

Teachers' lives can be made simpler by automating routine tasks and giving them tools to make the education process more engaging for students. Grade-book programs integrated with other school records can reduce grading tasks to one entry, thereby eliminating redundancies. Features such as teacher blogs, discussion boards, customizable quiz generator, and the ability to create and track assignments online should be options. Routines can be created that simplify and encourage teachers' communication with students and parents.

Most students love new technology. Some parts of an SIS can be designed specifically for direct student access to keep them interested in and involved with their own education by allowing them to monitor their progress, stay organized, track assignments, and access class resources. Communication with teachers and other students can be expanded through class blogs and discussion groups.

Educators know that parental involvement is a vital factor in student success. Giving parents an easy way to be proactive in their children's education and involved with the school community will enhance student learning. An SIS can create opportunities for parents to update their personal accounts, including contact information, and to fill in permission slips and other forms online, which also lessens management burdens for schools. Parents can sign up to volunteer for events, view their children's commitments and assignments, communicate with teachers, and receive progress reports.

An SIS should include specific modules designed for efficient management of school data. Brief descriptions of some key areas follow.

Calendars

An SIS must have the capability to create, manage, and share multiple calendars and events with minimal effort. As the school administrator, you may want to maintain a variety of different school-related calendars. Here are four suggestions:

- A *personal calendar* that includes all of the appointments and events for which you are specifically responsible. You may wish to maintain this calendar on your smart phone, as did the principal in the opening scenario of this chapter.
- A *school master calendar* that includes all special activities that are school related (see Figure 14.4).
- A *building utilization calendar* on which all reservations for public spaces are recorded such as the auditorium, gymnasium, cafeteria, and conference room
- A *personnel calendar* that indicates all the times when someone is *not* going to be in the building. This type of calendar is valuable when substitutes need to be hired or personnel need to be reassigned. Included would be teachers who will be at a conference or have requested a personal day and the times that administrators will be at meetings away from the school.

Once created, an entire calendar or a specific event should be able to be shared with an individual or a predefined group. School-related events can be made to automatically appear on the appropriate parties' calendars. For example, a student's homework assignments and exams appear immediately on his or her calendar once a teacher has posted the information. Teachers' calendars can be made to show schoolwide events, along with the many dates teachers must keep track of. Parents can easily see their children's commitments. All users should be able to subscribe to any particular group's calendars and determine which events need to be added to their own master calendar. Reminders from the master schedule can be sent prior to any scheduled event.

File Management

An SIS should allow administrators to create common folders and give read-only or read/write access to individual users or groups of users or give privileges based on a user's role. It should be possible to easily share files with anyone in the system, thereby avoiding multiple copies of the same file. When providing access to student data, remember, the restrictions established by the Family Educational Rights and Privacy Act (FERPA). Password control systems can provide access to only those eligible to view certain student documents.

Clinic Records

Student health information and medical records can be a critical part of the information maintained about students. Often these records are filed away in the school clinic, but in reality they are essential when emergencies arise. School nurses need to manage a variety of medical information: allergies, immunizations, prescriptions, emergency contact information, insurance, and a log of medication distributions. One of the components of a good school SIS is a retrievable file of student information. Records, of course, must be kept private; allow access only to eligible staff with a password protection system.

Sunday	Monday	Tuesday	Wednesday	Thursday	Friday	Saturday
N				**1**	**2**	**3**
4 **O**	**5** 3:20—Faculty Meeting	**6** ELECTION DAY Student Holiday	**7**	**8**	**9**	**10**
11 **V E**	**12** 3:20—Faculty Meeting	**13** NUTRITION DAY WORKSHOP 3:20—Leadership Team Meeting	**14** MAKE-UP DAY FOR PICTURES	**15** STUDENTS FROM LITTLE WORLD TO TALK TO K–5 9:30–12:00	**16**	**17**
18 **M B**	**19** 9:15—K & 1 Program Marty Silver Environmentalist 3:20—Faculty Meeting	**20** End of Third Month 9:00 2nd Grade Play K, 1, 3, & Multi-Age 9:15—4 & 3 Program Marty Silver Environmentalist 1:00 2nd Grade Play K, 4	**21** End of Six Weeks 9:15—2 & 3 Program Marty Silver Environmentalist 10:30 Singers leave for Gatlinburg 2:00 Singers Program at Gatlinburg	**22** THANKSGIVING HOLIDAYS	**23**	**24**
25 **E R**	**26** 3:20—Faculty Meeting	**27** The Clue That Turned Blue 10:00–K, 1st, 2nd Multi 10:30–3rd, 4th, & 5th 3:20—Leadership Team Meeting	**28** Progress Reports go out 8:30–11:30 Bledsoe—Ijani's Park Bivens—Airport	**29**	**30** Kindergarten— "Nutcracker"	

FIGURE 14.4 School Master Calendar

Report Generator

The SIS needs to be capable of extracting data from any module in order to generate, publish, and share reports that accurately convey a range of student and school information. The system should be able to track trends and view statistics for individual students, the entire school, or within-population subgroups. It should also filter retrieved data according to specific criteria—date, time, gender, grade level, age, and more. If a report fulfills a requirement for a regulatory organization, it should be possible for it to be customized so that it conforms to specific state reporting requirements. Remember to save the format for reuse next time the same report is needed. Examples of reports an administrator may wish to produce are listed next.

1. *Community Parent Profile.* This is a summary profile of all the parents of the children in the school, showing the percentage of each educational level, number of single-parent homes, type of occupations, percentage originally from outside the area, number of children in the family, and so on. Analysis of this type of information is useful in developing a better understanding of a student population and its needs.

2. *New Enrollee Analysis.* This report consists of a listing of the new enrollments for each year by month, with information regarding each student's previous school, condition of transfer, and success in your school using grade-point orange (GPA) or test score comparisons.

3. *Departing Student Analysis.* This is similar to the enrollment analysis.

4. *Excessive Absence List.* This is a list by name of all students with more than X number of days absent, showing total days enrolled and days absent. Also, dates and days of the week of each absence are indicated. The report might indicate which absences were not excused and if a disciplinary file, particularly truancy, exists on the student. A cross-check on the attendance of siblings is possible as well. If the list is to be used to contact parents, then their names, phone numbers, and addresses could be included as well to speed the follow-up process.

5. *Excessive Tardy Report.* This report could be similar to the excessive absence report. It might also be the basis for notification letters sent home using the merge feature on the word processor (part of good information management is keeping parents informed as well).

6. *Exceptional Student Report.* This is a list by grade and teacher, at the end of each grading period, of all students with a GPA greater than 3.5, 3.0 to 3.5, and less than 1.5. Special notations can be included for those who were not in these categories during the previous reporting period.

7. *Proficiency Test Report.* This is a list of those students by grade, teacher, and subject area who have not passed certain components of the proficiency test.

8. *Student Disciplinary Report.* A student disciplinary report can be a list of recent disciplinary cases by student and offense, or perhaps only a summary report indicating the number of cases, stating offense category and case disposition.

9. *Achievement Test Analysis.* This is a list of students showing achievement test score gains higher than expected over previous achievement test scores. It is also a list of all students showing achievement test scores lower than expected from previous achievement test scores reported by subject area and teacher.

Scheduling

Although school master schedules are discussed in detail in Chapter 12, they are part of the SIS system. Much of the information needed to construct a master schedule is drawn from the SIS databases. A good scheduling program analyzes available information and determines optimal class times to minimize potential conflicts, while taking into account classroom types, class size limits, student or parent requests, registrations holds, and course prerequisites. A good scheduler also supports irregular timing intervals, one-time class meetings, and holiday or early dismissal schedules. The program should be capable of creating schedules that are almost conflict-free with flexible, user-defined constraints for rooms, instructors, and students. Teachers and students should be able to view and print their daily schedules.

ISLLC 3

Student Records

The student record component of the SIS tracks a wide array of biographical, academic, and personal information in order to gain insight into the strengths, weaknesses, and character of each student in the school. The system should keep detailed records of a student's academic and personal information, allowing schools to maintain organized historical and current records. Vital information should be trackable from year to year. Access needs to be strictly limited to administrators to ensure that sensitive information is kept private. Demographic data—including ethnic background, languages spoken, and information about legal guardians and siblings—as well as emergency contacts and medical records are necessary to create a full picture of every student.

Report Cards

A report card program is most useful when integrated into the larger SIS. The SIS can be designed to provide opportunity to review, approve, and publish student report cards, progress reports, and transcripts. The software should set up a smooth workflow among administrators, teachers, and parents. Teachers prepare final reports, adding personalized or predefined comments, and send them directly to administrators for review and approval. Upon approval, the reports can be either printed or delivered electronically to parents. A good program will have security; that is, it will control access to sensitive information by determining who can view grades and specifying the grade level(s) to which each teacher has access.

Course Management Systems

Another approach to managing teachers' records is to use a course management system (CMS), which generally includes most of the record components of a grade-book program. A CMS is generally Internet-based software that creates and distributes course content, enabling teachers to extend the classroom beyond its traditional boundaries of time and space. Such a system can be used to supplement conventional courses by making available Web-based materials either posted directly by the teacher or via hyperlinks leading to other Web-based information. A CMS can help to completely organize a conventional course, by managing attendance, accepting completed assignments, administering exams, and providing opportunities for students to communicate remotely with each other or with the teacher via discussion boards, chat rooms, e-mail, and so forth. As students gain more direct access to the Internet via home computers, classroom computers, and portable devices such as laptops or cell phones, it is logical to begin to organize instruction directly on the Internet.

Although there are a number of good stand-alone CMS programs on the market, it is extremely desirable to have one that is linked directly with the SIS. A CMS program gives teachers an array of tools designed to lighten their workload. It should make readily available the information teachers need to monitor every student's academic progress. In fact, the CMS needs to be like a small SIS working on the teachers' behalf. This program should assist teachers to input and maintain grades, create and manage assignments, record attendance, and track disciplinary issues. It might also produce graphs and charts that allow teachers to identify particular types of students or track overall class performance, and have the capability of posting assignments online for students to download, complete, and return electronically or by hand.

A number of commercial CMS software packages designed for use with K–12 schools are available for purchase, for example, Blackboard Learning System.[21] There are, however, a growing number of excellent products that are free, open-source alternatives to Blackboard; Moodle, Claroline, and Sakai Project[22] are example. Even though these programs are in a sense free, they require a level of expertise and support that may not always be available in the local school. As a result, a number of software support service firms offer (for a fee) assistance in training teachers and managing operations for CMS products. A Google search can provide lists of such services.

Other Software Applications for Administrators

Classroom Supervision

The use of technology for teacher supervision has several powerful applications. Classroom observations can be greatly enhanced with software designed to operate on handheld devices such as a tablet computer, personal digital assistant (PDA), or smart phone with fully customized rubrics to meet criteria of individual school districts. As a teacher is observed in the classroom, class learning time, on-task time, teacher talk, wait time, attention to gender, divergent and non-divergent questioning, as well as questioning based on levels of Bloom's Taxonomy, can be evaluated with easily generated reports. The data allow administrators to create a database of observation results so that specific variables can be evaluated for individual teachers and building-level analysis can be conducted. A variety of software products are on the market to meet the different needs of principals.[23]

Video recordings of segments of teacher-taught lessons are a valuable source of local knowledge. As part of the principal's classroom observations, videos of good teaching practices in the building can be recorded and posted on a staff-development section of the school website for other teachers to watch. A Flip Video Camera[24] or a similar product can be carried in a pocket to use at a moment's notice. Such cameras have a recording capacity of one to two hours. For shorter recordings, a camera-equipped smart phone with a memory card also works.

ISLLC 2

Financial Accounting Systems

Financial accounting is one of the most common applications for computers. With the increasing demand for highly detailed accounting, the computer becomes a natural solution as a highly accurate labor-saving tool. Specialized packages for accounting are available from most computer stores. These packages are generally designed for business use, however. Most often, only the general ledger component is needed for school accounting, and in many cases it can be purchased as a separate component. Simple accounting procedures can also be created from a database management system or formulated on spreadsheet software (see Figure 14.5). Many school districts standardize all of their schools on a common financial accounting system. An Internet search reveals many current products.

FIGURE 14.5   Budget Spreadsheet

DEPARTMENTAL BUDGET, 2011
Mathematics Department
Southeast Elementary   Month   October

BUDGET AREA AND ITEM	ALLOWABLE	EXP. THIS MONTH	EXP. TO DATE	REMAINDER
TEXTS (B-4)				
5th Modern Math	$ 500.00	497.00		3.00
Programmed Texts and Temac				
Binders 21 @ $10.50	220.50		220.50	—
Supplementary Texts	450.00		275.00	175.00
EQUIPMENT (D-4)				
Volume Distribution Set (1)	60.00		60.00	—
Graph Board (multipurpose) (1)	35.00			
Tightgrip Chalkholder (6)	6.00	1.00		5.00
Rack of Compasses	12.00		12.00	—
Rack of Protractors	15.00		15.00	—
SUPPLEMENTARY (B-6)				—
Universal Encyclopedia of Math (2)	20.00	20.00		
Other References	50.00			
AUDIOVISUAL (D-7)				—
Overhead Projector	175.00		175.00	
DISCRETIONARY SUPPLIES	100.00			
SUBTOTAL	$1,643.50	518.00	757.50	368.00
PERSONNEL (A-3)				
2 Consultants 2 days each for				
in-service expenses	900.00			
SUBTOTAL	$ 900.00			
TOTAL	$2,543.50	518.00	757.50	1268.00

School Forms—Online Downloading

Many school forms and records can be maintained electronically. All schools have filing cabinets full of school forms needed for varying purposes: special education documentation, vocational programs, maintenance requests, technology repairs, purchase orders, tardy slips, lesson plans— the list can go on and on. Several levels of records management are available to the school. Most basic is to make available blank record forms in a portable document format (PDF) of all basic forms by creating a file of master school forms available to all stakeholders. This allows the downloading of any form to a local printer, so all forms will be readily available. If desired, access limits can be placed on the file, making forms available only to appropriate subgroups.

Electronic response forms.   An electronic system may allow on-screen completion of a specific school form, printing of the completed form, and electronic return of the completed form to the appropriate location. Examples of such forms are an application for a job, a permission slip for a field trip, and a parent review and updating of a child's personnel information—address, phone, health information, and so on.

Records progress tracker.   When records are being returned electronically by teachers, students, or parents, it is sometimes difficult to determine which records are complete and which are still in process. A tracking system can be added to the electronic record response program to keep track of which records are complete, in process, or have not been activated.

Document Management Systems

Document imaging and management systems, along with document scanning hardware, allow a school to create a computer document file of records it receives as hard copy and retrieve the file on the computer screen. Medical records, parent letters, certificates, and even student art work can be stored in such a system. Document descriptors are entered by which the document can be retrieved, sorted, or selected, just as one would do with a regular electronic database.

Security

Hardware Security

Computer equipment, being expensive but relatively lightweight and compact, is highly vulnerable to theft, particularly in the open setting of a school. Particular caution needs to be taken to reduce this threat. The following actions are recommended to reduce loss:

1. Record all serial numbers on computers and related equipment. This will assist police in their investigation should equipment be stolen. Serial numbers further allow the police to place listings of stolen property in the NCIC (National Crime Information Center).
2. Stencil or burn the school name and location on the exterior surface of the computer in plain view. Also place identification markings on an unexposed area of your equipment.

3. Obtain security anchor pads, if available, from your vendor at the time of purchase, noting that time and effort will be involved in removing a device. This will prevent equipment from disappearing from open offices or classrooms during the day.
4. Be security conscious but be careful not to be so restrictive that it becomes inconvenient to use the equipment.

Building Security

Video surveillance systems are an excellent technology tool to monitor school premises. They are useful in monitoring school grounds 24/7 to aid in the protection of property, and they can help monitor and control student behavior during school hours. The two purposes, however, are different and generally require very different installations and placements. Of foremost importance is to protect the privacy of students and staff by keeping cameras in public areas like cafeterias, administrative offices, gymnasiums, and outdoor areas like playgrounds and sports fields.

There are many factors to consider when setting up a security system in your school. Consider the following questions and factors when setting up security cameras:

- What types of facilities are you monitoring?
- What do you consider to be your most pressing security threat?
- What kind of security do you currently have in place? Does your school district have security protocol that you must follow?
- Are there problems with crime and violence in your surrounding area?
- Have you ever wished that you caught a specific incident on camera?
- Are there areas in your school where students congregate that have caused problems (e.g., vandalism in schoolyards or on lockers)?
- Cameras mounted near main entrances and in administrative offices can help you record visitors as they enter and exit your school. Cameras near exits can also help reduce truancy.
- Fixed cameras can be strategically placed to protect valuables such as computers, sound equipment, trophies, and books.
- Outdoor surveillance cameras in parking lots can help protect older students and staff when they are leaving school late or arriving early. These cameras can also discourage break-ins and vandalism during school hours.[25]

Summary

This chapter presented many of the current applications of technology to school administration. Some of the applications are simply extensions and improvements of existing practices such as computer-based scheduling or student record systems. Others, such as the use of social networks as communication tools, are relatively new phenomena for school administrators. Nothing is changing in education more quickly than the availability and use of technology. New and improved products of both software and hardware reach the market almost daily. Prices continue to fall while capabilities continue to rise.

Some of the new ideas integrate with educational practice wonderfully, whereas others do not stand the test of time and fade away. The task as a school administrator is to choose wisely, selecting those solutions that will make best use of your time and effort and create the most benefit to the children of each school.

ACTIVITIES

1. Review Case Studies 3, 6, and 9 at the end of this book. Analyze the problems presented and apply the concepts of computer utilization developed in this chapter. How might these problems have been prevented if a good computer system had been in place? What approach would you use in addressing the problems identified in these cases? Set forth a strategy to overcome the difficulties faced by the school in each of these cases.

2. What are the greatest impediments to full computerization of schools? Apply the concepts of strategic planning set forth in Chapter 4 and the ideas on human resources development outlined in Chapter 9 to the impediments you have identified. Outline your plan of action.

3. Turn to the ISLLC standards found in Appendix B. Review the functions listed with Standard 2. How well are the technology and management performances carried out in your school? What would be some ways to improve the management of your school with technology?

ENDNOTES

1. Thomas M. Siebel and Pat House, *Cyber Rules* (New York: Currency/Doubleday, 1999), p. 8.
2. International Society for Technology in Education National Educational Technology Standards (2009): http://www.iste.org/Content/NavigationMenu/NETS/ForAdministrators/2009Stardards/NETS-A_2009.pdf.
3. A webtop is an operating system that lives on the Internet rather than on your computer. A webtop can also be an online workspace that can be accessed from anywhere you have an Internet connection and Web-enabled devices. All your software, files, and so forth are there waiting for you, so no matter what computer you're at, you have the same experience and everything you need. No need to buy the latest version of anything because it's all hosted on a cloud where the provider takes care of all of that for you. In addition, many webtops support various types of smart phones, so you truly have access from just about anywhere. When you buy a new computer, typically you need software to get things done, which can cost thousands of dollars. Most webtops have that software built in and ready to go. It is all hosted online so you don't have to worry about buying the latest version. Most webtops can be run from a less expensive netbook computer. And most have equivalents of the popular office software available; all you have to do is pick your favorite software and go with it. Best part is you're never locked into it, because you can always switch to another.
4. Microsoft Office is a product of Microsoft Corp.
5. OneNote allows you to take notes, then helps you save, organize, and retrieve notes and information. It includes search tools and a shared notebook that makes working together easier.
6. One example of a newsletter is the Eaton Rocketeer; go to http://www.loudoncounty.org/schools/eaton.jsp.
7. Gaggle: https://www.gaggle.net.
8. parentlink.net, alertnow.com, schoolreach.com, and Connect-ED.com are a few of the companies (and their Internet locations) that were application service providers in 2010. A Google can identify many more.
9. Twitter is a free social networking and microblogging service that enables its users to send and read other users' updates known as tweets. It can be found at http://twitter.com/
10. http://twitter.com/; *www.instantsurvey.com/;* www.surveymonkey.com/; www.parentlink.net
11. http://www.facebook.com; http://www.teachertube.com/; http://www.linkedin.com/
12. http://en.wikipedia.org/wiki/blog
13. Edublogs.org is a blog site with limited free services dedicated to educational institutions. Other blog service sites include Blogger, TypePad, WordPress, and LiveJournal.
14. http://www.smartbrief.com/news/ascd/blogs.jsp; http://scholasticadministrator.typepad.com/
15. http://www.videopodcasts.tv/category/8/Education; the Education Podcast Network http://epnweb.org
16. Education Podcast Network: http://epnweb.org; Gabcast: http://www.gabcast.com/
17. http://www.principals.org/update; www.r.smartbrief.com; www.newsletters@edweek.org
18. Cell phone use policy: http://www.nxtbook.com/nxtbooks/ena/getconnected_200905/#/2/
19. Go to http://www.learninginhand.com/; Greenville. High School: http://gcschools.net/ghs/Default.asp. Other good cell phone education sites: Google Short Message Services: http://www.google.com/intl/en_us/mobile/default/sms.html;ChaCha: http://www.chacha.com/; Poll Everywhere: http://www.polleverywhere.com; and Gcast: http://www.gcast.com
20. Pearson Products is one of the large suppliers of SIS software for any size school with its PowerSchool and PowerTeacher products: http://www.pearsonschoolsystems.com/products/

powerschool/. Another well-known product is Skyward: http://www.skyward.com/.
21. http://www.blackboard.com/
22. http://moodle.org/; http://www.claroline.net/; http://sakaiproject.org/.
23. Several good souces of teacher observation software are: http://www.ecove.net; http://www.pes-sports.com; and http://austinsky.com.

24. Flip Video can be found at http://www.theflip.com/en-us/buy/educators.aspx.
25. There are many suppliers of video surveillance systems and the technology changes rapidly. A Google search with consideration to your specific needs will produce a number of leads for a vendor.

SELECTED READINGS

Brooks-Young, S. *Self-Assessment Activities for School Administrators: A Companion to Make Technology Standards Work for You* (Eugene, OR: International Society for Technology in Education, 2004).

Buck, F. "Saving Time and Paper with Basic Technology." *Principal* (January/February 2007): 18–21.

Felton, F. S. The Use of Computers by Elementary School Principals. Doctoral dissertation, Virginia Polytechnic Institute and State University, 2006.

Flanagan, L. and M. Jacobsen "Technology Leadership for the Twenty-First Century Principal." *Journal of Educational Administration 41,* no. 2 (2003): 124–142.

Hines, C., S. Edmundson, and G. W. Moore. "The Impact of Technology on High School Principals." *NASSP Bulletin 92,* no. 4 (2008): 276–291.

Richardson, W. *Blogs, Wikis, Podcasts, and Other Powerful Web Looks for Classrooms,* (Thousand Oaks, CA: Carwia Press, 2006).

Richardson, W., and R. Mancabelli. "The Ready Write Web: New Tools for a New Generation of Technology." *Principal* (January/February 2007): 12–17.

Shibley, I. A. "Technology Integrated Learning, Staff Development: It's a Total Package." *Educational Technology 31,* no. 6 (2001): 61–63.

Slowinski, J. "Becoming a Technologically Savvy Administrator." *Teacher Librarian 30,* no. 5 (2003): 25–29.

Vanderlinde, R., J. van Braak, V. De Windt, J. Tondeur, R. Hermans, and I. Sinnaever. "Technology Curriculum and Planning for Technology in Schools: The Flemish Case." *Tech Trends: Linking Research and Practice to Improve Learning 52,* no. 2 (2008): 23–26. (ERIC Document Reproduction Service No. EJ798648)

Yee, D. "Images of School Principals' Information and Communications Technology Leadership." *Journal of Information Technology for Teacher Education 9,* no. 3 (2000): 287–302.

Interacting with the External School Environment

The school leaders of the twenty-first century must have knowledge and understanding of emerging issues and trends that potentially impact the school community; the conditions and dynamics of the diverse school community; community resources; community relations and market strategies and processes; and successful models of school, family, business, community, government, and higher education partnerships. They should also believe in, value, and be committed to schools operating as an integral part of the larger community, collaboration and communication with families, involvement of families and other stakeholders in school decision-making processes, the proposition that diversity enriches the school, families as partners in the education of their children, the proposition that families have the best interests of their children in mind, resources of the family and community needing to be brought to bear on the education of students, and an informed public. The Educational Leadership Policy Standards: ISLLC 2008 Standard 4 supports these characteristics.

> **Standard 4: An education leader promotes the success of every student by collaborating with faculty and community members, responding to diverse community interests and needs, and mobilizing community resources.**

Likewise, the educational leader must have knowledge and understanding of principles of representative governance that undergird the system of U.S. schools; the role of public education in the developing and renewing a democratic society and an economically productive nation; the law related to education and schooling; the political, social, cultural, and economic systems and processes that impact schools; models and strategies of change and conflict resolution as applied to the larger political, social, cultural, and economic contexts of schooling; global issues and forces affecting teaching and learning; the dynamics of policy development and advocacy under a democratic political system; and the importance of diversity and equity in a democratic society.

The Educational Leadership Policy Standards: ISLLC 2008 Standard 6 supports these requirements.

Standard 6: An education leader promotes the success of every student by understanding, responding to, and influencing the political, social, economic, legal, and cultural context.

Part Four addresses these two standards and the functions that accompanies them.

15 The School and The Community

*"You will not teach or show that propagandist
Al Gore's film to my child ..."*

—PARENT PROTESTING THE SHOWING
OF *An Inconvenient Truth*

*"You know, I really like the Christmas season—the gift giving,
the decorations—but it does bother me that the teacher has
my little girl singing about the little Lord Jesus."*

—COMMENT BY A JEWISH PATRON OF THE
PUBLIC SCHOOLS IN A SMALL TOWN

*"Under legal pressure a rural school district canceled an
elective philosophy course on 'intelligent design.'"*

—NEWS RELEASE

Headline: *"Parents Outraged over School's Alleged Coverup
of Rape."* (A 12-year-old was accused of sexually assaulting
three first-graders over a several week period, but school
officials had taken no action.)

These quotations and stories are not imaginary. Three were reported in the daily newspaper of a large city; one was a personal conversation with one of the authors. The statements reflect community attitudes about things that are happening in schools. From films that bother some people, to book banning, to alleged infringements of student rights, and on to other issues—the publics have things to say about school practices. And over all the varied opinions loom federal and state regulations, court decisions, and school board policies. The role of school leaders in what often becomes a miasma of public controversy is complex.

Opinions will be expressed—sometimes loudly, sometimes in the courts, sometimes privately in the principal's office. The responses of school leaders and policymakers will determine the degree to which schools will have the support of the various publics.

Complicating the scene of school and community relations is this fact: Most communities are collections of diversity in background, in understanding, in belief systems, and even in a common regard for the importance of schooling. The word *community* is far removed from the root word *common*. Oh, there can be found here and there small, mutually dependent civil units—we would label these *gemeinschaft* cultures—but in the main, this does not describe many places in Western society today.[1]

The problem of keeping the publics well informed and generally supportive of the efforts of formal schooling is a continuing one and is most difficult in today's culturally pluralistic, multiethnic, religiously and ethically fractured society. Don't think so? Read the pages of the local paper: front section and second section, op-ed page, and letters to the editor. A seemingly simple—to you—issue is fraught with uncertainty and disagreement elsewhere among others.

When we write the word *public* as plural, that is what we mean. Any school practice, new or continuing, any reform, any new textbook or reading list, any cheerleader selection process, any hiring or firing of personnel or change of assignment, any location, relocation, or closing of a school is subject to manifold response from the publics, oftentimes rancorous and loud.

This chapter is organized into three parts. In the first part we describe some of the major issues that are likely to confront the school leader. Then, in the second part, we consider the complexity of the community and the issues that often produce controversy or, at least, differences of opinion. Strategies and techniques for good public relations are our focus in the third part of the chapter.

Hot-Button Issues

Maintaining a good course of positive interaction between school and the publics is quite possible, not to say necessary. It is not all bad news and potential conflict, although it is important to write about that as well. Most people in most communities are not unhappy about the operation of the school and have a generally positive regard for educators and formal educational policies.

From time to time, however, some things happen and some decisions are made that inspire negative reactions from this or that public. Sometimes, the reactions are the result of poor communication endeavors by educators; sometimes, they are the result of continuing social problems; and sometimes, they are the result of differences in basic belief systems.

Certain issues predictably will cause controversy and discord in some communities. Recognizing this and developing proper mechanisms to handle the controversy will make for less pain and less disruption. What are these potentially disruptive issues? They are not always distinct from each other and some meld in certain instances and controversies. Let's look at the more prevalent causes of complaint and discord.

Religious Beliefs

Nothing can be so rancorous or disruptive as charges from this religious group or that citizens' organization that the school is operating in a manner inconsistent with certain beliefs or contrary to common law and court decisions. The former charges are among the most difficult to handle, and the second are the most time-consuming and painful as legal underpinnings are disputed. Can you have a Bible Club? May you allow the distribution of religious tracts on school property? Is evolution demonstrable fact? And, sometimes one religious group will dispute attention that another is given in public school schools. Christmas celebrations have disappeared from most public schools. Halloween parties are no longer permitted in many schools; satanism is the fear. Many folks in the community care greatly about these issues. Keep your attorney handy. And, keeping one's perspective secular seems to be the best policy.

Books and Educational Materials

"Dirty books" is the allegation. Inappropriate placement of educational materials are some of the other charges. "*Huckleberry Finn* is racist! *Harry Potter* is satanic! *Of Mice and Men* has offensive language! *It's Perfectly Normal* focuses on homosexuality and has sexual content!" Sometimes there will be a protest because of reading assignments a teacher has made or because a certain book is alleged to be inappropriate for the grade level in which it is used, or because certain books are readily available to everyone who comes to the library.

A new group will form or one or two excited parents or community members will complain. A bunch of parents or neighborhood leaders stands outside your office. What *do* you do? Here are some things to consider: Do you have any policies to guide the selection of educational materials? Has the American Library Association list and policies been examined?[2] Is there an appeals committee in the school? Is there an appeals policy? Is it followed? See Figure 15.1, and stay safe.

FIGURE 15.1 Dangerous Reading?

The American Library Association (ALA) sponsors an annual Banned Books Week, which celebrates the freedom to read. In contrast, the books listed below have been pulled, by some citizen's demand, from some libraries or schools. These books were labeled *dangerous*; the reason for the label is given after the book title:

- *The Adventures of Captain Underpants*—causes unruly behavior
- *The Adventures of Huckleberry Finn*—racist language
- *Anne Frank: The Diary of a Young Girl*—sexually explicit
- *The Catcher in the Rye*—offensive language
- *The Handmaid's Tale*—sexually explicit
- *Harry Potter* (entire series)—occult
- *Little Red Riding Hood*—bottle of wine in Grandma's basket
- *To Kill a Mockingbird*—racist language
- *Miriam-Webster's Collegiate Dictionary*—offensive language
- *The Alice series*—sexuality, drugs, offensive language

If one or more of these books were challenged in your school, how would the challenge be addressed? Does your school have any policies for managing protest to educational materials used? In the past 20 years, there have been 8,700 reported book challenges.

School Closings and New Buildings

It is inevitable. Close a school for whatever reason—low enrollment, poor location, excessive costs for repair and remodeling—and there will be an outcry from some part of the school community or neighborhood. The answer, not always satisfactory to everyone but ultimately the only way, is for the school leaders to be certain of their facts and have anticipated the difference of opinions. Alumni of a closing school will nearly always be disturbed. Has there been any involvement of these folks? Nearby neighbors will be bothered. Their children will be inconvenienced and lifestyles disturbed. Have good arrangements been made to modify these inconveniences? Is the closing *really* necessary? Is there no hope for enrollment increasing or renovation? Are small schools unnecessary?

ISLLC 4

   In regard to a new school, location is always a concern. Again, has there been any community involvement? Will the construction occur in the "right" place or in a manner that will not interfere with community practices? That's hard to say, of course, but forming focus groups and exploring various options can bring different insights to the foreground. In one place, recently, it was discovered that a new building was planned to be built on historic lands; in another city, it was discovered that old Indian burial grounds were going to be disturbed. These sorts of concerns are often found out in a timely manner when there are processes in place that provide for local involvement.

Curriculum Strategies and Courses of Instruction

Even persons who have difficulty spelling *curriculum* care mightily about how the children and youth are being instructed and in what they are being instructed. And, *what* is being taught and *how* it is being taught have been, seemingly forever, issues of great debate in this group or that. Sex education? If and when? Physical education for everyone? How about someone's objection to this on religious or other grounds? How about a special program for my child who has ADHD? Shall it be the "whole-language approach" or shall it be "phonics"? Or both? Or some other approach? And on and on. Better stay familiar with the law and with good educational practice.

Violence in Schools

It is a worried and worrisome society. Incidents of shootings, mass murders, and drug use in school make the headlines of newspapers and become the lead stories on the television news. School leaders have responded with policies of zero tolerance and the expenditure of budgetary dollars for their own police forces, security gates, and special schools for transgressors. Is this concern new? Casella wrote:

> Concerns about violence have a long history. The first 19th century common schools were developed partly to curb teenage delinquency—to "tame" new immigrants and "savage" American Indians. Later in the 1960's and 1970's as greater numbers of students rebelled against injustice and authority, discussions about school violence became more heated, culminating in 1977 in the *Safe School Study* (National Institute of Education, 1977) mandated by the U.S. Congress.[3]

The Safe School Study found that violence was an important problem, and that inconsistent discipline contributes to the problem. Yet, little was done for 10 years, and then antidrug programs were established. It was not until the 1990s that other legislation, such as the Crime Control Act of 1990, was passed.

Based on this and later legislation, schools have passed policies such as zero tolerance to address the issues of violence, sometimes with success and sometimes not. School police forces, school protection devices, alternative schools, and zero tolerance are necessary steps, perhaps, to assist in the development of a safe school environment, but each must be used with good judgement. We wrote in Chapter 5 about ways to achieve positive student control, but we also need to return to a concern for good judgment. Zero tolerance means not putting up with unacceptable behavior. It *does not mean* one-size-fits-all punishment. That kind of policy can be seen as one for administrative convenience, not justice. Punishing everyone the same without regard for maturity, previous behavior, or mitigating circumstances is stupid behavior.

Helicopter Parents

Frequently, school leaders lament a lack of parent or caregiver interest in what happens at school. There is an opposite extreme to this lament, however, and that is the helicopter parent—the parent who cannot let go, who is seemingly forever in the office complaining about things "that have been done to my child." Small travesties or complex issues, if the particular child is involved, Mom or Dad is at the school calling for correction! Parents such as those are needy, overanxious, and sometimes just plain pesky, and schools at every level have to find effective ways to deal with them. They text message their children in middle school, use the cell phone like an umbilical cord, and have little compunction about marching into a second-grade classroom to scream at teacher about a grade.

What can be done about the helicopter parent? Active listening and examination of school practices and policies seem to be the best courses of action. If everything that the school has done is proper, then one simply relaxes and does one's best to deal with the irate parent. But dealing with the helicopter parent does take time, valuable time; nevertheless, deal you must. Just make sure school policies and procedures are sensible and applied fairly. Some schools, with the leadership of the principal and alert guidance cunselors, are developing seminars about how to interact with helicopter parents. Schools in Phoenix have developed a seminar called "Managing Millennial Parents" about how to handle micromanaging parents. Another major concern stems from micromanaging parents, namely, the ability of young people to become independent.

The Complex Community

> Multi-ethnicity and cultural pluralism characterize society, and the many groups and individuals that comprise a neighborhood, community, a neighborhood, and a city reflect varying points of view and hold diverse opinions about the several agencies that are established to deliver services to them.[4]

There are, of course, other issues of a public relations nature that from time to time confront the school leader, but these previously described ones seem to capture the most common concerns.

None is easily resolvable, but there are strategies that seem to work at least some of the time. The remainder of this chapter focuses on the communities in which these issues take place and on public relations strategies and practices that seem to make a difference.

A high-performing school requires broad-based community support, and support will come from communities that are well informed and well engaged in the educative processes that go on in the school. This does not happen automatically.

Communication between parents and other citizens, businesses, health- and social-care agencies, several levels of government, teachers, administrators, and students is essential and is the glue that binds the learning community. Establishing good communication processes is an essential task of the principal. It is not easy. Communities are diverse, attitudes vary, and formal and informal forces vie for attention and make demands on the school that are often contradictory and at cross-purposes. The territory is complex and so must be the school–community public relations program.

Schools do not exist apart from the society to be served. They get their support from the "outside" world, and those who make policy and those who permit policy to be made reside in the outside world. Inevitably and inexorably, individuals and groups attempt to establish policies and procedures in the school that are consistent with—indeed generative and supportive of—their values, beliefs, and ideals.

These are days of much individual school-based autonomy and in some places a mandated use of such decisional mechanisms as citizen and teacher advisory councils organized at the school level. The principal's role as a community relations expert has expanded and pressures have mounted for more effective ways to communicate with the "publics" composing the school community. These pressures are visited on teachers as well.

To perform this role even adequately well requires both knowledge about the makeup of the school community and about how best to communicate with community members. It is increasingly apparent that the strongest support base for the school is grassroots in nature, but there are seemingly infinite varieties of grass to be found in the lawns of many school communities. Moreover, it isn't only parents who feel they have a vested interest in schooling practices. Many other community members have a vested interest as well.

Also, one need not be a graduate sociologist to be aware of the impacts phenomena such as technocracy, urbanization, and the increasing complexity of social relationships have had on the nature of interaction between school and community. The increasing esotericism of professional educational practices, a concomitant of these changes, has widened the gap between school and community. The dissolution of the small, closely knit communities of years past has made schools and the people in the area unsure of each other. The same situation exists in the medical and legal professions as well as other welfare delivery agencies that attempt to address the varied and complex needs of people who live in a community.

The school is the closest community agency to residents, in both a literal and figurative sense. In geographic proximity, the school is "just around the corner" and often becomes the first line of communication with the area served. It is closer than the mayor's office; in most cases, it is even closer than the fire station. And, the school affects mightily the community's most prized possessions—its children and its pocketbook. It should not be surprising, then, that the schools are frequently the subject of perusal and subsequent criticism, and sometimes the result of the perusal is more visceral than cerebral.

Informal Community Forces

Influence and power are distributed unevenly throughout communities. Moreover, informal power must be distinguished from formal power. Formal power is manifest in the elected and appointed governmental offices of the community—the mayor, city council, police chief, superintendent, and board of school trustees, for example. *Informal power* refers to the ability of an individual or group to get certain things done in the community in a way that is satisfying to the individual or group. It may refer to individuals who are at or near the top of their respective social or occupational hierarchies. It may also refer to groups that are composed of, or individuals who represent, members of various special-interest groups, and who, on any given issue, mobilize substantial portions of the population to respond in a particular way.

ISLLC 6

The ability to influence depends on the presence of two elements: substantial resources and commitment. *Substantial resources* does not necessarily mean control of large sums of dollars; it may simply mean the control of large groups of people. People are a resource. Most of the early civil rights successes were characterized by displays of latent power and were conducted without huge sums of money, relatively speaking. *Commitment* refers to a singular belief in the basic rightness of whatever it is that is being proposed (i.e., the group "hangs together" no matter what), and when coupled with control of some resources, a formidable force is present.

Neighborhood Influence Systems

As communities have become more and more complex, neighborhood influence systems have become increasingly important. Such influence systems often reflect racial, ethnic, religious, or economic homogeneity.

Neighborhood influence systems may be especially important within the principal's sphere of interaction. We noted earlier that the individual school building remains, in most places, the closest community agency, certainly in terms of geographic proximity. Thus, it is handy, if nothing else, to members of the immediate neighborhood who have opinions to express. Moreover, school personnel, and especially the principal, are in an excellent position to feel the pulse of the surrounding area and to interact directly with that group.

Individual schools need to develop effective mechanisms to receive information from, and to dispense information to, neighborhood leadership. Research suggests that an individual community member's decision to support or not support any particular community issue is more often than not based on the influence of friends and neighbors rather than on the presence of any outside objective data. The school principal must become familiar with the leadership structure of the neighborhood that the individual school may serve.

Leadership structure exists in any community or neighborhood, except the most anomic. This structure may be readily identified, often through reputational means by surveying the storefront churches as well as the well-known churches, the local welfare agencies, the better *and* less well-known social clubs, and the membership of union locals, among any number of other somewhat formal sources. If a community is characterized by heterogeneity in racial, ethnic, or social makeup, more than the usual effort will be required, because well-known organizations may not reflect this heterogeneity. Furthermore a neighborhood leadership structure may not be composed of, or contain very many, people who are also parents of children attending the schools.

Traditional community groups often do not have a membership comprised of anything approximating the real nature of the community or the neighborhood served by the schools. In addition, there may exist a leadership structure that has not yet been recognized but that has important things to say about schools. An examination of the membership of local, formal parent–teacher organization and a comparison of certain characteristics of these people with general demographic characteristics of the student body of the school may reveal that certain groups of people are missing. If different kinds of people are missing, one can be sure that many key neighborhood influentials are not being reached by school messages.

Community Groups

The most intense memberships are held in groups that can be classified as *blut und bod.* These are groups with kinship and territorial bonds rooted in certain ethnic, racial, or historical ties.

> A common language, a common dietary, a common neighborhood, common experience with outsiders, a common history, make people feel more comfortable with one another, more at ease. They understand one another, they read one another; they get one another's messages. They feel they can count on one another for support. They constitute an in group; everyone else is an out group. *The bonds that hold people together also separate them from others; invisible lines are drawn to protect the boundaries between them and outsiders.* [emphasis added].[5]

Moreover, people in the community are also often members of an array of different formal and informal groups that may impinge on the schools. They are members of clubs and associations, some *blut und bod* in nature, for example, self-help groups such as the American Indian Movement, the League of United Latin American Citizens, the NAACP, or the National Organization of Women. People belong, as well, to unions and professional associations, to political parties, and to neighborhood improvement leagues. All of these organizations demand loyalty from their members and may from time to time oppose certain school system procedures, policies, and practices. Membership in what at times may be adversary groups can be the source of much conflict between community and school.

Pressure Groups

Pressure groups can be distinguished from the usual community decision-making systems because of the relatively short-lived nature of their activities and their tendency to form and re-form around issues or causes. Often, a group will form because of a specific decision made by the school leadership, which is perceived to have an impact on the group's life space or belief system.

It is clearly the right of citizens to protest when they feel that the school is failing to accomplish the right thing. Conflict may not be inevitable; in fact, it is frequent in any society. Conflict is not, however, necessarily disruptive or negative. Often, it is out of conflict that greater understanding results, provided the situation is characterized by openness, a willingness to compromise, and well-understood and agreed-upon procedures for resolution.

Pressure groups should not be dismissed lightly. They are a source of great disruption in many communities and sometimes a source of productive change. It is difficult to put the term *pressure group* in a noninflammatory context. Immediately, thoughts of book burnings, witch hunts, placard-carrying demonstrators, and impassioned pleas from the pulpit or the podium come to mind. One may also imagine school boards and superintendents hastily capitulating to the onslaught of such charges that the schools are "godless," that the English department is assigning lascivious literature, and that sex education is corrupting youth, among a host of similar kinds of charges, emotion-ridden in context and within which rational behavior often is nearly impossible.

But a pressure group may also consist of parents arguing persuasively for the return of an art program. It may be a collection of citizens raising important issues of equity or insisting on balanced reporting in textbooks about the contributions of minorities. It may be a group raising questions about district employment practices or the lack of bilingual programs, among other issues of equity. Most of the legislation and court orders ensuring or extending rights at local, state, and national levels have occurred because, early on, a small group of concerned citizens organized to call attention to an undesirable situation.

Negotiating with Pressure Groups.   From time to time, all school administrators will be confronted with requests from organized groups of people who represent a particular point of view about a school-related issue. Frequently, such pressure groups begin their inquiries at the school level in the principal's office. The issues may run the gamut, from complaints about teachers, textbooks, or specific courses of study to alleged institutional racism and demands for more equitable staffing or pupil assignment decisions. Often concerns are legitimate concerns, but legitimate or not, they must always be dealt with sensitively and sensibly. The following guidelines may help a besieged principal.

ISLLC 5

1. *Identifying.* An early identification should be made of the group that is in opposition to, or is likely to be in opposition to, certain school programs. Who are they? More importantly, who are the leaders?

2. *Discussing.* Can the leaders be talked with? Once the opposing group and the leader(s) of that group have been identified, it is appropriate to engage in a closed-door session to explore the elements of the issue. The principal may gain a more definitive notion of just what it is that is troubling the group. This meeting or series of meetings may result in ways, if the cause is legitimate, for the school to help the group achieve its goals. It may require great insight to find out what the real issue is, because stated "reasons" for opposition to this or that school issue are often at variance with the real causative factors. (At this point, it is also important to apprise the central office of the potential hostile situation and to seek counsel.)

3. *Analyzing.* After the informal meetings, it is important to reach a decision. Some important points must be considered at this time, including the question of how strong the opposition really is. Do they have a good chance to "beat" the school in its present position? Most importantly, do they have a solid point on which to differ with the school? At this time decision must be made about whether the issue will be fought on the basis of the initial positions of both sides or whether some accord is possible.

In all situations, it is important to determine what the real goal is, and what results or gains can be expected from the achievement of that goal. In other words, is the school's position or is the school administrator's position tenable? If so, evidence must be present to substantiate why it is tenable. Many school administrators have ended up in great difficulty because of a refusal to negotiate or compromise or because of an unwillingness to give up irrelevant points of contention.

4. *Negotiating.* Is there room for compromise? The political system under which a democracy operates functions on compromise. Politics is the delicate art of compromise. Desirable changes often can be achieved without compromising principles and without loss of integrity.

Of course, compromising may not be necessary. Perhaps simply sitting down with members of the pressure group and explaining the school's position and the facts may dissuade the group from further action. However, administrators who have engaged in community conflict situations over the years are likely to suggest that compromise and negotiation is the more likely process. The pressure group's motives may be highly complex. Its needs and goals are every bit as important to its membership as are the needs and goals of the particular administrator or school system in question.

In any effort to influence or achieve compromise, timing is important. One really can't wait until an organized campaign is under way to effect compromises or modify points of view. The time to influence a pressure group is before the particular group has launched its initial fusillade and before school personnel are totally and publicly committed to a position. Common sense suggests that it is increasingly difficult to change someone or some group when there will be much loss of face, real or imagined, by doing so.

5. *Marshaling Resources.* Seek help from other community members. Assuming that all efforts to negotiate with the opposition are unsuccessful, what does the administrator try next? The first step is to find out who is on the school's side, or who it appears ought to be on the school's side. Some community analysis can be conducted even at this stage and may prove fruitful. Who besides the school really stands to lose? Principals should not forget about other less-organized neighborhood groups of people who, though they seemingly may have a low potential for power, might have a high potential for unity on the particular issue and who could be called on for counsel and help.

Evaluating the Legitimacy of the Critic.   Members of the community have the right to legitimately question and criticize the schools, although defining the word *legitimate* in this context is difficult. One of the best benchmarks for judging legitimacy is to observe the behavior exhibited by the particular group. Is the group willing to meet with appropriate educational system personnel out of the glare of TV lights or without benefit of newspaper rhetoric? Is the group willing to consider other sides of the issue? Is criticism mostly characterized by reason and rationality, or does it seem mostly emotional in nature? Will the critics accept demonstrable facts? If these conditions are not met, then one may question the "legitimacy" of the critic and prepare for battle.

Anticipating Obvious Hot-Button Issues.   Why should a school leader be surprised when some parents express concern about some school books with themes or language that they consider inappropriate* or about a new school rule that requires a uniform dress code? Why should there be surprise when a school that has a multicultural or multiracial, or both, population evidences discord and prejudice or charges of "unfair" treatment? Or that there is concern about a poor showing on statewide or districtwide tests?

---

*Library materials as well as assigned published materials from the classroom are a constant source of parent and community complaint. The books in the J. K. Rowling *Harry Potter* series, for example, have come under fire from some members of the Religious Right. "Satanism and witchcraft" are the battle cries. These books actually promote friendship, loyalty, good over evil, and high ethical principles, and use great adventures to capture the attention of young readers.

Such issues have arisen historically and recur frequently. One is left to wonder why anyone would be unprepared for this sort of thing. The solution, of course, is to realize that such flashpoints will occur and to develop policies and procedures to handle them fairly.

Providing Well-Developed Policies. If conflict can be expected on educational issues, if ideological unity is not characteristic of many complex communities, and if criticism can be expected as a part of the normal life of the administrator of any public institution, what can be done to modify the divisive effects of such actions and instead capitalize on the rich diversity of views and opinions to improve the schools? Foremost is to provide a broad set of policies, both at the school district level as well as at the school building level, that establishes a framework within which diverging views can be heard in a regular and systematic manner. Such a framework provides, in effect, procedural due process whereby dissident factions in a community can formally register their concerns.

ISLLC 5

Figure 15.2 is a sample form that some districts provide to individuals who are objecting to the use of certain educational material. Such a complaint form could be adapted to other issues and, if used judiciously, provide a vehicle for citizens to make their views known in a rational and systematic way.

FIGURE 15.2   Citizen's Request for Reconsideration of Educational Medium

Title of medium _____

Type of medium: (circle)

Book   Film   Filmstrip   Recording _____
                                             (other)

Author/artist/composer/other _____

Publisher/producer (if known) _____

Request initiated by _____ Phone_____

Address _____

Complainant represents _____

_____ Self

_____ (Name of organization) _____

1. After having read/viewed/listened to the item in question, to what do you object, and why? (Please be specific; cite pages, frame, other)

2. What do you believe is the theme of this item?

3. What do you feel might be the result of students reading/viewing/listening to this item?

4. For what age group would you recommend this item?

5. Other comments

_____   _____

    Date   Signature of Complainant

Working with Review Boards.   Individual principals would be wise to establish some kind of review body on whom the principal could rely for advice, counsel, and the development of criteria for judging potentially controversial instructional materials. Involving an array of appropriate personnel in the development of policies to anticipate problems establishes a basis for information sharing and good decision making. Principals cannot be expected to know everything. The advice and counsel of the school staff, as well as the community, and the development of broadly based policies and policy review boards can provide for effective decision making and intelligent responses to questions that may come from groups or individuals in the community.

Working with Other Community Agencies.   Many community agencies and organizations in addition to schools have—or could have—an impact on the quality of children's lives. The school principal is in an uncommonly good position to coordinate the efforts of these agencies.

ISLLC 4, 6

It often happens that the principal serves in that role anyway, because the elementary school is usually the closest social agency available to patrons. And patrons look to their schools for all sorts of help that has to do with their families' well-being. The "closeness" of the school is for many as much a matter of psychological proximity as it is a physical proximity. Many community members look to the school for help in matters neither of the school's doing nor jurisdiction simply because they know of no other place to turn.

The sad fact is that in a complex society the important and varied welfare delivery agencies often operate in a most uncoordinated way. Principals frequently find themselves dealing with court orders, child protective services, police departments, city and state health and human services departments, and businesses and industries in an effort to help just one particular child or family. Sometimes these agencies even conflict with each other in their efforts and in their policies.

We are not aware of any administrator training programs that specifically prepare principals for this add-on role in the community. But it is there, and while it may not be a part of the job description, effective principals recognize the importance of developing good contacts with these outside agencies and providing referral and follow-up services to their patrons who may be in need.

Developing close relationships with the police department only makes good sense. Becoming personally connected with directors and counselors of child protective services, among other welfare delivery agencies, will pay rich dividends. Business partnerships such as adopt-a-school can provide enriched educational offerings as well as create an intimate involvement of the private sector in community service and form an important support base.

Formal Community Forces

> The biggest problem facing schools is fragmentation and overload . . . schools are suffering the . . . burden of having a torrent of unwanted, uncoordinated policies and innovations raining down on them from external hierarchical bureaucracies.[6]

Agencies at all three levels of government exert influence and control over the formal education system, often in direct prescriptive and regulatory ways. Even though locally managed and substantially supported by locally assessed taxes, as established by the law, public school districts are really state institutions; school boards of education members are state officers. In practice, of course, the support and control of the public school systems in this nation are vested in federal, state, intermediate, and local governments. A kind of partnership thus exists, although the nature and role of the partners vary among the states.

In the federal system of the U.S. government, education is a function of the separate states. Of course, no state may provide for a school system that violates the constitutional rights of citizens. The U.S. Constitution itself is strangely quiet about education. The state receives its authority to operate and control public education within its boundaries through the enactment of the Tenth Amendment to the Constitution.[7] Thus, the education system is established under powers reserved to the states, and the manner in which the system is maintained is a plenary responsibility of the state. Private, parochial, and charter schools also operate under the aegis of the states.

All of the state constitutions specifically provide for public school systems. The legal basis on which the schools are conducted and maintained may be found in state constitutional and statutory law and in the body of common law as it is established by judicial decisions. Opinions written by state attorneys general also have an impact on the operation of the schools until such time as these might be set aside by statute or by the judiciary.

The establishment of *magnet schools* has been a phenomenon. Magnet school operation creates especially complex relation problems between communities and schools, because of a widely dispersed school population. The decentralization of urban districts is also an effort to be responsive to more local needs.

The Local Board of Education

The policymaking body of a school district is the board of education. The board of education is a corporate and political body and has the power expressly and implicitly given to it by statute. In many communities, members of the board of education are elected by the people in the communities that they serve; others have appointed boards of education. The method of the selection of members for the lay governing boards of private and parochial schools varies widely.

Regardless of the method by which members are selected, the duties of the school board are both legislative and quasi-judicial. The local school board has great latitude in daily operation of the schools, subject always, of course, to constitutional and statutory limitations.

The size of boards varies considerably both within states as well as between the various states. Although uncommon, some local school boards have as many as 17 members. Legal requirements for school board membership are minimal, usually including no more than such prerequisites as being a registered voter in the district, being nominated for the office, and being elected. Age requirements are common, and certain people often may not serve on a board of education if they hold some other governmental position that would be deemed to be a conflict of interest.

What local boards of education can do is circumscribed by a host of state and federal law, court opinion at both levels, attorneys general opinions at both levels, and expressed local community expectations (see Figure 15.3).

We've already discussed the informal influences at the local level. Let us now turn to a discussion of school boards and the federal and state impingement on school board authority.

State Education Agencies

Within the limitations of a particular state constitution, the state's legislature has wide power to determine the purposes and the procedures for the subordinate levels of the education hierarchy.

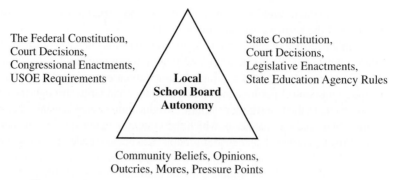

The Federal Constitution,
Court Decisions,
Congressional Enactments,
USOE Requirements

**Local
School Board
Autonomy**

State Constitution,
Court Decisions,
Legislative Enactments,
State Education Agency Rules

Community Beliefs, Opinions,
Outcries, Mores, Pressure Points

FIGURE 15.3   Circumscribed Local Authority for Schools

Usually, however, the laws issuing from the state legislature deal with general powers and purposes, leaving specific implementation to a state education agency and various intermediate and local school systems. The state education agency, or state department of education, itself is a creature of the legislature and is imbued with certain discretionary powers.

In order to carry out various legislative and constitutional provisions about education, any number of other boards of control exist, including controlling boards for higher education, vocational education, tenure, retirement, and similar activities. These are all in addition to a state board of education, which exists to determine policies that are then implemented by the state education agency. There are also a variety of agencies concerned with budgeting, accounting, building standards, health, school lunches, library services, civil defense, and myriad other activities in which the schools engage. In short, although the local school system is often viewed as an autonomous unit, it is subject to the controls and impingements from many other legally established community and state agencies.

All states have a chief state school officer who may be known as commissioner of education, state superintendent of schools, or a similar title. The number, term, and method of selection of members of a state board of education vary. Similarly, the method by which the state superintendent is selected varies.

Federal Influences on Education

Even though the U.S. Constitution is silent about a public education system, it is clear to even a casual observer that the role of the federal government has developed from one of "silence" to active, shared responsibility, with not a little control. The general welfare clause of the U.S. Constitution is most often cited as the constitutional provision that permits federal aid to public education. Federal programs tend to be categorical—that is, for an identified special purpose rather than generalized aid.

Categorical aid and specialized programs result in considerable federal influence and, inescapably, restrictions. Few would quarrel with the intent behind PL 94–142, the Education for All Handicapped Children Act, or with the legislation that resulted in the Occupational Safety and Health Act (OSHA),[8] for example. But the implementation of these pieces of legislation has not been without administrative frustration. At times, positive legislative intent gets caught up in a maze of rules that seem to inhibit rather than facilitate. Nevertheless, the school administrator's task is to make it work the way it was intended to work.

Federal interest has also resulted in the use of the schools as a tool for major social reform. This can best be exemplified by the 1954 Supreme Court decision in *Brown* v. *Board of Education of Topeka* in which the Supreme Court determined that "separate but equal" state provisions and *de jure* segregated educational systems in the United States were unconstitutional.

The federal interest is pervasive, and while it rises or declines in emphasis—depending on the philosophic stance of the executive and legislative branches of government—it nevertheless impinges greatly on the direction that local systems take.

An Interface of Levels

Each level of the government has its own areas of responsibility and autonomy. All of the levels interface, however, and there is both mutual obligation and dependence. Congress has authorized many educational programs for purposes that have been deemed to be especially important to the national interest. The U.S. Constitution itself grants to the states the responsibility for providing for public education. In turn, the states have delegated many of their powers to the local school district, while at the same time maintaining a vast number of regulatory controls over various aspects of the school operation, particularly in fiscal and program matters.

The previous sections established a contextual base for school and community relations. It is to the subject of the relationship of the publics and their *specific* schools that we turn. The focus now is on public relations practices and techniques of schools. The subject is how principals can build a solid citizen-support base and communicate effectively with school patrons.

Promising Public Relations Techniques: Dealing with Formal and Informal Forces

No one is in a better position to have a positive impact on the relationship between the school system and the community than the principal and the building staff. No single school district person is in a position to interact in person with greater numbers of community members than the principal. A district may spend huge sums of money on slick publications and a well-functioning, centrally located community relations office headed by a public information officer, but it is the principal who can be more influential on a day-to-day basis with individual school patrons. Even in this mass media environment, it is still the face-to-face encounter that provides the best basis for understanding and is the most influential in molding public opinion.

ISLLC 4

The greatest opportunity to influence and persuade, and to hear and feel the community pulse, occurs in the more intimate and often face-to-face settings likely to occur at the building level. Nevertheless, although the next section of the chapter will focus on public relations at the building level, some attention will be given to districtwide public relations activities as well.

School–community communication endeavors may take several forms, any one of which has limitations. An effective school–community relations program will make use of a variety of media, and an alert principal will tailor the particular message to be conveyed to the appropriate medium.

Getting the Message Out: One-Way Public Relations Techniques

There are numerous ways to broadcast a message from the school. Cooperative endeavors involving print and electronic media, building- or system-developed newsletters and brochures, and even the routinely sent report card can all be put to effective use. These are, however, one-way devices; there is little or no way to know if the messages were received or understood.

Print and Electronic Media

Few communities are not served by at least a weekly newspaper, and no community is outside the reach of radio and television. These mass media are commonly used to impart information about the various agencies serving the community.

Newspapers vary from weekly or biweekly advertisers, with perhaps a few columns reporting highly localized activities, to urban dailies with several editions. Depending on the kind of newspaper, a principal's role will. A principal may write news releases that will be published mostly word for word or meet with news reporters who will recast the stories in their own words. In any case, the development of good relations with the working press is essential. Reporters or editors will ask principals for information about developing stories or news items more often than for stories containing general information about what's going on in the schools.

The news media have their problems, too. Newspapers and television stations are businesses, with advertising to sell, bills to pay, and subscribers to satisfy. Some people are surprised to learn that 25 percent or less of newspaper space is devoted to stories and 75 percent or more to advertising. This percentage affects the amount of school news that will get printed. Moreover, news editors deal with many other agencies and pressure groups, each championing causes or matters for the "public good," so there is competition for available space.

A frequent complaint of reporters is that schools tend to engage only in "gold-star" story writing. The charge is that many school administrators are only too eager to publicize praiseworthy news items but will back away from or become upset about legitimate adverse criticism. An adverse story *is* legitimate news, and when such a story breaks, the school official and the newspaper both have a job to do. Covering up a weakness or refusing to respond to a legitimate inquiry about a potentially embarrassing situation can only lead to bad press relations, widening credibility gap, and, frequently, bad reporting.

Techniques for Dealing with the Mass Media.   News releases should be developed in a way that conforms to the requirements of the different media. Releases for radio and television must be shorter, more repetitive, and in a style that is more conversational than that used for newspapers.

Relationships with representatives of the various media, as well as district policy, will determine whether the person releasing the news concentrates on writing and distributing releases or on furnishing suggestions and information to journalists who in turn write their own material. In urban settings with large dailies and "live eye" television, reporters write their own stories, but they do need to be advised about promising sources, fast-breaking news, upcoming events, and policy changes. They also need to be provided with good background material.

In small towns and cities and in suburban and rural districts, local news will generally be disseminated by daily, biweekly, and weekly newspapers, ranging from miniversions of the large city dailies to four-page advertisers. In many of these places, a school official will frequently write an entire story with little assistance from an editor.

Articles and stories about scheduled events should be prepared well in advance, with photographs of speakers or others involved in the program provided to the news media *before* the event occurs. Often, as a matter of policy, newspapers will not print information about a past event. Follow-up reports should be prepared for the media as soon as possible after an event. The school principal should try to be aware of various media deadlines; missing a deadline means the story may never get printed.

Even small school systems are employing public information officers to facilitate and coordinate the flow of information from school to community. The duties vary and in some school systems the job may be only part time. Even where the job is full time and the public relations program is well developed, it is still the principal who will be sought as the prime source of fast-breaking news, and in time of crisis. Figure 15.4 contains eight practices to facilitate a good working relationship with representatives of the media.

District Policy Considerations. The latitude a principal has with the press will depend in great part on the press policy of the school district. News media personnel, however, are most sensitive to what they perceive to be censorship and normally respond negatively to the suggestion that every story or every interview must be cleared with the central office. A policy that requires all school personnel to refer reporters and editors to the central office rather than answer questions or that sends the news media to the central office for all information, will damage press relations, if rigidly enforced. Obviously, fast-breaking news items of a potentially explosive nature require discretion on the part of the school principal. But a principal standing in an obvious crisis situation does no service by saying, "I have no information" or "You must call the public information office."

The public information program needs continual evaluation. It really isn't very valuable to send out large numbers of news releases if few are used, and submitting too much material in an

FIGURE 15.4   Working with the Media

- Give reporters story ideas and information but remember it is editors and news directors who decide what should be covered.
- Be aware of when reporters' deadlines fall.
- Prepare articles about scheduled events well in advance and submit photographs at the same time.
- Make releases for radio and television shorter, more repetitious, and in a more conversational style than those for the print media.
- Avoid provoking reporters with "no comment" statements. Help reporters write potentially adverse stories by giving complete information and background.
- Anticipate the reporters' needs and have background information written ahead of time for distribution. (Don't trust that a "general beat" reporter knows much about schooling.)
- Avoid jargon and in-house language; it may not be understood, especially by a "general beat" reporter.
- Invite newspersons—reporters and their editors—to the school for lunch and periodic tours without trying to sell them on a story at the time. Get them acquainted with the school scene.

indiscriminate way may result in few stories being published. The lesson is clear: News media are most impressed by articles that contain only timely and worthwhile information. These will stand the best chance of getting reported.

School News Items File.   There are many missed opportunities to present the school to the public in a positive way. The typical school is a beehive of activity, much of which would be of interest to one segment or another of the public. The difficulty is that many schools have no central place where ongoing activities are recorded. Thus, when a reporter calls or an editor requests a story, a school often cannot adequately meet the need.

An especially effective practice is the use of a School News Item File, depicted in Figure 15.5. Many activities in the school are probably newsworthy, but without encouragement and facilitation, they will go unreported. Each staff member should have a supply of the news item forms to jot down projects that might be especially interesting, and on a regular basis these forms should be sent to the principal's office. The principal can then file the reports in a folder labeled according to the kind of project, and a news reporter can simply review the files, selecting any particular items to follow up. This practice helps both the reporter, whose responsibility it is to find news, and the principal, whose responsibility it is to provide news but not necessarily to write the story.

Newsletters and Bulletins.   The principal and school staff commonly attempt to communicate with the home and outside agencies through newsletters and bulletins. These can be useful if

It's news to somebody. Report it!

Type of News Item:

_____ Curriculum Project
_____ Activities of Staff
_____ School Awards
_____ Student Activities (field trips, special recognition, etc.)
_____ New or Interesting Instructional Techniques
_____ Continuing Difficult Problems
_____ Other

Title of Project or Item:

Description of Project or Item:

Persons Involved: (how many, and who—names, addresses, titles, etc.)

Dollars Involved and Sources of These Dollars:

Who to Contact for Further Information:

FIGURE 15.5   School News Item File

employed judiciously and if well done. But a bad message is conveyed when a newsletter arrives home crumpled in the pocket of a student, hard to read, and containing out-of-date information. If newsletters and bulletins are to be used, the format should be simple, the information conveyed should be written concisely and be free of educational jargon, and the method of getting these messages home should be via mail and e-mail. Newsletters sent home with children often do little but contribute to a neighborhood litter problem. If the newsletter is not produced with care and printed in an attractive manner, it is simply not worth the bother. Care should also be taken to recognize the multilingual nature of many communities.

Now it is easy to prepare newsletters and bulletins that appear professional in makeup. Desktop publishing programs produce an attractive product—complete with graphics.

Report Cards.   Report cards are often overlooked as public relations mechanisms, but they are the single-most regular way in which schools desseminate information to the home. Both teachers and parents like them to be uncomplicated. Yet, consideration of all of the ways in which a student is growing, developing, and learning defies summing up progress with a single letter grade. Thus, the development of an appropriate reporting procedure will require careful study by the staff and include a faculty–layperson committee to develop a report form that is easy to understand but that also contains important kinds of information relative to the student's progress.

If the purpose of a reporting system is to develop an effective communication link with parents and if parents value highly written reports, then the school should use some form of a written report card. A written report of grades alone is not adequate, however, and a more personal communication link, such as additional comments written by the teacher on the report card or a parent–teacher conference, should be added.

To effectively report a child's progress, a report card should provide three kinds of information. First, it should estimate the child's overall ability compared to other children the same age. This can be done through standardized tests or the teacher's judgment of the child's ability based on diagnosis and observations. Second, the report card should indicate the child's individual progress. During the elementary and middle grades, this should be based on estimated ability and a measure of the child's achievement in the classroom since the last marking period. This statement is not a comparison to other children; rather, it is the teacher's estimate of whether the child is achieving as much as possible. Finally, the report card should describe the child's conduct in school. Conduct may be rated with a check mark to indicate satisfactory behavior or with a code that indicates outstanding citizenship, satisfactory behavior, or unsatisfactory behavior.

The Fog Index

Writing well requires careful consideration of who it is that will be receiving the message. We've called attention to the need to consider the multilingual nature of many school communities, but effectively conveying information in writing requires more than using the native language of the intended receiver; it requires using that language meaningfully. That dictates straightforward sentences, unencumbered nouns and verbs, and common language. Simplicity, lack of clutter, and avoidance of jargon and pedagogical phraseology are required. And this can be done without talking down to people. Newspapers accomplish it daily. The messages should not rely on someone having a high school education to understand them. The nearer the messages come to a sixth- or seventh-grade reading level, the better. Many word processing programs have readibility statistics features. Microsoft Word, for example, uses both the Flesch-Kincaid Grade Level and the Flesch Reading Ease level for any selected passage.

Getting the Message Out and Back: Two-Way Public Relations Techniques

Information dissemination is not synonymous with *communication*. Because of the failure to make this distinction, many public relations efforts fail. In this final part of this chapter, let us focus on proven communication techniques.

The Message Was Sent—What Happened?

The *co* in communication suggests a closed loop. That is, the message was not only sent *but* it was received and responded to in a way that indicates it was understood. There are five important questions to ask when examining the quality of information devices:

1. If the message was received, was it read (heard)?
2. If it was read (heard), was it understood?
3. If it was understood, was it understood in the right spirit?
4. If it was understood in the right spirit, will it be acted on in a positive way?
5. How do you know?

The fifth question is an evaluation question. Of all the communication techniques and structures available, some approaches, seem the most promising for principals to use.

Community Advisory Councils

The trend to greater autonomy at the school building level has brought with it increasing use by principals of community advisory councils. In some states, legislation establishing greater school-unit autonomy and concomitant greater principal accountability has also mandated community advisory councils. Parents, teachers, and sometimes students are included in such councils.

Issues often arise about what is *policy advising* and what is *policy making*. Clearly, the reason for advisory councils is to have a formally established way for community and faculty representatives to share information with the principal and suggest alternative approaches to solving problems of schooling. In the best of worlds, the councils provides the principal with additional expertise and useful insights that will result in maximum feasible decisions. Note, though, that "advising" is not the same as "decisioning." Nevertheless, would it be a foolish principal who found himself or herself always operating contrary to the advice of the council?

Membership on the Advisory Council.   State law or local district policy may prescribe the nature of membership of the council and/or how members are to be selected. Lacking this, it seems fundamental that members, whether elected or appointed by the principal, should represent a cross-section of the local community.

Achieving Maximum Output from an Advisory Council.   Lack of clarity and understanding about the role of council members and about the difference between helping to make policy and policy implementation can become a source of conflict. People work best when they are aware of expectations and limitations. To establish a framework for advisory council activities, the school principal should follow these guidelines:

1. Establish the essential conditions that any solution, action plan, or policy must meet if it is to be acceptable. Are there financial, legal, or district policy considerations that must be taken into account? Are there activities that are known to not be in the best interests of learners? Are there activities that, in good conscience, the principal would not carry out? State limitations up-front so that everyone knows about them.
2. Help the group establish a specific time line and a set date for task completion.
3. Indicate what resources are available to the group.
4. Specify what specific outcomes are desired.
5. Establish the limits of the group's authority in the issue at hand. That is, is the principal asking for a final decision, for some alternative decisions, or simply for some advice?

Focus Groups

Research bureaus, professional associations, and advertising agencies, among other organizations, have used focus groups for years to define issues, anticipate problems, explore reactions to potential problems, develop alternative scenarios, and plan leaps into the future. A focus group is an example of a *nonprobability sampling* technique. The technique employs directional rather than quantitative data and can be used to great effectiveness as both a school public relations technique and a creative problem-solving technique. Focus groups, however, are not decision-making bodies nor are they even advisory bodies. Rather, they are groups of community members whose opinions about an issue the principal wants to learn. The purpose is both problem sensing and problem solving, but the problem "sensor" and the problem "solver" is not the focus group. The focus group provides feelings, attitudes, and information.

A focus group consists of a small number of people—8 to 10 are recommended. Each group represents a segment of the school/community population. The purpose of meeting with a focus group is to gain an assessment of how people feel about a school-related issue or problem—or anticipated problem. Typically, a meeting lasts no more than an hour, and no more than four questions are asked of the group. A moderator takes notes on the discussion, noting the key concepts, levels of intensity, and new information. Verbatim comments are recorded to the degree possible, absent editing. It is not important that the group meet in the school. A union hall, church basement, or apartment complex hospitality room might be a more convenient and comfortable choice for meetings.

Business and Other Community Partnerships

Many benefits, such as the following, can be gained from well-organized business/industry/education partnerships:

- Getting talented people engaged in the important work of educating children. Here are some example: the executives of a leading business have developed a training program in ethics and give their top staff released time to work with children in this program; a psychiatric hospital offers free counseling services to its "adopted school"; a leading manufacturer of computers releases its personnel to work with teachers and students in more effective use of computer technology (and not just in the use of the manufacturer's own computers, either); business sends school principals to its executive training program; another business employs science teachers in its research and development department during summers and at other times; companies offer in-service programs as well as tutorial services; a firm provides work opportunities for students who need financial help to stay in school; and the list could go on.

- Helping community leaders better understand the complexities of educating a child and helping them develop an appreciation for the problems and pleasures of teaching.
- Capitalizing on the technical expertise that is available in the community and using that expertise for staff updating as well as for program analysis and student tutoring.

To be maximally effective and to avoid costly misunderstandings, cooperative programs must be well coordinated. Although the principal doesn't need to be the one who manages the program, he or she is responsible for making sure that the program is well coordinated.

Key Communicators

Many principals capitalize on their knowledge of the community influence structure and develop a list of "key communicators." These are the persons to be contacted when there is a need to disseminate information quickly about the school. Key communicators are influential people in the immediate community who have an identified interest in the school. These people are influential because they interact with large numbers of people and are trusted. A loose organization of such individuals is easily formed. From time to time, the group might meet with the principal and other professionals in the building to discuss what is going on at the school that would be of general community interest. After an initial meeting, the key communicators are kept informed about such things as school budgets, new curricula, teacher turnover, and new construction. The group, as individuals and in collective feedback sessions, keeps the principal informed about "rumblings and rumors" in the community.

As always, care should be taken to see that all dimensions of the school community are tapped. The notion of using key communicators capitalizes on communications research, which continues to indicate that individual members of a community get most of the information from which attitudes and beliefs are formed in a word-of-mouth fashion—even in this mass media age.

Principal-Organized Interaction Sessions

In excellent schools, principals have regular "tell-it-to-the-principal" interaction sessions. Concerned about establishing and maintaining good relationships with students and parents, principals have initiated two kinds of sessions. One is a student–principal program conducted regularly in the principal's office or over lunch in a more secluded part of the school cafeteria. Attendance is limited to 8 or 10 students, and it is important that a representative sample of students participates. In these open-forum sessions, students express interests, discuss grievances, and make suggestions about the general improvement of the school.

The same sorts of session can be scheduled for parents and other community members. Patrons are invited to the meeting, and reservations are taken for a dozen or so patrons. Special invitations are necessary to ensure representativeness.

The rule for the meeting is that anything goes, except for personal complaints about individual teachers (which must be reserved for private, individual sessions). Two or three hours will provide an opportunity for an informal exchange of ideas. For the principal, the session is a good sensing mechanism to find out what patrons are concerned about and to get some notion of impending problem situations. For the patrons, it's a good opportunity to learn about the operation of the school and to raise questions about the educational practices.

One of the difficulties in engendering community support is the inadequacy of the information exchange between the school and the home. Organized, yet informal, parent–principal forums help. Complex ideas are difficult to express in the usual one-way bulletins or news stories that frequently serve as major sources of information for parents and other community members. Complex ideas are best tested in a face-to-face setting.

Parent–Teacher Conferences

Planned parent–teacher conferences can be an important element in a school–community relations program. Principal need to consider factors such as working parents, one-parent households, a parent's occupation that would preclude attendance at parent–teacher conferences scheduled during the normal school day, the language spoken, and transportation difficulties that might influence the success of the endeavor. These and other constraints can be overcome with diligent work on the part of school personnel.

Parent–Teacher Organizations

Historically, a PTA or PTO has served as the main, and sometimes only, organized school outreach program. Principals should use whatever devices are available to facilitate a two-way flow of information; in the case of PTOs, effectiveness has varied markedly throughout the country.

Nothing good happens automatically just because an organization is labeled in such a way as to suggest a formal relationship with the school. Parent–teacher organizations can provide a

useful avenue for interaction between school and community if meetings are organized to provide an opportunity for both formal and informal interaction and if the organization is given important tasks to perform. The key seems to be *active involvement in tasks*. Parent organizations, just like other community organizations, are competing for the time of their members. Whether a parent or a teacher elects to spend Thursday evening at a PTO meeting will depend on whether that time is viewed as productively occupied.

A good PTO will spend less time meeting formally and more time in subgroups considering important tasks to be performed around the school and the community. Organizing business–industry–education days for the career development program in the school, developing after-school programs for children and adults in the community, recruiting and training paraprofessionals, and working on curriculum review teams are the kinds of activities in which an effective PTO engages.

One common problem that inhibits the usefulness of a PTO as a communication device is the unevenness of the membership makeup. Even though the school may serve a heterogeneous population, the active membership is often almost entirely persons from only one thread in the societal fabric. Thus, the principal should examine the membership of the parent organization carefully. If the PTO is to be used as an effective communication device and the school community is heterogeneous, a membership that reflects the school community at large becomes most important. If the membership is not reflective, then it is likely that important opinions are not being heard and the organization is not promoting information exchange with the broader community.

In schools that are "magnets" and draw a substantial number of students from widely dispersed areas, a traditional parent–teacher organization may be difficult to maintain, even with the most intense efforts. Under such a circumstance, energy might be directed more efficiently to other involvement techniques—special clubs and booster organizations, for example.

Community Surveys

Surveying community attitudes and opinions can be effective, especially as a school district enters an evaluation phase in an effort to establish or review educational goals, objectives, and priorities. Such a survey can lead to community committees and a revitalization of community involvement in educational policymaking.

Educational surveys may be conducted in a variety of ways. The most common method is to mail questionnaires to a random sample of the population living in a particular school attendance area. A better technique to employ, if the time and person power are available, is to conduct house-to-house interviews using a structured interview technique and calling on a random sample of the population, making sure that all parts of the community are included in the sample. Telephone surveys may also provide a reasonable alternative.

When done properly, however, surveys are expensive to conduct. Often, too, the number of responses is disappointingly small—so small or so unrepresentative that the results are unreliable. Nevertheless, finding out periodically and regularly what community members think is very important. Demographics change, public opinion is fluid, and accurate information is essential to good administrative decision making. At the very least, the principal does not want to be blindsided. A crisis rarely occurs without some early indications, unrest, and dissatisfaction.

Summary

Developing good relations with the community and with persons in the school attendance area is one of the most important tasks for the principal. People live in a highly diverse society, and the children being educated belong to that society. Even in remote areas, differences exist and attitudes vary, affected, certainly by access to the Internet, television, books, and magazines. The schisms that separate many in society are often manifest in the relationships with public institutions such as schools.

School leaders are faced with the myriad of social changes that have occurred during the recent past. As a result of these changes—in societal makeup, in economic makeup, in technological change, and in global interactions, among others—the attitudes and orientations of the school's publics are at times confounding and always challenging.

This chapter has had both a macrofocus and microfocus. Schools exist as a part of the greater society and culture, but schools also exist in the smaller world of cities, suburbs, towns, villages, and, importantly, in neighborhoods. It is at the neighborhood level that the greatest interaction with the publics occurs. And it is in the neighborhoods that attitudes are formed. It is here where the school principal plays the important role. Certain hot-button issues can be anticipated and be dealt with in the neighborhood. School board policies can be best explained in the neighborhood. Citizens' advisory groups are most effective in the neighborhood, where action can be more easily implemented. For these reasons, the principals involvement is critical.

We have identified a number of community forces—some more local than others—and have presented strategies for working with those forces. Two-way means of information dissemination seem to be the most effective. These are also, however, the most complex of the public relations processes. But then, no one ever seriously wrote that being a school principal was easy.

ACTIVITIES

1. Reflect on Cases 2, 25, and 28. How will you respond in each of these situations?
2. Case Study 27 focuses on zero tolerance. How do you respond to the different situations in the case? What public relations issues might you foresee? What additional information would you seek?
3. Case Study 5 has controversial books as a central theme and a disturbed community group as a message bearer. Given the concepts in this chapter, what will be your approach?
4. Investigate the kinds of one-way and two-way information processing in your school programs. What means of evaluation are currently in place with regard to the effectiveness of these programs? What means might you suggest?
5. Collect some demographic data about the community(ies) in your school attendance area. Racial and ethnic data

will provide a starting point but investigate also housing patterns, public services, and commercial development. Check census tract information. Do a drive-about and note locations.

Then, examine the rolls of important school–community groups: advisory councils, booster clubs, PTA/PTO, and so on. To what extent is *active* membership in the identified groups representative of the nature of the adult population and the student population? Are there any differences in the makeup? What do any differences suggest about what kinds of public relations devices might better be employed?

6. Turn to the ISLLC standards in Appendix B. Review Standards 4 and 6. Which of the items in the standards relate to the concepts in this chapter? Relate one function in each standard to a concept expressed in Chapter 15.

ENDNOTES

1. The opposite of *gemeinschaft* is *gesselschaft.* The term *gesselschaft* identifies a community where there are many special interests and beliefs. It is a community where there is a general lack of knowledge about one's fellows and general anonymity. It is community that has—must have— many formal controls and laws because without these behavior would be uncontrolled, and there are many different organizations, some for political reasons, others for social reasons. *Gemeinschaft* is different. In the *gemeinschaft* community, ideological unity is paramount. There is a lack of special-interest groups because there are few special interests. Self-sufficiency and a strong sense of community identity exist. It's helpful to think of *gemeinschaft* and *gesellschft* as opposite ends of a sacred/secular continuum and communities as existing at various points along the continuum depending on the disposition of the community.
2. For the Most Challenged Books lists see details from the American Library Association at www.ala.org/.

3. Ronnie Casella, "Violence and Threats of Violence," in *Current Issues in School Leadership,* ed. Larry W. Hughes (Mahwah, NJ: Erlbaum, 2005), p. 21.
4. Larry W. Hughes, "Politics, Pressure Groups, and School Change," in *Current Issues in School Leadership,* ed. Larry W. Hughes (Mahwah, NJ: Erlbaum, 2005), p. 5.
5. Jesse Bernard, *Community Behavior* (New York: Holt, Rinehart and Winston), p. 358.
6. M. Fullen, *Change Forces: The Sequel* (Philadelphia: Falmer Press, 1999), p. 328.
7. "The powers not delegated to the United States by the Constitution, nor prohibited by it to the States, are reserved to the States respectively, or to the people."
8. As with much legislation, these two acts came about as a result of much concerted action on the part of the informal sectors of society—groups and individuals who exerted much pressure for federal action.

SELECTED READINGS

Blank, M. "Community Schools: Engaging Parents and Families." *Principal 83* (2004): 65.

Gretz, P. "School and Community Partnerships: Cultivating Friends." *Principal Leadership 3,* no. 5 (2003): 32–34.

Hughes, Larry W. (Ed.). *Current Issues in School Leadership* (Mahwah, NJ: Erlbaum, 2005).

Hughes, Larry W., and Don W. Hooper. *Public Relations for School Leaders* (Boston: Allyn & Bacon, 2000).

Jaksec, Charles M. *The Difficult Parent: Handling Aggressive Behavior* (Thousand Oaks, CA: Corwin Press, 2005).

Leighninger, M. "Working with the Public on Big Decisions." *School Administrator 60,* no. 10 (2003): 33–34.

McConnell, S. "Exercising the Power of Grassroots Advocacy." *Principal 84,* no. 3 (2005): 34–37.

Miller, T. N., L. Leslie-Toogood, and M. Kaff. "Creating Asset-Rich Communities." *Principal Leadership 5* (April 2005): 32–37.

Piltch, B., and R. Fredericks. "A Principal's Guide to School Politics." *Principal 84,* no. 3 (2005): 10–14.

Pitzel, G., A. Benavidez, B. Bianchi, L. Croom, B. de la Riva, D. Grein, J. Holloway, and A. Rendon. "Rural Revitalization in New Mexico: A Grass Roots Initiative Involving School and Community." *Rural Educator 28,* no. 3 (2007): 4–11.

Sanders, Mavis. *Building School–Community Partnerships* (Thousand Oaks, CA: Corwin Press, 2005).

Sharp, H. M. "After the Fact." *Principal Leadership 5* (January 2005): 39–41.

Voke, H. "Engaging the Public in Its Schools." *Educational Leadership 30* (July 2002): 68–79.

Wayson, William W., Charles M. Achilles, Gay Su Pinnell, M. Nan Lintz, Lila N. Carol, and Lavern Cunningham. *Handbook for Developing Public Confidence in Schools* (Bloomington IN: Phi Delta Kappa Educational Foundation, 1988). Do not let the copyright date fool you. This is still the best single guidebook around. It is practical, penetrating, *and* current.

Wherry, J. H. "Building on Respect, Humility, and Partnership." *Principal 84,* no. 5 (2005): 6.

Wittman, B. "Getting the Community Hooked." *Principal Leadership 8,* no. 2 (2007): 52–55. (ERIC Document Reproduction Service No. EJ779576).

Wooleyhand, C. D., D. Swietik, L. K. Winter, and Mark W. Mitchell. "Family Power." *Educational Leadership 65,* no. 7 (2008).

CHAPTER

16

Legal Rights and Responsibilities of Staff and Students

It is a litigious world in which we live. And so, one more important task of the principal is ensuring that the school operates in a legal manner, that staff operate in a legal manner, and that students' legal rights are ensured. It's more than simply staying out of court, it is behaving in a just way. Threats of lawsuits have seemingly become as commonplace as PTO potluck suppers. And, students, parents, and staff members may not always be right, but they always have rights.

—LARRY W. HUGHES[1]

No one expects a principal to be a legal authority, but knowledge of the laws under which the schools operate is an essential responsibility. There are many situations in which principals as well as teachers engage that have legal implications. School curricula, instructional practices, community expectations and demands, student behaviors, and the use of student records all have legal purviews.

The content of this chapter is about problem areas that may quickly result in litigation with a school district and particularly with principals and other educators as named parties. The chapter is also about the legal *and* ethical framework within which educators must operate to provide both a lawful and a humane school environment. Most administrator preparation programs provide coursework in school law. This chapter is not intended to replace such a course; rather, it highlights the continuing and prevailing situations that daily confront the school leader. Moreover, the chapter stresses the need for the school leader to stay abreast of new laws and court decisions that affect schooling. Various professional organizations, including the

National Association of Secondary School Principals and the National Association of Elementary and Middle School Principals, offer much help in this. (Reading a daily newspaper isn't a bad idea either.)

It is at the school building level that the policies of the local school board and the laws of the land that govern education are most often implemented. It is also at the school building level that most of the litigation involving the schools begins.

We begin this chapter by examining the federal, state, and local bases for schooling. After discussing certain fundamental rights—substantive and procedural due process, we review First and Fourth Amendment rights as these affect schooling and those to be schooled. Issues of equity are then considered—gender, racial and ethnic, disabling conditions, the homeless and sexual harassment. Following this is a discussion of common text liability settings in schools. There is a discourse, as well, about the elements of the Family Educational Rights and Privacy Act. We conclude the chapter by describing the development of good rules and regulations.

Legal Bases for Schools: Federal, State, and Local Perspectives

Historically, schools are creatures of the individual states, but in practice, the support and control of schools has been a partnership between local, state, and federal governments. Even private and parochial schools and school systems do not exist as autonomous entities, because these too must meet certain state curriculum and teacher certification standards. Also, certain federal regulations impinge when these schools accept available federal funds.

The legal framework within which school systems operate is manifest in the acts passed by federal, state, and local legislative bodies, court decisions, constitutional law, and rules and regulations enacted by regulatory and administrative bodies such as the state departments of education or other governmental departments. A further source of legal guidelines are the opinions of various attorneys general that stand until tested in a court of law or modified by subsequent legislative acts.

An extralegal impingement also exists: community sanctions, attitudes, and belief structures that modify, often very directly, the development and implementation of local policies. Within this framework, local administrators have latitude in the development of policies, rules, regulations, and procedures.

Limitations on local authority depend also on prevailing court philosophy in any state. In some states, the prevailing philosophy is that boards of education may adopt any reasonable policy not specifically prohibited by statute. In other states, courts insist that there be specific statutory permission before a particular policy can be adopted. Generally speaking, courts have tended to uphold the rule of reason—that boards of education may adopt any reasonable policy within the law. Courts in all states do insist on strict adherence to laws concerning management of public funds, however. School boards and administrators must find clear statutory authority for the expenditure of funds derived from public revenues.

Most of the individual rights enjoyed in this country derive from the Constitution of the United States and are largely located in the first 10 amendments of the Constitution (the Bill of

Rights) and in some subsequent amendments, notably the Fourteenth Amendment. Amendments of special relevance to the operation of schools are listed next:

- *Amendment One* deals with freedom of religion and expression and rights to peaceful assembly and petition. It grants the rights of all citizens to assemble peacefully and to petition the government for redress of grievances. Amendment One has often been cited in civil rights cases involving students and teachers.
- *Amendment Four* focuses on the rights of persons and states that the people and property shall be protected against "unreasonable searches and seizures," meaning that appropriate warrants must precede such police action. The educational implications here affect the confidentiality of records, interrogation of pupils, and the proceedings of juvenile court.
- *Amendment Five* guarantees the due process of law. It says that certain rights to life, liberty, and property are inviolate, and that people cannot be deprived of them without due process of law.
- *Amendment Six* provides for judicial procedure and guarantees a speedy public trial, an impartial jury, information about the nature of the charge, confrontation by witnesses against the party, the right of the accused to obtain witnesses in his or her own behalf, and the right to have counsel.
- *Amendment Eight* prohibits cruel and unusual punishment and excessive bail. The educational implications are clear, especially with regard to the question of corporal punishment, although undue mental anguish has also been cited as a "cruel and unusual" punishment.
- *Amendment Nine* guarantees the "rights of the people" and states that the enumeration in the Constitution of certain rights shall not be construed to deny or discourage other rights retained by the people. This simply means that even if the Constitution is silent, it does not imply that other rights are not enjoyed.
- *Amendment Ten* indicates that the powers that are not delegated to the United States by the Constitution nor prohibited by it to the states are reserved to the states respectively or to the people.

After the Civil War, the Fourteenth Amendment, the "States' Bill of Rights," was adopted. It states that "no state shall make a law which abridges the rights of citizens in the United States nor deny anyone the equal protection of the law." It states further that all persons, whether born or naturalized in the United States and subject to the jurisdiction thereof, are citizens of the United States and of the state wherein they reside. Thus, each state must guarantee the same rights to its citizens that are guaranteed by the U.S. Constitution. It is important to call attention to the phrase *all persons*. The amendment does not say all adults; it says all persons, and that includes children.

The courts have made it clear that constitutional protections apply to students both in and out of school. Freedom of expression and other basic rights, if not always clearly defined in the schools, are well established in the law. As the Supreme Court pointed out in *Tinker* v. *Des Moines School District,* "Students do not surrender their rights at the school house door."[2] Courts require specified procedures to safeguard those rights against the abuse of institutional authority. The matter of procedural due process, which will be discussed more completely later in this chapter, guarantees certain rights by the fair application of rules and regulations.

Nevertheless, even though students do have rights at school, these are balanced against the rights and responsibilities of administrators and teachers to maintain order and provide a good learning climate. The courts have been particularly careful to ensure that the school has the ability to effectively carry out the educational mission.

Application of the Laws

Of course, some rules of law are not universally accepted. Different courts often hand down conflicting decisions in seemingly similar cases, even within the same state. Also, the opinions of attorneys general vary over the years and between states. At the federal level, a change in the party controlling the executive branch often affects the rigor and vigor with which an attorney general or the Justice Department interprets and enforces the law and how the federal courts interpret a law.

Legislative acts at both state and federal levels vary from term to term as this or that current concern becomes law, or is countermanded by superseding law, or reaches a "sunset" provision. Also, the interpretation and the application of laws sometimes change over the years.

Due Process

The right to a fair warning and a fair hearing before a transgression is acted on is basic in American law. The general issue addressed by due process considerations is that of the constitutional rights of personnel and students balanced against the duty of school officials to control and protect the school system and to protect the rights of students to obtain an education. Two kinds of due process—substantive and procedural—must be considered and implemented.

Substantive Due Process

Substantive due process is concerned with the basic lawfulness of an enactment. School policies, rules, and regulations must stand the test of substantive due process. A person punished or denied the right to behave in some way by an existing law, rule, or regulation when that law, rule, or regulation is itself contrary to certain constitutional guarantees has legal recourse to set aside the punishment or denial and make the rule invalid. Moreover, substantive due process requires that there must be sufficient evidence or documentation of violation to warrant action by school officials or sufficient reason to believe that, if the rule is not invoked, current or subsequent acts by the parties involved will result in disruption of the educational process. The burden of proof rests with the school officials, not the alleged transgressor.

Tinker is often cited in reference to presumed disruptions.[3] Rules are invoked because the school principal says, in effect, "If this rule is not enforced and obeyed, the process of education in the school will be impeded." In *Tinker,* two important legal principles of a substantive nature were applied by the Supreme Court in holding for the students: There was no disruption; therefore, the presumption of the rule was false, and students had the constitutional right to defy the rule. The wearing of the armbands was analogous to free speech (a First Amendment guarantee), and the students had the right to express themselves.

Two rules of thumb must be applied: Will the behavior cause substantial disorder to the education process or normal operation of the school? Will the behavior be an invasion of the rights of others? The burden of proof rests on the school district and/or administrator. Courts are critical of administrative action predicated on presumption. The collection of sufficient evidence to show reason for administrative action is essential.

Guidelines to Ensure Substantive Due Process.   School policies, rules, and regulations, as well as the administrative actions enforcing them, should be subjected to the following guidelines:

1. *Legality.* Is there a basis in state and federal constitutional and legislative law for the policy, rule, or regulation? Are the constitutional rights of those for whom it was written protected?
2. *Sufficient Specificity.* Are the conditions under which the policy, rule, or regulation will be invoked detailed? Are the terms and phraseology used definitive? Vague and unclear statements are sufficient to cause the courts to abrogate.
3. *Reason and Sensibleness.* Does the rule or regulation really enhance the educational climate; that is, is it really necessary? Is there sufficient reason to believe that without the rule, the rights of others will be unprotected or the school will be disrupted? A rule may be declared unreasonable in and of itself or in its particular application.
4. *Adequate Dissemination.* Has information about the rule been distributed in such a way that persons affected can be expected to know about it, know what it means, and know what the penalties are?
5. *Appropriate Penalties.* Are the punishments appropriate to the nature of the infraction? Severe penalties for minor transgressions must be avoided.[4]

Procedural Due Process

Procedural due process is an orderly, established process for arriving at an impartial and just settlement of a conflict between parties. It entails fair warning and fair hearing.

Fair Warning.   Fair warning simply means that a person must be aware of the rules to follow, or behavior that must be exhibited, and the potential penalties for violation. The age of the person must be taken into consideration as well. Moreover, there must be a correlation between the severity of the penalty and the rule that has been broken.

Fair Hearing.   A fair hearing is composed of the following specific aspects:

1. *The individual must be given a written statement of the charges and the nature of evidence.* This is often called a Bill of Particulars. Clarity is important. The accused, and, in the instance of pupils, the accused's parents, must comprehend the contents of the written statement. The background and educational level of the individuals involved and the complexity of the statement should be taken into account. A personally delivered statement to the parents would provide an opportunity for clarifying charges and would be appropriate at times. The precise nature of the charges and the evidence must be incorporated in the statement. Vague rules and imprecise charges have resulted in the reversal of more school board and administrative decisions than any other defect.[5]

2. *The individual must be informed of certain procedural rights.* Having rights but being kept unaware of them is the same as not having rights. Individuals must be provided information specifying the appeal and defense processes available. Information such as to whom the appeal should be made, the time limit under which the appeal can be advanced, and other elements of procedural due process is necessary.

3. *Adequate time must be provided to prepare a defense.* In serious issues, ordinarily a minimum of 5 days should be provided for an individual to prepare a defense; 10 days almost certainly will sustain a court inquiry.[6]

4. *There must be an opportunity for a formal hearing.* Five components compose a proper formal hearing:

   a. The case must be presented to an impartial hearer. The school official bringing the charge may *not* also serve as hearer.

   b. The individual must have the opportunity to present evidence.

   c. The individual has the right to know and confront whomever brought the charges and to question that person or those persons.

   d. The individual has the right to produce witnesses and to cross-examine witnesses. The individual must have the opportunity to disprove the accusations of a hostile witness and include testimony of those who can explain the defendant's side of the issue.

   e. The individual has the right to counsel. This does not necessarily mean an attorney, but there is no reason why it could not be. It may be simply a friend, parent, or citizen on whose advice the defendant wishes to rely.

First Amendment Rights

The school's power to control students is not broad enough in scope to proscribe protected speech. In the *Tinker* case,[7] three students wore black armbands to publicize their objections to the Vietnam conflict. The Supreme Court held that wearing the armbands was protected because it was closely related to protected political speech. Political speech must be encouraged and protected because open speech is the basis of the nation's strength and of the "independence and vigor" of Americans. First Amendment rights, when allowed "in light of the special characteristics of the school environment, are available to teachers and students." Where there is no proof that the student has interfered with the school's work or the rights of other students, the school may not limit free expression merely because it fears a disturbance. The Constitution requires the risk of dispute to foster the democratic system.

In the banner *Hazelwood* decision (*Hazelwood School District* v. *Kuhlmeier*, 484 US 260, 1988) the Supreme Court ruled that a school newspaper was not a public forum, but rather "a supervised learning experience for journalism students." Rights of freedom of expression therefore are not unlimited. In a later court ruling a case involved the removal of a student-posted religious message. In the Eleventh Circuit, the U.S. Court of Appeals ruled that a principal did not violate a student's First Amendment rights of either free expression or of free exercise of religion by requiring the student to remove a religious message from a mural she painted for a school beautification process. A district court's ruling was upheld on the grounds that the beautification project did not constitute a public forum. The mural was a "school-sponsored" speech, and the principal's decision reasonably related to "legitimate pedagogical objectives (*Bannion* v. *School District of Palm Beach County*, Eleventh Circuit, October 12, 2004).

Freedom of Expression

There are limits on students' and on teachers' rights to freedom of expression in the school. In *Bethel School District No. 43* v. *Fraser* (106 S.Ct. 3159), the Supreme Court held in 1986 that a student's "lewd and indecent speech" is not protected by the First Amendment. Similarly, a teacher's rights to freedom of expression may be circumscribed. Several kinds of classroom speech are not within the protections of either academic freedom or the First Amendment. The repeated use of profanity in the classroom has been found not to be protected (*Martin* v. *Parrish,* 805 F2d 583) nor has using the classroom as a forum for criticizing school administrators or school policies (*Robbins* v. *Board of Education of Argo Community High School District,* 313 F.Supp 42). Political views and personal views unrelated to class subjects or the curriculum are also subject to proscription.[8]

Limits on student expression extend to slogans, matter that appears on clothing, and jewelry that may signify gang membership. For example, *Olesen* v. *Board of Education* (1987) upheld an antigang rule that prohibited the wearing of earrings by male students.[9] Similarly, dress codes that prohibited certain clothing that identified professional sports teams were upheld when the school showed that gangs wore these articles of clothing and that there was a large amount of gang activity in the school.[10] T-shirts and articles of clothing that depict lewd scenes or expressions have been found not to be within the bounds of student freedom of expression.[11] Where regulations are established for the purpose of protecting health and safety or for maintaining discipline, the courts are likely to be sympathetic. It is the responsibility of school officials to show that the rule bears a rational relationship to a legitimate state interest, however.

Student Publications

Scholastic newspapers fall within the ambit of the First Amendment's prohibition on censorship; therefore, a court would require a strong showing on the part of the school to uphold any censorship. The school would have to show that publication of the forbidden articles would materially and substantially interfere with the requirements of discipline in the operation of the school. Students are *not* free to publish without supervision, however, and administrative review has been held to be appropriate. In *Nicholson* v. *Board of Education, Torrance County Unified School District,* for example, the court held:

> Writers on high school newspapers do not have an unfettered constitutional right to be free from pre-publication review. The special characteristics of the high school environment, particularly one involving students in a journalism class that produces a school newspaper, call for supervision and review by faculty and administration. The administrative review of a small number of sensitive articles for accuracy rather than for possible censorship or official imprimatur does not implicate First Amendment rights.[12]

This same court also held that the school possessed a substantial educational interest in teaching young student writers journalistic skills that stressed the tenets of accuracy and fairness.

As we previously wrote, a case involving the First Amendment rights of students was decided by the Supreme Court in 1988 in *Hazelwood School District* v. *Kuhlmeier.* Former high school students who had been staff members on the school newspaper filed suit in federal district court, alleging that their rights had been violated by the deletion of two pages from an edition of the paper. Included in the deletion were two articles. One of the articles described school

ISLLC 6

students' experiences with pregnancy; the other discussed the impact of divorce on students at the school. The newspaper was written and edited by a journalism class and the class was a part of the regular school curriculum.

Pursuant to the school's practice, the teacher in charge of the class had submitted page proofs to the principal, who subsequently objected to the pregnancy story. He objected because, even though no names were used, he believed that the pregnant students might be identified from the text and because he believed that the references to sexual activity and birth control were inappropriate for some of the younger students.

The principal objected to the article about divorce because the page proofs he had been furnished identified by name (deleted by the teacher in the final version) a student who complained of her father's conduct. The principal indicated he thought the parent should have been given an opportunity to respond to the remarks or to consent to their publication. Believing that there was insufficient time to make the changes if the paper was to be issued before the end of the school year, the principal directed that the pages be removed even though other unobjectionable articles were included on the same pages.

The Supreme Court held that the First Amendment rights of the students had not been violated, that such rights were not automatically coextensive with the rights of adults in other settings, and that such rights must be applied in light of the special characteristics of the school environment. In the opinion of the Court, the school need not tolerate student speech that is inconsistent with its basic educational mission, even though the government could not censor similar speech outside of the school.

School facilities may be deemed to be public forums only if school authorities by policy or by practice have opened the facilities for any indiscriminate use by the general public, or by some segment of the public, such as student organizations. Otherwise, no public forum has been created and reasonable restrictions may be imposed on the speech of students, teachers, and other members of the school community. The school, in this case, was found not to have deviated from its own restrictive policies.

School Library Books

To what extent do school boards (and, by implication, administrators) have discretionary authority to remove books and materials from a school library? Courts have held that although a school board has broad discretion in adding books to a school library, it may not remove books simply because it dislikes the ideas contained in those books. The school may not remove books in order to "prescribe what shall be orthodox in politics, nationalism, religion or other matters of opinion."[13] The question of whether the removal of the books is an unconstitutional abridgment of a student's First Amendment rights is decided on an analysis of the board's intention. The board may not remove books to prevent access to ideas that it disapproves of or when ideas fall under the protection of the First Amendment. The circumstances that permit exception to this principle are narrow. However, it would be permissible to remove books that were "pervasively vulgar" or educationally unsuitable.

These latter issues, of course, require definition. The wise principal will work with the staff to develop criteria to determine "educational suitability." Help is available from the National Council for the Teaching of English and from the American Library Association. Whatever the court meant by "pervasively vulgar" is unknown—such phrases lack definition and are useless to the school leader.

Required Reading Materials

In *Grove* v. *Mead School District No. 354*,[14] a student and her parents argued that the use of a particular book that was a part of the English curriculum violated the First Amendment's prohibition of state establishment of religion. The court held that the factors that must be considered were whether there was a heavy burden on the individual's exercise of religion; if there was a compelling state interest justifying that burden; and if there could be some accommodation that would not impede the school's objective. The court decided that the burden on the student's exercise of religion was minimal because she was allowed to read an alternative book and avoid the classroom discussions of the other book.

This accommodation was made in order to allow the school to continue to provide a well-rounded public education; to do otherwise would have critically impeded the school's function. When there is no coercion used with the student, and the school is pursuing a valid end of public education, such an accommodation does not violate the student's right of free exercise of religion. But if a student (or parent) objects to the use of a required book because it infringes on religious beliefs, the wisest course would be to have, *if educationally possible,* an alternative reading assignment available.

Prayer and Religion in Public Schools

The subject of prayer and religion can become a problem of great significance and a source of headaches for principals in a public school, elementary or secondary. Permitting prayer or accommodating religious groups need not be a problem, however, except insofar as a particular community insists on *prescription* by the schools. The key word is *voluntary.* The courts—the Supreme Court, in particular—have clarified the issue on many occasions. (We will cite only a few representative ones here, but the reader can find ample formal citation on the Internet using these search words: religion and school prayer.)

ISLLC 4

As noted earlier, the First Amendment to the Constitution states, "Congress shall make no law respecting an *establishment* of religion, or prohibiting the *free exercise* thereof." [emphasis added]. The federal and state courts have held in many cases that every governmental body (including school districts) must remain neutral with respect to religion. Schools are prohibited from taking any kind of action that tends to either "establish" or support religious beliefs *or* tends to prevent the "free exercise" of religion. The courts mean that public school personnel may not require, lead, or encourage the study or discussion of scripture or any other religious activities during the school day or in connection with school-sponsored extracurricular activities.

May students study about religion when it is directly related to curricular offerings? Generally, yes. For example, a history teacher developing a lesson about the early settlement of what became the United States could certainly examine the centrality of religious beliefs to the migration of the Pilgrims to this continent and the degree to which those beliefs affected their lives. Also, for example, it would seem impossible not to discuss the Spanish Inquisition or the effect of the spread of Islam on the development of the Mediterranean region, including parts of southern Europe, if a class was engaged in a study of Western civilization. And, how could one introduce such plays as *The Crucible* without examining the basis for the Salem witch trials?

Yet, issues in a religious context continue to trouble some schools and certainly some school principals. "To pray or not to pray" seems to be a continuing matter of public concern in some communities. And here we refer to formal prayers offered before school events. The courts have disallowed this continually in recent years, but the subject continues to come up. Frequently, a school group or a collection of students, often with supporting parents, will propose to offer "nondenominational" prayers before a school event—an athletic contest perhaps or a commencement ceremony. The "prayer" will be one the student has developed. Others attending the ceremony or event will not be required to participate. It is "all voluntary." Can it be done? Not according to the courts and not according to many attorneys general. The issue is a politically charged one and principals will wish it hadn't come up because some members of the community will be incensed at being denied this practice. The principle is this: Any individual may pray privately at any time but prayers offered to an assembled group or sanctioned by the public school are *not* legal under the Federal Constitution.

In 2000, the issue was further addressed by the Supreme Court. In *Santa Fe Independent School District* v. *Doe,* the Court outlawed school-sponsored prayer at high school football games (120 U.S. 2206). School-sponsored religious activities are constitutionally prohibited. But the controversy goes on and arises from time to time regardless of court actions. One community group or another frequently tests schools and principals on the issue and school boards often collapse in the face of this pressure, and back to court the school goes. What are principals to do? Stay within the prescribed law and be prepared seems to be the best policy.

Religious Clubs.   If the school has an open forums policy, and the formation of after-school clubs of a noncurricular nature that meet on school grounds is permitted, then such nonschool-related clubs as chess clubs, science fiction clubs, and Bible study groups are permitted. But this is permitted only to the extent that the groups are student sponsored and not school sponsored and are not held during school hours.[15]

Students may also distribute religious tracts on school grounds *if* other groups are permitted to distribute materials about their organizations. If a school regularly permits students to distribute noncurricular, nonreligious materials in the hallways, then it must allow students to distribute religious materials. Our advice is to not permit any noncurricular materials to be distributed by students. Such a policy will prevent a lot of unnecessary headaches and hurt no one.

Objectionable Materials.   What about objections of this or that religious group to instructional materials being used or to certain events such as Halloween parties? In an elementary school in Wheaton, Illinois, a supplementary reading program for K–5 students was introduced after a curriculum review committee screened the series for educational suitability and quality. The series included the work of Dr. Seuss, C. S. Lewis, Ray Bradbury, Maurice Sendak, A. A. Milne, and other noted authors. Some parents filed suit and alleged that the series fostered a religious belief in the existence of supernatural beings including "wizards, sorcerers, [and] giants." They further alleged that the material "indoctrinates children in values directly opposed to their Christian beliefs by teaching tricks, despair, deceit, parental disrespect and . . . denigration of Christian symbols of holidays." Even the *Harry Potter* books by J. K. Rowling have been assailed by the Christian religious right.

Ultimately, the courts held that the burden on the parents was, "at most, minimal"; they were free to provide religious instruction on their own, and "the use of the series did not compel their children to affirm or deny any religious doctrine." The teaching of reading and creativity was viewed by the court as a fundamental and compelling governmental interest, and the court noted that the tolerance of religious diversity is among the appropriate values for public schooling.[16]

The selection and use of instructional materials should always be subjected to careful review by teachers. Moreover, good educational practice requires that the development of new curriculum be subjected to such criteria as suitability and quality, and that the formation of curriculum review committees only makes good sense in any case. Although prudence and sensitivity are always important, principals and teachers should not be intimidated by parents' religious beliefs. Efforts to "cleanse" the curriculum by this or that religious group in accordance with any particular religious orthodoxy is harmful—indeed, it is at extreme cross-purposes to the reason that schools exist. This does not mean that a discerning excusal policy may not be advisable, but it does mean that wholesale elimination of educational materials in the face of parental complaint is a dereliction of duty and contrary to good educational practice. It is sound practice to have a standing academic review committee for advice on such matters.

Now to Halloween and other such celebrations: The schools have also been accorded latitude here in the instance of parental objection on religious grounds. In Florida, some parents objected to Halloween celebrations as satanic celebrations that inculcated a belief in witches. The court held that "witches, cauldrons, and brooms in the context of school Halloween celebrations appear to be nothing more than a mere 'shadow,' if that, in the realm of establishment clause jurisprudence."[17]

Fourth Amendment Rights

A particularly difficult legal issue is that of conducting searches of students and their property. Freedom from unreasonable searches and seizure of property is a Fourth Amendment right. The Fourth Amendment's prohibition of unreasonable searches and seizures applies to searches conducted by public school officials. In carrying out searches and other disciplinary functions pursuant to school policies, administrators act as representatives of the state, not merely as surrogates for the parents, and they cannot claim the parents' immunity from the strictures of the Fourth Amendment.

Although school officials may search students or their possessions when it is "reasonable" to do so, the court has not given specific examples of what is reasonable, although "possible cause" is a common determinant. Whether a search is reasonable depends on the factual context of the search. The search of a child's person or property is a violation of the expectation of privacy of the student; however, this expectation of privacy is balanced against the interest of teachers and administrators in maintaining discipline and security.

These principles lead to the following test of the legality of a search: Is the search reasonable under all of the circumstances of the search? More specifically, is the search justified at its inception, and is the search related in scope to the circumstances that justify the interference in the first place?

Under ordinary circumstances, a search by a school official will be justified at its inception when there are reasonable grounds for suspecting that the search will show that the student has violated or is violating either the law or the rules of the school. The severity of the violation is a factor, however. One shouldn't search a student for minor infractions.

The Supreme Court has addressed the issue from yet another perspective: random testing of students for the purpose of determining if individuals were using prohibited drugs. The Supreme Court decided in June 2002 that it was permissible for a school to have a drug policy that established random, suspicionless urinalysis testing of any student participating in extracurricular competitive activities (*Board of Education of Independent School District No. 92 of Pottawatomie County v. Earls* [No. 01–332]). The Court held that the Tecumseh, Oklahoma, schools' drug-testing policy "is a reasonable means of furthering the School District's important interest in preventing and deterring drug use among its school children and does not violate the Fourth Amendment."

In a 1995 decision, *Vernonia School District 47J v. Acton* (515 U.S. 646), the Supreme Court determined that drug testing of students participating in athletics was permissible. The Tecumseh decision expands that to include competitive activities in addition to athletics. One can assume that even extracurricular activities such as choirs and debate teams would also be subject of random testing if the school determined this was a good policy. The Court addressed the privacy issue when it said that students who participate in extracurricular activities have "a limited expectation of privacy" because of the voluntary nature of these activities.

Sexual Harassment

Complaints of sexual harassment between adults and between adults and children have increased exponentially, it seems. It is a serious issue and truly one of the fastest-growing areas of potential school district and school administrator liability. Failure to respond to allegations of sexual harassment most frequently gets school officials into difficulty.

Strahan[18] wrote, "Sexual misconduct by a professional employee . . . is a fact situation that often results in both contract termination and a criminal complaint." The situation becomes especially electric when the allegations involve a teacher or an administrator and a student. Those instances where cases have been about teachers permitting one student to sexually harass another, or a teacher being sexually involved with another student, or even a faculty member dating a student, have been resolved against the professional staff member.[19]

The *Davis* v. *Monroe* case (1999) is especially interesting because of some far-reaching implications.[20] In this case, a fifth-grader revealed that she was sexually taunted by a male classmate, including suggestions to come to bed with him and being touched on her breasts. Despite repeated complaints by the girl's mother, school officials failed to do anything to stop the boy. (The local sheriff had also been advised of her complaint.)

In 1994, Davis sued the board of education under Title IX of the 1972 Education Amendments, which cover public education at all levels. The school board won in lower courts but, because it was only one of a myriad of peer sexual harassment suits filed nationwide and these suits had yielded conflicting judicial opinions, the Supreme Court took the case on appeal. The Supreme Court ruled that in the case of harassment, a student could sue under Title IX if it could be shown that school officials knew of and were deliberately indifferent to the misconduct.

What is the lesson of these and other harassment allegations? School leaders must review every allegation, investigate the basis for each, and be prepared to take appropriate action. Indifference clearly will not be tolerated.

The implications of the *Davis* case extend well beyond the particulars. Title IX as a legal point—a prohibition against sex bias in schools that receive federal aid—was the issue. Women's rights groups applauded the decision as a victory, as did gay rights groups who use Title IX to fight abuse of gay and lesbian students by their peers.

Common Tort Liability Settings

A tort is an act *or an omitted act,* including breach of contract, that results in damage, injury, or loss to the injured person(s), who then may seek relief by legal action. Torts may be intentional, may result from negligence, or may be caused by carelessness. School employees are liable for their failure to carry out prescribed duties or the failure to carry out these duties correctly. Individual staff members are expected to behave in a reasonable manner in the discharge of their duties, avoiding acts that are capricious, arbitrary, or negligent.

Tort liability suits require adequate evidence of the following:

ISLLC 6

- A prescribed or implicit duty on the part of the defendant for the care of the plaintiff
- An error of commission or omission by the defendant
- Damage, loss, or injury sustained by the plaintiff
- Indication of a cause-and-effect relationship between the error and the circumstance at issue
- Absence of contributory or offsetting comparative negligence on the part of the plaintiff[21]

The best defense against lawsuits is precaution. Principals and teachers cannot be expected to be prescient, but they should anticipate possible dangers. The discussion that follows will examine common liability settings and describe certain aspects of the legal environment.

Pupil Injuries

A school is not usually a hazardous place, but young people frequently do sustain injuries in and about the school. Most of these injuries are accidental and minor, the result of normal behavior. Nevertheless, teachers and administrators do have a responsibility to provide reasonable and prudent protection for their charges, and they are legally liable in tort for injuries arising from their negligence.[22] The main test of negligence is *foreseeability.* That is, the behavior of an individual would be called negligent if an ordinarily prudent person would have foreseen that certain actions, or a failure to act, would lead injury to another.

The principal is responsible for taking all steps to promote the well-being of the students within the school and to guard the welfare of the staff. Therefore, to both staff and students, the principal has a particular duty to plan and supervise in a manner that will minimize the possibility of injury. At the very least, this involves providing information to staff members about their legal responsibilities and developing a set of rules and regulations that, if carefully followed, will result in protection for students.

Schools should be especially cautious in instances where it is "foreseeable" that student injury might result. Certain parts of the school environment present particular problems.

Physical Education, Field Trips, and Other Extracurricular Programs.   Field trips, other extracurricular programs, and physical education are inherently more hazardous than the regular academic program. Greater supervision is required to avoid liability as a result of negligence. Carefully developed and well-understood written rules and regulations for the governance of these activities are important.[23] Adequate regulations cover such categories as pupil conduct while a participant or spectator, medical examinations for participants, medical care for sick and injured participants, transportation to and from the activity, duties of teachers and other supervisors, and notification and approval in advance by a parent or guardian.[24] But approval *does not* foreclose the right of the injured party to sue.

Laboratories and Shops.   These two instructional areas present more hazards than any other in the school. Even general science classes engage in experiments within the classroom, often involving chemicals as well as common electric- or gas-powered laboratory equipment. Moreover, good educational practice in teaching science involves such outside classroom events as off-campus field trips and on-campus outdoor activities.

Similarly, greater emphasis on career education and career exploration means that more and more middle and elementary schools are developing prevocational shops with at least rudimentary power equipment as well as common hand tools. In addition, classes such as cooking and sewing continue in popularity and require power-and hand-operated equipment.

Constant and immediate supervision is expected of teachers functioning in these instructional spaces. Teachers must adequately instruct students in the care and use of equipment they will be operating. If there is evidence that a student has been permitted to use a particular tool, or perform an experiment, before being trained and told the consequences of improper usage, negligence will be difficult to disprove. Greater care is expected of teachers supervising students who are exposed to dangerous equipment. Even a brief teacher absence from a room where a class in engaged in hazardous activities is risky.[25]

Playgrounds.   Where supervision is regular, planned, reasonable, and proper, a negligence charge in case of pupil injury on the playground is not likely to be sustained. Consideration should be given to the kind of playground equipment in use, the size of the playground, and the number and age of the pupils to be supervised.

The courts generally appreciate that a teacher is unable to keep every child within view and out of hazard at all times. Nevertheless, negligent supervision is often held to be the proximate cause of injury. If, for example, a teacher permits a child to leave a supervised group and the child is injured in a known, existing hazardous condition, then the teacher may be liable. If a teacher assigned to playground duty leaves a post for no good cause and a child is injured in a known or foreseeable dangerous condition, there may be tort liability because of negligence. Also, although teachers would not be expected to repair playground equipment, permitting pupils to use equipment known to be faulty, or beyond the maturity level of the child, could result in a claim of negligence.

The principal has three major responsibilities. First, proper rules of behavior, consistent with good safety practices, must be developed and implemented. Second, adequate adult supervision on the playground should always be provided when children are present. Third, the principal must arrange for frequent and regular inspection of the playground and playground equipment and for a reporting system about any hazardous conditions. Staff and students must be apprised of these, and action should be taken to have the conditions corrected.

Classrooms.   Teachers are normally in charge in the classroom and thus are most frequently held responsible for the safety of the children there. However, the principal has some responsibilities that, if not met, may result in a charge of negligent behavior. The primary responsibility of the principal with regard to classroom activities is to ensure that there is a teacher or a responsible adult present at all times. The principal should always be aware of a teacher's absence from the classroom. Failure to have a plan to provide for pupil supervision when a teacher becomes ill or is tardy to class could cause the principal to be charged with negligence if an injury resulted while the students were unsupervised. A common practice is to have a check-in sheet for teachers in the morning. The principal, thus, can know immediately of any unanticipated absence or tardiness of personnel who have responsibility for the supervision of students.

Generally speaking, however, a temporary short-term absence from the classroom by a teacher would not, in and of itself, be considered a negligent act of general supervision. If, for example, a student misbehaves and in so doing injures another student during a teacher's brief absence from the room, a court would not ordinarily find negligence, because the teacher's absence was not the proximate cause of the accident. However, in all cases, the age, maturity, and intelligence of the student will bear on the question of teacher negligence in such absences. The best rule is not to leave students unattended.

Regulating Student Conduct

In even the best-run schools, students misbehave. Principals and teachers may prescribe reasonable controls against the misconduct of children. Many kinds of disciplinary action are available to school administrators and teachers when pupils violate school policies and rules. These include such minor punishments as short-term removal from the classroom, withholding certain privileges, detention after school, isolation from the rest of the class, being sent to the principal's office, and so on. The courts have generally upheld the right of school administrators and teachers to impose such minor punishment. Other forms of disciplinary action, however, such as suspension and expulsion from school[26] or the use of corporal punishment, are more often tested in the courts, and school administrators and teachers must take great care in the prescription of these punishments. Figure 16.1 depicts a basic information form to document disciplinary action.

In any case, the question of both substantive and procedural due process is important.[27] The reasonableness and legality of the rule or regulation violated must be examined with care, and the legal issue of whether the student has a right to a prior hearing is important. Clearly, administrators should take care in imposing minor as well as major punishments to ensure that pupils or personnel are treated fairly and are not victimized by capricious or arbitrary action.

Corporal Punishment.   *Corporal punishment* is disciplinary action by the application of physical force. As a means of modifying behavior, it is probably the oldest disciplinary tool. It also is one of the least efficacious. Acts of corporal punishment are probably the cause of more court cases than anything else.[28] Many school districts have developed policies that prohibit corporal punishment by teachers and by principals. So, contrary to what the laws of the state might permit, this policy would take precedence. Without a policy, however, under *in loco parentis,* the courts continue to uphold the right of teachers and principals to use "reasonable" force to ensure proper conduct or to correct improper conduct.[29]

ISLLC 3, 6

ISLLC 3

FIGURE 16.1   Report of Disciplinary Action: Randall Bury Junior High School

Date: _____

Student's Name: _____ Homeroom: _____ Grade: _____

Time: _____

Person Reporting: _____

Title of Person Reporting: _____

Nature of Offense:

Student's Account:

Action Taken:

I have had a chance to tell my side. _____

(Student Signature)

Date of Hearing: _____ Person Conducting Hearing: _____

Time: _____ Other Person(s) Present: _____

Infraction: State Law: _____ School Policy: _____

Board of Education Policy: _____

Central Office Policy: _____

Teacher Rule: _____ Common Sense: _____

In the *Baker* case,[30] the court held that corporal punishment may never be used unless the student was informed beforehand that specific misbehavior could occasion its use. The court also said that corporal punishment should never be employed as a first line of punishment. Another official also must be present and be told of the wrongful act in the presence of the student, to give the student an opportunity to protest spontaneously. A written explanation must then be sent to the parent, stating the reasons for the punishment.

Important guidelines must be followed if the use of corporal punishment is to be adjudicated as prudent and reasonable. Corporal punishment is generally held to be prudent under the following conditions:

- The state law and the local policy permit it.
- The punishment takes into consideration the age, size, gender, and health of the student and is not excessive.

- There is no malice; the punishment is given for corrective purposes only and is not immoderate.
- The student understands why punishment is required.
- An appropriate instrument is used.

Sometimes courts consider other attendant circumstances such as whether there was permanent injury as a result of the punishment.

To ensure the fairest treatment possible for the student, the principal and the teacher must establish reasonable rules and make sure that the punishment for breaking these rules is suitable. They also must reasonably administer the rules and apply them equally to all students. It is possible to administer a reasonable rule so improperly that it becomes unreasonable. Any vindictiveness or viciousness in administering corporal punishment must be avoided. If the teacher or the principal knows that he or she is uncontrollably angry, then it is not time to punish the child corporally—or in any other way.

Suspension/Expulsion. *Suspension* is a dismissal from the school for a specific, but relatively short, length of time. *Expulsion* means permanent or long-term dismissal from school and, in most states, can be accomplished only by the board of education; permanent exclusion from school is outside the authority of the school administrator.

Attendance at a public school is generally viewed as a right rather than a privilege, but the enjoyment of this right is conditioned by the student's willingness to comply with reasonable regulations and requirements of the school. Violations of these may be punished by suspension or, in extreme cases, by permanent exclusion. Under a suspension, a student is usually required to meet some set of conditions established by the administrator before being readmitted.

The dividing line between a short- and a long-term exclusion from school is not clearly defined, but as a result of *Goss* v. *Lopez* has probably been established as 10 days.[31] In *Goss,* the court clearly established the right of school administrators to suspend students to maintain order in the school system. However, in this case, the court did find that school officials had violated the student's constitutional right to procedural due process. Nine students were temporarily suspended from school *without a hearing* and thus were held to be denied due process. The school board had contended that due process was not applicable to suspensions because there was not a "constitutional right" to public education. The court disagreed with this, saying:

> Although Ohio may not be constitutionally obligated to establish and maintain the public school system, it has nevertheless done so and has required its children to attend. Those young people do not "shed their constitutional rights at the school house door. . . ." The authority possessed by the State to prescribe and enforce standards of conduct in its schools, although concededly very broad, must be exercised consistently with the constitutional safeguards.[32]

The school board had argued that even if public education was a right that was protected by due process, in this instance the due process clause should not apply because the suspensions were limited to 10 days, and this was neither a severe nor a grievous infringement on the students' right to an education. The court disagreed here also and faced the question of what kind of process is due in the instance of short-term student suspensions. The court held that only rudimentary process was required to balance student interests against the educator's need to take quick disciplinary action. The court said:

> The student [must] be given a written notice of the charges against him, if he denies them, an explanation of the evidence the authorities have and an opportunity to present his side of the story. . . . There need be no delay between the time "notice" is given and the time of the hearing. In the great majority of cases the disciplinarian may informally discuss the alleged misconduct with the student minutes after it has occurred. We hold only that, in being given an opportunity to explain his version of the facts at this discussion, the student first be told what he is accused of doing and what the basis of the accusation is.[33]

This is important because it implies that while due process provisions must always be present, even in less than major punishment, the nature of the punishment and the infraction will determine the degree to which one must engage in elaborate vestments of due process. In minor infractions it would be necessary only to provide rudimentary forms of hearing. Even here, however, the important lesson is that the child to be punished must in all instances be treated fairly and that there must be clear indication of the absence of capricious action. Expulsions are a different matter. In the case of an expulsion, it would seem clear that all of the vestments of due process be clearly applied.

Opposition to the use of suspensions and expulsions as punishment for misconduct is growing. More often, schools are developing a disciplinary procedure called *in-school suspension* as a means of avoiding the disruption and negative effects of being denied instruction for long periods of time. The in-school suspension usually involves taking the student out of the regular classroom for a period of time and placing the student in another learning situation within the school building, either in an independent learning situation with supervision or in a designated special class. When this procedure is coupled with counseling by the principal, the guidance counselor, or some other clinician to diagnose and treat the problem, it is a sound practice.

Detention.   It is well established that principals and teachers have the authority to temporarily detain students from participating in extracurricular activities and even to keep students after school as a punishment, providing, of course, that the students have a safe way of getting home. As in other punishments, the detention must be reasonable. False imprisonment may be claimed if the principal or a teacher either wrongfully detains a student or detains a student for an unreasonable amount of time as a punishment. In this, as in all other punishments, the main test is one of fairness. If school officials act fairly and in good faith in dealing with students, their actions will probably be upheld by the courts.

Privacy and Confidentiality of Student Records

The question of the confidentiality and accuracy of student records is important, and since the passage of Public Law 93–380, Family Educational Rights and Privacy Act of 1974 (FERPA), the issue has been legally clarified. This act states that students and parents are permitted to inspect and review records and must be given a copy of any part or all of the educational record on

ISLLC 6

request. It also requires that in any dispute concerning the contents of a student's educational record, due process must be provided. Where a record is found to be inaccurate, the inaccuracies must be expunged. FERPA essentially requires that the schools and other agencies permit an individual to determine what relevant records are maintained in the system of records; to gain access to relevant records in such a system of records; to have copies made; and to correct or amend any relevant record.

Furthermore, records about an individual may not be disclosed to outsiders except by the consent of the individual in question. The consent must be in writing and must be *specific* in stating to whom the record may be disclosed, which records may be disclosed, and, where applicable, the time frame during which the records may be disclosed.

In some instances, disclosures may be made without the consent of the pupil or the pupil's parents. Information may be disclosed within the school to teachers or guidance counselors who have a "need to know"; where there is a court order; where there is required disclosure under the Freedom of Information Act; and for routine usage, such as the publication of names of students who made an honor roll or information for a directory such as class lists or sports brochures, which might include such information as the student's name, address, gender, or birthplace. Even in this latter instance, however, it would be best to get prior permission through some sort of routine process. The district may be held liable for a common law tort for the disclosure of private facts about a student without consent if the disclosure results in any unwarranted publicity.[34]

Guidelines to assist principals in developing fair policies about student records include these:

1. Develop procedures to ensure that parents and students know what kind of information is contained in school records at a given time and are informed of their rights concerning control over the process of information collection and recording.

2. Encourage mature students and their parents to inspect the records. The rights of parents to do this are now well established, but most parents are unaware of these rights. Increased communication and greater trust on the part of the parents will be major benefits, and such a policy might provide a substantially more accurate record.

3. Develop systematic procedures to obtain explicit and informed parental or pupil consent before information contained in school records is released to outside parties, regardless of the reasons for such release or the characteristic of the third party. Most schools will, on occasion, give out information to law enforcement or other agencies without obtaining consent from the student or the parents. Aside from the possible legal implications of a violation of privacy, this practice can have no other effect than that of discouraging a trustful relationship among the parent, the child, and the school.

Issues of Equity

Increasing attention has been placed on the need to ensure that all persons have equal access to the fruits of education, regardless of gender, race, ethnicity, or any disabling condition. A host of laws, often federally generated, have been promulgated and much litigation has occurred in the

ISLLC 5

effort to ensure equity. Of special relevance to the school principal are the laws, court decisions, and educational guidelines with respect to gender discrimination, desegregation, provision of the least restrictive educational environment for students with disabilities, and employment opportunities for people with disabilities who are otherwise qualified.

Gender Discrimination

Issues of gender discrimination have arisen in both academic matters and cocurricular matters, but mostly in the cocurricular realm.

In academic matters, gender discrimination has occurred most often in class assignments and admission to programs or schools. Gender has been determined to be an illegal criterion for assignment and admission. It has been held also to be a violation of the equal protection clause of the Fourteenth Amendment to use higher admission standards for females than for males for admission to an academic school. The circuit court, in *Berkleman* v. *San Francisco Unified School District,*[35] said that merit is the only sound basis for admission, not such "unsupported" needs suggested by the school district officials' position that "an equal number of male and female students is an essential element in a good high school education."[36]

Nevertheless, the "separate but equal" concept with regard to schools for boys and girls is still viable where a school district (or any educational unit) can show that genuinely equal educational opportunities are provided to students in these schools, when these schools are compared to all other schools or units in the system.[37] The burden of proof is on the school system, however.

In some schools, too, females have been excluded from certain specialized vocational and prevocational courses. This practice has been challenged, and in most such cases, females were admitted to the courses before the cases came to trial. Clearly, even though there is little in the way of case law, such exclusion practices are contrary to the current thrust of the law. Unless the school administrator or the school board can show some rational basis for excluding one gender or the other from a course or program, there should be no policy that would differentiate the enrollment. It is doubtful that such a basis could be developed; few human activities are physiologically determined.

An ongoing controversy involves interpretations of the Title IX provisions. This controversy has to do with whether local districts can determine a particular school or program to be of service to only one gender. It comes about as some districts desire to create all-boy or all-girl schools in an effort to address different learner needs that may exist that appear to be gender related. For example, there is some indication that boys, especially African American boys from underprivileged urban neighborhoods, perform better in schools that do not also enroll girls. This may be true, as well, of boys who are not black, and it may also be true that some girls perform better in situations where they are not competing with boys. There is little definitive research about this issue, but there are some remarkable stories of learner success in single-gender schools for both boys and girls.

In January 2002, President George W. Bush signed into law in the No Child Left Behind Act, an amendment on the provision of single-gender schools. The amendment by Senator Kay Bailey Hutchison, with bipartisan support, allowed for single-gender schools "consistent with applicable law."

For almost 40 years, the "applicable law" has been Title IX. Title IX of the Educational Amendments of 1972, which amended the Civil Rights Act of 1964, was signed into law by President Richard M. Nixon. It states:

> No person in the United States shall, on the basis of sex, be excluded from participation in, be denied the benefits of, or be subjected to discrimination under any education program or activity receiving Federal financial assistance.

Advocates of the No Child Left Behind amendment say, however, that this is an instance where Title IX has been incorrectly interpreted and is not meant to ban single-gender programs and schools. Those who reason this way indicate that the law prohibits such schools and programs *only* if the other gender does not have access to the same quality of courses, services, and facilities. The U.S. Department of Education has prepared guidelines for the implementation of single-gender schools. Lawsuits will follow—of that, the school administrator may be assured. Such groups as the American Civil Liberties Union and the National Organization for Women have already raised the issue in the instance of some particular schools.

Most of the litigation focusing on gender discrimination has concerned participation in cocurricular activities, specifically participation in athletic competition. Title IX of the Education Amendments of 1972 (PL 92–318) is a bulwark against gender discrimination in the cocurricular realm. Title IX established, among other things, that organized athletic programs in the public schools must be accessible regardless of the gender of the aspirant.

There are two situations in which claims have arisen. The first is the failure of a school district to fund and provide a team for a specific sport for its female students, and then, while not providing a team, also prohibiting female students from participating on the team it does have. The issue in these cases is not whether a female student has a constitutional right to participate in a particular sport but whether the state, having provided an athletic program, can deny an opportunity to participate to members of one gender. The asserted protective purpose in maintaining separate teams is frequently stated this way: Girls cannot compete effectively with boys in sports because of the inherent physical differences between the sexes; thus, it is argued frequently, separate teams are reasonable and indeed even necessary. Several courts have accepted this conclusion but have held that they could not sanction a failure to provide a separate athletic program for girls.[38]

Separate but equal athletic programs are also statutory law in section 86.41 of Title IX(B), "Administration of Athletics." But, there is a provision that states if a school district does not fund and offer separate athletic programs, it must allow members of the excluded sex to try out for the team it does have, unless the "sport involved is a contact sport."

Some courts have determined that even in cases of contact sports, a school must allow a girl to participate if there is no girls' team. For a school to maintain different teams for boys and girls, the reason for the disparity in treatment must be "substantially related" to the achievement of an important government objective; however, "overbroad and archaic" generalizations about differences in the genders are not acceptable.[39]

When a school attempts to use safety as a rationale for forbidding coeducational teams, the school must show that there is a sufficient relationship between the announced goal of safety and a rule that would automatically exclude one gender.[40] Accordingly, girls must be given the opportunity to demonstrate that the presumption they are more prone to be injured is invalid. "They must be given the opportunity to compete with boys in interscholastic contact sports if they are physically qualified."[41]

Single-Gender Classes and Schools

There has been an increase in the number of school districts providing schools for girls or for boys as well as classes that are segregated by gender. The U.S. Congress expressed support for same-gender education by means of the No Child Left Behind Act. (Earlier than this, some districts in the nation had been permitting same-gender classes, as well.) The official guidelines allow public schools to open same-gender schools or single-gender classes *as long as they are voluntary* and there is a "substantially equal" opportunity for the other gender. Research is mixed about whether students perform better in single-gender environments, but there have been instances of success.

Arguments in support of single-gender classes often cite that boys and girls learn differently, and separating them will permit teachers to tailor the lessons to take advantage of this difference. But there has been too little research about the issue to reach a definitive conclusion. Some members of organizations such as the National Organization for Women have deplored the practice stating that separate is never equal.

Education for the Disabled

Public schools historically have been involved in the education of the young who are disabled, but now such activities have taken on a more precise and legally defined basis. Legislation culminating with the Education of All Handicapped Children Act of 1975 (PL 94–142) has mandated the provision of the "least restrictive learning environment" for children who are disabled. Public Law 94–142 provides for ready access to appropriate public education for these children between the ages of 3 and 21 and mandates the integration of these children into settings that formerly may have been limited to nondisabled children.

Public Law 94–142 is buttressed by other federal laws: PL 94–143, the earlier PL 93–112, and the Individuals with Disabilities Education Act (1990), which have established certain rights to education and fair treatment for children with disabilities.[42] The rights include these:

- Right to a free appropriate education at public expense, without regard to severity of disability
- Right to service in the least-restrictive setting when the disability requires service in something other than the normal school setting
- Right to prior notice before any decision is made to change services given to a child
- Right of parents to give consent before their child is evaluated, placed in a special program, or changed in placement
- Right to full due process, including representation by legal counsel, right to confront and cross-examine school personnel, right to a verbatim transcript, right to appeal, and right to be heard by an impartial hearing officer (not a school employee)
- Right to assignment and program placement without discrimination on the basis of gender, race, or culture, and to placement in a facility that is comparable to that offered to nondisabled clients of the system

- Right to be served in accordance with an individual program plan that states annual goals, measurable intermediate steps, the names of persons who will provide services and their qualifications, a timetable for beginning each step in the service and its anticipated duration, a schedule for evaluating the success of the program, and the right to be transferred if the program is failing
- Right to be protected from harm through the use of unregulated experimental approaches, untrained staff, inclusion in a program with others who are physically assaultive, freedom from unreasonable corporal punishment, and freedom from work assignments without compensation
- Right to see all records and to contest them in a hearing, with the right to place in the record information that the client feels presents a balanced picture

The passage of PL 94–142 was the culmination of many years of litigation and legislation to protect the civil rights of children who are disabled. The legislative act ensures specified substantive and procedural provisions for such children, as well as an escalating funding formula to ensure a free and appropriate public education for all students who are disabled. Of specific importance to school principals is that the law insists on the following items:

- A zero reject policy
- Specific due process procedures
- Nondiscriminatory testing
- A written and promulgated individual educational plan for every child who is disabled (to be developed jointly with parents and reviewed at least annually)
- Provisions for a least-restrictive environment

The act's "stay-put" provision directs that a child who is disabled "shall remain in his or her then current educational placement" pending completion of any review proceedings, unless the parents and state and local educational agencies otherwise agree.

The stay-put provision prohibits school authorities from unilaterally excluding children with disabilities from the classroom for dangerous or disruptive conduct growing out of their disabilities *during the pendency of review proceedings.* The act is unequivocal in its requirement that the "child *shall* remain in the current educational placement."

Doe and Smith, students who were emotionally disturbed, were suspended indefinitely for violent and disruptive conduct, pending the completion of expulsion proceedings by the school. In *Honig* v. *Doe and Smith*,[43] it was held that the implementing regulations under the act allow the use of normal, nonplacement-changing procedures, including *temporary* suspensions for up to 10 school days for students posing an immediate threat to others' safety, and allow for interim placements where parents and school officials are able to agree. Further, the act authorizes schools to file a suit for "appropriate" injunctive relief where such an agreement cannot be reached. In such a suit, there is a presumption in favor of the child's current placement, but school officials can rebut only by showing that maintaining the current placement is substantially likely to result in injury to the student or to others.

The Individual Education Plan. For each child, there must be developed a formal individual educational plan (IEP). The IEP is developed by a team, including the appropriate professional educators (e.g., diagnosticians, teachers, psychologists, and principals) and the child's parents. Parents must give consent before a child with disabilities may be placed in a program. The IEP must contain:

- The child's current level of performance
- A statement of goals and objectives
- The nature of the educational services to be provided
- The place(s) and time(s) the services will be provided
- The kinds of teachers, diagnosticians, and other professionals who will be working with the child

The litmus test is whether the IEP is "reasonably calculated" to enable the child to advance from grade to grade.[44] Moreover, removing a child who has a disability to a disciplinary setting may be a change in placement and thus requires that the school comply with the act's procedures.[45] If the school cannot meet the needs of the child in the normal school year, the act requires a program longer than the normal year.[46]

The Supreme Court has held that schools may be required to reimburse parents for expenditures incurred in private school placement if the court ultimately determines that the private school placement is proper and that the school district's proposed IEP is not proper under the act.[47]

Individuals with Disabilities Education Act (IDEA).   Passed by Congress in 1990, this is the so-called inclusion act. It requires that the educational placement of each child who has a disability is to be determined at least annually, that the plan is based on the child's individual education program, and that the child is educated as close as possible to his or her home. Unless the IEP requires some other arrangement, the child is to be educated in the school that would have been attended had there been no disability. In selecting the least-restrictive environment, consideration is to be given to any potential harmful effect on the child or on the quality of services needed. Simply put, these regulations require the school to make a substantial effort to find an inclusive solution for the child. Federal courts have held that this act requires that children with very severe disabilities must be included in the regular classroom they would otherwise attend if not disabled (even when they cannot meet the academic expectations of the class) *if* there is a potential social benefit, *if* the class would stimulate the child's linguistic development, or *if* the other students could provide appropriate role models for the student.[48] Thus, the question asked is, Can the IEP be implemented in the regular classroom with supplementary aids and services?

ISLLC 5, 6

Parents are increasingly aware of these rights and have shown a willingness to go to the courts to force school districts to include their child in "regular" classes, even when the child who is disabled may not be able to keep up with the standard work of the class. The burden for showing both the parent and the court how exclusion is in the best interests of the child rests on the school.

Aside from the legal implications of IDEA and PL 94–142, the implications of these acts with regard to teacher training and in-service development are immense. Inclusion is clearly a way of reconceptualizing the method by which special services are delivered to children with disabilities. Rather than sending the child to a special class full time or to a school in the district that houses only special classes, the new model requires that the special education services be brought to the child.

Employment Issues

School administrators have the responsibility to practice fair employment policies and provide equal opportunity for job aspirants. Increasingly, greater authority for employment decisions is being placed at the school site level. Thus, the principal and the school staff need to be aware of federal and state laws and court decisions that regulate decision making about personnel selection and termination.

At the federal level, the Equal Employment Opportunity Commission (EEOC) is specifically charged with the enforcement of Title VII of the Civil Rights Act of 1964 (race, color, religion, sex, and national origin); the Equal Pay Act of 1963; the Age Discrimination in Employment Act of 1967; the Rehabilitation Act of 1973; the Americans with Disabilities Act of 1990; and the Federal Civil Rights Act of 1991. The EEOC actively follows up complaints to obtain full compensation and benefits for employees who have been discriminated against in an unlawful manner.

Americans with Disabilities Act (ADA)

This 1990 piece of federal legislation specifically protects the employment rights of the disabled. The law is sweeping in its protection for such persons in employment and in state and local government services. Organizations in both the public and private sectors come under the act, whether or not the particular entity receives any federal funds. Students and employees are covered and certain accommodations are required. Generally speaking, the following guidelines apply to employment practices:

ISLLC 5, 6

1. All positions are open to qualified applicants with disabilities.
2. Openings must be posted in places that can be reached by people who are disabled.
3. Applicants may not be asked if they have a disability or how it was caused. Only those questions that have to do with the ability to perform essential job functions should be asked.
4. Medical information on an employee's disabilities must be kept in a separate file.
5. Employers must accommodate employees who are disabled unless the changes would impose an "undue hardship." (Widening doors and lowering chalkboards, for example, have not been found to be unreasonable accommodations.)
6. Readers, interpreters, and attendants should be provided unless that would be a "hardship."
7. Preemployment testing cannot discriminate against persons with sight, hearing, or speaking limitations.

The implications of the act to the school administration seem clear. Essential job skills will need to be even more carefully established and demonstratively related to the tasks that need to be performed before an otherwise qualified person with disabilities is denied employment because of a presumed inability to carry out job responsibilities. The burden for showing that a job requires specific physical or educational requirements will rest with the school district and the school administrator.

Racial and Ethnic Discrimination

With the *Brown* v. *Topeka* case in 1954 (*Brown* v. *Board of Education of Topeka,* Supreme Court of the United States, 347 U.S. 483), the issue of publicly supporting systems of schooling in which enrollment was determined by one's ethnicity or race was settled. "Separate but equal" education was determined by the Supreme Court to be illegal and *de jure* segregation was an improper use of local board of education responsibility.

A host of court cases followed as some school districts sought relief from this law and attempted to avoid racial and ethnic mixing. A pattern of desegregation practices soon followed, ranging from pairing schools to providing magnet programs. In many districts, mass busing of students resulted, as well. An agonizing 30 years followed the original and subsequent Supreme Court decisions and the subsequent lower court decisions that were in support of the framework supplied by the Supreme Court.

There are still many school districts under federal mandate to follow approved plans of desegregation. Over the years, however, in many other districts a judgment has been made that the schools are now "effectively desegregated" or at least that the plan has been effectively implemented and the court mandate has been removed. The fact is, however, that school desegregation has not really occurred in many cities. Migration and housing patterns have caused this. What has happened is that boards of education are not setting up attendance rules and boundaries in such a way to cause segregation.[49]

Youth in Poverty: Reauthorization of the Elementary and Secondary Education Act (ESEA)

The reauthorization of ESEA contains some new wrinkles, most of which focus on expanding educational equity. Title I has been redesigned to address the National Education Goals in a more specific manner. Addressed is the belief that all students can achieve high standards of excellence and that local districts should have greater flexibility in designing programs to increase achievement.

The funding formula for Title I has been revised to target more dollars to schools with the highest concentration of poverty. Equally important is the provision that permits schools to use Title I money to upgrade the entire school's educational program. Title I money may be combined with other resources, as well. Under the provisions, a school may develop a program to include the entire school *if* 50 percent or more of its students come from low-income families.

ISLLC 1

Among other provisions are grants for projects designed to focus on the unique problems of urban and rural schools with high-poverty populations. The projects must focus on ways to close the achievement gap between disadvantaged students and students in more affluent areas.

Homeless Youth

In the United States, the Department of Education has reported that more than 800,000 school youth are homeless each year. Because of a federal law reauthorized in 2001, public schools have become refuges for these homeless youth, providing bus fare, school supplies, and free lunches. The Mckinney–Vento Homeless Assistance Act requires school districts to immediately enroll homeless youth, even if they lack the usually compulsory immunization records, school transcripts, and proof that they meet residency requirements. Specifically, the law reads:

> It is the policy of the Congress—
>
> 1. Each State educational agency ensure that each child of a homeless individual and each homeless youth has equal access to the same free appropriate public education, including a public school education as provided to other youth;
> 2. in any State that has a compulsory attendance law or other laws, regulations, practices, or policies that may act as a barrier to the enrollment, attendance, or success in schools of homeless children and youth, the State review and undertake steps to revise such laws, regulations, practices, or policies to ensure that homeless children and youth are afforded the same free, appropriate public education as provided to other children and youth;
> 3. homelessness is not sufficient reason to separate students from the mainstream school environment; and
> 4. homeless children and youth must have access to the education, and other services needed to ensure such children, and youth have an opportunity to meet the same challenging State student performance standards to which all children are held.

The law also requires a school district to designate a liaison to identify youth living in shelters, motels, and other provisional housing; to help enroll these youth in school; and then to ensure that they get the proper immunizations or adequate health records. The task of the liaison is to make referrals for dental, medical, and mental health services, notify caregivers of educational programs, and arrange transportation for the students.

Homeless people move a lot and instability reigns in these families. The law provides that school districts provide transportation to the child's school of origin in order to provide more stability. Often districts will also provide remedial studies and tutoring at homeless shelters but this is not an aspect of the law. Interestingly—and importantly—in many schools these services, except for transportation, have always been provided to homeless youth. "Just part of what we do," some principals would say.

Rules and Regulations

No school will function well without a consistent body of rules and regulations to guide student and staff conduct. It simply makes sense—rules and regulations provide a sound basis for school operation. So, types of behavior, student attire, items that cannot be brought to school, and similar matters are subject to codes that are established, often with the participation of faculty and students. This is good: Folks who know what is expected can behave in reasonable ways. Everyone's rights are respected that way.

But problems have arisen and prevail. In an effort to clarify and simplify punishment for a violation of rules or regulations, the procedure called *zero tolerance* for certain transgressions has been invoked. Commonly, carrying weapons or things that can be turned into weapons, or bringing controlled substances, or not dressing according to the established school dress code, brings an immediate punishment. The offender might be placed in another school, sent home, turned over to legal authorities, or put into detention. Punishment depends on the nature of the transgression.

Zero tolerance may have made the job of school officials simpler in some cases. In other instances, however, dumb application of the principle has created great difficulty and much embarrassment for school officials. In Alabama, a student was disciplined for hugging another student whose parent had just died. This hug was in violation of the school's zero-tolerance policy about physical contact among students. In Ohio, a boy in junior high school was punished for bringing a knife to school. The knife was a Civil War saber that had been in his family for years and he was bringing it to a history class for display. In California, a high school girl was punished for bringing an aspirin to school for self-use. Her parent had wanted her to take it during her lunch break. In Oklahoma, a Muslim student was suspended from school for wearing her *hijab*. (She is being represented in court by a civil liberties group.) In many schools, good sense seems to have given way to zero tolerance.

The issue of religious wear is often a difficult dilemma for principals, however, because of two reasons. Dress codes are becoming more and more strict, and religious groups are becoming more vocal about their right to religious accommodation. This is not a new situation. Seventh-Day Adventists and Jehovah's Witnesses have made inroads about the issue, and now with a greater Islamic population in the country, these believers also have become assertive about their rights.

Dr. James May, principal of Kempner High School in the Fort Bend (Texas) Independent School District clarifies the problem: "The 64,000 dollar question is, is this part of your religious exercise or is this an opportunistic fashion statement?"[50] Attire that is claimed to be a religious statement is subjected to an interview with the individual student. Steven Amstutz, principal of Lee High School in Houston—perhaps one of the most diverse schools, with students from 72 different countries—agrees with May. Students at Lee who request a religious accommodation must meet with Amstutz. He says, "It really isn't hard to discern when a student is sincere or genuine. I don't know any religion that requires kids to wear Yankee ball caps."[51]

Zero tolerance as a policy is a time-saver, but it should not be used without some thought about the circumstances of individual cases. When applied with reason, zero tolerance does establish that the school will be operated in a safe manner.

Summary

What guides the principal and the school? Although federal and state laws and court decisions provide the legal framework, Fossey wrote:

> [But] school boards do not have unfettered discretion over what goes on in the classroom, however. They may not make curricular decisions that support a religious agenda; and they may not reject texts or library materials simply because they disagree with the ideas contained in them.[52]

In fact, of course, school boards do interpret and apply the laws of the nation and the state to the local community and, in the absence of law, develop their own policies with regard to teachers and students. Nevertheless, what freedom that permits is often circumscribed by local customs and desires. That is where the greatest difficulty begins, because local customs and desires are often truly "local" and sometimes in disagreement with both the law and with the customs and desires of some other local group.

School board members are but mere mortals subject to their own biases and often inadequate knowledge of the law. At least, we hope, the school principal will be soundly grounded in what is legal and what is just.

This chapter focused on bringing clarity to both the legal issues and the "customs and desires" issues. Our goal was to provide a legal footing, an understanding of the nature of communities, and a good means of communicating with the publics.

ACTIVITIES

1. Read Case 23. What are the issues of employment at Whisler Elementary that might cause you to seek the advice of the school's attorney? Develop a short paper about these issues and describe what you believe would be the best course of action.
2. Case 30, also an employment issue, has to do with dismissing an employee. Read the case. Will you proceed with the dismissal notice? On what grounds?

3. Case 18 involves an instructional assignment to which some are objecting. Is the teacher in a legally defensible position?
4. Turn to the ISLLC standards in Appendix B. Review the functions listed in Standard 6. Identify two functions related to material in Chapter 16 and describe situations in your school that are pertinent.

ENDNOTES

1. Larry W. Hughes, written for this chapter.
2. *Tinker* v. *Des Moines Independent Community School System,* 393 U.S. 503, 89 S.Ct. 733 (1969).
3. Ibid. See also *Burnside* v. *Byers,* 363 F 2d. 744 (5th Cir. 1966).
4. Procedures and punishments must be tailored to fit the offender and the offense. See, for example, *Rhyne* v. *Childs,* 359 F.Supp. 1085 (1973), affd. 507 F.2d. (5th Cir. 1975.)
5. Full disclosure requires an explanation of the evidence the school officials have against the student. See *Goss* v. *Lopez,* 419 U.S. 565; *Board of Curators of the University* v. *Horowitz,* 435 U.S. 78 (1978); *Keough* v. *Tate County Board of Education* 748 F.2d. 1077 (5th Circuit 1984), for example.
6. Although procedural due process is required by the U.S. Constitution, the courts have a different fact pattern in each case. There is no set formula for what is sufficient to establish that there has been procedural due process. Although this process appears to take on vestments of a court of law, it is *not* a court of law. Rather, it is simply a procedure for fair and impartial treatment. After the process is completed, the accused still has the right to take the case to court if he or she feels the issue was decided wrongly or the punishment is improper.
7. *Tinker* v. *Des Moines Independent Community School System.*
8. *Goldwasser* v. *Brown,* 417 F.2d. 1169 (1969), *Moore* v. *School Board of Gulf County Florida* 364 F.Supp. 355 (1973).
9. 676 F.Supp. 820.
10. *Jaglin II* v. *San Jacinto Unified School District,* 827 F.Supp 1459 (1993).

11. For example, see *Pyle* v. *Hadley School Committee,* 861 Fed. Supp. 157 (1994), *Gato* v. *School District 411,* 674 F.Supp 796 (1987).
12. 682 F.2d. 858 (1982).
13. *Board of Education, Island Trees Union Free School District No. 26* v. *Pico,* 853 U.S. 457 (1982).
14. 735 F.2d. 128 (1985).
15. *Lamb's Chapel* v. *Center Moriches Union Free District,* 124 L.Ed. 252 (1993). See also *Westside Community School Board* v. *Mergens,* 496 U.S. 226 (1990) for a definition of a "noncurriculum-related school group." In the latter judgment, such a group was defined briefly to be any student group that does not directly relate to a body of courses offered by the school. If a school permits student groups such as a scuba diving club, a political club, and so on, to meet at school facilities during noninstructional time (before or after the school day), it must also permit *student-organized* religious groups to meet. The only way school officials could deny access to a group that wished to advance the teachings of Jesus or Mohammed or Confucius or Karl Marx or others would be an open forum or public forum policy. The only way that a judge could be convinced would be to convince the judge that the group was advocating the violent overthrow of the government or that that group's presence will lead to violence, damage to property, or injury to persons, or the like.
16. *Fleischdresser* v. *Directors of School District 200,* 15 F.3d. 680 (1994). See also *Mozert* v. *Hawkins County*

Public Schools, 627 F 2d 1058 (1987), *cert denied* 108 S.Ct. 1029 (1988).

17. *Guyer* v. *School Board,* 634 F.2s. 806 (Fl Dist. Ct. App. 1994)

18. Richard D. Strahan, in *Principal as Leader,* ed. Larry W. Hughes (Upper Saddle River NJ: Prentice-Hall, 1999), p. 313.

19. See, for example, *Board of Education of Santa Fe Schools* v. *Sullivan,* 740 F.2d. 119 (1987), *Katz* v. *Amback* 472 NYS 2d, and *Davis* v. *Monroe County School Board,* 199 S Ct. 791; 142 L.Ed. 2d 655 (1999)

20. Ibid.

21. "Contributory negligence" is determined by whether or not the party who was injured exercised the degree of caution others of the same age, gender, maturation level, and experience would have exercised under the same conditions. "Comparative negligence" requires that the plaintiff be charged with proportional liability for his or her acts that contributed to the injury if the plaintiff is old enough to be held accountable for those injuries. Obviously, more supervision is expected of those in charge of young children. Personnel in elementary schools are less likely to be able to claim contributory liability than those who supervise older students. Nevertheless, whatever the age, a student who disregards or acts in direct defiance of an admonishment of a supervising adult would probably be found guilty of contributory negligence if the refusal resulted in an injury.

22. Of course, not all injuries to students are actionable; some are unavoidable, the result of pure accident. Only those injuries resulting from negligence provide a basis for legal action.

23. For example, the failure to provide safety equipment when sports are being played is negligence or the failure to give proper instruction in the way to perform physical ability tests in the instance that that was occurring.

24. However, note that advance notice to a parent or caregiver does not foreclose the right of a student to sue if injury has occurred.

25. Greater care than usual is required. In a New York case, for example, a student dropped chemicals from a school window and those chemicals were later retrieved by a young child who was injured by the chemicals. The failure either to keep the chemicals under lock and key or to supervise the student using the chemicals was held to be negligence (*Kush by Marszalek* v. *City of Buffalo,* 462 NYS 2d 26, 1983).

26. *Suspension* is generally defined as dismissal from school for a specific, although relatively short-lived, period of time. Normally, this is for three or four days and often a week at maximum. Usually the principal of the school has the right to suspend. *Expulsion* is defined to mean permanent dismissal and is most usually an action that can be taken only by the school board.

27. In the instance of suspension, one of the most limiting cases was that of *Mills* v. *Board of Education,* 348 F.Supp. 866, 1972, in which the court ordered that there must be a hearing prior to a suspension invoked for more than two days. In *Goss* v. *Lopez,* 95 S.Ct. 729, 1975, the Supeme

Court ruled basically that school officials must accord students and school employees their constitutional rights to due process even in routine disciplinary actions. *Goss* held that a junior high school student suspended for as much as a day is entitled to due process. And, in *Wood* v. *Strickland,* 95 S.Ct. 992 (1975), the Supreme Court ruled that school board members and school officials can be held personally liable for pecuniary damages when students are denied constitutional rights, even by omission.

28. If a teacher or a principal uses excessive force or causes untoward injury, he or she may be held liable for battery. There is often confusion between the terms *assault* and *battery.* Battery is the actual unlawful inflicting of physical violence on another. Assault is the threat to commit battery. There can be assault without battery.

29. The Supreme Court has affirmed the right of school personnel to use corporal punishment as long as there is no state law or local policy prohibiting it. Lower courts have issued rulings that corporal punishment may be administered provided "reasonable force" is used and provided that the student knew beforehand that certain behaviors could result in physical punishment. *Ingraham* v. *Wright,* 430 U.S. 651 (1975) and *Baker* v. *Owen,* 385 F. Supp. 294 (1975).

30. *Baker* v. *Owen.*

31. *Goss* v. *Lopez.*

32. Ibid., p. 736.

33. Ibid., p. 740.

34. *Klipa* v. *Board of Education of Anne Arundel County,* 54 Md. App. 644, 460 A 2d 601 (1983).

35. 501 F.2d. 1264 (9th Cir. 1974). See also *Bray* v. *Lee,* 337 F.Supp. 034 (D. Mass. 1972).

36. Ibid., p. 1269.

37. *Vorcheimer* v. *School District of Philadelphia,* 532 F.2d. 880 (3d. Cir. 1976).

38. For example, *Brenden* v. *Independent School District,* 343 F.Supp. 1224 (D. Minn. 1972), aff'd 477 F. 2d. 1292 (10th Cir. 1973); *Herver* v. *Meiklejon,* 430 F.Supp. 164 (D. Col. 1977).

39. See *Clark* v. *Arizona Interscholastic Association,* 695 F. 2d. 1129 (9th Cir. 1082).

40. *Force by Force* v. *Pierce City School District,* 570 F.Supp. 1020 (W.D. Mo. 1983).

41. *Yellow Springs Exempted Village School District* v. *Ohio School Athletic Association,* 433 F.Supp. 753 (S.D. Ohio 1978).

42. PL 94–143 is entitled "Developmentally Disabled Assistance and Bill of Rights Act." PL 93–112 is "Rehabilitation Act" and was enacted in 1973.

43. 484 U.S. 305; 108 S. Ct. 592; 98 L.Ed. 2d. 686 (1988).

44. See *Board of Education of Hendrick Hudson Central School District* v. *Rowley,* 458 U.S., 176 (1982).

45. See *Adams Central School District* v. *Deist* 334 N.W. 2s. 775 (Nebraska 1983).

46. See *Board of Education for the City of Savannah* v. *Georgia Association of Retired Citizens,* 52 U.S.L.W. 3932 (1984).

47. *School District of the Town of Burlington Mass.* v. *Mass. Dept. of Education,* 53 U.S.L.W. 4509 (1985).

48. See, for example, in *Board of Education, Sacramento* v. *Holland* (786 F.Supp. 874, 1992) the court ordered the school district to place a child with an IQ of 44 in a regular second-grade class and rejected the district's complaints about expenses as exaggerated. In *Oberti* v. *Board of Education of the Borough of Clementon School District* (789 F. Supp. 1322, 1992) the court rejected the claim of the school district that a child would be so disruptive as to significantly impair the education of other children.

49. Two books may be of especial use to review for further insights into the legal issues of desegregation and the various plans and efforts to achieve this. See Michael W. LaMorte, *School Law: Cases and Concepts,* 7th ed. (Boston: Allyn & Bacon, 2002), Chapter 5, and Larry W. Hughes, William M. Gordon, and Larry W. Hillman, *Desegregating America's Schools* (New York: Longman, 1980).

50. As reported in the *Houston Chronicle,* September 17, 2006, P.B3.

51. Ibid.

52. See Richard Fossey, "Censorship: Who Controls School Material and Teaching Materials," in *Current Issues in School Leadership,* ed. Larry W. Hughes (Mahwah NJ: Erlbaum, 2005), pp. 90–92.

SELECTED READINGS

Anderson, J. K. "What Schools Can Say about Johnny?" *Principal Leadership (Middle School Ed) 4,* no. 4, (2003): 67–70.

Berlin, L. F. "Public School Law: What Does It Mean in the Trenches?" *Phi Delta Kappan 90,* no. 10 (2009): 733–736.

Brooks, M. "Sexual Harassment." *Principal Leadership 3* (2003): 71.

Brooks, M. "Janie's Got a Gun; Call Her Parents?" *Principal Leadership 5* (2005): 63–64.

Cambron-McCabe, N. "Balancing Students' Constitutional Rights." *Phi Delta Kappan 90,* no. 10 (2009): 709–713.

Cases in Point, a legal update service to members of the National Association of Secondary School Principals. See www.nassp.org

Conn, K. "Cyberbullying: A Legal Review." *Educational Leadership 66,* no. 6 (2009): 16–18.

Essex, N. "Student Distribution of Religious Fliers in Public Schools: Ten Ways to Invite a Lawsuit." *Clearing House: A Journal of Educational Strategies, Issues and Ideas 79,* no. 3 (2006): 138–143. (ERIC Document Reproduction Service No. EJ745139)

Essex, Nathan L. *School Law and the Public Schools* (4th ed.) (Boston: Allyn & Bacon, 2007).

Fossey, Richard. "Censorship: Who Controls the School Curriculum and Teaching Materials?" in *Current Issues in School Leadership,* ed. Larry W. Hughes (Mahwah, NJ: Erlbaum, 2005).

Hyde, W. B., and L. Soronen. "Reducing Liability for Sexual Harassment." *Principal Leadership 84,* no. 3 (2004).

Marshall, J. M. "Religion and Education: Walking the Line in Public Schools." *Phi Delta Kappan 85,* no. 3 (2003): 239–242.

Osborne, Alan G., and Charles. J.Rosso, *Special Education and the Law: A Guide for Practitioners* (2nd ed.) (Thousand Oaks CA: Corwin Press, 2006).

Rosenblith, Suzanne. "Religious Controversy," in *Current Issues in School Leadership* ed. Larry W. Hughes (Mahwah, NJ: Erlbaum, 2005).

San Antonio, D., and E. Salzfass. "How We Treat One Another in School." *Educational Leadership 64* (2007): 32–38.

Wiener, Kevin G., and Wendy C. Chi. *Current Issues in Educational Policy and the Law* (Charlotte NC; Information Age Publishers, 2008).

Zinkely, P. "Bullying: A Matter of Law?" *Phi Delta Kappan 85,* no. 1 (2003): 90–91.

Zirkel, P. A. "Privacy of Student Records: An Update." *Principal 82* (2003): 10–13.

SOME INTERNET SOURCES

For general legal research of court cases and opinion:
www.findlaw.com
For the Library of Congress:
www.loc.gov/index.html

For Federal Laws Since 1973:
www.thomas.loc.gov

APPENDIX A

Case Studies in School Leadership and Management

Problem Analysis, Decision Processing, and Decision Making: Introduction to the Cases

In order to arrive at the maximum feasible decision, it is first necessary to define the problem correctly. Then, one needs to think about the decision processes that are available to resolve the problem. Many response patterns are open to any executive. Selecting the right one will determine whether the problem will be resolved or at least mitigated or whether even greater problems result. Anticipating the consequences of any particular process or act is more than an intellectual exercise.

A school leader's day is characterized by one encounter after another with staff members, students, parents, community members, politicians, and others—the kinds of individuals or subgroups are myriad and diverse. For the school principal, a simple walk down the hall from the office to resolve a problem in the cafeteria may result in half a dozen or more encounters with this or that teacher, custodian, parent, or child, all of whom have questions and requests and problems that the principal is asked to solve. Hurried answers are shouted over the shoulder. The principal is thrust into a maelstrom during the routine of most days. The rapidity and intensity of encounters and the life span of the problems will vary. Frequently, the time frames will be short and the databases will seem too meager.

But, few problems have to be solved at the moment. There is almost always some time—albeit often not much—to reflect on the nature of the problem and the likely decision process that will result in a satisfactory solution. The fundamental questions to be asked are these:

- Do I have at hand the information necessary to solve this problem?
- Whose support will be necessary in order to effect a long-term solution?
- How likely is it that I will get this support if I go ahead and make the decision on my own?
- Does this problem need immediate attention?
- On what rationale, value, or theory am I basing my decision?
- What specific, or implicit, references or citations in this text can give you guidance in the analysis and/or solution to this problem?

On the pages that follow are case studies about problems that occur in and around schools—student problems, angry clients, budget crunches, maintenance issues, staff appraisal difficulties, dilemmas about curriculum, conflicts about a multitude of issues—most not simple. In any given case, select analytical processes that seem to you to be most appropriate. The Maier and Vroom–Jago models (Chapter 3) may be especially helpful, but whatever approach you choose, be prepared to defend your reasoning.

As you analyze the cases, make only those assumptions that are reasonable, given the limited number of facts that are provided. But remember, *you* are the executive who is confronted by the issue, not someone else. It is *your* problem; however, you don't have to solve the problem. Your task is to analyze the issue and set in motion a process that you believe will result in a good solution. Determine what you believe is the main problem or issue and indicate any subproblems or issues.

Case Studies: Primary Subject Matter and Decision Level

CASE	ISLLC STANDARD	CURRICULUM	PERSONNEL	STUDENTS	PUBLIC RELATIONS	FINANCE
1	2, 5, 6		X			
2	2		X	X	X	
3	2, 3, 4	X			X	X
4	1, 2, 4		X		X	
5	1, 4	X			X	
6	3					X
7	1, 2	X	X			
8	2, 4, 5		X	X	X	
9	3					X
10	4, 5, 6		X	X	X	
11	2, 5		X		X	
12	1, 4, 6			X	X	
13	1, 4	X	X		X	
14	2, 3, 4, 5		X	X	X	
15	2, 4		X		X	
16	4, 5, 6	X		X	X	
17	2, 3		X			
18	1, 2, 4, 5		X	X	X	
19	2, 5			X		
20	1, 2, 3	X				X
21	3, 6			X	X	
22	3, 6		X	X	X	
23	4, 5		X		X	
24	2			X		
25	4, 6			X	X	

26	1, 2			x	x	x	
27	3, 4, 6				x		
28	2, 5, 6	x		x		x	
29	2, 4			x			x
30	3, 4			x		x	
31	1, 4, 6	x			x	x	
32	2, 3, 6			x	x	x	

LIST OF CASE STUDIES

Case Studies

Case 1: A Different Applicant

Recruitment activities are well underway. As principal of a large middle school, you have filled almost all the upcoming vacancies. You are still seeking a person to teach at least three remedial mathematics classes as part of a load. Usually it is difficult to find teachers for these classes because the students who are assigned are generally not prepared and sometimes difficult to handle.

One candidate, Eileen Duvall, seems well prepared for the assignment. She last served as an instructor in an educational program managed by the state department of prisons for inmates. She has not yet met with your faculty selection committee, but you have some time cleared on your calendar today and decide to interview her a day or so before the committee does because of convenience.

As your secretary escorts Ms. Duvall into your office, you are surprised by her appearance. She is well groomed and dressed professionally, but she is not more four feet tall and she walks haltingly. She clambers into the chair you have for those being interviewed and the interview begins.

On paper, Ms. Duvall is well qualified. Her credentials are good. Her manner is pleasant. She explained her reason for leaving her latest employment: She trained to be a public school teacher but could not locate a job. She is tired of the institutional life under which prisoners must live. She wants to be with young people and is once again seeking a position in a public school.

Neither of the other two candidates is academically as strong or as experienced as Ms. Duvall. But, as you know, Ms. Duvall will be assigned the "worst" students in the school—mostly boys and a few girls who either have been retained at least one grade or have had previous assignments to alternative schools for those who have had serious behavioral problems.

So, what do you do?

Note: These cases have all been developed by and written by Larry W. Hughes, Ph.D. Dr. Hughes holds the copyright for each.

Case 2: Satanism!

You are principal of an elementary school with an enrollment of 550. A small group of parents is meeting with you in your office. They belong to a neighborhood denominational church. You have seated them around a small table.

The problem, the spokesperson says, is one of your sixth-grade teachers. She is having a Halloween party and the children are to come in any costume they wish. "We object to this! Halloween is nothing but a pagan holiday and is contrary to what we teach in our church. This holiday has no place in a school." Your school has no policy with regard to certain holidays. What do you tell the parents? What actions, if any, will you take?

Case 3: Don't Mess with My Budget

You are the principal. As you conduct a review of the school's science program, you are aware of the following:

1. Students from your unit do not do well on the SAT or similar tests and complain about not being able to get into prestigious colleges and universities.
2. Enrollments in advanced science classes have been dropping steadily over the past five years.
3. Many of your science teachers did not major in science; it is their second teaching field.
4. Some members of the community have been clamoring for "a better science program."
5. The superintendent of schools and the deputy in the district's division of instruction have just mounted an effort to persuade the board of education that massive additional resources need to be expended on reading programs in the schools.
6. Principals in your district have considerable latitude in the development and implementation of an instructional budget.
7. The amount of your instructional budget is determined by a basic allotment plus a factor, which is largely a result of the average daily attendance in the previous year.
8. There is a good bit of jealousy among the academic departments about matters of budget.
9. A change of attendance zone boundaries has recently occurred because a new freeway displaced several hundred families. The impact of this on your school is a 15 percent increase in students from homes in which English is not the primary language.
10. No overall increase in your budget for next year can be expected. Your average daily attendance is about the same from year to year.

How will you proceed to make budget allocations for next year?

Case 4: Trouble Brewing at Scott Larry Middle School

You are the new principal of Scott Larry Middle School. The school has had three different principals in the past five years. It is August 1 and school will be opening soon. You have the following facts at hand:

1. Enrollment is 1,200 students in grades 5 through 8 and the school is in an urban setting.

2. Although the total population of the school is relatively stable, there is much transience. About 35 percent of your students will "turn over" in any given year, some leaving and returning within the year, many just leaving or entering.

3. Your student population is 30 percent African American, 35 percent Hispanic, and about 10 percent Asian, mostly Vietnamese. Projections are for an increasingly declining white population. Many of the white parents in the attendance area send their children to one of two private schools, one of which is parochial.

4. A little more than one-quarter of the students come from a nearby public housing project.

5. About one-fourth of the students are bused in because of a special extended day program that your district maintains in a few of its middle schools.

6. The attendance area that your school serves has an adult population composed of 65 percent white, 12 percent black, 13 percent Hispanic, and 5 percent Asian. Socioeconomic status indicators suggest a wide range of economic levels. Housing ranges from upper-middle class to substandard housing. Recently, young married couples with no children have been taking advantage of some housing bargains in one of the neighborhoods and there has been a substantial in-migration of these couples.

7. The teaching staff has a 20 percent annual turnover and is bimodal in teaching experience—that is, a large number of teachers are in their first three years of teaching and a large number have over 15 years of experience. Only a few of your teachers are in their intermediate years.

8. There doesn't seem to be a very active PTO.

9. Your predecessor left no plans for the three-day staff in-service program that is to begin each school year.

Case 5: The Library Patrons

You are the principal of David Thomas Elementary School (K–8) with an enrollment of 840 students. The community the school serves is in a growing area of exurbia with an increasingly diverse population. A new group has formed, labeling themselves The Library Patrons. The group is not formally affiliated with the school and, in fact, before today, you had never even heard of it. The group has targeted a number of books in the library that the members have determined are inappropriate for your school's age group and have sent you a paper demanding the establishment of a citizens' committee that would establish "age-appropriate policies for the selection and distribution of books with sexual, gay, and drug themes and those with 'bad' language." The group wants some of these books banned entirely. It also insists that key members of the group be included on the citizens' committee. The paper has several signatories, some of whom are well-known community activists.

Among the books on the list are *Silly Duck* by Harvey Firestein, *The Perks of Being a Wallflower* by Stephen Chobsky, *Of Mice and Men* by John Steinbeck, the Harry Potter series by J. K. Rowling, and the anonymously authored *Go Ask Alice*. The first two on this abbreviated list have "sexual or gay content," Steinbeck "uses offensive language," the Harry Potter books have a heavy focus on wizardry and magic and seem "antireligious," and *Go Ask Alice* deals with drug use among young persons. The other books listed have similar features.

The group wants to meet with you in the next week and to help you decide who should be on the citizens' review committee. The group also wants immediate removal of the cited books until the committee meets and makes its recommendations.

Case 6: Where Will the Money Come From?

You are the principal of Lori Albright Middle School. You have an Activity Fund that has proved useful to your program. Many of the "extras" that can be provided to teachers are paid for from this account. Field trips to places that charge admission, special events performances, gifts for outstanding students and teachers, transportation costs for some interscholastic events, clothing for children in need, and other beneficial extras are not a big problem for your middle school. There always seems to be an adequate amount of money in the Activity Fund. With adequate preplanning, there are few extras that cannot be provided. Until now, that is.

Your middle school has an enrollment of 925 students, most of whom come from homes of modest means. About 65 percent of the young people receive free or reduced-price school lunch. Many participate in your breakfast program.

The problem is a decided movement in the larger school community to reconsider the machine sale of snack foods and soft drinks. Some children avoid the regular lunch and fill up on snack foods. Moreover, with increasing concern about poor diets and obesity of young people, feelings about getting rid of the temptations of snack foods and sugary soft drinks are running high. It is clear that a decision is about to be made at the central-office level to discontinue the practice in all schools.

Under current conditions, your Activity Fund will not survive this lack of income, because the main source—probably as much as 85 percent of the money—comes from sales of snack food and soft drink. Your students need the extras that the fund provides. But, of course, good sense indicates that the source of this money is not the best.

So, what are you going to do?

Case 7: Which Textbook Will It Be?

You are the principal of a middle school, grades 6 through 9, and there is need to review the social studies series currently in use. You have a strong opinion that the current series does not adequately depict the contributions made by minorities and women. Because your own teaching field is social studies, you have more than a casual interest in and knowledge about the issue. The social studies department seems split on the matter. Two teachers do not want to use any text at all, several teachers are satisfied with the current text, and three others favor at least two other series. The board requires one adopted text series but does permit supplemental works when it can be shown that there is good reason to do so. It is now January; a recommendation is due in the central office one month from today.

The chairperson of the department is undecided on the matter and requests that you "do something." A review of staff evaluations reveals that one of the teachers who wants no text at all is among the top-rated teachers in the school. She is unhappy with the more conservative posture of many of her colleagues and has indicated that unless a more positive stand on the multicultural nature of society is taken by the department, she will go elsewhere. A *cause célèbre* looms.

Case 8: The Banquet or the Test or Both?

You are the principal of Douglas Edward High School, which has an enrollment of 850. It's 5:00 P.M. but before leaving for home this day, you review the mail that came in much earlier in the day, which you have only just now time to sit down and read. One letter is disturbing. It is from a person who is ordinarily supportive of what goes on at the school.

> Dear [You]:
>
> This evening, my daughter, Grace, was forced to make a difficult choice between preparing for an unannounced test or attending the Spring Sports Banquet. Whether she should forego the banquet and the recognition of the school and her peers—she was elected captain and most valuable player—is not my concern for writing, however. I am bothered that the school, through lack of planning, puts students in this situation.
>
> Students are encouraged to participate in sports and other activities sponsored by the school. Yet, it then punishes them for that participation by failing to recognize what the pressure to do well on tests can cause and scheduling conflicting evening activities without regard to academic matters.
>
> My daughter made an effort to learn what was upcoming in her classes on last Thursday. She was going to be absent on Friday because of attending a district student leadership conference and didn't want to miss an assignment. No mention was made of the tests. Yet on Monday four of her teachers indicated they would be giving grade-period-ending examinations on Wednesday. The banquet is scheduled for Tuesday evening. Four major tests in one day are bad enough. But having these occur the day after a sponsored evening event is ridiculous. My daughter decided not to go to the banquet.
>
> You don't need to answer this letter but you do need to be aware that I am not the only parent who is bothered by this lack of planning.
>
> Sincerely,
>
> (Mrs.) Cynthia Norris

Information for the reader: The banquet *was* planned for two days before the tests. The athletic director *is* new. The teachers in question *are* experienced. The grading period ended a few days after the tests were given. Grace is a struggling student who often just manages to stay eligible to participate in the organized sports programs, despite a strong effort to do her schoolwork.

What action do you take?

Case 9: The New Photocopier

Losses in enrollments because of population shifts and an eroding tax base have resulted in deep budget cuts. You, as the principal, must trim all nonessential expenditures. You have decided to investigate whether your office needs the large, fast, highly flexible copier currently in use. It could be replaced with any of a number of cheaper machines on the market; a substantial cost savings would be effected. You have the specifications for both the current and the smaller machines and the salespersons have advised you of the various features of each, including fidelity of reproduction, copies per minute, number of copies collated (if at all), and other features. Other useful information is readily available from your staff as well as the business office.

It is clear that your support staff prefers the current machine, some outspokenly so. They are not as concerned as you are about costs and are well aware of the many advantages the current machine has in making their own workload easier. Moreover, if you had a smaller machine installed, there would be the need to improvise on some of the larger jobs, or, from time to time, to take work over to the district office. Some of the staff could make life more difficult for you by making up reasons to take work "downtown." It would not be possible to develop a policy to fit every contingency, so you would either be in position of constantly monitoring the reproduction tasks or of running the risk of flagrant misuse of the district's equipment, which would be charged against your operating budget, as well as a waste of time of some of your support staff.

Nevertheless, even though they will all be affected, the staff members know that a substantial amount of money is involved. Most also believe that making these kinds of decisions is what you are being paid for.

Case 10: How Safe Is the School?

You are the principal of an urban high school. Numerous break-ins and incidents of violence have characterized several of the high schools in the district. Your high school is one of these. The window breakage alone in the district required $375,000 for repairs last year. Beyond this, the costs for repainting and other building repairs exceeded national averages by far.

Teachers are complaining that they do not feel safe, and some parents complain that their children have had money extorted from them by other "students" on their way to and from school as well as on the school grounds. Also, within recent months, there was a parking lot incident in which a teacher was shot at by an unidentified youth.

The restroom walls always seem to need cleaning; spray-painted scatology abounds in the restrooms and on sidewalks. School equipment doesn't seem to last long—it breaks or it disappears.

And now, an enterprising news team from a local TV station has started a well-watched series "How Safe Are Our Schools?"

Case 11: Mrs. Davis Is a Bad Teacher

You are the principal of Ubben Elementary School, a prekindergarten through grade 5 school with a population of 530. It is nearly the end of the school day and you are reviewing your mail. A letter from a parent captures your attention. It reads as follows:

> Dear Principal, Assistant Principal, and School Board:
>
> My husband and I, as parents of a third-grader and a fourth-grader at Ubben Elementary, would like to bring to your attention some problems in Mrs. Davis's class. Our daughter Rebecca is in Mrs. Davis's third grade. In the past few weeks, our conversations

with Rebecca have turned up some disturbing facts about Mrs. Davis's interactions with her students. Among other things that Rebecca reports are the following: The entire class is denied recess if any one child misbehaves. Mrs. Davis repeatedly tells her students that they are "dumb," "stupid," "ignorant fools," and that their behavior is much worse "than her two-year-old."

We concede that an eight-year-old's perceptions can be very different from those of an adult—after all, missing recess on several occasions for something you didn't do is very upsetting for an eight-year-old. However, I have sat in on Mrs. Davis's class and have observed her behavior in the classroom. On one occasion, she and the class were returning from lunch and some of the children were talking and moving about, which I think is normal for eight-year-olds. She yelled at the children to sit down and then screamed, waving her arms. Everyone sat down. As an adult, I was frightened. Can you imagine what an eight-year-old would feel? If she demonstrated that kind of behavior while I was present, I can't imagine how she is when she is alone with the children. We also have evidence of unfair grading practices.

We are requesting that Rebecca be transferred out of Mrs. Davis's class immediately. This, of course, is only a partial solution—it won't solve the problem for the rest of the class. There is a complete lack of a positive learning climate.

Verbal abuse is just as destructive as physical abuse. We have always had a high regard for the district and we are shocked that someone like Mrs. Davis could be employed. Surely others have complained.

We would like to hear from you immediately.

Sincerely,

David and Lori Hughes

Case 12: Dress Code Violated

You are principal of a suburban high school with an enrollment of 1,300 students in grades 10 through 12. There is a dress code approved by the student council and a faculty advisory group.

Four students, new to the school, appear in your office one morning in September. They have been sent to the office by their homeroom teacher. The three girls are dressed in long "dresses" and are wearing burkas. The boy has a light beard, just beginning to sprout and become dark, and also wears a "cap." Facial hair is not permitted in the school and neither are hats during class times inside the building.

The students are unhappy about being sent to the office for their dress and appearance. They complain that the dress code is contrary to Muslim practice and that they are being subject to unfair discrimination.

Now you understand the call-back note on your desk from the parents of one of the students confronting you in your office.

So, there you sit with four upset students, a dress code that your teachers and most of the students support, facing a charge of religious intolerance.

What do you do immediately? What is your following plan?

Case 13: Back to the Basics

You are the principal of a large junior high school. Your school system is on a back-to-the-basics mode, reflecting the outspoken criticism of several board members and their constituencies. This, coupled with a new educational reform bill passed in the state legislature, is having a negative effect on your district's highly successful prevocational education program and, to a significant degree, on the fine arts program. Your school has achieved special state recognition for its efforts and achievements in both. Nevertheless, the school board has decided that prevocational education should be eliminated and has reduced the budget amounts to be spent districtwide in the fine arts to the barest of minimums.

You are now faced with counselors, teachers, and parents who are very concerned about the demise of the prevocational education and physical education programs. Counselors are concerned that the career counseling load will now fall on them.

Complicating the matter is what to do about the current full-time career counselor. She relates very well to adolescents and has been able to "turn tough kids around." Parents are supportive as well. Her teaching fields are history and Latin. Latin has not been offered in years at your school and the history department "runneth over." You would hate to lose this fine teacher.

The parents are upset on several counts, not the least of which is the lack of attention to the fine arts program and physical education.

Your superintendent is waiting for your staffing plan and budget proposals for next year. These are due in two weeks.

Case 14: A Parent Complains; The Teacher Doesn't Respond

You are the principal of John Harrison Elementary School, which has 700 students. A telephone call has been referred from a parent with the following story:

Her third-grade son is failing in science. She wants to know how to help him, but despite two notes to his teacher, the parent has not received a response. What should she do? You recommended that she make another contact. The parent was in the school doing some volunteer work today and you asked if she had received any response from the teacher. She said no. You placed a query in the teacher's school mailbox asking about the situation.

The following day the teacher comes storming into your office. "I have been ill and out of school last week and am only now just back from that absence. Now, you are sending me a note about not contacting a parent. I sent an announcement to all parents at the first of the year about the days and times when I am available for conferences. Let her come in or call me during those times! I can't be responding on every occasion to notes from parents."

What are your actions now?

Case 15: Welcome: Please Change Janie's Teacher

You are the new principal of Selter Elementary School. It's the third day of school and you've had a reasonably smooth opening. Selter is a large elementary school (average daily attendance = 790) and houses grades 1 through 5. Your predecessor retired after a 30-year career in the district and is now enjoying the fruits of a successful tenure. She is on a world-spanning vacation after which she will relocate in a small town some distance away.

You are reviewing your mail and come across a letter from the president of the PTO, whom you have met but once, briefly, at a preschool opening reception. She welcomes you in her first couple of lines and then turns to another subject. The final paragraph of the letter reads:

> "Oh yes, I am not happy with Janie's class assignment. You have placed her with a Level I teacher—a Miss Burket. Lovely person, so young and pleasant. But Janie requires some special help, as I'm sure you've seen from her records. Certainly a novice is ill prepared to deal with this. I know you have a number of Level II teachers but I especially admire Dr. Norris who is a Level III "Master Teacher." Janie and I were most disappointed that she was not assigned to her class. Your predecessor had indicated that this would be done. Could you arrange for Janie to be placed with Dr. Norris, please? Thank you very much."

Case 16: We Object!

You are the principal of a high school (grades 9 through 12) with an enrollment of 1,500. It is mid-November. You have been at a statewide professional meeting for the past three days and have just returned to your office. The letter below is among other first-class mail that you find in your in-box. The letter arrived on Monday; today is Thursday.

> Dear Principal:
>
> We, John and Grace Michael, request that our daughter Heather be dismissed from her fifth-period class, Health, for the remainder of the semester. We are basing our decision on the fact that materials used in the classroom and methods of teaching are in complete disharmony with the values and beliefs we have tried to implement in our home. At such a vulnerable time in their lives, it is difficult, at best, for young people to be strong in the beliefs they have been taught and then stand up against the pressure of their peers. But it's something the youth of today face on a daily basis and we parents, as a collective group, hope and pray that our youth make the right choices and develop a stronger character because of those choices.
>
> But when the adults who have a direct influence on our child, through teaching, begin to promote a value system that has been rejected in our home, just consider the impact on our child (or any other) and how it will affect the decision-making process when that young person is once again faced with peer pressure.
>
> During a recent conversation with Ms. Blackstone and Ms. Weaver, it was interesting to us how we were told repeatedly that teachers cannot tell students what is right and what is wrong; they must choose for themselves. Yet, in the same conversation, we were told that because many students have sex and many students drink, it is okay to teach "safe sex" and "responsible drinking." If this isn't at the very least a contradiction, then certainly you must agree that it is a compromise in values. As it has become obvious to us, it must also be obvious to you that we simply do not agree with the standards being practiced and

taught. It is at this point that we have reached the conclusion that Heather should be re-moved from this course.

Sincerely yours,

John and Grace Michael

Case 17: Mike Is the Best You Have

Mike Flynn is your best mathematics teacher. His students always excel and he doesn't always get the best students to begin with. His classes range from Algebra I to a special advanced place-ment group in concepts well beyond calculus and differential equations. Parents of all students are highly supportive of Flynn. Moreover, he is frequently used by the district as an in-service training leader.

For as long as anyone can remember, Mike has had first period as his planning period. He comes to school late every morning because of his avocation, which is raising roses and doing other kinds of hybrid gardening. "Early morning hours work best for this," he says, "especially for watering, pruning and fertilizing."

You are Mike's new principal. Two teachers have come to you within the past few days, each complaining of the favoritism being shown Mr. Flynn. They have asked why they cannot leave school during their planning period to tend to their personal business. Also, they have fur-ther suggested that first-period-off privileges should be extended to everyone. "Nobody else gets to do this," they say.

Case 18: Write Your Legislators

You are the principal of James Burket Middle School, a school that now has an enrollment of 1,225 students. This morning, among other phone calls, three calls have been about a similar subject. One was from the superintendent, one was from a member of the school board, and one was from a local state legislator. All were either complaining about or reporting an assignment apparently made by one of your social studies teachers. The assignment was for each student to write a highly charged letter to an identified legislator or the governor about proposed cuts to state school financing; the cuts would include reduced health care benefits and less state aid for teacher salaries.

You investigate and discover that, in fact, the teacher made such an assignment. Further in-vestigation indicates that the teacher arranged for the mailings but did not read the letters and that the students had been "coached" on the issues about which to write. The legislator produced copies of the letters he had received. These were not badly written but the authors were very firm in their statements about the injustices that would be done by reduced funding. Many students pleaded with legislators to spare field trips, to better fund textbooks, and to save teachers' salaries from the ax of budget cutters.

The school board member insists that the teacher has violated the school system's standard of professional conduct. Some others on the board agree. The legislator seems less bothered of all but is curious, in his words, about "what *is* being taught in social studies these days." The local newspaper has picked up on the story and has it featured in its well-read "What's Happening in Our City" section.

The teacher, to this point in his career, has an unblemished record. In fact, just two years ago, he won the districtwide best teacher award. His annual job reviews have always been good to outstanding.

Several board members ultimately indicate they think the teacher should be dismissed for unprofessional conduct.

The superintendent has asked for your recommendation. What is your recommendation and on what basis do you make this recommendation?

Case 19: I Wish I Was Dead

You are the principal of a prekindergarten through grade 5 elementary school with an enrollment of 530. It is 10.00 A.M. and you have just returned from a morning tour of the building. You are reviewing mail, memos, and notes from various staff that have accumulated since late yesterday afternoon when you were attending an all-district administrators' meeting at the central office.

Among other things, there is a short note from one of your fifth-grade teachers, written the afternoon before. It reads: "I thought you ought to see this." Stapled to the note is a piece of tablet paper containing the last part of an essay by one of her students, a boy named Timmy. The assigned topic for the essay was My Favorite Things. Timmy's essay concludes, " . . . but I'll never get to have these things. Sometimes I wish I was dead. Sometimes I want to kill myself."

Case 20: Who Gets the Money?

You are the principal of Kevin Arthur Middle School. The school has an enrollment of 950 students in grades 5 through 8. Most of the students are Anglo (86 percent) with some African American and a few Asian students. As principal, you are the chief fiscal officer of the school, although you do have a well-trained bookkeeper. It is budget development time and the district office has requested your budget proposals for next year within two weeks. As usual, departmental requests have exceeded the possibilities. You would be disappointed if that did not happen because it is an indication that the staff is ambitious. But there are some tough choices to be made between departments, thousands of dollars at stake, and some faculty will be unhappy.

Two departments—English and science—are requesting new computer programs that are very expensive. The athletic department insists that its equipment needs have increased because of a new foray into interscholastic lacrosse and an expanded effort in football for the sixth-graders. This influences staffing as well as equipment. A fourth aspect of your program, the library, insists that two more paraprofessionals are needed, and the library's new book proposals are about double the request for last year. A greater emphasis on multicultural works is part of this increase in needs.

You have two weeks to complete your proposal. You decide . . .

Case 21: Gun in the School

You are the assistant principal of Ubben High School, a school with an enrollment of 1,500 students. Ubben has a multiethnic student body and is located in a small city. It's Friday.

Two students approach you during second period and say a girl has brought a gun to school because she wants to scare a boy who continues to sexually harass her. The girl is in a class on the second floor; the student who allegedly has been harassing her is not in that class. The bell to change classes will ring in 15 minutes.

Case 22: Late Practice

You are a junior high school principal. A parent has just come in to discuss an issue concerning her 13-year-old daughter, Ashley Jane. She is complaining about the girl's basketball coach. Apparently, he has been giving special after-practice instruction to her daughter and to two other ninth-grade girls, although not on the same days. He meets with these students after the rest of the team has been dismissed.

The parent indicates that several times Ashley Jane has arrived late for dinner. The parent relates, "The coach always drives her home, but the time will frequently be as much as half an hour after we have started our evening meal. Last evening she arrived late, again, but this time she had been crying."

She would not tell her parent what the difficulty was, saying only, "I wasn't good enough." The parent assumed she was talking about her playing ability and let the matter go while offering a comforting word or two.

Later, the parent noticed that her daughter's T-shirt was torn, so her suspicions were heightened. "What is he doing with these girls?" she asks. The parents of her daughter's two friends were of no help. Their daughters had been home by dinnertime even after the late practices.

As principal, you decide . . .

What other actions, if any, will you take?

Case 23: Who Gets the Job?

You are the principal of Whisler Elementary School, a six-grade school with a preschool program and an extended day schedule. It's April and you have just completed interviewing teachers for positions next fall. Each of the prospective teachers you have interviewed has already met with a committee of teachers and been recommended for further consideration. This committee has rated the candidates either 4 or 5 on a list of persons with whom they would be happy to be colleagues. (Candidates are rated on a 5-point scale with 5 being the highest rating.) You will have only one vacancy for a fifth-grade spot for which three individuals are qualified. Two of these have received ratings of 4s and 5s—and those are very good ratings. The third candidate has a rating of 5 from all the teachers.

In your mind, the best choice is a young, single mother with two children of elementary school age. This is also the person that the teachers have rated most highly. One troubling fact is that the teacher has her children enrolled in a local school sponsored by a fundamentalist church.

She has expressed firm unwillingness to transfer these children to Whisler or to any public school in the district. You learn, as well, that other administrators and teachers have grave reservations about the quality of the school to which the applicant sends her children. There is also a general expectation in the community that teachers and administrators should have their own children enrolled in the local public schools.

You must make your staffing recommendations to the central office by the end of the week. It is now Tuesday.

Case 24: More Fights

"He called me the 'N' word," shouted the 12-year-old boy. "Did not," said the other boy, an Anglo youngster a year older and several inches taller. "You're always lookin' for trouble and you're always crying prejudice. Even the teachers are sick of it." The boys lunge at each other but are held back. They have been brought to the office by two of your teachers who remain in the room.

"What happened?" you ask the teachers. "We weren't there until the fight started, so we have no idea what happened."

It is just one more fight among your junior high students. Even the girls are squaring off with each other. And, mostly—but not always—it seems to have racial or ethnic overtones.

You are the new principal of Joy Phillips Junior High, a new school in the county and a school where about half of the students are bused in to a magnet program. The student population is diverse—economically and ethnically.

You think about your next steps, first with these students and then with the problems the school seems to be confronted with in regard to the student population.

Case 25: Students Are "Hanging Around" in the Shops

You are the principal of Barton Herrscher High School, a school with grades 10 through 12 and an enrollment of 1,350 students. The students are mostly from middle-class to upper-middle-class homes in a neighborhood community that is considered to be "well off." It is late afternoon and you are reviewing the mail of the day. You have just read a letter from the president of the local affiliate of the Chamber of Commerce. It reads as follows:

Dear [You]:

I've been asked by our public relations committee to write you about what they see as a developing problem involving some students from your school. For the past few months, we have become aware of a large number of teenagers congregating in various mall stores. The proprietors of the theatre and two stop-and-shop stores are particularly bothered, although other merchants have also indicated concern. The police have been notified on several occasions about rowdy behavior and even some drinking of alcoholic beverages. (We think drugs have also been involved.) The police have been helpful in moving larger groups of kids out of certain areas but the kids don't stay away very long. Lately, some of our merchants have reported an increase in shoplifting.

Now, we don't know if the young people are all your students. Some may be from other communities, but we do need your help because many of the kids *are* students of Herrscher High. They wear letter jackets and other identifying clothes.

This is serious. We've always been very supportive of school activities but this is getting out of control. Will you help us? What do you suggest? We would be glad to meet with you as soon as you can.

Sincerely,

Patricia Holland, President
Winstead Chamber of Commerce

What is your action?

Case 26: Why Can't Graceilla Go to College?

The school year has just begun. You are in your first year as principal of Wilford Weber Senior High School. Weber has an enrollment of 1,465 students who are 70 percent Anglo, 20 percent African American, and nearly 10 percent Latino—largely immigrants from Central American nations. A small percent of Asians also compose the population. The Anglos represent a range of income levels, the African Americans are also mixed, and the Latinos mostly are struggling day workers living in low-cost public housing. It's late Friday afternoon and you are finally getting around to the mail. One handwritten letter in particular catches your attention.

Dear [You]:

We are new to Weber High School and to this community. So far, we have been happy with Weber and the teachers but now our daughter Graceilla is having difficulty. This is her third high school in the past two years. But now, it seems we have made the last of our moves and Graceilla will finish at Weber.

A few days ago she came home quite upset because of a conference she had with Mr. Fossey, her guidance counselor. Mr. Fossey had just told her that she needed to give up her interest in going on to college because of her low grade-point average. Probably Graceilla has had difficulty because of all of our moves. We moved a lot when she was in grade school, too. But she is determined to improve and likes all of her teachers. She is motivated! Or at least she was until the meeting with Mr. Fossey.

We don't think people like Mr. Fossey should be discouraging students this way. This seems to us to be a very bad attitude for counseling people to have—especially with new kids. Will you tell us what, if anything, you will do about this very bad situation?

Sincerely yours,

Carol Barritta

What action will you take?

Case 27: Zero Tolerance

Background. You are the principal of Howard L. Jones High School with an enrollment of 1,475 students. The makeup of the student body is 55 percent Anglo, 20 percent African American, 20 percent Latino, and 5 percent Asian. This is quite a change from last year, brought about because of a new school building and a realignment of attendance boundaries. "It's a real mixed group," says one of your colleagues during the first week of the school year. Last year 90 percent of the students were Anglo.

Your district has a zero-tolerance policy with regard to drugs, weapons, and violence. It reads in part: "The student shall not be in possession of any prohibited weapon at any school or any school function."

"Weapons" are defined (in part): "Prohibited weapons are defined as follows: 1. A firearm [and the policy goes on as firearms are described], 2. An illegal knife as defined by law (knife with 5 inches or more, or a hand instrument designed to cut or stab another . . .) or by local policy." (The state penal code is then cited.) And the policy goes on through four more items listing various weapons and dimensions. It ends with the statement "or any other object used in a way that threatens or inflicts bodily injury to another person."

Drugs are defined in the policy with the statements: "A student may be expelled or at least sent to the Behavioral Care High School for a semester if while on school property or attending a school sponsored activity on or off school property if the student 1. Sells, gives, or delivers to another person any amount of marijuana or a controlled substance as defined by 21 U.S.C. Section 801 et seq.; or a dangerous drug otherwise defined in the State Safety Code or . . ." and the policy goes on. The penalty is immediate assignment to the Behavior Care High School for one semester.

School district policy is clear on disciplinary procedures with regard to students with disabilities: "Students with disabilities may be disciplined in the same manner as nondisabled students." And the policy goes on to describe the kinds of discipline open to the administrator. These include suspension and assignment to a special school for disruptive students. In your district that school is the Behavioral Care High School.

Situation. Two students sit in the outside office. Two different teachers have sent them. One student an African American girl, a senior, who was discovered taking a pill that she says is an antiallergy medication. It is in a plain metal pillbox. There is no note in her file that she is under a physician's care. The other student, a 16-year-old Anglo boy, is enrolled in the school's program for students with ADHD. His teacher discovered that the boy was carrying a long, slim, nail file—about five inches long—in his front pocket. It had been sharpened.

What actions do you take?

Case 28: Test Travesty

You are in your office preparing notes for an address you have been asked to give to the School Advisory Council and a neighborhood meeting. The address is to be about the testing program in your state. The testing program has been induced by the No Child Left Behind acts of the U.S. Congress. Schools are certified in your state depending on how much improvement is shown in the way students perform on the annual test. The test for high school juniors is scheduled for next week.

The local newspaper today is featuring a column by a popular political reporter who has just visited one of the other schools in your district. His remarks are damning with regard to the preparation teachers are making for students taking the tests. He reports about a review sheet one of the history teachers is using. (It had been left for a substitute teacher who is drilling students for the test.)

In part, the review sheet states in its first three statements: "If it is a question about the Revolutionary War, the answer is George Washington or Thomas Jefferson. If the question is about the women's rights movement, the answer would be Susan B. Anthony. If the question is about a civil rights leader, the answer is likely Martin Luther King." The review sheet goes on for three more pages with dates and definitions spelled out. The newspaper reporter ends the article by stating that the sheet "presents a reflecting pool of U.S. history a centimeter deep and 200 years wide, filled with murky water." The reporter ends his column by asking about the nature of education in the local schools. "What are we doing to these kids?" he asks.

The chairperson of your School Advisory Council has just stopped in to discuss the article. "Please address this issue in your remarks to the council and the guests this evening. Teachers surely are not doing this sort of thing, are they?" He then leaves your office and the school.

You ask your history teacher about the list. He remarks, "The truth is I hated the feeling that I had to make that list that reviews material the students had in the eighth grade. It's not a reflection of my teaching, but it is an aid to those students who need last-minute help. This test has serious implications to our school and to evaluations of my teaching effectiveness." He goes on to lament the negative effect of the state's reliance on such tests for the evaluation of school effectiveness. You ask him, "Is everybody doing this?" His reply: "Everybody I know."

You return to your notes to get ready for your talk tonight. Your notes are as follows . . .

Case 29: Where Should the Money Go?

You are the principal of a large high school. Booker T. Washington is almost a leftover from the days of racial discrimination. Most of the 2,800 students come from the nearby projects. Even though you have a magnet program in the fine arts, few potential Anglo or Latino students elect to come to the school. There are no Asian students, either. So, even the magnet program has a large African American population. The issue before you at this time is not racial balance of the students, however. It is faculty assignments.

Your school population is growing at the rate of 50 or so per year and an increased recruitment effort on the part of the magnet coordinator is paying off. There are sufficient personnel funds for three new positions, but there is a lot of discord about what those positions should be. The fine arts department insists it must add a staff member. The science department needs a specialist in physics. Your music department wants to add a person experienced in strings. The English department has two persons about to retire and has demonstrated the need for two additions. Your football team has been successful and the athletic director has threatened to resign unless he is given two more coaches. (Coaches have only a half-time instructional load.)

So, there you are. Budget proposal sessions are coming up. The district office wants your recommendations in three weeks. You have a personnel committee that functions only irregularly and that has members who rarely agree. You do have some flexibility. All or part of your personnel budget may be expended for instructional aides. An aide costs about half the salary of a certificated teacher.

What is your approach to this problem?

Case 30: Fire Her and I'm Going to the Board!

You are one of two assistant principals in an urban junior high school. The enrollment is 1,100 students and is mixed racially and ethnically. You've been with the district for four years and have just applied for a principalship in a new junior high school just about to be opened in the district. You are on the short list.

One of your current responsibilities is the supervision of instructional aides. Supervision includes systematic evaluation and a written annual review of performance. You have just recommended the dismissal of an aide who assists in a seventh-grade alternative class for students with ADHD. Recommendations about employment have been sent out to all personnel during the past two weeks. The particular aide disputed your charges of incompetence and appealed to the principal. The principal rejected the appeal, citing the evidence you had provided in the file. That evidence included reports of three occasions earlier in the school year when you met with the teacher to discuss the aide's poor attendance and insufficient handling of poor behavior on the part of a student. The teacher who was working with the aide was not of much help to you and he, himself, has been recommended by the principal for transfer to another assignment next year.

The aide is an Anglo female who has been with the district four years but at your school just one year. Her previous evaluations have not been high, but no one has recommended termination before this year.

Today, you were visited by a parent of one of the students in the alternative class. She is unhappy about the aide's termination notice. She is a leader in the school community and an African American who has actively supported the election of two school board members. She is irritated when you tell her that the teacher's appeal to the principal has been denied. You are being "unfair," she says.

There is time for you to withdraw your recommendation. The board has not met yet. Your principal has indicated her support for whatever you decide to do. She does not seem troubled by the incident and, apparently, would not be bothered if the aide returned for another year. Aides are difficult to find. The pay is not high.

So, you have a couple of days to think about the issue. What do you decide to do?

Case 31: What Next for Billy?

You are an assistant principal of a junior high school with an enrollment of 1,100. An aspect of your responsibilities is to chair special education admission, review, and dismissal meetings (ARD) in compliance with legal requirements when educational programs and actions for disabled students are to be established. These students include those who are emotionally disturbed.

Billy is the subject of the agenda today. Billy has a history of being disruptive in schools and he has once again come to your attention. He takes a medication for hyperactivity but recently it seems to have diminishing effects. His behavior, according to teachers, has been getting progressively worse. Billy is now scheduled to be in a self-contained classroom each school day.

In your school's regular program, most students who are in attendance are "normal" adolescents and go to the usual classes. So, Billy and his emotionally disturbed colleagues do have opportunities to interact with and attend some classes with the normal student body—usually physical education and art classes. Also, there are opportunities in after-school events and in the cafeteria at lunch times.

Regardless of the situation, Billy simply does not get along well. He fights, bites, and scratches his fellow students and screams at teachers and other students alike.

The intermediate service unit to which your school district belongs has just opened a centrally housed unit for the emotionally disturbed. You mention this possibility to Billy's parents and they object strongly. "You will turn Billy into a hoodlum! He'll only become worse. Why can't you manage this in your own school?" Both parents want Billy mainstreamed into the regular program "as IDEA requires," they say. A lawsuit is threatened. The parents go on to state that Billy's teacher is "against Billy" and they insist that their child be removed immediately from his current assignment.

Midterm ARD meetings are being scheduled to begin next week. Billy is due for a midterm review.

What actions will you take?

What legal bases will guide you?

Case 32: Why Can't I Play?

One of your responsibilities as one of two assistant principals is to manage the student activities programs in the freshman and sophomore classes. That involves more than 700 students. Another assignment is administering the school's athletic program. Your plate is full.

You are sitting at your desk at the end of a long day and the freshman football coach comes in. "You've got to help," he says. "Two girls showed up at our first practice this afternoon and asked for gear and uniforms." He goes on, "I'm not going to have girls playing on the football team. I sent them home."

The coach leaves the office. Your phone rings. It is the parent of one of the girls. He is unhappy and curious about why his child cannot play football.

- Your response is . . .
- You tell the parent . . .
- You tell the coach . . .

On what do you base your actions?

APPENDIX B

Educational Leadership Policy Standards: ISLLC 2008[*]

Standard 1: *An education leader promotes the success of every student by facilitating the development, articulation, implementation, and stewardship of a vision of learning that is shared and supported by all stakeholders.*

Functions
a. Collaboratively develop and implement a shared vision and mission
b. Collect and use data to identify goals, assess organizational effectiveness, and promote organizational learning
c. Create and implement plans to achieve goals
d. Promote continuous and sustainable improvement
e. Monitor and evaluate progress and revise plans

Standard 2: *An education leader promotes the success of every student by advocating, nurturing, and sustaining a school culture and instructional program conducive to student learning and staff professional growth.*

Functions
a. Nurture and sustain a culture of collaboration, trust, learning, and high expectations
b. Create a comprehensive, rigorous, and coherent curricular program
c. Create a personalized and motivating learning environment for students
d. Supervise instruction
e. Develop assessment and accountability systems to monitor student progress
f. Develop the instructional and leadership capacity of staff
g. Maximize time spent on quality instruction

Source: as adopted by the National Policy Board for Educational Administration on December 12, 2007.

[*]ISLLC = Interstate School Leaders Licensure Consortium.

    h. Promote the use of the most effective and appropriate technologies to support teaching and learning

    i. Monitor and evaluate the impact of the instructional program

Standard 3: *An education leader promotes the success of every student by ensuring management of the organization, operation, and resources for a safe, efficient, and effective learning environment.*

Functions

    a. Monitor and evaluate the management and operational systems

    b. Obtain, allocate, align, and efficiently utilize human, fiscal, and technological resources

    c. Promote and protect the welfare and safety of students and staff

    d. Develop the capacity for distributed leadership

    e. Ensure teacher and organizational time is focused to support quality instruction and student learning

Standard 4: *An education leader promotes the success of every student by collaborating with faculty and community members, responding to diverse community interests and needs, and mobilizing community resources.*

Functions

    a. Collect and analyze data and information pertinent to the educational environment

    b. Promote understanding, appreciation, and use of the community's diverse cultural, social, and intellectual resources

    c. Build and sustain positive relationships with families and caregivers

    d. Build and sustain productive relationships with community partners

Standard 5: *An education leader promotes the success of every student by acting with integrity, fairness, and in an ethical manner.*

Functions

    a. Ensure a system of accountability for every student's academic and social success

    b. Model principles of self-awareness, reflective practice, transparency, and ethical behavior

    c. Safeguard the values of democracy, equity, and diversity

    d. Consider and evaluate the potential moral and legal consequences of decision-making

    e. Promote social justice and ensure that individual student needs inform all aspects of schooling

Standard 6: *An education leader promotes the success of every student by understanding, responding to, and influencing the political, social, economic, legal, and cultural context.*

Functions

    a. Advocate for children, families, and caregivers

    b. Act to influence local, district, state, and national decisions affecting student learning

    c. Assess, analyze, and anticipate emerging trends and initiatives in order to adapt leadership strategies

INDEX